The Flower Gardener's Bible

The Flower Gardener's Bible

Time-Tested Techniques, Creative Designs,

and Perfect Plants for Colorful Gardens

LEWIS AND NANCY HILL

Photographs by JOSEPH DE SCIOSE

STOREY
BOOKS

The mission of Storey Publishing is to serve our customers by publishing practical information that encourages personal independence in harmony with the environment.

Edited by Gwen W. Steege and Nancy J. Ondra
Art direction by Cynthia McFarland
Text design by Kent Lew
Text production by Kent Lew and Susan Bernier
Indexed by Susan Olason, Indexes & Knowledge Maps

Printed in the United States by R. R. Donnelley
10 9 8 7 6 5 4 3 2 1

Library of Congress Cataloging-in-Publication Data
Hill, Lewis, 1924–
    The flower gardener's bible : time-tested techniques, creative designs, and perfect plants
    for colorful gardens / Lewis and Nancy Hill.
        p. cm.
    ISBN 1-58017-462-0 (pbk. : alk. paper) — ISBN 1-58017-463-9 (hardcover : alk. paper)
    1. Flower gardening. I. Hill, Nancy. II. Title.
SB405 .H536 2003
635.9 — dc21

To our very special editor and friend, Gwen Steege, who has worked tirelessly with us on many projects with great skill, patience, thoroughness, and creativity, making it all fun.

In addition to Gwen, we are grateful to talented photographer Joe De Sciose, who made our words come alive with his artistic eye, and Elayne Sears, exceptional artist, who transformed garden concepts into colorful works of art.

Many thanks to the other skillful people who made this book a reality: Nancy J. Ondra, expert gardener and editor; and Cynthia McFarland, consummate art director and gardener. Thanks, too, to Kent Lew, for his wonderful design, and to Susan Bernier, for her skillful production.

We are grateful to Tobi and Sally von Trapp, who welcomed us into their beautiful gardens to photograph. And finally, a huge thank-you to John and Martha Storey, with whom we have greatly enjoyed working over many years.

Lewis and Nancy Hill
November 2002

Contents

PART III: A FEAST OF FLOWERS   213

An alphabetical listing of plants with species-by-species information
on each plant's characteristics and how to care for it.

The Pleasures of the Garden

WHEN WE WERE PLANNING OUR FIRST backyard perennial garden, a visitor from England told us that it takes a minimum of 50 years to create a fine garden and, if possible, one should allow 200 years. We were still young, but 50 years seemed like a long time, and the prospect of an outstanding border became dim. Fortunately, he was wrong. Although our gardens have never rivaled those at Sissinghurst or Kew, they have been a joy to us, which was all we asked of them.

In the early years, we made many mistakes, and when we were discouraged, it was tempting to remove the herbaceous plants and grow rows of shrubs instead. In retrospect, we realize that if we had been better educated on plant growth and maintenance, we could have avoided most of the problems.

Initially, we experimented with many types of gardens, each consisting of all bulbs, annuals, or perennials. Finally, however, we realized that including several types of plants together in one flower garden would make it more interesting than using any one of them alone. Certain wildflowers, as well as bulbs, shrubs, herbs, ornamental grasses, and vines, also proved valuable for adding variety and interest. As we experimented with different combinations, our gardens improved. We found that combining several

different types of plants has many advantages: Annuals, for instance, bloom for most of the gardening season, while perennials provide a display that changes every two or three weeks. Spring bulbs supply flowers very early, flowering shrubs offer year-round substance, and evergreens contribute color to the winter scene. Vines add a vertical dimension to the garden, and ornamental grasses have contrasting foliage and fall blooms.

In the following pages, we offer you descriptions of many different plants, with the hope that these will help you decide which to include in your own garden. Plus, we share what we've learned about caring for our own plants, to help you avoid making the same mistakes we once made. We hope that building your gardens and working in them gives you a great deal of pleasure!

PART ONE

The Joy of Flower Gardening

When we started our first flower garden many years ago, we knew almost nothing about flowering plants. Thanks to advice from our gardening friends and our own painful experimentation and mistakes, we began to grow more and more plants successfully. Eventually, we could show off our backyard garden with pride.

We are happy to share what we've learned with you, beginning with advice on planning and design. We explain how to improve soil pH, texture, and fertility — basics for success. When it's time to plant, you'll find the techniques we like to use, including how to start seeds, naturalize bulbs, and move shrubs. If you decide to expand your garden, you will discover how easy it is to propagate plants by taking cuttings, layering, or dividing. And if your garden occasionally hosts pests or diseases that need your attention, we offer solutions that we have found helpful. Finally, we take you through the cycle of seasons with a checklist of what needs to be done when. We hope this practical advice will translate into successful gardens and pleasure in every plant you grow.

CHAPTER 1

The Fascination of Flowers

MANY THINGS IN LIFE can make us happy — some for a day, others for a month. But if you want to be happy for a lifetime, our experience tells us that the best prospect comes with being a gardener. It would be untrue to say that gardening is all joy and that beautiful roses appear with no bugs, disease, or frost damage. Nevertheless, compared to most pursuits, gardening offers enough rewards, challenges, and pleasures to satisfy nearly anyone.

Among the many wonderful things about a garden is the fact that you can never say it is finished. A carpenter can complete a house, and a writer a book, but because a garden is alive, it goes on as long as we nurture it. During a few months of winter there are no weeds to pull and no bouquets to gather, but a true gardener is always planning, studying, and waiting for the chance to start once again. Like life itself, gardening's perfect moments come and go, but the constant change makes it unendingly interesting.

It Takes All Kinds to Make a Garden

LIKE MANY GARDENERS, we have moved gradually through several phases that we can see only in retrospect. In the beginning we simply liked flowers and admired gardens with absolutely no idea as to how they were created. People gave us plants, so we dug holes and casually stuck them in the ground, often without adequately preparing the soil. One by one, we learned the names of plant species, but we remained unaware of the different cultivars. To us, irises were simply red, white, brown, and yellow.

Gradually we came to know more about plant habits —when they bloomed, how high they grew, how vigorous they were, and whether their foliage remained attractive throughout the season, as is the case with peonies, or needed to be cut back, as is necessary for delphiniums and Oriental poppy (*Papaver orientale*). We learned to recognize when to divide a plant and which of the vigorous species we needed to restrain. Over time we finally learned to plan *before* we planted to achieve pleasant color combinations and to arrange

different cultivars to get bloom throughout the garden during the entire growing season. We began to set out the plants in particular groups and locations, rather than jamming them in arbitrarily. Finally, we learned the hardest lesson of all: to be ruthless and to actually throw away healthy plants if they had bad habits or contributed little to the garden.

Discerning eyes and a garden regimen gradually developed. We realized that a border didn't look finished if an edging was missing, that it was important to weed and fertilize on schedule, and that we must deadhead the fading blooms. As we became more knowledgeable, we searched for outstanding cultivars. A peony simply labeled "red" was no longer satisfactory, so we ordered the selection 'Karl Rosenfield' because it had the distinctive, large, double, dark red blooms that would look smashing in the spot we'd chosen for it.

Just as great cooks must know their ingredients in order to cook great meals, the most successful gardeners need to understand the components of a garden

GROWING WITH YOUR GARDEN. Two midsummer gardens—
a shady retreat [LEFT] and a sunny border [ABOVE]—overflow with
plants of different colors, sizes, and textures. Finding the perfect
new hybrid daylily [RIGHT] is an ongoing challenge and pleasure.

and be able to combine them with imagination and skill. We are always in the process of learning, and forever will be. The more we know about plants, the more we enjoy the gardening experience. No two gardeners want the same thing from their gardens, however, and the world is full of people who are completely happy cramming a lot of plants into a small bed, combining unharmonious colors, and never learning their Latin names. If you are one of these, that is fine. Enjoying your garden is really all that matters. But if you want to learn more, we know you'll enjoy the experience as much as we have.

Over the years, we have gotten away from specialty gardens and broadened our vision of what a flower garden should be. Now we have fun with a variety of plants. There are no rules to proclaim that small shrubs, ornamental grasses, wildflowers, background vines, and evergreens shouldn't have a place in a flower border, alongside perennials, bulbs, and annuals. Each contributes a unique quality to the garden.

Getting to Know the Terms

Perennials live more than two years. The word encompasses hardy shrubs and trees, as well as hardy herbaceous plants. It also includes plants like geraniums (*Pelargonium*) and begonias that are perennials in warm climates but killed by low temperatures in colder areas; these are commonly called "tender perennials."

Annuals are plants that grow from seed each spring and live only one season. Cosmos, calendulas, and marigolds are popular annuals.

Biennials sprout and grow the first year the seed is planted, then produce flowers, make seeds, and subsequently die in their second year. This sequence may vary if a plant sprouts very early and blooms the first year, or if it lives for more than two years, as may happen in areas with a short growing season. Canterbury bells (*Campanula medium*), sweet William (*Dianthus barbatus*), and common foxglove (*Digitalis purpurea*) are well-known garden biennials.

Perennials: Powerful Partners

From studying the new garden catalogs in mid-January to tucking mulch in among the plants just before the winter snows arrive, gardening is full of delightful surprises and never monotonous. As soon as the snow melts in the spring, we hurry out to discover which perennials are peeping through the wet earth after their winter hibernation. With the first spring shower, many that had seemed dead on first inspection suddenly sprout green buds, and we know that more delights will appear each day until the cycle of seasons brings gardening to a close once again.

It is this quality of metamorphosis that attracts us to herbaceous perennials. They are fascinating because most bloom for only short periods and seldom look the same two days in a row, or two years in succession. Our early morning walks reward us with a changing display of blossoms and an endless variation of plant textures, heights, and fragrances. We wait expectantly to see if the new hybrid iris we splurged on last fall will be as spectacular as the catalog description promised, or if the blooms of the peony that were disappointingly small last summer will improve this year.

Perennials are the mainstay of the flower border, adding variety with their many different heights, colors, foliage textures, and blooming times. They don't need replanting every year, and they are especially prized by those who garden where winters are too severe to grow many flowering shrubs. Because perennials die to the ground over the winter, they can actually have an easier time surviving the winter in areas with a reliable snow cover than in warmer zones. Certain perennials, such as some hybrid delphiniums, prefer cool weather during the growing season, too, and will fade out after just a year or two where summers are hot. Other species positively thrive where winters are warm and summers are sizzling hot.

PERENNIAL FAVORITES. Black-eyed Susans *(Rudbeckia)* and purple coneflowers *(Echinacea purpurea)* [ABOVE] are dependable late summer bloomers. Old-fashioned *Campanula* 'Kent Belle' [RIGHT] is striking where height and summer color are needed.

COLOR WHERE YOU NEED IT. For color throughout the season, depend on glowing petunias [ABOVE] and brashly brassy marigolds [RIGHT]. Keep both deadheaded, and you will have a colorful display all summer long, in garden beds as well as in containers.

Annuals: Adaptable Allies

The annual flowers that grow, bloom, produce seed, and die the same year are lovely, colorful, and predictable throughout the summer. They are inexpensive, especially when you start them yourself from seeds, and they require little summer care other than deadheading and regular maintenance. The huge variety of annuals makes it easy to choose appropriate colors and heights, and the small size of many makes them easy to protect from late spring or early fall frosts. Most need no staking.

Gardeners in cool regions treat some perennials as annuals because the plants aren't winter hardy in much of North America. Geraniums *(Pelargonium)*, petunias, and impatiens, for example, flourish year-round in frost-free areas but need protection elsewhere. They bloom for most of the season, and, if we want, we can dig and pot them before the first frost and use them as houseplants during the winter.

Bulbs: Bold Beauties

Bulbs have an important place in an all-season garden. Bulb-type plants include not only daffodils and other spring bloomers that brighten the end of winter but also those that appear in summer and fall — the lilies, irises, dahlias, and many more that add so much to the joy of gardening. Like perennials, bulb clumps increase in size each year, and you can divide them every few years to expand your planting or give to friends.

When the first snowdrops *(Galanthus)* peep through the snow in late winter or early spring, we're elated. Later, the daffodils, crocus, tulips, and hyacinths provide bright spots of early color even when the lawn appears dead. Throughout the summer, bulbous plants such as crocosmias, lilies, lily-of-the-valley, ornamental onions *(Allium),* oxalis, Persian buttercup *(Ranunculus asiaticus),* and spider lilies *(Lycoris)* add interesting blooms and foliage textures.

COMFORTABLE COMPANIONS. Daffodils nestle with heather *(Calluna vulgaris),* which will continue to bloom after the bulbs' foliage dies away.

A TOUCH OF THE WILD. This columbine *(Aquilegia canadensis),* a native, reseeds freely and is dependable for years.

Wildflowers: Familiar Faces

Planting wildflowers in the cultivated flower garden can be a debatable subject. Most are better suited to a more natural setting, and many require shade, especially in summer. There are notable exceptions, however: Violets fit nicely into even the most formal perennial garden, for instance, while bunchberries *(Cornus canadensis)* make great edging plants. In our own yard, we enjoy a clump of maidenhair ferns *(Adiantum)* in a shaded part of our back border, and wild columbine *(Aquilegia canadensis)* has seeded itself beautifully in part of one sunny bed. Wild shrubs, such as flowering raspberry *(Rubus odoratus)* and red-flowering currant *(Ribes sanguineum),* add some interest as well as beauty to a planting, and wild roses can make a nice impenetrable background.

Wildflowers fit well into certain specialty gardens. Many are ideal for rock gardens, some are suited for shade gardens, and others are perfect for bog plantings or dry areas. Useful wild plants, like the mints *(Mentha),* American ginseng *(Panax quinquefolius),* and wintergreen *(Gaultheria procumbens),* are good choices for medicinal herb plots.

Never dig any endangered plants from the wild or buy plants from someone who sells wild-collected plants. Keep in mind, too, that many wildflowers have a favorite environment and special light, moisture, temperature, and soil requirements, and consider these conditions when you choose wildflowers for your garden. You'll find more inspiration for using wild plants in flower gardens on page 138.

Shrubs: Season Stretchers

Shrubs have been described as the "bones of the garden." Dwarf shrubs are the best ones to plant among annuals and perennials, and in recent years, nurseries have introduced many new compact deciduous and evergreen shrubs. Numerous low-growing, deciduous, flowering shrubs are available, including cinquefoils *(Potentilla)*, cotoneasters, forsythias, French hydrangea *(Hydrangea macrophylla)*, and roses. Small, broad-leaved evergreens, such as compact rhododendrons and azaleas, furnish a riot of color in spring.

Dwarf needled evergreens also have a place in the garden: They are green when the leaves of deciduous trees and shrubs have fallen and the world looks drab, so they add brightness to perennial gardens, rock gardens, and slopes during the winter months. Many dwarf evergreens are no larger than a clump of iris, so it's easy to fit them into a border. Some good choices for the garden include selections of arborvitae *(Thuja)*, false cypresses *(Chamaecyparis)*, firs *(Abies)*, hemlocks *(Tsuga)*, spruces *(Picea)*, and pines *(Pinus)*.

Where space permits, taller shrubs can be used as accents or to provide a windbreak and backdrop to a garden. You can even use them to support the stems of tall-growing flowers, such as delphiniums and hollyhocks *(Alcea rosea)*. Many flowering shrubs serve as nostalgic reminders of old-fashioned gardens, and they deserve their reputations: Lilacs *(Syringa)*, mock orange *(Philadelphus coronarius)*, and wisterias fill the air with sweet perfume in the spring, and many shrub roses bloom for most of the summer, pouring out their fragrance over a large area.

One of the most valuable contributions shrubs of all sizes can make to a garden is furnishing form, texture, and color to the border throughout the year, even after perennials and annuals are gone. Forsythia and daphnes are among the first blooming shrubs of spring, making them a welcome sight after a long winter, while others brighten borders in summer and fall. Many shrubs also provide beautiful foliage color during the last days of fall. Burning bush *(Euonymus alatus)* and blueberries *(Vaccinium)*, for instance, have brilliant red leaves at the end of the season, while others welcome the shortening days with shades of yellow, pink, or bronze. A number of deciduous shrubs and some evergreens, including junipers, hollies *(Ilex)*, and yews *(Taxus)*, have attractive berries or small fruits and furnish food for birds and other wildlife. Some fruits, such as those of the American highbush cranberry *(Viburnum trilobum)*, hang on for most of the winter.

Once established, shrubs require less care than perennials, and you don't need to replant them each spring, as you do annuals. The true dwarf cultivars need little, if any, pruning, and except for roses, most are not bothered by insect and disease troubles.

SHIFTING SHADES. Summer hydrangea [BELOW] and fall burning bush *(Euonymus alatus)* [LEFT] glow with color.

Vines: Vertical Variety

Because they need support, upright-growing vines are not usually found within a perennial bed, although they may be ideal to cover the arbor that forms an entrance to it. Their foliage and blooms can also be attractive when covering a fence, wall, or trellis that provides a background for other plants. Other uses of vines include hiding deck supports, screening a porch, climbing lampposts, and trailing over arbors, rocks, or even shrubs. If space is limited, you can grow them over a wire fence to act as a hedge. Your choice of vines isn't limited to heavy ivies or wisterias: Sweet pea *(Lathyrus odoratus),* morning glories *(Ipomoea),* and scarlet runner bean *(Phaseolus coccineus)* are ideal choices for lightweight supports, such as strings or netting.

Vines are particularly useful for providing vertical beauty in a small urban, suburban, or rooftop garden where space is limited or where the border backs up against a wall. Within a bed, they can climb a structure to provide an accent point.

Grasses: Graceful Elegance

Ornamental grasses come in a wide range of sizes, textures, and foliage and bloom colors. When the right grass is in the right place, it can add pizzazz to a perennial bed, meadow garden, or other natural area, and tall specimens form nice background plants in the flower garden. Many grasses have lovely arching stems and showy flowers, some of which persist into the winter and brighten the bleak landscape. Some, such as giant reed *(Arundo donax),* are gigantic in size and suitable only for large estates or parks, but there are also miniature grasses that fit in well in rock gardens.

If you are considering some of the ornamental grasses, check out their growth habits before letting them into your garden. Some can spread quickly by creeping roots, and you need to give them room to run or else confine them with root barriers, because they are not easy to control once established. Vigorous spreaders can still be very effective in a spot where they can grow freely, and their textures, foliage colors, and blooms can dress up an otherwise drab area.

Before planting grasses, visit a nursery or display garden that grows a wide variety of them, so you can

FOR FOUNTAINLIKE EFFECTS. Japanese wisteria *(Wisteria floribunda)* [TOP] flows gracefully over the top of a brick garden wall. A variegated ornamental grass [BOTTOM] contributes sparkle and textural contrast to a large-scale garden.

see for yourself how big they'll get. A great many are hardy only up through Zone 5, so select those that are right for your region and for your specific conditions. Some will withstand drought well, for instance, while others are tolerant of wind and salt spray. If you are fond of a grass that has the potential to take over, confine it in a large plastic tub with the bottom removed. Sink the tub so the top rim is just above ground level, fill it with soil, and set the grass inside. Every year or so, remove the plant and divide it to keep it from becoming rootbound.

Latin for Gardeners

Although you can have a magnificent garden without knowing the botanical names of your plants, you'll avoid a lot of confusion if you learn them early. Scientific nomenclature absolutely defines the plant to which people refer, no matter what their language. A gardener in one area may talk about a yellow daisy, for example, while another discusses a marguerite; however, both are talking about the plant known botanically as *Anthemis tinctoria.* Knowing and using botanical names also makes sure you get the specific plant you want when you shop. If you asked for honeysuckle at a garden center, for instance, you might be shown a vine, a shrub, a wildflower, or a perennial. But if you asked for *Lonicera × heckrottii,* you'd receive exactly what you were looking for: a beautiful flowering vine.

While most botanical names stay the same, others change on occasion, as botanists learn more about the plants and their unique characteristics. That's why a plant with a familiar name, such as *Coleus,* may suddenly have a totally different name (in this case, *Solenostemon).*

GENUS AND SPECIES. The scientific name categorizes a plant into the correct genus (the first, and capitalized, part of the name) and the species within that genus (indicated by the second, descriptive word in the name). All members of the gladiolus genus, for example, are *Gladiolus,* and the popular glad shown here is *Gladiolus callianthus.* (When mentioned after the first reference in a text, it is written "*G. callianthus.*")

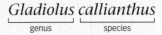

Gladiolus callianthus
genus — species

The species name (formally known as the specific epithet) may describe a particular quality of a plant, indicate the country or region where it originated, distinguish its native habitat, or describe its appearance (its leaves, stem, blooms, fruit, or habit of growth). For example, here are some scientific adjectives that provide clues about a plant:

canadensis	of Canada
japonica	of Japan
orientalis	of the Orient
montana or *alpina*	of the mountains
sylvaticus	of the woods
aquatica	of the water
gigantea	large
brevi	short
colorata	colored
arborescens	woody
mollis	soft
annuus	annual
nanus	dwarf
multiflora	many-flowered
alba	white
triphyllum	three-leaved
barbatus	bearded

CULTIVAR. Plants within a species sometimes show an unusual trait, such as an out-of-the-ordinary flower color, leaf marking, or growth habit. Commercial growers may select that variation, give it a name, and propagate it to retain its special characteristics. These unique plants are called cultivars. The cultivar name is capitalized and placed in single quotes. For example, the gladiolus cultivar 'Karen' is written as *Gladiolus callianthus* 'Karen'.

Gladiolus callianthus 'Karen'

A Perfect Marriage

IT IS ALWAYS TEMPTING to choose the flowers for your garden by their appearance alone, but, as in choosing a spouse, you need to be aware of what is unseen before you take the plunge. The thousands of different garden species vary widely in their growth and blooming habits, and each has different needs that must be met in order to thrive.

With their stunning photos, garden catalogs are fun and inspirational, and it takes a strong will to resist reaching for your checkbook when they arrive early in the winter. The descriptions tend to be enthusiastic, especially those for new cultivars that are just being introduced into the garden trade. You will be much better off, however, if you wait to see a plant for yourself, or at least do some research on it, before you spend your money.

Even Beautiful Garden Flowers Can Be Weeds

Because we were anxious for quick results when we first started gardening, we made the mistake of planting too many overly aggressive perennials, including yellow daisy *(Anthemis tinctoria),* mountain bluet *(Centaurea montana),* and old-fashioned daylilies *(Hemerocallis).* These fast growers soon crowded out the more refined phlox, irises, and balloon flowers *(Platycodon grandiflorus),* causing no end of frustration and work. Now we limit the number of the more vigorous plants, watch them carefully, and don't hesitate to remove part of the clump whenever our flower beds become threatened by unfriendly takeovers.

When we know a plant is a possible problem, we keep a close eye on it in our gardens. Perennials on our "watch list" include bee balms *(Monarda),* bugleweeds *(Ajuga),* English daisy *(Bellis perennis),* forget-me-nots *(Myosotis),* goldenrods *(Solidago),* loosestrifes *(Lysimachia),* lupines, mountain bluet, peach-leaved bellflower *(Campanula persicifolia),* stonecrops *(Sedum),*

CHEERFUL THUGS. Goldenrods *(Solidago)* are colorful additions to the late summer garden, but given the right conditions, they can become invasive and therefore need to be kept under control.

sweet rocket *(Hesperis matronalis),* tawny daylily *(Hemerocallis fulva),* yarrows *(Achillea),* and yellow daisy *(Anthemis tinctoria),* as well as most grasses. All have shown a tendency to take over our beds with the slightest encouragement.

Some spreaders can be more than minor nuisances. Certain attractive, innocent-looking plants have become a major problem in some areas of the country. Vigorous programs are currently in force in the United States to eradicate hostile immigrants like purple lythrum and Japanese bamboo.

Of course, perennials aren't the only spreaders. Certain annuals, such as calliopsis *(Coreopsis tinctoria),* and biennials, such as foxgloves *(Digitalis),* can scatter enough seeds to become a problem. A few shrubs, including red-twigged dogwood *(Cornus alba)* and common juniper *(Juniperus communis),* may also drop their seeds and spread more than you'd like. Trailing shrubs and vines sometimes grow roots along their branches and form new plants that keep spreading, although you can usually contain these by a regular cutting back. Even some of our often used bulbs, such as grape hyacinths *(Muscari),* lily-of-the-valley *(Convallaria majalis),* and crested iris *(Iris cristata),* can be invasive.

It is unfair to rigidly classify all super-vigorous plants as weeds, because each can be attractive and useful in the proper location and for the right purpose. The vigor of a plant may vary considerably according to soil and climatic conditions, too, and plants that have become thugs in our garden might be ideal in yours. Naturally, if you are one of those gardeners who likes to see a wild array of plants competing with each other, ignore our warnings and enjoy your display.

Something Old or Something New

When buying plants, you sometimes have a choice between new hybrids and the older, tried-and-true kinds. Of course, you want the best for your garden, but how can you judge which cultivars (especially new ones) will be right for your plan and growing conditions?

Hybrids result from a cross between two different species or varieties. Such crosses are usually possible only within the same genus. Although some new introductions are accidents of nature, most result from the careful planning of horticulturists who attempt to combine the best qualities of different plants. Hybrid cultivars often have more spectacular flowers than those of their ancestors and are well worth seeking out in your local garden center or in nursery catalogs. In addition to improved color, bloom size, and vigor, traits such as a compact growth habit or a longer bloom season may make hybrids more suitable for your garden. 'Blue Fountain' delphiniums, for example, are among our favorite hybrids. They are as attractive as the popular giant Pacific hybrids, but since they are much shorter, staking is unnecessary even in our windy area.

Keep in mind that, in the plant world, "new" does not automatically mean "better." In the search for bigger and brighter flowers, breeders occasionally overlook traits like vigor, disease resistance, and fragrance. For example, we have heard friends lament that many new hybrid pinks *(Dianthus),* like many newer sweet peas *(Lathyrus odoratus)* and roses, do not have the same delightful scent of earlier species. This lack leads some people to prefer old-time or heirloom cultivars, which have proven their worth to generations of gardeners.

Virginia bluebells *(Mertensia pulmonarioides)*

Appreciate the Ancestors

Many plants were introduced to this country by the first European settlers, who brought their favorite growing things along with their personal necessities. When we were young, our neighbors had a large clump of bluebells of Scotland *(Campanula rotundifolia)* in their yard, and they often told us of how their grandparents had brought a root from the Isles with them in a small ship a century earlier. That dark blue campanula seemed to us a living bit of Europe, and we sometimes speculated about how much it must have meant to those homesick settlers during their first difficult years here.

In addition to the plants imported by immigrants or by early American missionaries and other people who traveled abroad, many others were discovered by professional horticulturists who visited foreign lands to seek new species of plant life. Some of the imports felt so much at home in this country that they quickly became unappreciated weeds. The common dandelion *(Taraxacum officinale),* devil's paintbrush or orange hawkweed *(Hieracium aurantiacum),* oxeye daisy *(Leucanthemum vulgare),* tansy *(Tanacetum vulgare),* and many others arrived as garden flowers or medicinal herbs but rapidly spread throughout the countryside. Of course, not all garden perennials are immigrants. In fact, a fair number of them are natives of North America's fields and woods. Wildflowers such as the yellow lady's slipper *(Cypripedium calceolus),* bee balm *(Monarda didyma),* and Virginia bluebells *(Mertensia pulmonarioides)* were admired by the early settlers and transplanted into private yards and gardens. In recent years, there has been growing interest in using native plants in gardens, so now we can buy nursery-grown selections of these special plants instead of digging them from the wild.

CHAPTER 2

Designing Your Flower Garden

MANY YEARS AGO a retired farm couple gave us a tour of their perennial garden. All of their flowers were planted in neat cultivated rows, just like their vegetables, quite contrary to all the rules of garden design. As we walked up and down the rows, they described each plant's background, where they had acquired it, and a bit of its lore. They proudly displayed their collection of beloved flowers the same way some people

show bottles or seashells, and they were so enthusiastic that we enjoyed the tour as much as they enjoyed giving it. Clearly this was the right garden for them.

During our years in the plant business we have visited hundreds of gardens, and each is as different as the person who created it. We have become convinced that there is no one "right" way to design a planting. Still, a few basic guidelines of good design can serve us well as we plan our own gardens.

Where Does Your Garden Grow?

BEFORE YOU CHOOSE the specific site for your garden, first step back and consider the characteristics of the whole area where you live. North America has a wide range of climates, from areas with year-round ice and snow to tropical paradises. Foresters, farmers, and gardeners rely on the United States Department of Agriculture's hardiness zone map (page 348) for choosing the plants that will grow well in their climate. Updated periodically, the map classifies each region according to its average annual minimum temperature. Some maps also show average dates of first and last frosts. Zone 1 is near-tundra, and Zones 2 and 3 have low winter temperatures and short growing seasons. Much of the continental United States falls into Zones 4, 5, 6, 7, and 8, where a wide range of plants grow well. Since Zones 9 and 10 have little or no frost, people there can raise many tropical and semitropical plants.

Gardeners in the South, especially, may want to check the American Horticultural Society's Plant Heat Zone Map (page 349), which gives the average numbers of "heat days" for each of the 12 zones shown. Heat days are those when the temperature rises over 86°F (30°C) — the point at which plants begin to suffer damage from the heat. Zone 1 has less than one heat day per year, while Zone 12 has more than 210. Use this map to help select plants that should perform well in your climate and avoid those that are likely to struggle in warm regions.

Some climates aren't cold enough for certain plants. A few northern conifers and alpines, as well as peonies and tulips, for example, won't survive in an area unless they get the required number of "chilling" days (when the temperature falls below freezing) each year. Of course, heat and cold are only two factors that affect how plants perform in a particular climate. Gardeners must also take into account other growing requirements, including moisture, light, soil pH, and fertility, and these may vary depending on the different zones.

SOME LIKE IT COLD. Peonies *(Paeonia)* [ABOVE] grow only in areas that receive a certain number of days when temperatures fall below freezing each year, whereas tender shrubs, like most fuchsias [RIGHT], are hardy enough to stay outdoors year-round only in Zones 9 and 10; elsewhere they must be grown as annuals.

The Best in Both Worlds

Gardening in the North

If you have moved recently to a northern or mountainous climate, you may be distressed to see how much it limits the growing of some of your favorite trees and shrubs. You will also find, however, that there are many wonderful woody plants that thrive there, and that the climate is ideal for most annuals and herbaceous perennials. Many species grow best and bloom over longer periods in areas where summers are cool and evening dews are heavy.

Frigid winter temperatures do not affect perennials as much as they do woody plants, because their tops die down before winter, and snow often mulches the roots. Friends of ours who moved from Zone 6 in eastern Massachusetts to our mountain village in Zone 3 hardly missed their rhododendrons and mountain laurel *(Kalmia latifolia)* because they were so captivated by the many perennials and alpine plants that thrived in their new backyard.

Gardening in the South

If you garden in a southern region, you obviously face more problems with heat, and possibly drought, than with cold. An unexpected frost can strike even in citrus country, but ordinarily you can grow beautiful semitropical plants that Northerners envy. In a hot, dry climate, some years you will need to water daily throughout the summer to keep the gardens thriving, and you may find it necessary to shade fragile plants during the hottest weather. Heavy, humus-rich soils are desirable in warm, dry regions, because they stay cooler than light, sandy ones. Mulches are extremely valuable, since they help keep the soil cool and prevent moisture from evaporating rapidly. Trees, hedges, tight fences, and walls can give valuable protection from drying winds and provide light shade during the heat of the day. August is a resting period for many plants in such a climate, and you can take a break from many gardening chores for a few weeks. With cooler days in September, the garden—and the gardener—becomes active again, and you can look forward to enjoying a long fall season of asters, chrysanthemums, cannas, and similar plants.

If you garden in a very hot, humid region, or one that gets a lot of rainfall during certain seasons, you may need to increase air circulation and possibly sunlight by thinning out trees or other plants in the garden. A bit of judicious pruning may help your plants avoid mildew and other troubles caused by too

much moisture. You can save much time and labor if you choose the plants best suited to your particular southern location. Most garden catalogs list the recommended planting zones for each plant, and you may be able to get helpful advice from your gardening neighbors, local nurseries, or Cooperative Extension Service.

Understanding the Quirkiness of Each Plant's Needs

While hardiness zone and heat day ratings go a long way toward helping gardeners choose plants that are adapted to their climate, they are not absolute guarantees that a particular plant will thrive in a certain area. When plants considered "hardy" are raised in a warmer climate, for instance, they may suffer when they are moved to a colder zone. A smoke bush *(Cotinus coggygria)* that is rated as hardy in Zone 4 but raised in Zone 6 may resent a move to the colder zone and either die or suffer dieback for several years until it acclimates.

Often, the temperature of the soil, rather than the air temperature, is the critical factor affecting plant survival. Snow is a wonderful insulator for the soil, keeping the earth evenly cool but preventing it from freezing deeply. That's why gardeners who can depend on a generous amount of snow each winter may have better luck overwintering a plant than another gardener in the same hardiness zone but with no snow cover. If you garden where the mercury drops below 0°F and a protective layer of snow is not certain, plant only the hardiest perennials, unless you are able to cover them with thick mulch each fall and uncover them at the proper time in the spring. An insulating material like leaves, straw, or wood chips around the plants helps keep the soil from the alternate freezing and thawing that can heave plants out of the ground, exposing the roots to cold damage. A cover of evergreen boughs that doesn't pack and smother the plants also provides good winter insurance.

THE FROSTING ON THE CAKE. Japanese anemones *(A. × hybrida* and *A. japonica)* [ABOVE] bloom late, sometimes even after light frosts. Blue wood aster *(Aster cordifolius* 'Little Carlow') [BELOW LEFT] blossoms from late summer through midfall. Although these plants are hardy in Zones 4–8 and 5–8, respectively, their flowering times may be cut short where early heavy frosts are common.

Winter temperatures alone should not govern your choice of plants in the North. The timing of the first frost is another consideration. Plants such as chrysanthemums, dahlias, fall-blooming anemones, gentians, hardy asters, and rose mallows *(Hibiscus)* flower late in the season and may bloom for only a short time, if at all, where frosts come unusually early.

Our gardens have taught us to be patient and tolerant of the whims of nature. We now realize that despite good intentions, the best-laid plans of gardeners everywhere can be upset by violent storms or other unusual weather, by surprise epidemics of diseases and bugs, and by unexpected demands on their time. But, like baseball fans, we who grow plants never despair. There's always next year, when everything will grow and bloom to perfection, and we'll be proud to show our backyard to the likes of the legendary gardener Gertrude Jekyll herself!

The Site That Is Right

PART OF THE FUN of designing a garden is uniting your chosen plants with a unique location. No other garden in the world will be exactly like yours, because the design of your home, the natural features of the landscape, and the surrounding vistas will make it as distinctive as a fingerprint. Even if you live in a city and have little or no choice of sites, you can still create a garden with its own character.

If all gardens followed the example of many formal European borders, it would seem that the only place for a proper garden is in a lawn that is as large and level as a ballroom floor. That kind of area can serve as the setting for a magnificent garden, of course, but most of us are neither so ambitious nor so fortunate as to garden in such a setting. As the Japanese have demonstrated so well, a garden can fit nearly any available space.

If your lot is bare, with no trees, pool, hedges, or shrubs, you will be able to plan your dream garden with great freedom. The possibilities are endless, no matter

what size or shape plot you have: Set up a shrub border that encloses a secret gazebo, install a water garden brimming with water lilies and lotus, build a pathway that winds through a bed of lavender, arrange colorful annuals around a boulder, plant a bed of roses, or consider any of the theme gardens described in Part 2 as inspiration.

If trees, pools, hedges, and shrubs are already installed, you'll want to choose plantings that complement these features. A flower bed always looks best if it relates well in size and design to the buildings and other plantings near it. Certain spots are naturals for a flowering border, so look at any existing features that could be used as boundaries for a garden. These include fences, walls, hedges, walkways, driveways, buildings, terraces, a brook, a pool, or a specimen tree. One of our borders snuggles up against a tall clipped arborvitae (*Thuja*) hedge that surrounds the backyard, and another smaller border lies comfortably alongside an old barn. Take advantage of whatever you already have in your landscape and use it as the backbone of your plan to create new spaces.

MAKING THE GRADE. A raised-bed garden [ABOVE], backed by fencing, makes a pleasing transition between lawn areas.

One Size Does Not Fit All

If you like flowers and enjoy creating beauty, gardening is undeniably pleasant, but most of us have many other demands on our time. The solution would seem simple: Start with a small garden, and stop expanding the minute it becomes more work than fun. Unfortunately, it seems to be just as difficult for an avid gardener to resist acquiring more plants as it is for a compulsive eater to go on a diet or for a gambler to give up casinos. Tempting new cultivars beg to be grown, and many of the perennials already in the ground must be divided regularly. Who is hard-hearted enough to throw away beautiful surplus plants? For most of us, it is easy to decide that a little more lawn must go to make room for expanding plantings, but it can be difficult to properly maintain it all.

Our nursery customers often thought perennials were the answer, assuming that, like roadside trees, they pretty much take care of themselves year after year. But most gardeners spend a lot of time mulching, weeding, deadheading, dividing, watering, feeding, coping with insects and disease, and getting the garden ready for winter. Low-maintenance plants, such as hostas, peonies, and daylilies (Hemerocallis), need little attention if placed in an ideal spot, but even these are not completely carefree if you want them to prosper over time.

A flower garden, like a vegetable plot, is more beautiful, productive, and satisfying when kept to a manageable size. The Chinese have a saying to which all gardeners should pay heed: "Praise large gardens, plant small ones." Whatever your plans for a garden may be, let quality rather than quantity be your goal.

Getting the Light Right

While some plants insist on full sun and others demand shade, most flowering plants are somewhat flexible in their light requirements. A plant described as needing full sun may actually grow beautifully with only a half day of full sun, as long as it gets plenty of "skylight" for the remainder of the day. (*Skylight* can be defined as light from an "open" sky, with shading provided by a vertical surface, such as a wall, hedge, or building, rather than by the canopy of a tree or building overhang.)

The amount of light a plant needs for good growth and flowering can be affected by the latitude in which it is growing. A variety that needs shade in the South may be happiest with full sun in the North because the light is less intense there, especially as the days shorten rapidly after mid-August. Likewise, a plant that prefers full sun in the North may suffer badly with that exposure in a hotter climate.

Light exposure affects plants in other ways. In some cases, it can change their bloom time. Peonies grown on the west side of a building, for instance, bloom later in the season than they would in a sunny southeastern exposure. Plants like chrysanthemums bloom earlier if they are grown where they get some afternoon shade, because their bud formation is triggered by diminishing light conditions. Occasionally, the flowers of some plants are more beautiful when grown in shaded conditions. Daylilies, for example, generally bloom best in full sunlight, but the blossoms of certain red and pink cultivars are brighter when partially shaded from the bleaching effects of hot afternoon sun.

Ideally, your garden will grow for many years in the same spot, so you should not only make a note of the present light conditions but also try to anticipate how those conditions may change in the future. If young trees are nearby, the amount of shade they provide will increase as they grow, which will necessitate some pruning, or even complete removal of trees, to ensure adequate sunlight for continued good growth and blooms in the flower garden. The future is not always easy to predict, of course. We have friends who saw their beautiful backyard garden wither away in deep shade when a six-story apartment building replaced the small house next door. They recovered by planting a new garden with shade-loving perennials, like ferns, astilbes, and hostas.

It is interesting to note that certain flowers tend to face the source of light when they are planted in a garden that is shaded for part of the day. Daffodils, most daisy-type flowers, pansies and violets *(Viola)*, and spiky flowers such as beardtongues *(Penstemon)* all have this habit, so if you have a garden facing a deck or terrace and plan to grow more than a few of these flowers, you may want to position your garden to take best advantage of this tendency. You may also want to avoid planting flowers that are likely always to face their "backs" to you.

Shelter from Wind

If high winds are the rule where you live, choose a sheltered spot for your garden or create a protected area with hedges or fences. We are pleased with the 12-foot evergreen hedge that serves as our back boundary, because it allows us to grow tall, fragile plants such as hollyhocks *(Alcea rosea)*, lavateras, and sunflowers *(Helianthus annuus)*, even on our windy hilltop. A basket-weave or picket fence will also offer wind protection, but a solid fence may create more problems than it solves. Unless the confined area is small, a tight board fence or one made of fiberglass panels can create powerful downdrafts and cause winds to swirl uncontrollably among the plants, which can inflict as much damage as a direct gale.

Getting to the Root of the Problem

Trees and shrubs adjacent to a flower garden can be a problem not only because of their shade but also because their large roots are likely to creep into the beds and rob your plants of nutrients and moisture. It is difficult to gauge what might be an adequate distance to separate a garden from a tree, since the roots of a large shade tree growing in shallow soil can extend 100 feet or more from the trunk. If the area gets plenty of sun, it is possible to garden near trees, tall hedges, and shrubs, as long as you are prepared to provide enough moisture and nutrients to nourish both your garden and the larger plants. Some gardeners bury a metal or concrete barrier 2 or more feet deep between a newly planted hedge or shrub border and the garden to keep the roots from venturing where they are not wanted.

The Garden as a Neighborhood of Plants

THE LAYOUT OF THE GARDEN is as important to its appearance as its siting. The concept of clumping has long been basic to good garden design. In most backyard gardens, a single medium-sized plant — one flowering or evergreen shrub, for instance, or an established lupine *(Lupinus),* peony, or shasta daisy *(Leucanthemum × superbum)* — has enough presence to be a "clump." With smaller plants, such as coral bells *(Heuchera sanguinea),* petunias, and primroses *(Primula),* you may need three, five, seven, or even more of the same cultivar to create a similar visual impact. As in art, odd numbers of plants seem to work best in garden design. To create the masses of color and the various shapes and textures that make a border attractive, repeat the same clumps at intervals throughout the garden to create a strong pattern.

When spacing the plants, allow plenty of room initially for the natural expansion of each clump or shrub, so that it will not impinge on neighboring plants. Leaving enough space takes discipline, because we all have a tendency to set new small plants too close together. Estimating eventual size as you design the garden is a tricky business, even for an experienced gardener, because the different cultivars of one species grow to different heights, and even identical cultivars may grow to varying sizes, depending on the quality and type of soil, light conditions, and climate.

Planning for Breadth and Height

Guess the mature size as closely as you can, then allow at least 6 inches between each plant within a clump, and a foot or more between the separate clumps. A vigorous-growing plant, such as a dwarf shrub, daylily, gloriosa daisy *(Rudbeckia hirta),* or peony, will fill an area 2 or more feet in diameter within only a couple of years. After a few seasons of gardening, you will be better able to judge how plants grow in your area, and then you can make experienced decisions about how far apart to space them. The small perennials in your newly made garden will look very sparse, so stick some annuals between them for the first year or two, until the others grow.

Another method of design is to space plants much further apart than is necessary, and then apply a heavy mulch between them to prevent weed growth. Because this garden style is easy to care for, it is often used for industrial and commercial landscaping.

Common sense dictates that plants should be arranged according to height, so that short plants such as sweet William *(Dianthus barbatus)* and pansies will not be completely hidden behind a tall clump of lupines at

A PLANT OF SUBSTANCE. A single specimen of some plants, such as the bright orange butterfly weed *(Asclepias tuberosa)* in this garden group, is enough to form a substantial clump. A few more plants of the yellow coreopsis *(Coreopsis lanceolata)* will most likely be required to provide a similar visual impact.

The Long and the Short of It

Tall-Growing Perennials (4 or more feet)

Asters, some cultivars (*Aster*)

Astilbes, some cultivars (*Astilbe*)

Boltonia (*Boltonia asteroides*)

Bugbanes (*Cimicifuga*)

Chimney bellflower
    (*Campanula pyramidalis*)

Common foxglove, most cultivars
    (*Digitalis purpurea*)

Common rose mallow
    (*Hibiscus moscheutos*)

Common sneezeweed
    (*Helenium autumnale*)

Daylilies, some cultivars, especially
    Altissima hybrids (*Hemerocallis*)

Delphiniums, most cultivars
    (*Delphinium*)

Desert candles (*Eremurus*)

Elecampane (*Inula helenium*)

Globe thistles, most cultivars (*Echinops*)

Golden glow
    (*Rudbeckia laciniata* var. *hortensia*)

Hollyhock (*Alcea rosea*)

Joe-Pye weed (*Eupatorium purpureum*)

Lilies, many hybrids, including
    'Black Dragon', 'Copper King',
    'Moonlight', and others (*Lilium*)

Meadow rues (*Thalictrum*)

Monkshoods (*Aconitum*)

Plume poppy (*Macleaya cordata*)

Valerian (*Valeriana officinalis*)

Wild senna (*Cassia marilandica*)

UPS AND DOWNS. Combining plants of varying heights gives a natural effect.

Dwarf Plants (less than 1 foot)

Avens, some cultivars (*Geum*)

Basket-of-gold (*Aurinia saxatilis*)

Bloody cranesbill
    (*Geranium sanguineum*)

Blue fescue (*Festuca glauca*)

Bugleweeds (*Ajuga*)

Carpathian bellflower
    (*Campanula carpatica*)

Catmint (*Nepeta* × *faassenii*)

Coral bells (*Heuchera sanguinea*)

Dwarf bearded iris (*Iris pumila*)

English daisy (*Bellis perennis*)

Fringed bleeding heart (*Dicentra eximia*)

Grass pink (*Dianthus plumarius*)

Iceland poppy (*Papaver croceum*)

Lady's mantle (*Alchemilla mollis*)

Lesser periwinkle (*Vinca minor*)

Moss pink (*Phlox subulata*)

Mountain avens (*Dryas*)

Perennial candytuft (*Iberis sempervirens*)

Plumbago (*Ceratostigma plumbaginoides*)

Primroses (*Primula*)

Rock speedwell (*Veronica prostrata*)

Snow-in-summer (*Cerastium tomentosum*)

Stonecrops (*Sedum*)

Thrifts (*Armeria*)

Tunic flower (*Petrorhagia saxifraga*)

Wall rock cress (*Arabis caucasica*)

Woolly speedwell (*V. spicata* subsp. *incana*)

blooming time. We have met gardeners so impressed by this reasoning, however, that their borders are rigidly arranged with tall plants in the back row, medium-sized ones in the middle, and low-growing ones in front, like a set of stairs. They plant island gardens the same way, in tiers like a wedding cake, with the tallest plants in the center. Unfortunately, such inflexible arrangements result in an artificial appearance. A garden is more pleasing to the eye if plants of different heights, colors, and varieties are arranged as if they were growing naturally, at random throughout the garden. An irregular arrangement of heights is made easier because perennials bloom at different times throughout the season. You can, for instance,

place a 2-foot-tall globeflower (*Trollius*) near the front of a bed, because it will be finished blooming and you can cut it back before the shorter coral bells behind it start to flower.

Height charts are useful, but only as guides, because plants may behave somewhat differently given different growing conditions. This is why most of us move plants around so much. But to help you with your planning, The Long and the Short of It (above) offers some suggestions of useful garden perennials that are particularly tall or especially short. The majority of other perennials fall somewhere in between. A description of the plants listed above and their planting zones can be found in Part 3 of this book.

Planning for Blossoming Times

Just as it is difficult to estimate the mature height of plants, it is also hard to tell exactly when each species will bloom. Various soils, light conditions, and climate variations can cause identical plants to flower at different times. And identical plants may behave differently from one year to the next. A warm spring could accelerate the blooms; an unexpected late winter or cool spring may delay the flowering period. In our short growing season, spring often arrives late, and some years the daffodils, leopard's banes *(Doronicum),* lungworts *(Pulmonaria),* and tulips all bloom at the same time, along with the lilacs *(Syringa).*

Charts are useful as broad guidelines, but the expertise of your neighboring gardeners is likely to be more valuable if you are a new gardener or gardening for the first time in an unfamiliar climate. Even so, like us, you will probably shuffle plants around for as long as you garden in order to achieve a satisfying design. We keep a notebook handy to record blooming times, as well as plant heights and combinations that we like, and we place plastic tags or signs next to those plants that are to be moved when the time is right. Each spring we get plenty of exercise rearranging our plants.

Using Annuals Effectively

Annuals, or bedding plants as they are sometimes called, are a gardener's secret weapons for ensuring bloom throughout the season in flower beds. Not only are annuals good "fillers" among sparse plants in a new bed, but they provide color when perennials are not blooming in an established perennial garden. They beautifully cover the spots left after the spring bulbs have bloomed and died down; you can even set the smaller growing ones directly on top of deeply planted bulbs, such as daffodils. Choose annuals with heights and colors that complement the established perennials in your garden. A single color in each clump is usually most effective, but if you mix them, choose compatible colors.

Choosing Accent Plants by Size and Blossom Time

By selecting a few basic accent plants for each of the blooming seasons, you'll find the rest of the garden falls easily into place. Accent plants — the strong, prominent perennials, annuals, and shrubs that form the backbone of your display — have attractive blooms and furnish interesting foliage for most of the season. You can plant an entire garden with such plants, of course, but most gardeners like to set some smaller, less robust plants among the stronger growers to supply additional beauty, interest, and color to the garden. Accent plants may find a special place in your heart. One lady we knew gave individual names to each of her favorites and would sometimes call to ask why her Lady Macbeth was not thriving the way Hamlet was.

Some annuals and biennials that make good accent plants are Canterbury bells *(Campanula medium),* castor bean *(Ricinus communis),* cosmos *(Cosmos bipinnatus),* lavatera *(Lavatera trimestris),* tall marigolds, and spider flower *(Cleome hassleriana).* A few accent perennials are delphiniums, Japanese iris *(Iris ensata),* foxgloves *(Digitalis),* common rose mallow *(Hibiscus moscheutos),* orange coneflowers *(Rudbeckia),* shasta daisy *(Leucanthemum × superbum),* and, as shown at the right, lilies *(Lilium).*

Most gardeners either start their own annuals (see page 82) or buy started flats or pots from a nursery or greenhouse, rather than sowing seeds directly in the garden. Not only does starting seeds save the trouble and risk of direct sowing, but the blooms appear much earlier. Except when you use them as an edging, clump your annuals like perennials and give each enough space to grow to its full beauty without crowding. Ten to 12 inches apart is seldom too much, and large-growing types, such as spider flower, lavateras, and 'Crackerjack' marigolds, need even more room.

With their innumerable colors, shapes, and sizes, annuals serve many purposes in our garden. We tuck in bachelor's buttons *(Centaurea cyanus)*, calendulas, China asters *(Callistephus chinensis)*, zinnias, and many others to provide consistent color throughout the summer. Sweet alyssum *(Lobularia maritima)*, dwarf marigolds, and other compact annuals make attractive, low-growing edgings. We often use medium-sized marigolds as fillers because they need less deadheading (see page 118) than most other annuals, and they also repel some harmful insects from the garden. Petunias are beautiful both in planters and in large beds, and although older cultivars need frequent deadheading, many excellent new petunias, such as 'Lirica Showers', are "self-cleaning" and will continue to bloom prolifically even if you do not remove the faded blossoms. Our latest favorite for beds and borders is marguerite *(Argyranthemum)*, a tender perennial from the Canary Islands and Madeira that produces daisylike flowers all summer long on a neat, compact plant.

Many annuals serve the double purpose of being good cut flowers. We usually grow bachelor's buttons, calendulas, China asters, cosmos, sweet peas *(Lathyrus odoratus)*, zinnias, and many perennial daisy-type plants, such as blanket flower *(Gaillardia)*, feverfew *(Tanacetum parthenium)*, gloriosa daisy *(Rudbeckia hirta)*, shasta daisy *(Leucanthemum × superbum)*, and yellow daisy *(Anthemis tinctoria)*, in borders as well as in our cutting garden. If you don't have room for a real cutting garden, it does no harm to snip a few of these flowers from your border for bouquets.

EDIBLE LANDSCAPING THAT GLOWS. The greens and purples of ornamental kales and cabbages *(Brassica)* pair with burnt-orange chrysanthemums in this vibrant color scheme.

A Garden for Bouquets

A FRIEND ASTOUNDED US RECENTLY by saying that she never picked any flowers to bring indoors because they were so messy and often covered with ants, earwigs, or slugs. She may have a point, but her argument does not deter us from enjoying fresh bouquets in the kitchen, dining room, living room, bedrooms, and even the bathroom from early spring until fall frosts, and dried arrangements throughout the winter. Blooms from our garden go into church arrangements, wedding and anniversary bouquets, corsages, and decorative dried bunches, as well as to sick friends in the hospital and nursing homes. We use them as hostess gifts and cut impulsive bouquets for our visitors. Our cut flowers make us feel wealthy.

In our fairly small garden, cutting flowers for use in a bouquet or to dry often means choosing each bloom carefully so we don't spoil the current display. If you need large quantities of cut flowers for your own pleasure or to exhibit or give away, you may want to do as we do and grow them separately in what the Victorians called a "cutting garden." In such a garden you can pick to your heart's content without concern about the effect on the bed when you've finished.

ROW BY ROW. By setting out cutting flowers in rows like vegetables, you can use a small tiller for weeding, as well as get to the plants easily when it is time to pick.

A cutting garden is not designed to be a spot of great beauty throughout the season, so it shouldn't be located in immediate view. Ours is in a corner of our vegetable garden, where it is accessible and easy to tend. With this kind of bed, we are unconcerned about plant heights, color clashes, or blooming times.

Even though appearance in the cutting garden does not matter as it would in a show garden, a few chores are essential. We thin the annuals and weed everything frequently so the plants won't be crowded or deprived of nutrients and moisture. We provide adequate water and fertilizer to obtain the maximum number of flowers, and, of course, we deadhead regularly to prevent seed formation.

What to Grow

There are few limits to what you can grow in your cutting garden, except for the usual restrictions of light and climate. You can raise annuals, perennials, bulbs, and even shrubs such as roses and French hydrangea *(Hydrangea macrophylla)*. We have planted viburnums to furnish foliage and berries for bouquet fillers. Even ornamental grasses and wildflowers can have a place in such a planting, if you wish.

We also use our cutting garden for other purposes. It is an ideal spot to try out new cultivars and combinations we aren't ready to admit to the regular borders, as well as plants with offbeat colors or odd forms. We find this to be a good place to experiment with new specimens, with the welcome benefit that it keeps our mistakes out of sight.

Perennials. By selecting perennials that bloom at different times, you can have cut flowers from early spring until the first light frost, and even later if hardy asters and chrysanthemums are among your choices. Although almost any perennial can be used in a flower arrangement, some are far better than others, not only because of their beauty but also because the cut flowers last longer. Certain astilbe cultivars shatter immediately after picking, and an arrangement of daylilies *(Hemerocallis)* will obviously not look the same on the second day. Our list of the best perennials for cutting is

Good Flowers for Cutting Gardens

Perennials

Asters *(Aster)*
Baby's breath *(Gypsophila paniculata)*
Beardtongues *(Penstemon)*
Bellflowers *(Campanula)*
Blanket flowers *(Gaillardia)*
Bleeding heart *(Dicentra spectabilis)*
Carnation *(Dianthus caryophyllus)*
Chrysanthemums *(Chrysanthemum)*
Crocosmias *(Crocosmia)*
Delphiniums *(Delphinium)*
False dragonhead
     (Physostegia virginiana)
Gayfeathers *(Liatris)*
Globeflowers *(Trollius)*
Globe thistles *(Echinops)*
Gloriosa daisy *(Rudbeckia hirta)*
Irises *(Iris)*
Japanese anemone *(Anemone × hybrida)*
Lilies *(Lilium)*
Lupines *(Lupinus)*
Monkshoods *(Aconitum)*
Mountain bluet *(Centaurea montana)*
Painted daisy *(Tanacetum coccineum)*
Peonies *(Paeonia)*
Sages *(Salvia)*
Shasta daisy *(Leucanthemum × superbum)*
Sneezeweeds *(Helenium)*

Speedwells *(Veronica)*
Stonecrops *(Sedum)*
Sunflowers *(Helianthus)*
Tickseeds *(Coreopsis)*
Torch lilies *(Kniphofia)*
Yarrows *(Achillea)*
Yellow daisy *(Anthemis tinctoria)*

Flowers for Miniature Bouquets

Candytufts *(Iberis)*
Coral bells *(Heuchera)*
Forget-me-nots *(Myosotis)*
Leopard's banes *(Doronicum)*
Lily-of-the-valley *(Convallaria majalis)*
Pansies and violets *(Viola)*

Annuals and Bulbs

Bachelor's buttons *(Centaurea cyanus)*
Calendula *(Calendula officinalis)*
Celosias *(Celosia)*
China aster *(Callistephus chinensis)*
Daffodils *(Narcissus)*
Dahlias *(Dahlia)*
Freesias *(Freesia)*
Gladioli *(Gladiolus)*
Lavatera *(Lavatera trimestris)*
Snapdragon *(Antirrhinum majus)*
Stock *(Matthiola incana)*
Sunflowers *(Helianthus)*
Sweet pea *(Lathyrus odoratus)*
Tulips *(Tulipa)*
Zinnias *(Zinnia)*

A BUCKETFUL OF SUNSHINE. An old watering can is easy to carry into the garden filled to the brim with water, so flowers need never be high and dry. It can also serve as a container for an informal arrangement.

presented above, but yours will undoubtedly be somewhat different depending on your preferences and experience. For plant descriptions, including growing zones, please see Part 3.

Annuals and Bulbs. Most cutting gardens include a generous number of colorful annuals and bulb-type plants that make good cut flowers. Each year we plant short rows of our favorite "bouquet" annuals including annual baby's breath *(Gypsophila elegans),* bachelor's buttons *(Centaurea cyanus),* calendulas, cosmos, lava-teras, nasturtium *(Tropaeolum majus),* sweet pea *(Lathyrus odoratus),* and statice *(Limonium sinuatum),* which we use for dried bouquets. We also include some spring bulbs, such as tulips and daffodils, and for summer, lilies, gladioli, dahlias, and lily-of-the valley *(Convallaria majalis).* Herbs, too, make beautiful scented bouquets. We use parsley *(Petroselinum crispum)* and others as greenery for small-scale bouquets, dill *(Anethum graveolens)* for its large, showy flowerheads, and lavenders for fresh and dried nosegays.

Gathering and Arranging Cut Flowers

The best time to pick flowers is in the morning, when their stems are filled with water and the plants are covered with dew. Take a pail of tepid water with you to the garden, along with sharp scissors, clippers, or a knife. Select only prime flowers: those that are just opening or have recently opened. Cut the stem on a slant or straight across; we've found it doesn't matter which, as long as the instrument is sharp and does not crush the stem tissue. Take stems as long as possible so that when you begin to arrange them, you have plenty to work with. Remove the bottom leaves so they won't pollute the water as they decompose. Immediately place the cut flowers in the water, and store the pail and flowers in a cool place out of the sun until you are ready to use them.

Some flowers are easy to combine informally in a bouquet by simply placing them in a container and arranging them loosely, one by one, until you get the effect you want. In other cases, you may desire a more formal arrangement and need to use devices you can purchase from a garden shop: Instant Oasis, a block of light, porous material, which is reusable; a pinholder (needlepoint holder); and floral clay or tape. Oasis is invaluable in arrangements because it holds the stems wherever you want them. Never let one flower depend on another to hold it upright. It won't work for long.

Cut the Oasis slightly smaller than the container and push it onto a needlepoint holder that you've covered with a small piece of nylon panty hose. (The nylon makes it easier to cleanly remove the Oasis.) If the holder doesn't stay in place, fasten it to the bottom of the container with floral tape or clay. Soak the Oasis in lukewarm water for a minute or two before you set any flowers in it.

The container you choose should be clean so the flowers will stay fresh, and the flowers should relate well to it. Neutral-colored containers show off blooms to best advantage, but use your imagination to create unusual combinations. Hide plain jars and cans in baskets, an antique kettle, or other receptacle, for example.

When you enter a flower show, rules restrict your choices, but for home use you need only consider a few tips. Before you begin, consider where the arrangement will go so you can design it to fit in the intended space. Will it be seen from one side only, perhaps on a mantel, or from all sides, as a table centerpiece?

For a professional appearance, arrange the height of the bouquet in proportion to the height of the container. If the vase is too tall, the flower heads will barely peek out over the top. Ideally, the container should be no more than one-third the height of the arrangement. Before you begin, decide on the shape of your arrangement — triangular, circular, or perhaps linear. Cover the Oasis with greenery so it will be invisible. Recut the stems as you place them in the Oasis, using the heavier flowers (those that are larger or darker in color) in the center, and the lighter, smaller ones near the perimeter. Express yourself and enjoy the colors and shapes of the beautiful flowers you have grown.

GATHERING THE PROPS. Keep stems of fresh-cut flowers immersed in water from the time they are cut. Florist's Oasis (a foam specially formulated to absorb water) and a variety of other plant supports, including the needlepoint holder in the blue bowl, are some of the tools that make it easy to control your flower arrangements.

FLOWERS THAT LAST. Cut flowers for air-drying when there is no moisture on the plants. Strip the leaves, tie the stems tightly, and hang in a warm, dry, airy place for several weeks [LEFT]. Once they dry, arrange them in appropriate containers [ABOVE].

Flowers for Drying

When we visited Colonial Williamsburg one November, we regretted not seeing the gardens when they were in bloom. But the beautiful dried arrangements in each home nearly compensated for what we missed. For as long as people have gardened, they have dried flowers to enjoy during the cold seasons, and modern techniques have made it easy to dry even those species that were once difficult to dry successfully.

Many perennials are effective in dried arrangements, including artemisias, yarrows *(Achillea)*, pearly everlastings *(Anaphalis)*, small globe thistle *(Echinops ritro)*, sea hollies *(Eryngium)*, baby's breaths *(Gypsophila)*, and Chinese lantern *(Physalis alkekengi)*, as well as acrocliniums *(Rhodanthe)*, strawflower *(Bracteantha bracteata)*, honesty *(Lunaria annua)*, love-in-a-mist *(Nigella damascena)*, and numerous other annuals. Many ornamental grasses, such as hare's tail *(Lagurus ovatus)*, go well in dried arrangements, as do plants with interesting seed clusters and pods. Certain herbs are also worth drying. Look for the easy-to-dry plants listed in garden catalogs.

We air-dry a surprising number of the above flowers the old-fashioned way: by stripping off the leaves, tying the blooms together by the stems, and hanging them upside down out of the sunlight in our warm, dry, ventilated attic or garage for 2 to 4 weeks. Then we store the dried flowers in paper bags.

Another common way of drying flowers is to pack the blooms carefully in silica gel, a sandlike compound containing blue crystals that turn pink when they have absorbed maximum moisture. Silica gel draws moisture out of the flowers so rapidly that their form and color are almost completely retained. It is available, with directions for use, at garden centers and from seed companies. You may also wish to experiment with borax and dry sand for the same purpose.

Silica gel is also used for microwave drying, another popular preservation method. Place the flowers in a nonmetallic container, cover them with the gel, then place them in the center of the oven with a cup of water near them. Timing is crucial, and you'll need to experiment. Carnations usually take about 1 minute, roses 1½ minutes, and other blooms up to 3 or 4 minutes. Wait until the silica gel has cooled before moving the container.

Because the stems of dried flowers are often fragile and break easily, use floral wire or pipe cleaners to strengthen, lengthen, or even replace them. Conceal the wire by wrapping it with green or brown floral tape, available from florists.

Arrange the dried flowers to your pleasure, using Oasis or simply gathering them into a loose bouquet. You will have no worries about their wilting, harboring bugs, or running out of water.

Using the Bulb Family

Bulbs add a lot of exciting color to the garden, and not just in spring. There are also summer-flowering lilies, fall beauties such as autumn crocuses *(Colchicum)*, and the tender dahlias, gladioli, cannas, tuberous begonias, and caladiums, which also bloom in summer.

Different bulbs vary in life span. Daffodils, grape hyacinths *(Muscari)*, and snowdrops *(Galanthus)* live for many years if they are planted at the recommended depth, kept fertilized, and divided when they become overcrowded. Most cultivars of tulips and hyacinths are much shorter lived and must be replaced every year or two unless they are dug up after they have died down in early summer and stored for replanting in the fall. Various lilies also differ in endurance. Many older favorites such as Henry lily *(Lilium henryi)*, regal lily *(L. regale)*, tiger lily *(L. lancifolium)*, and live for decades, as do certain Asiatic hybrids, such as 'Enchantment'. Some of the recently developed lily hybrids, however, have short life spans and must be replaced every few years. This is not a good reason for omitting them from the garden, however, and some devoted lily lovers treat them as annuals.

Intermingling bulbs with herbaceous plants presents some challenges. Some bulb leaves disappear during the growing season. The foliage of magic lilies *(Lycoris)* and autumn crocuses, for example, comes up early and then disappears; the flowers do not appear until late summer. Daffodils and other spring bulbs leave no aboveground sign after they have died back in early summer, and summer bulbs like crocosmias often are tardy in appearing. It's easy to mistakenly dig into the hidden bulbs.

The solution is to give these bulbs their own spots within the bed, set aside by visible markers if your memory is not perfect. We plant our spring bulbs at the very front. As their foliage yellows, we plant annuals among them to camouflage and then take their place for the summer. The autumn crocuses have their own home at the ends of the bed, and the crocosmia spaces are marked by inconspicuous, short wooden stakes.

Set bulbs in clumps where they will make a statement. One gladiolus, for example, looks like the odd man out in a perennial border, but gladioli set in clumps of five or seven are attention-getters.

What's what: **A.** *Muscari* (bulb) **B.** *Crocus* (corm) **C.** *Ranunculus* (tuber) **D.** *Eranthis* (tuber) **E.** *Scilla* (bulb) **F.** *Galanthus* (bulb)

Just What Is a Bulb?

The roots of many plants, both hardy and tender, are often called bulbs because they are fleshy, but they do not meet the strict definitions that horticulturists reserve for true bulbs. Ornamental onions *(Allium)* and tulips grow from true bulbs — modified buds with fleshy scales — but other bulb-type plants grow from rhizomes, corms, or tubers. In this book we refer to all these bulb-types as bulbs, but it's helpful to understand the distinctions:

RHIZOMES. Bearded irises are one example of a plant with rhizomes, which are fleshy underground stems that grow close to the surface of the ground and are used for food storage by the plant.

CORMS. Gladioli and crocuses grow from corms, which are similar to bulbs but are more solid and lack scales.

TUBERS. Dahlia roots are tubers, which are large, fat, underground stems with "eyes" from which sprouts grow.

Bulbs for Every Season

Starting with the very earliest bulbs, like the aptly named snowdrops *(Galanthus)*, through to the brilliant autumn crocuses *(Colchicum)*, there truly is a bulb that blooms in every season. This photo gallery is just a sampling of the colorful flowers you can introduce into your garden with bulbs.

A. Snowdrops, *Galanthus* (late winter)

B. Tulips, *Tulipa* (spring)

C. Irises, *Iris* (late spring and early summer)

D. Lilies, *Lilium* (midsummer)

E. Autumn crocuses, *Colchicum* (fall)

Dutch crocus (*Crocus vernus*)   Siberian squill (*Scilla siberica*)   Pinks (*Dianthus* 'Bath's Pink')   Speedwell (*Veronica*)

Plan a Succession of Blooming Bulbs and Perennials

The first flowers in early spring are always a thrill, but the actual month the blooms appear varies widely, depending on where you live. In our Zone 3 climate, for example, often only snowdrops and crocus bloom before May. By midsummer, however, the long days have enabled most of the summer- and fall-blossoming bulbs and perennials to catch up, so their flowers appear in the North at nearly the same time as they do further south. This list of plants therefore refers to season of bloom, rather than specific months. You will learn by experience when "early spring" comes to your neighborhood.

Plants marked with a ❀ are especially good choices for beginning gardeners because they are easy to grow and are desirable in the border. Some are extremely vigorous, however, and must be kept under control (see the section on weedy plants, pages 12–13, chapter 1). Note that some genera, such as speedwells (*Veronica*), include many species and cultivars that may bloom at different times.

The first list, Perennials That Bloom Over a Long Season, contains plants that are especially valuable because they usually bloom for many weeks and can be depended on while others come and go.

Perennials That Bloom Over a Long Season

Alpine forget-me-not (*Myosotis alpestris*)
❀ Blanket flower (*Gaillardia aristata*)
❀ Carpathian bellflower
   (*Campanula carpatica*)
Common torch lily (*Kniphofia uvaria*)
❀ Coral bells (*Heuchera sanguinea*)
False dragonhead (*Physostegia virginiana*)
❀ Fringed bleeding heart
   (*Dicentra eximia*)
❀ Horned violet (*Viola cornuta*)
Large-flowered tickseed
   (*Coreopsis grandiflora*)
❀ Mountain bluet (*Centaurea montana*)

Late Winter Bloomers

❀ Crocuses (*Crocus*)
❀ Daffodils (*Narcissus*)
Hellebores (*Helleborus*)
Netted iris (*Iris reticulata*)
Siberian squill (*Scilla siberica*)
Snowdrops (*Galanthus*)
Spring heath (*Erica carnea*)
Winter aconite (*Eranthis hyemalis*)

Early Spring Bloomers

Basket-of-gold (*Aurinia saxatilis*)
❀ Bleeding hearts (*Dicentra*)
Blue phlox (*Phlox divaricata*)
Bugleweeds (*Ajuga*)
❀ Catmint (*Nepeta* × *faassenii*)
❀ Columbines (*Aquilegia*)
Crimean iris (*Iris lutescens*)
Cushion spurge (*Euphorbia polychroma*)
Early meadow rue (*Thalictrum dioicum*)
Early speedwell (*Veronica pectinata*)
❀ English daisy (*Bellis perennis*)
Heart-leaved bergenia (*Bergenia cordifolia*)
❀ Iceland poppy (*Papaver croceum*)
Marsh marigold (*Caltha palustris*)
❀ Moss pink (*Phlox subulata*)
❀ Mountain bluet (*Centaurea montana*)
❀ Pansies and violets (*Viola*)
❀ Perennial candytuft
   (*Iberis sempervirens*)
❀ Primroses (*Primula*)
Purple rock cress (*Aubrieta* × *cultorum*)
Virginia bluebells
   (*Mertensia pulmonarioides*)
Wall rock cress (*Arabis caucasica*)

Midspring Bloomers

Baneberries (*Actaea*)
Basket-of-gold (*Aurinia saxatilis*)
Bishop's hats (*Epimedium*)
❀ Bleeding hearts (*Dicentra*)
Bugleweeds (*Ajuga*)
❀ Catmint (*Nepeta* × *faassenii*)
❀ Cranesbills (*Geranium*)
Creeping buttercup (*Ranunculus repens*)
Cypress spurge (*Euphorbia cyparissias*)
❀ English daisy (*Bellis perennis*)
❀ Globeflowers (*Trollius*)
Grass pink (*Dianthus plumarius*)
❀ Irises (*Iris*)
Jacob's ladder (*Polemonium caeruleum*)
❀ Leopard's banes (*Doronicum*)
❀ Lily-of-the-valley (*Convallaria majalis*)
❀ Lupines (*Lupinus*)
Maltese cross (*Lychnis chalcedonica*)
Mountain aster (*Aster alpinus*)
Musk mallow (*Malva moschata*)
❀ Painted daisy (*Tanacetum coccineum*)
❀ Pansies and violets (*Viola*)
❀ Perennial candytuft (*Iberis sempervirens*)

Flanders poppy (*Papaver rhoeas*)   Torch lily (*Kniphofia*)   Yellow daisy (*Anthemis tinctoria*)   Aster (*Aster oblongifolius* 'Raydon's Favorite')

Perennial flax (*Linum perenne*)
❀ Primroses (*Primula*)
Saxifrages (*Saxifraga*)
❀ Sneezeweeds (*Helenium*)
Snow-in-summer (*Cerastium tomentosum*)
❀ Speedwells (*Veronica*)
Stonecrops (*Sedum*)
Sweet rocket (*Hesperis matronalis*)
❀ Sweet William (*Dianthus barbatus*)
Sweet woodruff (*Galium odoratum*)
Thrifts (*Armeria*)
Thymes (*Thymus*)
Tree peony (*Paeonia suffruticosa*)
❀ Virginia bluebells
    (*Mertensia pulmonarioides*)
Woolly yarrow (*Achillea tomentosa*)

Early Summer Bloomers

Avens (*Geum*)
Baby's breaths (*Gypsophila*)
Beardtongues (*Penstemon*)
❀ Bee balms (*Monarda*)
❀ Bellflowers (*Campanula*)
Butterfly weed (*Asclepias tuberosa*)
Campions (*Lychnis*)
❀ Coral bells (*Heuchera*)
❀ Daylilies (*Hemerocallis*)
❀ Delphiniums (*Delphinium*)
English daisy (*Bellis perennis*)
❀ Foxgloves (*Digitalis*)
Gas plant (*Dictamnus albus*)
❀ Globe thistles (*Echinops*)
Heron's bill (*Erodium manescaui*)
❀ Hollyhock (*Alcea rosea*)
❀ Iceland poppy (*Papaver croceum*)
❀ Loosestrifes (*Lythrum*)
Mountain bluet (*Centaurea montana*)
❀ Oriental poppy (*Papaver orientale*)
❀ Painted daisy (*Tanacetum coccineum*)
❀ Peonies (*Paeonia*)
Poppy mallow (*Callirhoe involucrata*)
❀ Siberian iris (*Iris sibirica*)

❀ Speedwells (*Veronica*)
❀ Sweet William (*Dianthus barbatus*)
Woolly yarrow (*Achillea tomentosa*)

Midsummer Bloomers

Astilbes (*Astilbe*)
Avens (*Geum*)
Balloon flower (*Platycodon grandiflorus*)
Bearded irises (*Iris*)
Beardtongues (*Penstemon*)
Betonies (*Stachys*)
❀ Blanket flowers (*Gaillardia*)
Blue bugloss (*Anchusa azurea*)
Campions (*Lychnis*)
❀ Daylilies (*Hemerocallis*)
❀ Delphiniums (*Delphinium*)
❀ Foxgloves (*Digitalis*)
❀ Goat's beard (*Aruncus dioicus*)
Hollyhock (*Alcea rosea*)
Lilies (*Lilium*)
❀ Meadow phlox (*Phlox maculata*)
Meadowsweet (*Filipendula ulmaria*)
❀ Monkshoods (*Aconitum*)
❀ Painted daisy (*Tanacetum coccineum*)
Pincushion flower (*Scabiosa caucasica*)
Sea lavender (*Limonium latifolium*)
Shasta daisy (*Leucanthemum × superbum*)
❀ Speedwells (*Veronica*)
Stokes' aster (*Stokesia laevis*)
Torch lilies (*Kniphofia*)
❀ Yarrows (*Achillea*)
❀ Yellow daisy (*Anthemis tinctoria*)

Late Summer Bloomers

Baby's breaths (*Gypsophila*)
Balloon flower (*Platycodon grandiflorus*)
❀ Bee balms (*Monarda*)
Boltonia (*Boltonia asteroides*)
Border phlox (*Phlox paniculata*)
Bugbanes (*Cimicifuga*)
Common rose mallow
    (*Hibiscus moscheutos*)

False dragonhead (*Physostegia virginiana*)
False sunflower (*Heliopsis helianthoides*)
Flaxes (*Linum*)
❀ Gayfeathers (*Liatris*)
❀ Hostas (*Hosta*)
Large-flowered tickseed
    (*Coreopsis grandiflora*)
Perennial lobelias (*Lobelia*)
Pincushion flowers (*Scabiosa*)
❀ Silvermound (*Artemisia schmidtiana*)
Sneezeweeds (*Helenium*)
❀ Speedwells (*Veronica*)
Turtleheads (*Chelone*)
❀ Yellow daisy (*Anthemis tinctoria*)

Early Fall Bloomers

❀ Asters (*Aster*)
Azure monkshood
    (*Aconitum carmichaelii*)
❀ Blanket flower (*Gaillardia aristata*)
Boltonia (*Boltonia asteroides*)
❀ Border phlox (*Phlox paniculata*)
Bugbanes (*Cimicifuga*)
❀ Chrysanthemums (*Chrysanthemum*)
False dragonhead (*Physostegia virginiana*)
False sunflower (*Heliopsis helianthoides*)
Gayfeathers (*Liatris*)
Gloriosa daisy (*Rudbeckia hirta*)
Japanese anemone (*Anemone × hybrida*)
Lobelias (*Lobelia*)
Mistflower (*Eupatorium coelestinum*)
❀ Perennial pea (*Lathyrus latifolius*)
Purple coneflower (*Echinacea purpurea*)
❀ Rose mallows (*Hibiscus*)
Sages (*Salvia*)
Sneezeweeds (*Helenium*)
❀ Speedwells (*Veronica*)
Stokes' aster (*Stokesia laevis*)
Stonecrops (*Sedum*)
❀ Sunflowers (*Helianthus*)
Turtleheads (*Chelone*)
White mugwort (*Artemisia lactiflora*)

Designing with Color Coordination in Mind

AS IN INTERIOR DECORATION, you can use colors in gardens to create special effects and moods. Blue, green, white, and pale shades of lavender and yellow are cool colors. Orange, red, and bright yellows are warm. Red and other vibrant colors make a display of perennials seem closer than it is and create the illusion that the garden is larger. Blues, on the other hand, make a garden appear smaller and more distant.

Our perception of each color changes according to whatever shades surround it and, of course, the amount and quality of lighting it receives. Plants look quite different in sunlight than they do in shade. Bright hues often appear less brilliant on a sunny day than on a cloudy one, and colors seem to change considerably, no matter what the weather, from morning to high noon to dusk. We have noticed that our bed of daylilies seems to look best in the twilight of a summer evening.

Annuals are easier to conceptualize in the garden because the same plants stay in bloom all season, but when perennials are part of the mix, the color scheme constantly changes as different plants come into blossom. It is challenging to design a garden that appears full of bloom throughout the season, while keeping plants of different heights from obscuring each other. But it can be even more daunting to arrange the plants so their colors remain harmonious as blossoms change from week to week.

It has been said that Mother Nature can throw together colors of all kinds and they don't clash as they would in a manmade environment. In our early gardening days we took those words to heart and paid no attention to the color scheme of the garden. Merrily we planted bright orange and pink lilies side by side and seed mixtures with a jumble of reds, oranges, and yellows. As we visited gardens that had been color coordinated, however, it became obvious that our capricious methods were not the best. Even in nature, colors can clash. Gardens that have been planted in thoughtful color combinations have an overall beauty that a hodgepodge just can't match. If you have any doubts, take a color photo of both types of borders and compare them.

EYE-CATCHING COMBOS. 'Profusion Orange' zinnias [ABOVE] create a dynamic color combination with neighboring *Ageratum houstonianum* 'Red Top'.

A SPIN ON COLOR. **A**. Primary colors (red, yellow, and blue) make a strong statement. White astilbe in the foreground provides visual relief. **B**. Analagous colors (those next to one another on the color wheel [BELOW]) create a unified look in the purple-red-orange flow of a fall garden. **C**. A monochromatic garden (shades of one color) can be very effective, especially when accented with white. *Astrantia* echoes the variegated foliage in this shady garden that features a range of greens.

My Favorite Things

Once, we had the pleasure of helping an elderly lady with her gardening chores for the summer. Of her several small perennial gardens, her special favorite was a blue-and-white border enclosed by a low stone wall. Delphiniums provided accent points at the corners, and masses of bellflowers *(Campanula)*, hostas, irises, Jacob's ladder *(Polemonium caeruleum)*, perennial candy-tuft *(Iberis sempervirens)*, snow-in-summer *(Cerastium tomentosum)*, shasta daisy *(Leucanthemum × superbum)*, and other flowers bloomed at various times throughout the spring, summer, and fall. Since that pleasant intro-duction to a color garden, we have admired many other effective beds created with a single color — pink, red, yellow, or blue — combined with white. Some were planned with the gardener's favorite color in mind, while others included colors that complemented their backgrounds — an aging shed of weathered boards, a tall stone foundation where a barn once stood, a sheared evergreen hedge, a wooden fence, or a reflecting pool.

We feature a blue-and-white garden design in Part 2. (See True Blue, the Zenith of Gardens, which includes a list of some of the most common blue flowers; pages 196–98.) Check out each species and cultivar before you plant it to be sure it is the shade you prefer, since colors vary greatly even within the same species.

STRENGTH IN NUMBERS.
Get the most out of each flower
by planting types and/or colors
in masses that are repeated
throughout the border. Here,
low-growing, light yellow
thread-leaved coreopsis
(*C. verticillata* 'Moonbeam')
echoes the taller yellow daisy
(*Anthemis tinctoria*).

Creating Masses of Color

In a color-coordinated garden, plant a number of clumps of the same variety and the same shade, rather than a grand mixture. A half-dozen pink primroses planted together, for example, have a more impressive visual impact than a multicolored grouping. The validity of this concept is obvious in parks where large, formal beds of the same cultivar of geraniums, petunias, or marigolds are so effective. When you have chosen the colors for each grouping, arrange them so they don't clash with their surroundings. A simple way to do this is to use white flowers as mediators to "cool" and separate brilliant shades. Masses of white also make bright colors appear even brighter and create the illusion that the bed is larger than it is.

When developing a harmonious color design, your good sense will often tell you what goes best with what. Or, like Gertrude Jekyll, the great English gardener and writer, you can scientifically plan the bed according to the color spectrum. Nearly a century ago, Jekyll established an enduring reputation as the leading authority on color by filling huge borders with long color masses, which she termed "drifts." Using the color spectrum, she arranged the reds at one end, followed by orange, yellow, blue, and violet. She never planted primary colors side by side, instead separating them with paler shades of the same color or white so that each led into the next without a sharp contrast.

To include the entire color spectrum, a garden would need to be large, and most of us obviously cannot duplicate Miss Jekyll's 300-foot-long, 14-foot-wide borders. For a smaller version, choose whichever parts of the color spectrum appeal to you. Position pale colors to flow into vivid shades, then progress back to pale or white flowers. If drifts of more than two colors are used, they should be proportionate to each other and to the garden as a whole.

Our own border is small and contains a large variety of plants. We modify Jekyll's methods by separating the clumps of vivid hues with groupings of white or pale-colored flowers in the same part of the color spectrum. Further along the border we try to duplicate a similar grouping of the same plants. Thus, when the eye falls on one group of red sweet William (*Dianthus barbatus*), it is drawn along to an identical group farther on, and then another in a continuing scheme throughout the garden.

The color symmetry of such a planting should not be as repetitive as a wallpaper pattern, but it should be orderly enough that the design has continuity. Showy accent plants such as deep blue delphiniums, bright red Russell's hybrid lupines, gloriosa daisy (*Rudbeckia hirta*), or others of special size, brilliance, or beauty make good focus plants, and the smaller plants with more subtle shades can be interspersed among them.

The Many Colors of Foliage

In a garden, just as in a bouquet of cut flowers, blossoms seem barren without a background. Walls and fences are useful for the back border of a bed, but the foliage of hedges and shrubs is usually more attractive. Masses of green within the garden separate the different colors of flowering plants, and the leafy textures of certain plants add beauty even when they are not in bloom. Green leaves are predominant in most gardens, but gray foliage plants such as silvermound *(Artemisia schmidtiana)* or lamb's ears *(Stachys byzantina)* also provide striking contrast. Some shrubs and perennials have variegated leaves in interesting red, bluish, or yellow hues. Certain plants, such as hostas, are grown more for their foliage than for their flowers, as are annuals like coleus and caladiums. Ornamental grasses with unusual foliage also spice up the garden.

Plants with "golden" or pale leaves (some hostas and perennial grasses, for example) can appear to be sick and undernourished unless they are used skillfully. You may want to put in more than one plant of each cultivar to indicate that the planting is deliberate, and separate each grouping with clumps containing green foliage for contrast. The massive blue-leaved hostas, for example, are much more striking when interplanted with green-leaved cultivars.

When we started gardening, we chose our plants primarily because we liked their blooms. Now, with more understanding, we consider plants for their foliage as well, since many have interesting and attractive leaves. Even when there are few or no flowers, the masses of lacy, delicate maidenhair ferns *(Adiantum)*, rubbery-leaved stonecrops *(Sedum),* and sturdy orange coneflowers *(Rudbeckia)* contrast nicely with the spiky foliage of irises and daylilies. The foliage clumps of massive peonies and lupines are quite unlike the shapes and textures of phlox and the tall globe thistles *(Echinops).* Although we enjoy their blossoms in season, we have also discovered that the widely different leaves of mounded cranesbills *(Geranium)*, speckled lungworts *(Pulmonaria),* and scalloped coral bells *(Heuchera sanguinea)* make beautiful front-of-the-border plants throughout the summer. A seasoned gardener, like a stage director or artist, gives attention to the mood created by the backdrop of the scene.

BEYOND GREEN. Let foliage colors and patterns add their own dynamic to your garden. Some of the many choices include [A] oxalis, [B] cockscomb *(Celosia* 'Forest Fire'), [C] dusty miller *(Senecio cineraria* 'Silver Queen'), [D] hosta, [E] coleus *(Solenostemon* 'Red Creeper' and 'Fairway Ruby'), and [F] brunnera *(Brunnera macrophylla* 'Jack Frost').

Designing the Garden on Paper

IF ARRANGING PLANTS TASTEFULLY according to height, bloom sequence, and color seems puzzling to you, treat it as a game. Designing a plant layout can be as much fun as doing a crossword puzzle, and the results are much longer lasting. It can simplify the buying process, pinpoint potential mistakes, and speed up planting, since it limits last-minute decisions in spring. By making notes on the plan throughout the summer, you'll have a permanent record of your garden and ideas for changes when you redo your plan next winter.

One graphic way to design a garden uses cutouts of appropriately colored paper to represent each plant or group of plants. Four tracing paper overlays represent parts of the growing season. By isolating on each sheet the plants that come into bloom at about the same time, you can visualize whether the balance throughout the garden and throughout the season is what you hope to achieve. The following steps tell how it's done.

1. List all the plants you intend to grow according to their blooming season. Divide each of these blooming categories into color groups (see sample list at right).
2. To make the Master Plan, outline your garden on a piece of graph paper. Include in it any permanent features, such as a pathway, fence, building, or existing tree or shrub. The graph paper helps you make your drawing to scale (for instance, 1 square = 1 square foot).
3. Cut out pieces of colored paper to represent the plants on your list. Allow 2–3 feet for each ordinary-sized clump and 3 or more feet for each large clump or accent plant. (Use the same scale as in step 2.)
4. Try out the colored paper cutouts in various positions on the plan until you like the arrangement. Trace around each cutout to reserve a space for it on the plan.
5. Label four pieces of tracing paper using the seasonal headings shown (see facing page). Working season by season, shift each cutout to the page it belongs on.

Master Plan (see key in plant list at right)

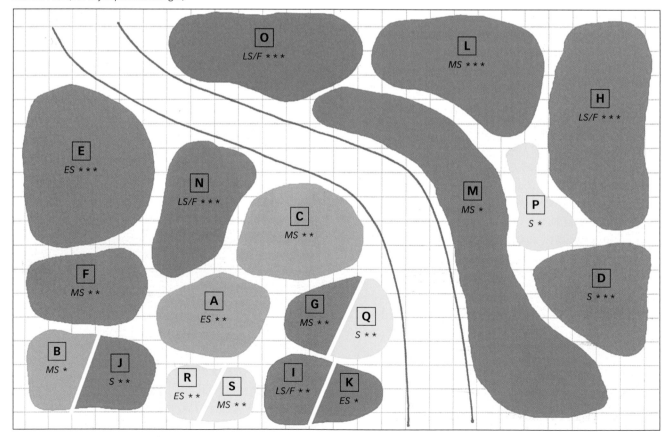

Master Plant List *(see step 1 at left)*

	Plant name	Height	Season
A	Willow blue star *(Amsonia tabernaemontana)*	⋆⋆	ES
B	Floss flower *(Ageratum houstonianum)*	⋆	MS
C	Balloon flower *(Platycodon grandiflorus)*	⋆⋆	MS
D	Tree peony *(Paeonia suffruticosa* 'Largo')	⋆⋆⋆	S
E	Mountain laurel *(Kalmia latifolia)*	⋆⋆⋆	ES
F	Astilbe *(Astilbe* 'Peach Blossom')	⋆⋆	MS
G	Sage *(Salvia × sylvestris* 'Rose Queen')	⋆⋆	MS
H	Hydrangea *(H. paniculata* 'Grandiflora')	⋆⋆⋆	LS/F
I	Stonecrop *(Sedum* 'Frosty Morn')	⋆⋆	LS/F
J	Drumstick primrose *(Primula denticulata)*	⋆⋆	S
K	Dwarf bearded iris *(Iris pumila)*	⋆	ES
L	Butterfly bush *(Buddleia davidii)*	⋆⋆⋆	MS
M	Horned violet *(Viola cornuta)*	⋆	MS
N	New England aster *(Aster novae-angliae)*	⋆⋆⋆	LS/F
O	Burning bush *(Euonymus alatus)*	⋆⋆⋆	LS/F
P	Daffodils *(Narcissus)*	⋆	S
Q	Tulips *(Tulipa)*	⋆⋆	S
R	Crocosmia *(Crocosmia* 'Lady Hamilton')	⋆⋆	ES
S	Daylily *(Hemerocallis* 'Hyperion')	⋆⋆	MS

Tip: If you place the tracing paper over the Master Plan when you do this, it will be easy to identify the correct location for each plant by matching its shape to the tracing you made in step 4.

6. Study your plan and make any adjustments necessary to achieve a balance of heights and color each season. Lay the pieces of tracing paper over one another so that you don't inadvertently make an adjustment that results in planting "on top of" another plant. Once you're satisfied, transfer the information from each season to the Master Plan. This is what you will take into the garden when you begin to plant.

KEY: HEIGHT. Asterisks (⋆) indicate plant height: ⋆ for plants 12 inches or less; ⋆⋆ for those that grow up to about 30 inches; and ⋆⋆⋆ for tall plants. **BLOOM TIME.** The growing season is here divided into 4 parts: *S* (spring), *ES* (early summer), *MS* (midsummer), and *LS/F* (late summer through fall). **COLOR.** Paper cutouts represent the color of the blossoms or, in some cases, foliage. Note that several cutouts show two colors for one clump. These indicate areas that contain spring bulbs or other early-blooming plants that die back and are replaced by longer-lasting plants later in the season. **PLANT IDENTIFICATION.** The large, boxed capital letters refer to the plant list above.

Tracing Paper Overlays *(see step 5 at left)*

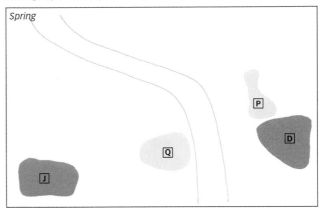

Spring

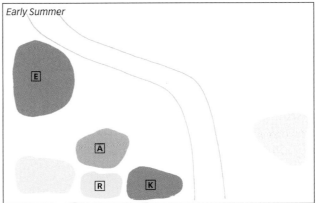

Early Summer

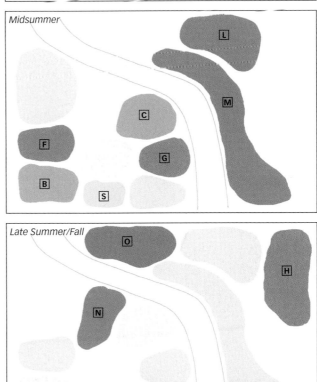

Midsummer

Late Summer/Fall

Ornaments in the Garden

FEW SUBJECTS stimulate more heated discussion than aesthetics. Everyone has an opinion about what constitutes beauty, and the feelings are apt to vary considerably when it comes to enhancing a garden with ornaments and lighting.

Not long ago, we visited an exquisite small garden near a restored farmhouse. The owners had used the granite foundation of a former barn as a backdrop and combined it successfully with a stone statue they had picked up on a visit to Spain. The sculpture served as a focal point next to a tiny pool, and the colorful flowering plants in the garden were complemented by the manmade objects. We found the spot charming.

We know of another garden in another nearby village that is filled with painted wooden cutouts: windmills, animals, an overweight woman bent over ostensibly picking flowers, pink flamingos, gazing globes, and more. Obviously, the owner, an elderly lady, feels

happy in such a garden, although most of us prefer a more natural setting with the plants predominating. Inanimate objects either enhance or detract from the overall effect of a garden, depending upon their beauty and how you place them. Statuary (even though whimsical), planters, urns, sundials, and garden furniture should blend into the landscape and complement it rather than stand out as prominent features that distract the viewer from the plantings.

Choosing and Positioning Garden Ornamentation

If you are starting a garden from scratch, first install any walls, terraces, patios, pools, large fountains, pathways, steps, bridges, or other basic features that will become an integral part of the total landscape design. Avoid placing such permanent fixtures in a spot where it may be necessary to disturb them at some point. We know of occasions when people have had to wreck much of their landscape because they needed to have someone dig up their water, sewage, or power lines.

HEAVENS ABOVE. Weather and other observation instruments like this antique armillary sphere [ABOVE] make perfect garden ornaments.

It can be a pleasure to select manmade objects to enhance your garden, and you probably have certain spots that suggest a particular one: perhaps a bench placed where the garden opens with a view to the sea or mountains, a rail fence lining a country pathway, Grecian urns that flank the entrance of a formal garden, or an arched rose arbor that connects two gardens.

Another approach is to build your garden around a particularly impressive ornament, as our friends did with their Spanish statue. A sundial or a rock, real or artificial, makes an ideal center for a low-growing herb garden. A fountain or waterfall used as a focal point will add movement and a soothing sound. To introduce other kinds of motion and sound, hang wind chimes or bells unobtrusively from the branches of a nearby tree, or attract birds with a few birdhouses, feeders, and a birdbath.

It is helpful to experiment with any unusual new accessory before you set it permanently. View it from various spots around the grounds and from indoors if it will be visible from your home.

As with interior decorating, the objects you use should contribute to an integrated whole. For instance,

unless you are skilled at breaking the rules of design successfully, whatever fixtures you choose should be appropriate to your home. A contemporary sculpture that would be suitable for a modern home might seem out of place near an Early American homestead. Likewise, a flagstone pathway and rail fence would probably be in character near a Colonial-style home, but a path of modern paving blocks or a basketweave fence might not.

Earth-toned paint for larger structures such as a tool house, bench, or potting shed; weathered material for gates, arbors, or trellises; and real, rather than artificial, rocks will blend into the landscape better than white-painted or colored objects. Natural wood is especially attractive and appropriate, but you should treat it with a wood preservative or sealer unless it is cypress, redwood, or other type that will stand up to weathering.

It works best to choose objects that are sized in proportion to your garden and its surroundings. At the Huntington Gardens in San Marino, California, rows of large classical statues flank a long lawn with a view to the hills, making an impressive and memorable scene. Even one of those statues would be completely out of place in our small backyard garden. On the other hand, our tiny sundial would be lost in the broad expanse at Huntington.

Everyone has an opinion about the tastefulness, or lack of it, of using small ornaments in the garden. We feel that they can be fun as long as they're not overdone. We enjoy our 18-inch-tall, classic stone statue of Saint Francis, given to us by friends when they had to move their garden. Each summer, he hides unobtrusively in the midst of our lavender, where one can come upon him quite unexpectedly. Similarly, a cast-iron frog or a stone gnome in the right place can add a touch of whimsy to a flower bed, but if the garden has more than a few toadstools and "Snail Crossing" signs, your attention is likely to gravitate toward them instead of the flowers. And if you place a bright plastic ornament in the garden, you may find to your dismay that your friends think you love them and give you a lot more. Then you will have a problem.

GENTLE GUARDIAN. We especially love a classic stone statue of St. Francis that we have had in our garden for many years, moving it from place to place among the plants over the season.

Illuminating Your Garden

UNLESS WE GO on a moonlit walk (or make the effort to go outdoors with a flashlight), most of us never see our flowers at night. If you entertain a great deal on summer evenings, however, or use your garden areas at night near a swimming pool, deck, or patio, for instance, you may want to cast light on your garden. Garden lighting also enables people who work during the day to enjoy their plantings once the sun goes down. Although our garden is not fully lighted, we're

glad to have our floodlight and post lantern when we entertain in our backyard or when we want to show our flower beds to evening guests. One friend told us she especially enjoys entertaining at night on the terrace near her lighted garden because the semidarkness effectively conceals many of the weeds that show so glaringly in bright sunlight.

You have several lighting choices, such as using regular house current, installing low-voltage or solar systems, or relying on old-fashioned candles and torches. Illuminating a garden for decorative effect is quite different from installing lights for safety or security. A professional outdoor lighting expert will spend many hours moving lights around to achieve just the right balance between light and shadow, and there's no reason why you can't do the same thing by experimenting with portable ones.

It is helpful to visit other lighted landscapes before you invest heavily in such a project so you can compare the type of light from each kind of bulb. Mercury vapor, quartz, incandescent, fluorescent, and others each shine with a different quality of light and distort to some degree the natural colors of foliage and flowers.

For large projects wired into house current, you will want the help of an experienced electrician. He or she will make certain that the wire used is of an adequate gauge for everything wired to your system, as well as for any extra fixtures you might want to add later. The wires should be enclosed in a steel pipe that is buried deep enough that it is not likely to be disturbed. Make a chart noting the location of the pipes so you can access the wiring later, if necessary, and be careful to avoid digging or driving metal posts in those areas.

LET THERE BE LIGHT. Nonelectric lights, such as gaslights, tiki torches, luminarias, or Japanese stone lanterns, are all attractive for evening entertaining. It is not easy to achieve all the lighting effects you want in the garden without electricity, but the charm and mystery of a garden in flickering light cannot be duplicated by an incandescent bulb.

Coping with Bugs

Because lights in the summer are likely to attract clouds of moths and other insects, you may want to consider using the type of colored lights that are less inviting to insects or setting up electronic, sonar repellents in unobtrusive spots.

DRAMATIC EFFECTS. Softly uplit by a spotlight hidden in nearby foliage, this multi-trunked tree becomes a focal point in the garden. White-edged, variegated hosta and white-painted chairs make the area even more inviting for an evening spent enjoying conversation and the rest of the garden. In such a setting, take care to position the light so that it doesn't shine into people's eyes.

Placing Your Lights Effectively

🕯 Hide the light source. Obscure the bulbs high in the foliage of trees or low behind shrubbery. If you set up a high overhead light shining downward, use a second light beamed upward so the source of the upper one will be hidden. Downlighting emphasizes the foliage of trees and nicely illuminates flowers, paths, pools, and garden decorations.

🕯 Light a terrace, patio, or pathway from a spot high enough that the light doesn't blind or glare. Add a dimmer switch if you want to be able to adjust the lighting and make it more subtle.

🕯 Illuminate a garden outside a picture window by mounting a floodlight on the house so that the beam shines toward the garden.

🕯 Light a rock garden from the front and above, or from lights placed behind large rocks or shrubs at the sides of the garden, like footlights.

🕯 Place submerged pool lights on the side from which the pool is seen so they won't shine in the viewer's eyes. Install lighting for a shallow reflecting pool in such a way that only the plants or objects to be reflected are illuminated.

🕯 Illuminate running water in a fountain or waterfall either from behind or below, to highlight the shimmering effect.

If you'd like to install your own system, you might want to consider either solar-powered or low-voltage lighting for your garden. Solar systems need no underground wires, because they use sunlight to charge their batteries, and the lights come on automatically at dusk. They give a soft light, and their size makes them easy to place anywhere. You can use them as security lights, as luminaries to light pathways, in areas you use for entertaining in the garden, or to watch your phlox by night. Low-voltage lighting is connected to the house wiring with a transformer that reduces the voltage, making it safer for use around the grounds and easy to install. The wires can be concealed in neighboring shrubbery or buried in the ground.

The Effect of Light on Plants

When you plan your garden lighting, be aware that lights can sometimes affect the growth and flowering habits of nearby plants. If the lights are left on all night, or even for several hours in the evening, the plants will experience what amounts to a long summer day.

This extension of daylight hours can encourage faster growth and earlier flowering of certain plants, such as carnations (*Dianthus caryophyllus*) and many annuals, but after midsummer, it is likely to delay the blooming of chrysanthemums, fall asters, and other plants that flower only as the days get shorter. Small amounts of light have no effect on most perennials.

Bright lights left on for long periods can have a detrimental effect on certain nearby shrubs and trees if their different stages of growth are triggered by the amount of light they receive. Some plants, if they get extra light in the fall when daylight hours would ordinarily be shortened, may not respond as if winter is coming and fail to develop their leaf and flower buds for the following spring. Many plants need a shortened day to stop growing and harden their new growth before the first frost. If the growing season is artificially lengthened, such trees and shrubs may be full of sap and in lush growing condition when the first hard frost arrives, and the entire plant or tree can be killed. Careful gardeners use garden lighting only occasionally, if at all, during the month preceding the first likely fall frost.

CHAPTER 3

Nurturing Your Garden Soil

WHEN WE WERE GROWING UP, our parents often quoted the proverb "Well begun is half done." This bit of wisdom is particularly fitting for making a flower garden that is expected to last for years without annual tilling and replanting.

If you are lucky, the location you choose for your garden is already endowed with deep, rich topsoil containing an abundance of moisture-retaining humus. More likely, however, you are faced with the job of converting a grassy lawn, former hayfield, old vacant lot, sand dune, or other challenging site into a thing of beauty. If your garden contains mostly poor, worn-out soil that lacks humus and nutrients, all your plants will probably struggle and never  achieve the large root systems you want. And as if the importance of your soil's fertility, texture, and acidity level weren't enough, it is also essential to rid the soil of all weeds and weed roots before you plant or you will be confronted with a monumental weeding task forever after.

Evaluating Soil Texture

MOST PLANTS IN YOUR GARDEN need a deep, rich soil with lightweight texture if they are to thrive. Slightly moist but well-drained soil is ideal. The earth should never dry out completely, nor be soggy for extended periods. Sandy soils dry out too quickly, which causes the plants to suffer from lack of moisture; heavy, wet, clay soils become so compacted that the air necessary for good root growth is forced out of them.

Dig up a spadeful or two of your topsoil and squeeze it with your hands. Does it feel like modeling clay, or does it slip, like sand, through your fingers? With luck, its texture will be somewhere between these two extremes, with particles of mineral matter (in the form of clay and sand) mixed with organic matter to create a material that is light and sponge-like when moist.

SOMETHING TO STRIVE FOR. Even within small geographical areas, soils differ widely. The soil at the right is heavy clay; notice how it holds its shape. In the middle is nearly pure sand. And at the left, we show the ideal, rich loam.

Organic Matter: The Life of Your Soil

Organic matter — and the humus that's produced from it — is the "life blood" of your soil. It stores moisture and nutrients for future use, keeps the soil loose, allows aeration, and encourages the bacterial and earthworm activity necessary for healthy plant growth. Although no one would recommend setting a plant into a material that is 100 percent organic matter, such as peat moss or rotted manure, a soil containing a high percentage of organic matter will help your plants thrive.

Compost is an ideal source of both nutrients and organic matter. In many places, it is available from municipal waste-processing plants. Garden centers sell compost in bags as well as in unbagged truckloads. In the country, some farmers convert part of their manure and other farm wastes into compost to sell. Many home gardeners like to make as much of their own compost as possible out of garbage, leaves, and garden wastes.

The words *compost pile* have a different meaning for each gardener, since the term can refer to just a heap of materials rotting in a corner of the backyard or to a scientifically layered pile of various organic materials placed in an elaborate container made of wood, fiberglass, or concrete. By turning the pile frequently and using activators, you can encourage the contents to rot quickly without odor.

Although entire books are devoted to the subject of how to build a compost pile, our method is uncomplicated. It works well for people who don't take the time to do all the extras and are in no hurry for fast compost. Near our vegetable garden we have two adjacent 6-foot-square, 3-foot-high bins, each framed with cement blocks on three sides. In one bin we alternate layers of organic material (table scraps, garden wastes, weeds, leaves, and grass clippings) with layers of soil and layers of manure during the year. We keep it

Swampy, Wet Soil

If the spot you want for your garden is wet, consider draining it with ditches or drain tile. Then add light, sandy topsoil to raise the potential garden area a foot or more. First check with the local authorities about wetland regulations, however, since it may be illegal to alter areas over a certain size. An easier option, of course, if it is possible, is to leave the area as it is, grow some of the interesting plants that thrive in water or dampness, and build your flower garden in a more favorable spot. See the section on water gardens (pages 164–69) for more information.

Improving Your Soil's Texture

Once you have identified your soil's texture, use these methods if it needs improvement:

CLAY SOIL. Lighten heavy clay or clay-loam soil by tilling in peat moss, manure, compost, or all three. If the soil is heavy and appears to have a good supply of organic material but doesn't drain well, till in some sand every five years or so. You may need to spread as much as 6 inches of sand and work it into the top 6 inches of soil. Alternatively, you could spread a layer of light topsoil 6 inches or more deep and plant in a raised bed.

SANDY SOIL. To improve a light soil that tends to dry out quickly, add peat moss, manure, or compost, and till in one or more cover crops. If you don't want to take the time to improve the soil in this way, or if it is in particularly bad condition, buy some rich topsoil instead; spread it 6 or more inches deep on the spot, and till it thoroughly.

BEYOND SOIL ADDITIVES. If your soil appears to need a major amount of improvement and you feel that additives are not enough, it makes sense to delay planting for a year. Till the soil and then grow a cover crop in the area for a season. In the fall, till the crop into the soil before it goes to seed. Not only will the cover crop add a lot of humus, but it will choke out many weeds as well. You can purchase cover crop seeds at local garden centers or farm stores or by mail order. We've successfully used annual oats and annual rye as cover crops.

moist in the summer to hasten decomposition. We also turn it occasionally to cool any material that may be overheating, since too much heat can cause depletion of the valuable nitrogen in the pile. As decomposition slows down and the pile cools, it comes alive with earthworms, which break down the materials further into rich, black humus. When one bin is full, we cover it with lawn clippings or old hay, and let it rest until the composting process is completed. Then we begin filling the second bin in the same fashion. It takes about a year for all the materials to decompose, and if it isn't completely finished by then, we dig the compost we need from the bottom of the pile.

For faster decomposition in your compost pile, shred leaves and any coarse stalks, such as those of sunflowers. Also, avoid adding shavings, chips, or woody prunings, since they take a long time to rot.

A MIRACLE IN THE GARDEN. Composting can seem almost magical to the uninitiated. This pile still contains stems and weeds that have not yet broken down. But the entire pile will soon convert to the dark, rich humus that is already forming, especially if it is turned frequently and kept moist.

A Look at Soil Fertility

ALTHOUGH THE TEXTURE of your soil is important, you must also be concerned with its fertility. Consider the effects of soil nutrients on your plants in the same way you'd think about the results of a diet of food for yourself. Without good nourishment, your health would obviously suffer and you would feel worn out and bedraggled. Plants have similar problems when they are not fed properly.

Although you may be tempted to plant your garden first and pour on plant foods later, it is far better to have plenty of organic nutrients mixed throughout the soil initially so they will be available at all stages of a plant's growth. If your soil is nourished, your plants will thrive, and you will enjoy them far more.

The primary elements needed for healthy plant growth are nitrogen (N), phosphorus (P), and potassium (K). These three are listed in that order on packages of both chemical and natural fertilizers, whether in liquid or dry form (pelletized products are easier to pour and spread). When a fertilizer label reads 5-8-10, it means that the fertilizer is 5 percent nitrogen, 8 percent phosphorus, and 10 percent potassium. The other 77 percent is an inert filler.

The Chemical Approach

Advertisers continually make elaborate claims about the fantastic results you can expect if you use their miracle chemicals on your garden. Determining the correct amount of chemical fertilizer to use is tricky, however. When too much is applied to the soil, the rapid availability of chemicals can cause the "burning" of the foliage, sometimes enough to kill it outright. Even if burning does not occur, overfeeding can cause such rapid growth that it results in weak plants that are susceptible to easy breakage in wind, as well as to attacks by insects and diseases. In an attempt to overcome the problems of overfeeding, manufacturers have developed a variety of slow-release fertilizers that can be applied once, in early spring, and more safely provide food for the plants throughout the growing season. Dedicated organic gardeners like to avoid these products, too, because in hot weather their nitrogen

is released faster, which can cause problems. If you decide to use chemicals of any kind, be sure to follow the directions exactly, and remember that more is almost never better.

The Organic Approach

We prefer to use organic plant foods because they are slow-acting and feed the plants over a long season. We are also convinced they produce healthier plants. Organic fertilizers, such as kelp, fish emulsion, dried manure, bonemeal, and finished compost are excellent sources of nutrients, and, unlike chemical fertilizers, will not harm the plants if you accidentally give them an overdose.

Some organic products have certain drawbacks. Fresh farm manure usually carries an abundance of weed seeds, so it's best to compost it for a year before adding it to the soil. Unless you have a good supply nearby or gather your own materials, organic plant food is likely to cost more than chemicals. In addition, the nutrient value of various organic products differs widely from brand to brand.

While well-rotted farm manure and finished compost are great sources of organic matter and supply some nutrients, they may not have all those that your plants need. You may need to add cottonseed meal, soybean meal, alfalfa pellets, or bloodmeal to supply additional nitrogen. Greensand, wood ashes, and granite dust can provide potassium; bonemeal and rock phosphate are good suppliers of natural phosphorus. Natural substances such as seaweed, composted leaves, and fish oils are not only rich in basic nutrients but also provide trace elements such as boron and manganese. These and others are needed by some plants in minute amounts for good growth but are often lacking in worn-out soils. Fortunately, you need not buy each product separately; complete organic fertilizers in formulas such as 5-7-9 and others are now available.

When using any commercial manure fertilizer, carefully follow the directions that come with the product. If there are none, spread commercially dried cow or sheep manure at the rate of at least 10 pounds over each

Some Common Natural Soil Additives

A. COTTONSEED MEAL (contains nitrogen). Stimulates plant growth.

B. BLOODMEAL (contains nitrogen). Promotes rapid growth and dark green foliage.

C. ROCK PHOSPHATE (contains phosphorus). Encourages early root development; aids flower formation.

D. KELP MEAL (contains nitrogen and potassium). A brown seaweed; is an excellent supplement to other organic soil additives.

E. GARDEN GYPSUM (contains calcium and sulfur). Improves water and air penetration; minimizes salt damage; promotes root growth; maximizes effect of fertilizers.

F. ALFALFA MEAL (contains nitrogen, as well as other macro- and micronutrients). Stimulates plant growth.

G. BONEMEAL (contains phosphorus and nitrogen). Helps create sturdy root systems; stimulates plant growth.

H. POTASH (contains potassium). Helps develop vigorous plants and disease resistance.

100-square-foot (10-foot-by-10-foot) plot before the final tilling. Fresh farm manure, if it is available, has a much higher moisture content than dried manure, so 100 pounds per 100 square feet is the recommended ratio. Poultry manure is richer but very strong, so, whether fresh or dried, use it carefully, at no more than half the above rates. Be sure to till any manure into the soil promptly before it dries out. When it is left exposed to the sun and air, the nitrogen, which is especially volatile, will evaporate.

Know Your Plant Food Elements

Nitrogen, phosphorus, and potassium are known as the *primary elements* needed for healthy plant growth. In addition, plants require other elements in smaller amounts, including *secondary elements* and *micronutrients* (sometimes referred to as *trace elements*). The following charts provide advice on the function and sources of each element, as well as what symptoms indicate its deficiency or excess.

Primary Elements

Nitrogen — N

FUNCTION: Gives dark green color to plant. Increases growth of leaf and stem.

DEFICIENCY: Light green to yellow leaves. Stunted growth.

EXCESS: Dark green. Excessive growth. Retarded maturity. Loss of buds or fruit.

SOURCES: Manure, bloodmeal, fish emulsion

Phosphorus — P

FUNCTION: Stimulates early formation and growth of roots. Gives plants a rapid and vigorous start. Is important in formation of seed.

DEFICIENCY: Red or purple leaves. Cell division retardation.

EXCESS: Possible tie-up of other essential elements.

SOURCES: Superphosphate, rock phosphate, bonemeal

Potassium — K

FUNCTION: Increases plant vigor and disease resistance. Encourages strong, stiff stems. Promotes production of sugar, starches, oils.

DEFICIENCY: Reduced vigor. Susceptibility to diseases.

EXCESS: Coarse, poor-colored fruit. Reduced absorption of Mg and Ca.

SOURCES: Muriate or sulfate of potash, greensand, wood ashes, seaweed

Secondary Elements

Magnesium — Mg

FUNCTION: Aids photosynthesis. Key element in chlorophyll.

DEFICIENCY: Loss of yield. Chlorosis of old leaves.

EXCESS: Reduced absorption of Ca and K.

SOURCES: Magnesium sulfate (Epsom salts). Dolomitic limestone is ⅓ Mg.

Sulfur — S

FUNCTION: Helps build proteins.

DEFICIENCY: Looks like nitrogen deficiency.

EXCESS: Sulfur burn from too low pH.

SOURCES: Sulfur, superphosphate

Calcium — Ca

FUNCTION: Part of cell walls. Part of enzymes.

DEFICIENCY: Stops growing point of plants.

EXCESS: Reduces the intake of K and Mg.

SOURCES: Limestone, basic slag, gypsum, oyster shells

Elements from Air and Water

Carbon — C

FUNCTION: Keystone of all organic substances.

DEFICIENCY: None known.

EXCESS: None known.

SOURCE: Air (carbon dioxide)

Oxygen — O

FUNCTION: Respiration

DEFICIENCY: Wilting.

EXCESS: None known.

SOURCES: Air and water

Hydrogen — H

FUNCTION: Necessary in all plant functions.

DEFICIENCY: None known.

EXCESS: None known.

SOURCE: Water

SOURCE: Adapted from *Down-to-Earth Vegetable Gardening Know-How,* Dick Raymond

Micronutrients

Zinc — Zn

FUNCTION: Aids in cell division. In enzymes and auxins.

DEFICIENCY: Small, thin, yellow leaves.

EXCESS: None known.

SOURCE: Zinc sulfate

Iron — Fe

FUNCTION: Chlorophyll formation.

DEFICIENCY: Yellowing of leaves, the veins remaining green.

EXCESS: None known.

SOURCES: Iron sulfate, chelated iron

Manganese — Mn

FUNCTION: In enzyme system.

DEFICIENCY: Mottled chlorosis of the leaves. Stunted growth.

EXCESS: Small dead areas in the leaves with yellow borders around them.

SOURCE: Manganese sulfate

Copper — Cu

FUNCTION: Enzyme activator

DEFICIENCY: Multiple budding. Gum pockets.

EXCESS: Prevents the uptake of iron. Causes stunting of roots.

SOURCES: Copper sulfate, neutral copper

Molybdenum — Mo

FUNCTION: Helps in the utilization of N.

DEFICIENCY: Symptoms in plants vary greatly.

EXCESS: Poisonous to livestock.

SOURCE: Sodium molybdate

Boron — B

FUNCTION: Affects absorption of other elements. Affects germination of pollen tube.

DEFICIENCY: Small leaves. Heart rot and corkiness. Multiple buds.

EXCESS: Leaves turn yellowish red.

SOURCE: Borax

Organic Fertilizers

Fertilizer	Uses / Amount
Bloodmeal N 15% | P 1.3% | K 7%	**USES**: Supplies readily available nitrogen. Speeds decomposition of compost. **AMOUNT**: Up to 3 lbs. per 100 sq. ft. (more will burn plants).
Bonemeal N 3% | P 20% | K 0% | Ca 24–30%	**USES**: Raises pH. Excellent source of phosphorus. Good for both bulbs and flowers. **AMOUNT**: Up to 5 lbs. per 100 sq. ft.
Cow manure N 2% | P 1% | K 1%	**USES**: Because slow releasing, a valuable soil additive. If fresh, will burn plants. **AMOUNT**: 40 lbs. per 50–100 sq. ft.
Cottonseed meal N 6% | P 3 % | K 2%	**USES**: Acidifies soil. Lasts 4–6 months. **AMOUNT**: 2–5 lbs. per 100 sq. ft.
Fish emulsion, fish meal N 5–8% | P 4–6% | K 0–1%	**USES**: In early spring, as a foliar spray. Fish meal lasts 6–8 months. **AMOUNT**: Emulsion: dilute 20:1. Meal: Up to 5 lbs. per 100 sq.ft.
Gypsum Ca 23–57% | S 17%	**USES**: When both calcium and sulfur are needed and soil pH is high. **AMOUNT**: Up to 4 lbs. per 100 sq. ft.
Kelp meal, liquid seaweed N 1% | P 0% | K 12%	**USES**: Contain natural growth hormones and trace minerals. Use sparingly. Kelp meal lasts 6 months. **AMOUNT**: Meal: Up to 1 lb. per 100 sq.ft. Liquid: dilute 25:1.
Sulfur S 100%	**USES**: Lowers pH in alkaline soils. Increases crop protein. Ties up excess magnesium. **AMOUNT**: 1 lb. per 100 sq. ft. to lower pH 1 point. As fungicide, 3 tablespoons per 1 gallon of water.

SOURCE: *The Able Gardener,* Kathleen Yeomans

The True Test

If you are doubtful about the kind and amount of nutrients in your soil, have it tested by your Co-operative Extension Service. Some extension services offer soil testing through their websites. For information about what is available in your area, see the U.S. Department of Agriculture website at www.reeusda.gov. Some garden centers also offer a soil-testing service, or you can buy a kit at most garden centers and test your soil yourself. When you have determined what the soil is lacking, you can add the proper fertilizer to improve it.

1 Dig soil samples from several places in your garden, because soil can vary widely even in a small area, depending on what treatment it has had in the past.

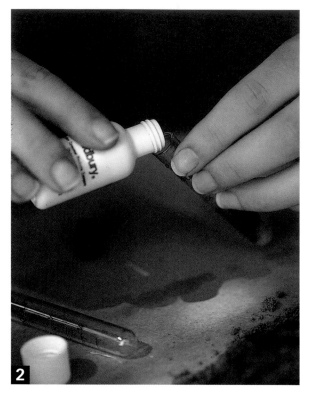

2 Following the test kit directions, mix the soil with the solutions provided.

3 Match the soil mixture against the kit's color chart to determine pH or nutrient content.

Sweet or Sour Soil?

IF YOUR SOIL IS WELL SUPPLIED with organic matter and nutrients, the plants will probably grow well, and soil pH—the measure of its acidity or alkalinity—should not be a great concern. But if the soil is extremely acidic (sour) or alkaline (sweet), nutrients become "locked" in it and many plants are unable to make use of them. If you suspect that the pH of your soil is at one extreme or the other, either buy a small soil pH test kit and check it yourself or ask your Cooperative Extension Office about a test. (You can find the address and phone number of your local office in the "Government Offices" section of your phone book.)

The pH scale chemically measures acidity on a scale of 1 to 14. 1 is the most acid, 14 the most alkaline, and 7 is neutral. The type of mineral and organic matter present in the soil determines its pH. Soils containing high amounts of aluminum, sulfur, iron, peat, decayed pine needles, or oak leaves tend to be acidic, and those with calcium are more alkaline. Most garden plants grow best in soil with a pH that ranges from 6.5 to 7. Heaths *(Erica),* heather *(Calluna vulgaris),* wild orchids, and broad-leaved evergreens prefer a pH of 4.5 to 5, conditions far too acidic for most other plants, while delphiniums, clematis, and lilacs *(Syringa)* favor a pH of nearly 7. The description of each plant in Part 3 lists any special soil requirements it may have.

To make acidic soil more alkaline (to *raise* the pH): Mix 10 pounds of lime or 20 pounds of wood ashes into 100 square feet of soil to raise the pH one point. Since lime leaches away in the rain, you'll need to repeat the application every two or three years.

To make alkaline soil more acid (to *lower* the pH): Add peat moss, cottonseed meal, sulfur, or the composted bark or sawdust of oak, pine, or hemlock; or apply an acidic fertilizer of the type used for blueberries and azaleas. Three to four pounds of sulfur per 100 square feet will lower the pH one point.

KNOW THEIR PREFERENCES. Heaths *(Erica)* [TOP] flourish in soils too acid for most other plants, while lilacs *(Syringa)* [BOTTOM] prefer slightly alkaline conditions.

Be careful when correcting soil pH, because too much lime can lock up nutrients as much as too little. An excess of wood ashes or lime on a garden makes the soil too alkaline for many crops and also discourages earthworms and soil microorganisms. If your soil is excessively alkaline, rather than struggling continually to make it more acidic, you may find it is easier to avoid growing broadleaf evergreens, blueberries, and other acid-loving plants and grow the ones that are better suited to your type of soil.

The chart on pages 54–57 gives broad preference ranges for selected plants.

pH chart

Please note that the soil's nutrient content and texture work in combination with pH to affect plants' ability to prosper. This chart should be regarded as a starting point only. You may have different results in your own garden.

ACID   ALKALINE

4.0	4.5	5.0	5.5	6.0	6.5	7.0	7.5	8.0

Alkanets (*Anchusa*)

Amaranths (*Amaranthus*)

Aster, New England (*Aster novae-angliae*)

Aster, New York (*Aster novi-belgii*)

Astilbes (*Astilbe*)

Azaleas (*Rhododendron*)

Baby's breaths (*Gypsophila*)

Bachelor's button (*Centaurea cyanus*)

Balloon flower (*Platycodon grandiflorus*)

Beardtongues (*Penstemon*)

Beautybush (*Kolkwitzia amabilis*)

Bee balms (*Monarda*)

Black-eyed Susans (*Rudbeckia*)

Black-eyed Susan vine (*Thunbergia alata*)

Blanket flowers (*Gaillardia*)

Bleeding hearts (*Dicentra*)

Boltonia (*Boltonia asteroides*)

Bridal wreath (*Spiraea × vanhouttei*)

Bugleweeds (*Ajuga*)

Butterfly bushes (*Buddleia*)

Butterfly weed (*Asclepias tuberosa*)

Calendula (*Calendula officinalis*)

Candytufts (*Iberis*)

Canterbury bells (*Campanula medium*)

Cardinal flower (*Lobelia cardinalis*)

Celosias (*Celosia*)

Chaste tree (*Vitex agnus-castus*)

Chinese lantern (*Physalis alkekengi*)

Clematis (*Clematis*)

Coleus (*Solenostemon scutellarioides*)

Columbines (*Aquilegia*)

Coral bells (*Heuchera*)

Coreopsis (*Coreopsis*)

Cosmos (*Cosmos*)

Cranesbills (*Geranium*)

Crocus, fall (*Crocus speciosus*)

Crocuses, autumn (*Colchicum*)

Crocuses (*Crocus*)

pH	4.0	4.5	5.0	5.5	6.0	6.5	7.0	7.5	8.0

Cyclamens (*Cyclamen*)

Daffodils (*Narcissus*)

Dahlias (*Dahlia*)

Daylilies (*Hemerocallis*)

Delphiniums (*Delphinium*)

Deutzia (*Deutzia gracilis*)

Euonymus (*Euonymus*)

False dragonhead (*Physostegia virginiana*)

False indigo, blue (*Baptisia australis*)

False indigo, yellow (*Baptisia tinctoria*)

Flag, blue (*Iris versicolor*)

Flowering quince (*Chaenomeles japonica*)

Flowering tobaccos (*Nicotiana*)

Forget-me-nots (*Myosotis*)

Forsythias (*Forsythia*)

Fothergillas (*Fothergilla*)

Four o'clock (*Mirabilis jalapa*)

Foxgloves (*Digitalis*)

Fritillaries (*Fritillaria*)

Fuchsias (*Fuchsia*)

Garden heliotropes (*Valeriana*)

Gayfeathers (*Liatris*)

Gladioli (*Gladiolus*)

Globeflowers (*Trollius*)

Grape hyacinths (*Muscari*)

Heather (*Calluna vulgaris*)

Hellebores (*Helleborus*)

Hollyhock (*Alcea rosea*)

Honesty (*Lunaria annua*)

Honeysuckles (*Lonicera*)

Hyacinth (*Hyacinthus orientalis*)

Hydrangeas, blue (*Hydrangea*)

Hydrangeas, pink (*Hydrangea*)

Hydrangeas, white (*Hydrangea*)

Hypericums (*Hypericum*)

Impatiens (*Impatiens*)

Iris, crested (*Iris cristata*)

Iris, Japanese (*Iris ensata*)

Irises, bearded (*Iris*)

Jack-in-the-pulpit (*Arisaema triphyllum*)

Jacob's ladder (*Polemonium caeruleum*)

Japanese anemone (*Anemone × hybrida; A. japonica*)

Joe-Pye weed (*Eupatorium maculatum*)

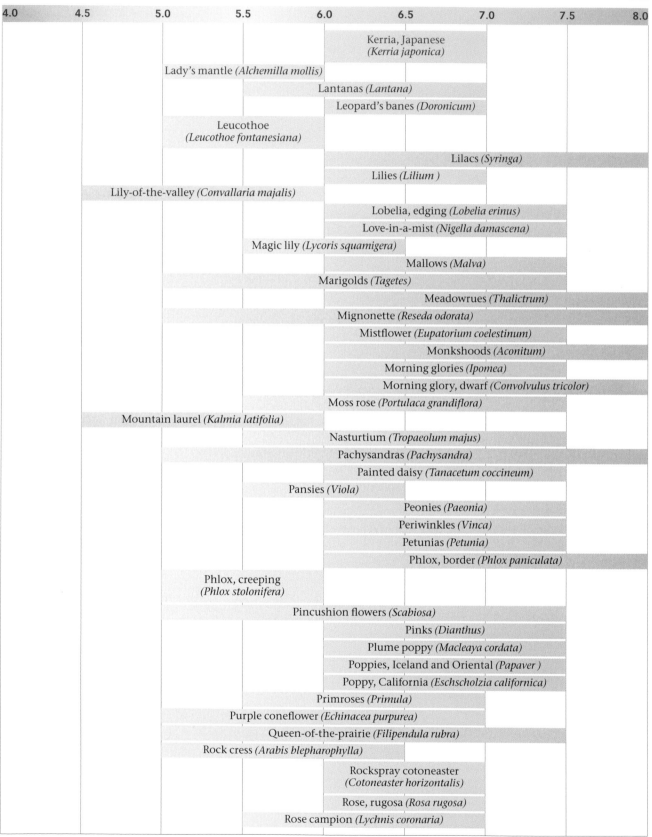

4.0	4.5	5.0	5.5	6.0	6.5	7.0	7.5	8.0

Kerria, Japanese *(Kerria japonica)*

Lady's mantle *(Alchemilla mollis)*

Lantanas *(Lantana)*

Leopard's banes *(Doronicum)*

Leucothoe *(Leucothoe fontanesiana)*

Lilacs *(Syringa)*

Lilies *(Lilium)*

Lily-of-the-valley *(Convallaria majalis)*

Lobelia, edging *(Lobelia erinus)*

Love-in-a-mist *(Nigella damascena)*

Magic lily *(Lycoris squamigera)*

Mallows *(Malva)*

Marigolds *(Tagetes)*

Meadowrues *(Thalictrum)*

Mignonette *(Reseda odorata)*

Mistflower *(Eupatorium coelestinum)*

Monkshoods *(Aconitum)*

Morning glories *(Ipomea)*

Morning glory, dwarf *(Convolvulus tricolor)*

Moss rose *(Portulaca grandiflora)*

Mountain laurel *(Kalmia latifolia)*

Nasturtium *(Tropaeolum majus)*

Pachysandras *(Pachysandra)*

Painted daisy *(Tanacetum coccineum)*

Pansies *(Viola)*

Peonies *(Paeonia)*

Periwinkles *(Vinca)*

Petunias *(Petunia)*

Phlox, border *(Phlox paniculata)*

Phlox, creeping *(Phlox stolonifera)*

Pincushion flowers *(Scabiosa)*

Pinks *(Dianthus)*

Plume poppy *(Macleaya cordata)*

Poppies, Iceland and Oriental *(Papaver)*

Poppy, California *(Eschscholzia californica)*

Primroses *(Primula)*

Purple coneflower *(Echinacea purpurea)*

Queen-of-the-prairie *(Filipendula rubra)*

Rock cress *(Arabis blepharophylla)*

Rockspray cotoneaster *(Cotoneaster horizontalis)*

Rose, rugosa *(Rosa rugosa)*

Rose campion *(Lychnis coronaria)*

	4.0	4.5	5.0	5.5	6.0	6.5	7.0	7.5	8.0

pH preference ranges for plants (continued):

Plant	Approximate pH range
Roses, hybrid tea (Rosa)	5.5–7.0
Scarlet runner bean (Phaseolus coccineus)	6.0–7.0
Scarlet sage (Salvia splendens)	5.0–6.0
Sea lavender (Limonium latifolium)	6.0–7.0
Shasta daisy (Leucanthemum × superbum)	5.0–6.0
Snapdragon (Antirrhinum majus)	6.0–7.0
Sneezeweed (Helenium autumnale)	5.5–7.0
Sneezewort (Aconitum ptarmica 'The Pearl')	6.0–7.0
Soapworts (Saponaria)	6.0–7.0
Speedwell (Veronica longifolia)	5.5–7.0
Spring beauty (Claytonia virginica)	5.0–6.5
Spring heath (Erica carnea)	4.5–6.0
Spurges (Euphorbia)	6.0–7.0
Squills (Scilla)	6.0–7.5
Stocks (Matthiola)	6.0–7.0
Stokes' aster (Stokesia laevis)	5.0–6.5
Stonecrops (Sedum)	6.0–8.0
Summersweet (Clethra alnifolia)	5.0–6.0
Sunflower (Helianthus annuus)	6.0–7.5
Swan River daisy (Brachyscome iberidifolia)	6.0–7.5
Sweet alyssum (Lobularia maritima)	6.0–7.5
Sweet rocket (Hesperis matronalis)	5.0–6.0
Sweet William (Dianthus barbatus)	6.0–7.5
Sweet woodruff (Galium odoratum)	4.0–7.0
Torch lilies (Kniphofia)	6.0–7.5
Transvaal daisy (Gerbera jamesonii)	6.5–7.5
Trilliums (Trillium)	4.5–5.5
Tulips (Tulipa)	6.0–6.5
Turtleheads (Chelone)	5.0–6.0
Verbenas (Verbena)	6.0–7.5
Violets (Viola)	5.5–6.0
Wallflower, English (Erysimum cheiri)	6.0–7.5
Wallflower, Siberian (Erysimum × allionii)	5.5–6.0
Weigelas (Weigela florida)	6.0–6.5
Wisterias (Wisteria)	6.0–8.0
Witch hazels (Hamamelis)	5.5–6.0
Yellow daisy (Anthemis tinctoria)	6.0–7.5
Yuccas (Yucca)	6.0–8.0
Zinnias (Zinnia)	5.5–7.0

4 Planting Your Flower Garden

UNTIL YOU ACTUALLY dig the first hole, dip your fingers in the loose soil, and set in the first plant, gardening is an intellectual exercise. When it becomes physical exercise, the real fun begins. You are like the pianist who finally plays the first sonata after long practice of scales or the artist who paints the landscape after careful study of color and technique.

As you plant, be faithful to your plan and resist the temptation to fill up the bed quickly with easily available plants that you may not like in the future. There  is rarely any reason to do all of your planting immediately, unless you are preparing for a wedding or the arrival of the garden club. Most borders of perennials and shrubs look sparse when they are newly planted; if you want a full bed the first season, fill in the bare spots with annual bedding plants.

Putting In a New Garden

IT IS POSSIBLE to start a new garden successfully from scratch in the spring and many gardeners do so, but the ideal time to prepare a new bed is in early fall. By digging or tilling it deeply then and again in the spring before planting, you can eliminate most of the weeds.

Starting a garden by spading or tilling heavy sod can be a formidable project. You can save a great deal of work by starting even earlier: In midsummer, cover the site you've chosen with clear plastic for several weeks to kill off any existing plant life. The sun will bake the plants under the plastic, as well as kill most of the dormant weed seeds as they germinate.

You can also destroy grass and weeds with an herbicide. Chemicals are fast and efficient, but unless you use the right products and application methods they can have a detrimental effect on the soil and harm future plant life. If you opt for herbicides, ask your garden store or Cooperative Extension Service which ones are currently recommended, read the labels carefully, and follow the directions exactly.

If your plot is small, you can dig it up with a spade and muscle power, but for a larger area, a rotary tiller is a great help. Rent one at a garden center or home rental store. Avoid using a large farm tractor tiller, if possible, because the heavy machinery will compact the soil nearly as much as it loosens it.

To give your plants plenty of room to grow, dig or till to a depth of at least 12 to 15 inches. Remove all weed roots and rocks at this time, because it will become much more difficult to get rid of them after you have planted the garden. If your soil is in fair shape, it may need enrichment only with compost or manure. Simply apply these after the first tilling, and then till again to mix the organic matter into the soil.

As we said before, buying *good* topsoil and spreading it where you want the garden is the fastest way to remedy a bad soil condition. Unfortunately, obtaining good topsoil is difficult in many areas, and it is never dirt cheap. A less expensive option is to plant a cover crop, fertilize it well, and till it in at the end of the growing season. Till the area once again in the spring, just before planting. With the soil in great shape, you are ready to begin planting your dream garden.

To help transfer your design from graph paper to the soil in your prepared bed, you may want to use a splash of ordinary flour or garden lime to mark the spots where you will set the plants. A 50-foot metal measuring tape will help you measure lengthwise, and a short carpenter's folding rule works well to mark the distances from front to back and between plants. If you have purchased container-grown plants, you are now ready to make your paper garden plan a reality.

You May Think You'll Remember But . . .

Directly after planting, place an unobtrusive label near each kind of plant. The labels will clearly identify them when your chart is not handy, and they'll mark the spot so you won't absentmindedly dig into a plant when it is dormant. After years of using wood, plastic, steel, and aluminum labels, we have settled on the last. They are the most permanent, because the imprint of the pen on the soft label lasts indefinitely and is not affected by weathering. They come in different styles. Some have wires that you can use to affix them to short stakes placed near the plant, or to the plant itself if you wish. Others are made to stick into the soil. You'll find them in most garden centers and nursery catalogs.

Preparing the Bed

1 In midsummer the year before planting, till and rake your garden smooth, then cover the entire area with clear plastic. Weight the edges with boards or stones so the plastic does not come loose. Allow the area to remain covered all summer, while the sun kills not only weeds but often also certain disease organisms.

2 In early fall, remove the plastic and add a layer of compost 2–3 inches deep. You may also wish to add manure and other soil amendments, as needed. Till in these additions and again rake the area smooth.

3 Spread the area with a cover crop of annual winter rye. The seeds will germinate and grow over winter. When you dig the plants into the soil in spring, they will add valuable nutrients to the soil. (Use only annual seeds.)

TRY TO COMPACT THE SOIL AS LITTLE AS POSSIBLE when working, both at planting time and later. Don't walk on it unless necessary, especially when it is wet, because compacted soil is hard for roots to grow through. You can reach into a narrow garden from outside its borders, but if the bed is wide, you may want to lay down boards to walk or kneel on, to distribute the pressure of your weight.

Transplanting Perennials, Shrubs, and Vines

IT IS IDEAL TO BUY perennials, shrubs, and vines in containers. Container plants do not suffer transplant shock when replanted, because their roots are intact and not damaged by recent digging. You can also move established woody or herbaceous plants that are freshly dug from a nursery or garden in the spring or fall when they are dormant. In addition, most herbaceous perennials can be transplanted all summer if you do it carefully. Summer is actually the best time to move those perennials that go into a short, partly dormant period directly after blooming — bleeding hearts *(Dicentra),* leopard's banes *(Doronicum),* bearded irises, Virginia bluebells *(Mertensia pulmonarioides),* peonies, and Oriental poppy *(Papaver orientale),* for instance.

SHOPPING TRIPS. Every gardener looks forward to the first visit to a local nursery in spring. Inspect plants carefully for unhealthy-looking foliage or any signs of insect damage.

Some Rules of Thumb for Planting Depth

SHRUBS AND VINES. Plant these about an inch deeper than they grew in the nursery. Look closely at the crown — the point from which new shoots arise — and you should see the soil line.

MOST PERENNIALS, ANNUALS, AND ORNAMENTAL GRASSES. Set these at the same depth at which they were previously growing. It is easy to find this level if the old soil line is still visible on the stems. But if you aren't sure what the proper depth is, arrange the plant so that the top of the root area (the bottom of the crown) is an inch or two below the soil surface. Notable exceptions to this rule are peonies and bearded iris (see pages 86 and 123).

BULBS. See the chart on page 67, as well as individual listings in Part 3.

Watering

Like broken records, we tell people over and over that careful watering is the most important thing you can do for all of your plants. After the initial watering of new plants, continue to water them every two or three days for two or three weeks, unless it rains hard. Thereafter, during the first season, whenever the top inch of the soil becomes dry, you will need to water them again. After the first season, well-established and mulched herbaceous perennials, vines, and shrubs should need extra water only during extended dry periods.

Most of us don't water often enough or heavily enough. Be sure to use enough water each time that it soaks down to the very bottom of the roots. A light sprinkle or shower may do more harm than good, because it encourages shallow roots. It may take as much as a half pailful, poured on slowly, to properly water a shrub. For large plantings you may want to use a soaker hose. Laid in the garden on top of the soil, where they can be hidden by foliage, these hoses have tiny holes throughout their length that allow a small amount of water to trickle out and soak in gradually. Such hoses are easy to install, supply water precisely where it is needed, and waste very little in runoff.

Transplanting a Container-Grown Plant

Dig a hole somewhat larger and deeper than the size of the pot, and add some compost-and-soil mix to the bottom of the hole. We feel this encourages deep rooting, which helps the plant stand dry weather better and also grow and get established more quickly. Pour a quart to a half gallon (depending on the size of the rootball) of water into the hole. To get the plant growth off to a fast start, add liquid fertilizer to the water in the hole at a slightly weaker dilution than is recommended in the package directions.

1 Water the plant thoroughly before you begin, so that the roots are completely soaked.

2 Remove the plant from its container. Usually it will pop out easily if you turn it over and tap it gently on the bottom, but if it sticks, insert a knife around the edge, just as if you were taking a cake from its tin, or slit open the pot.

BALLED-AND-BURLAPPED PLANTS. When planting a tree or large shrub with the roots wrapped in burlap or similar material [BELOW], dig the hole two or three times wider than the rootball and deep enough that you can place some good soil at the bottom. Remove any outer layer of plastic. Unless the plant has been recently watered, soak the rootball thoroughly. Cut off the burlap carefully so you don't disturb the roots. Untangle, loosen, or cut off any roots that are beginning to encircle the root system, a sign the plant has been in storage too long. (Encircling roots can eventually girdle and strangle the plant.) Pour water in the hole and plant as described for container-grown plants.

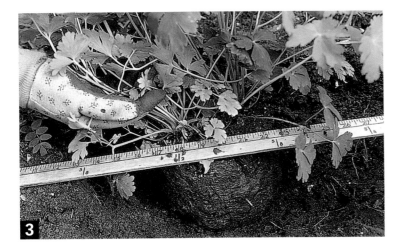

3 Keeping the root mass intact, set it an inch or so below ground level to allow space for a "saucer" in the soil around the plant. (Position a stick across the hole as a gauge.) Fill the hole with good topsoil or soil mixed with compost or dried manure. Carefully pack the soil around the roots, leaving a depression (the saucer) to catch rain and waterings. Water thoroughly to help firm the soil and expel any air that might dry out the roots.

Planting Bare-Root Plants

MAIL-ORDER NURSERIES often offer a wide variety of plants, especially if they specialize in only a few genera of plants. Many mail-order nurseries grow perennials in containers and ship practically year-round, but some dig their woody plants in the fall, store them in cellars or refrigerated sheds, and ship them as bare-root plants in the spring. They also may ship freshly dug plants in the fall. If you live in the northern zones and need plants in the fall, try to get the nursery to ship early or you may find the stock arriving in a snowstorm. In cold areas, it is important that fall-planted, bare-root shrubs and vines get somewhat established before they face freezing temperatures. In Zone 5 and warmer regions, fall and spring planting are equally good. Mail-order herbaceous perennials are dug when they are dormant in early spring and refrigerated until they are shipped to keep them from sprouting. It is important to plant them as soon as they arrive, before they dry out.

Whether herbaceous or woody, when a bare-root plant arrives from a mail-order nursery, the roots are usually covered with sphagnum moss or some other moisture-retaining material. When your plant arrives, unpack it immediately. If it looks dry, soak it in a pail of water that is only slightly warm — five to ten minutes for a perennial and as long as overnight for a dry woody plant. Careless treatment of bare-root plants before planting is responsible for more unnecessary casualties than all other poor planting techniques together.

To avoid the drying effects of weather, always keep the roots covered with moist burlap or a wet towel

BAREST ESSENTIALS. Rose bushes are one of the plants that are often shipped bare-root from mail-order nurseries.

while you are digging the holes. If you must wait a few days before setting the plant in your garden, moisten the packing material around it and store it in a cool, dark place. Evenings or cloudy days are the best times to plant bare-root stock, because the plants won't dry out as quickly as in the sun. Set the plant into the ground according to the directions that come with it, or refer to the photos on the facing page for our favorite planting method — "puddling." Not everyone uses the puddle method, preferring simply to set the plant in the loosened soil and water it well afterward. Whatever method you choose, however, always create a saucer around each plant to ensure that future waterings reach its roots, and press the soil firmly enough to ensure there are no air pockets left to dry them out.

Pre-Planting Pruning

Unless your bare-root deciduous shrubs and trees come already cut back, prune them either before or just after planting. We like to cut back the tops and branches about a third, cutting each limb to a bud. If you neglect this important step, the tops will begin to grow a few weeks before the roots have started enough to support them. With this pre-planting pruning, the plant will grow much faster than it would otherwise. Balled or potted plants need no cutting back.

The Puddling Method

With a shovel or trowel, dig a hole at least twice as wide and several inches deeper than the root clump. Don't try to squeeze a plant's roots into a small hole. As the old saying goes, "Never put a ten-dollar plant in a two-dollar hole." Loose soil should surround the roots so they can begin to grow rapidly. Unless your soil has recently been supplied with fertilizer and compost, mix a cup of compost and a few tablespoons of dry manure into the soil you removed from the hole.

1 Put a layer of the soil you have prepared back into the hole so the plant will be at the proper soil level. Be sure to note where the bare roots extend from the top part (called the crown) so that you will know how deep to set the plant. Fill the hole half full with water. This old-time practice, called *puddling,* ensures that you will have crucial moisture at the base of the roots.

2 Set the plant into the hole, spreading out the roots as you plant.

3 Finish filling the hole with the soil mix. The muddy mixture will force out any air pockets that might dry the roots.

4 Firm the soil carefully around the roots, but leave a slight depression, or saucer, around each plant to catch the rain and future waterings.

Getting Bulbs Off to a Good Start

PLANT SPRING-BLOOMING BULBS in early fall so they will have a chance to develop roots before the ground freezes. Lilies and other hardy, summer-blooming bulbs and bulb-type plants may be planted in either spring or fall, but tender, summer-blooming, bulb-type plants such as dahlias, gladioli, and begonias should be set in the ground in spring, after the danger of frost is over.

Nurseries sell bulbs by mail-order or in garden centers, and some department stores also offer them. Buy mail-order bulbs only from reliable firms, and if buying them in bulk in a store, select those that are large,

firm, and healthy looking. Plant them as soon as possible. Except for the sturdy, naturalizing-type bulbs or corms, most kinds need to be in a cultivated, weed-free bed if they are to thrive. To learn more about naturalizing, see page 68. For advice on planting bulbs in beds, see below.

Even though spring- and fall-blooming bulbs remain vibrant for only a short time, they still need regular fertilizing, dividing, and other care in future years, just like other perennials. Every two or three years, spread a bulb fertilizer over the bed in early spring.

Planting Bulbs in Garden Beds

Set the bulbs in well-prepared soil, at the appropriate depth, with the sprouting or pointed end up. Plant rhizomes and tuber-type bulbs at the recommended depth, laying them flat in the hole. For guidance on how deep to plant bulbs, follow the advice on the package label or refer to the chart on page 67.

1 To plant masses of large bulbs, such as tulips, remove all the soil to the proper depth for the bulb being planted. Add compost or other soil enhancers to the bottom of the hole, if necessary.

2 Arrange the bulbs, top side up. In circular beds and clumps, place the flat side of the bulb out. The first leaves will come from this side and, when facing outward, will look more attractive and natural. Replace the soil.

FOR A NATURAL LOOK.
When planting tulips in a garden bed, plant at least ten to twelve bulbs of a single color in each grouping, rather than lining the plants in rows.

Proper Planting Depth at Bulb Base

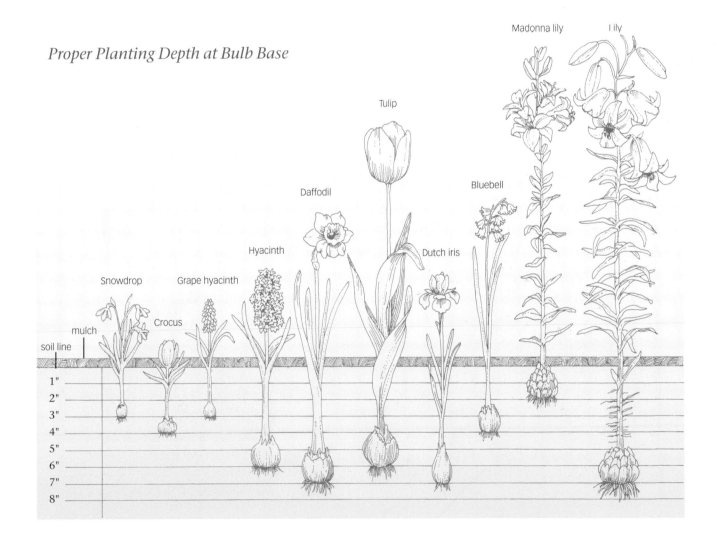

Naturalizing Bulbs

Crocuses, most common daffodil cultivars, and many of the so-called minor bulbs, such as grape hyacinths *(Muscari)* and snowdrops *(Galanthus),* have more vigor than other bulbs, so you can plant them in a semi-wild area for naturalizing. The fragrant, old-fashioned, double-flowered daffodils and the 'King Alfred' trumpet type, for example, will flourish and compete well with grass if you mow it after the foliage dies down in early summer. Most bulbs should not be set in a place that will need early mowing, such as the lawn, because the tops need to die down naturally as the nutrients return to the bulb. Without this refresher, the bulbs will suffer and next year's flowers, if they bloom at all, will be less beautiful. Fertilize the area lightly every three years, and divide and replant the bulbs every six to eight years. See below for two ways of achieving a naturalistic effect.

A HOST OF DAFFODILS. Narcissi are favorites for naturalizing.

Planting Bulbs for Naturalizing

1 The time-honored method is to take handfuls of bulbs and gently toss them over the ground, planting them where they fall.

2 Use a trowel, bulb planter, or dibble to dig individual holes for the bulbs.

SMALL BULBS. For bulbs that do not need to be set very deep, such as crocuses, grape hyacinths *(Muscari),* and glory-of-the-snows *(Chionodoxa),* simply lift up flaps of turf instead of digging hundreds of individual holes, tuck in the bulbs, and replace the turf.

Planting Annuals

IN MANY CLIMATES you can sow the seeds of annuals directly in well-prepared soil in your flower bed, right next to your perennials and bulbs, just as you would plant seeds in a vegetable garden, and thin them as they grow. If you do this, be careful when you weed and cultivate any established plants in the area, or you may disturb the annual seedlings. (For advice on sowing seed directly in the garden, see page 80. For information on starting seed indoors, see page 82.)

In cool climates with a short growing season, it is advantageous to set out most annuals as started seedlings, either your own or those from a nursery, after the danger of frost is over. You will enjoy much earlier blooms, avoid the chore of thinning, and save a great deal of weeding among the tiny seedlings.

If the plants are coming directly out of a greenhouse or warm room, harden them off by setting them outside in a sheltered spot for a few hours each day for two or three days during warm sunny periods.

Use the puddling method we described for planting potted perennials (see page 65). Pop the plants out of the containers, and arrange them according to your garden plan. Plant them in groups, slightly deeper than they were growing in the flat, and visualize the ultimate size of the plant, so that you don't crowd them. Cosmos, spider flower *(Cleome hassleriana),* and lavateras, for instance, need far more room than dwarf marigolds and sweet alyssum *(Lobularia maritima).* Be sure to water the plants thoroughly and frequently until they are established and growing well. Add liquid fertilizer, liquid seaweed, fish emulsion, manure tea (see box on page 115), or liquid chemical fertilizer to the water at planting time, and also about once a week until the plants are well established.

Moving Plants

OFTEN WE NEED TO MOVE an established clump of perennials, a shrub, or a vine. Move woody plants only when they are dormant, in early spring or late fall. It is best to move perennials at those times, too, but if necessary, you can move established clumps during the summer if you do it carefully. See Transplanting to a New Location on the next page for advice on how best to transplant. Choose a rainy spell or, if that is impossible, a cloudy day or evening when less wilting will occur, and cut back the tops by about two-thirds. (You can usually move lilies during the growing season without cutting back the tops if you put a cardboard box or paper bag over them for a few days after the move.) If you can't replant immediately, keep the roots moist, and do not expose the clump to wind or sun.

EASING THEM INTO OUTDOOR LIFE. Plants that have been grown in greenhouses or indoors under lights must be gradually acclimated to outdoor life through a process called "hardening off."

Transplanting to a New Location

Prepare the new site by digging a hole about twice as wide and several inches deeper than the root clump. Place a layer of good soil at the base to encourage the plants to begin forming new roots quickly.

1 If there are blooms and a mass of leaves on the clump, cut them back by about two-thirds in order to prevent moisture loss.

2 With a spade or spading fork, cut vertically, deep into the soil, encircling the plant and taking with it a good-sized ball of soil.

3 Move the clump to its new hole, setting it at the same depth at which it had been growing. Add some soil around the clump, and fill the hole halfway with water. Let the water settle in, then finish filling the hole with soil. Firm the soil around the roots, and create a saucer around the plant.

4 Water well once more, allowing the saucer to fill with water and soak generally into the root area.

The Many Advantages of Mulch

BECAUSE YOUR NEW PLANTS are likely to be small, your garden will have a considerable amount of bare soil exposed after planting. If the soil is left open to sun and wind, weed seeds in the soil will sprout easily. The solution is mulch. After using it for many years, we would never attempt to garden without it. Mulch not only protects the soil but also improves the garden's appearance, checks the growth of weeds, and keeps the plants clean by preventing soil from splashing onto them during a hard rain. A layer of mulch preserves moisture, saves watering chores, and helps protect plant roots from extreme changes of temperature. Earthworms work busily in the moist, cool soil beneath the mulch, aerating it and creating a loose medium in which roots can grow more easily. Mulches are also useful as protectors for the roots of tender perennials, vines, and shrubs over the winter (see Fall Chores, page 121). As a bonus, decomposing organic mulch adds valuable humus and nutrients to the soil.

Mulch Materials

Each fall, we cut down our perennials and tuck a layer of newly raked maple leaves 3 to 4 inches thick around them. If it does not rain right away, we water the leaves so they will settle in and not blow away in the first wind. If we need additional mulch at other times, we buy shredded bark, wood chips, chopped hay, or whatever other suitable organic material is readily available in our area.

Depending on where you live, you can usually find many different materials to use for mulch. Near farms, you can often buy old hay, ensilage, or straw; a woodworking mill may provide rotted shavings, wood chips, or shredded bark; and in some areas, citrus pulp, peanut hulls, marsh hay, or beet pulp may be available. Nurseries and garden centers sell mulch, both bagged and in bulk. We like to use lawn clippings for mulch, though we never have enough of them. They decompose nicely and don't harbor weed seeds. We save pine needles or oak leaves for our acid-loving plants.

In spite of its many advantages, mulch isn't always beneficial. In some areas, slugs hide under a cool layer

PROTECTIVE COVERING. A 2- to 3-inch layer of mulch, such as shredded bark, will suppress weeds and keep soil moist. Leave air space at the plant base to prevent moisture buildup and disease.

of wood chips or grass clippings during the day and make a feast of the garden at night. And not all organic materials are ideal. Fine sawdust packs together too hard to allow rain to penetrate it, and it locks up nitrogen whenever it mixes with the soil. Paper doesn't let water pass through easily either, and it can look unsightly. Black building paper can be toxic to the soil.

Although inorganic mulches such as coarse gravel, marble chips, flat stones, fiberglass, and plastic weed-check fabrics do not add humus or fertility to the soil, they do have other advantages: They thoroughly check weeds and last a long time, and some are good looking. For cutting gardens and formal plant collections, black polyethylene laid between the rows is an acceptable mulch material, but it is unsuitable for a flower border because it is unattractive and difficult to fit around the clumps. A plastic cover also makes it hard to divide and move plants.

Living on the Edge

AN EDGING DEFINES EXACTLY what is garden and what is not, and it gives the bed a finished appearance, often making the difference between a fine garden and one that looks mediocre. In addition to the aesthetic boost, it protects the flower bed from weeds that are likely to sneak in from the sides. Even if the edging's purpose is to finish off your garden, it is best to install it *before* you plant anything, though it is also possible to add an edging to an established garden, if necessary.

There are numerous ways to define an edge. In many gardens it is simply a narrow strip of bare earth about 8 inches wide between the flowers and lawn. These strips were once very popular and the edging tool used to create them—a sharp, curved blade on a straight handle—was an indispensable piece of equipment for the serious gardener. Such a cut-out edging is attractive, but because such edgings must be recut frequently, they are less common today.

HANDS ON

Installing Edging

To install steel, aluminum, or heavy plastic edging for a straight-edged border, use a taut string tied to stakes at each end, as a guide to mark the bed. To mark an irregular or curved bed, use a rope, clothesline, garden hose, or other flexible guideline.

1 After marking the edge of the border, use a spade to cut a slit straight down to the necessary depth. Sink the edging, keeping it as vertical as possible.

2 Replace the soil behind and in front of the edging, making sure the top of the edging is level with the soil so it won't be visible or interfere with mowing the lawn.

Strips of steel, aluminum, or heavy plastic, usually from 4 to 8 inches in width, make "invisible" edgings and are available at most hardware and garden stores. They take longer to install initially but are effective, long-lasting barriers. You can bend them easily to fit beds of any shape, which makes them useful for an island garden or pathway planting, as well as for a straight border.

The depth of edging you need depends on the type of plants growing in the garden bed and the ones surrounding your garden. A 4-inch depth will keep out shallow-rooted weeds and most lawn grasses, but 8 inches will do the job better. Edgings that are 2 or more feet in depth — and possibly constructed of concrete — are necessary to halt the deep-roving roots of shrubs and hedges.

Not all edging materials need to be hidden, of course. A visible edging can add a decorative touch to the garden. Depending on the appearance you want to create, you might use bricks (placed either horizontally or at an angle), flagstones, paving blocks, stone chips, tiles, concrete, wooden timbers, or similar materials. If you decide on a wood edging, choose cypress, redwood, or another long-lasting type, or treat less durable woods with a nontoxic preservative. Avoid old railroad ties or other timbers that have been soaked in creosote or toxic chemicals, such as pentachlorophenol.

You can also make attractive edgings of living plants. A low, tight hedge of dwarf shrubs, perennials, or annuals, such as boxwoods *(Buxus),* lavenders, pachysandras, thymes, lilyturfs *(Liriope),* perennial candytuft *(Iberis sempervirens),* thrifts *(Armeria),* sweet alyssum *(Lobularia maritima),* or alpine strawberry *(Fragaria vesca),* is often used as a live edging, especially in large formal gardens. Though beautiful, live edgings require more maintenance than an inanimate edging and, unless wide, are not as effective in keeping out weed roots.

Installing an edging is time-consuming, but it can save a great deal of work in the future. Aesthetically, the finished look it gives a garden can be compared to enhancing a fine painting or photograph with the right matting and frame.

A HARD EDGE. A visible edging can add an attractive finishing touch to your garden. Choose materials that blend with the other hardscape of your yard or that complement the style of your garden. A stone edging [TOP] laid flush with the ground blends nicely with the natural stone steps that the garden flanks. Brick [BOTTOM] is a traditional edging for more formal gardens.

Reviving an Old Perennial Bed

A FLOWER BED THAT IS OVERGROWN and neglected can be hard to face, and like the old woman who lived in a shoe, a gardener who has acquired one may not know what to do. Whether such a spot came with the property or your own border has simply gotten out of hand because you haven't had the time or energy to care for it properly, don't despair. It can probably be salvaged and made into a thing of beauty once again.

Your first decision must be whether to try to restore what is there or to rip out all the plants and start over. If you can't identify the various kinds or tell which are weeds, ask another gardener for help, and tag them if you have a short memory. A neglected bed is likely to contain weeds and vigorous, older perennial species, such as Johnny-jump-ups *(Viola tricolor),* yellow loose-strife *(Lysimachia punctata),* phlox, ancient daylilies *(Hemerocallis),* and lupines gone mad.

Remaking an old bed is usually easier than starting from scratch, and it is exciting to find the treasures hidden among the weeds. The plants you salvage are likely to be fully acclimated, larger than those you would buy, and waiting for a chance to be free to grow. Furthermore, the only expenses will be fertilizer, peat moss and/or compost, and, of course, your labor.

When All That's Needed Is a Good Weeding Out

If you decide things are not completely out of hand and suspect your neglected border could thrive if given the right encouragement, first list which plants are worth saving and which should go to the compost pile. After you have made the two lists, draw a new garden design. Sketch in the plants you intend to leave in place and omit those you want to move to a new location and those you plan to discard.

Although you can remake a perennial bed during the summer or fall if you are careful, the best time is in early spring, as soon as you can identify the plants but before much growth has taken place. Transplanted plants reestablish themselves quickly at this time.

The first task calls for a sturdy back to dig out the weeds and the perennials you intend to assign to the compost pile. Be forewarned: They will be robust after years of neglect! Choose a day for digging when the soil is fairly dry, if possible, because it will be easier then to shake the soil from the roots.

The nutrients and organic matter in the soil will have become depleted, so you will need to supply additional fertile topsoil where you have dug out the unwanted plants. If the remaining plants look healthy and the soil seems in good condition, however, all you may need are a few bales of peat moss, some manure or compost, and possibly lime. (See Chapter 3.) Work these into the soil around the plants you have left in place and into the empty spots where you plan to set new ones.

Move phlox to end of border —

Move foxglove to blank bed —

MUSICAL PLANTS. The tall-growing foxglove and phlox need to be moved to another spot to make room for a groundcover around the flowering crabapple tree.

A Full-Scale Remodeling

If your border has become hopelessly overgrown, you'll have best results if you dig everything out and start over with an entirely new garden plan. The best time to renew an aging perennial garden is in early spring or fall, when the plants are dormant.

1 Sort out the plants as you dig them, shaking off all the soil from the weeds and unwanted perennials before placing them in the compost pile for recycling. Carefully dig up the treasures you want to save and keep their root-balls intact. Remove weeds from the clumps of plants you plan to keep. This is a good time to separate old plants that need rejuvenating, so you may want to divide any overgrown clumps.

2 Set the rescued plants close together in a shady spot on a piece of plastic or tarp, and cover them with damp cloths (old quilts, burlap, or anything else that holds moisture well).

3 Prepare the empty bed as if you were starting from scratch: Dig or till fertilizer, peat moss, and compost into the soil. Remove all the weeds and weed roots as described in Chapter 3. With your garden plan in hand, replant the clumps you have saved as well as any new additions to the bed.

CHAPTER 5

Making More Plants

A SUCCESSFUL BUSINESSMAN who dabbles in the stock market tells us that propagating plants is the gardening chore he most enjoys. He happily compares dividing his plants to the splitting of stocks, and the volunteer seedlings that appear in the border are his dividends. And he refers to the weeds and bugs that sneak into his beds as an attempted "hostile takeover."

One of the nice things about many plants is that they naturally multiply rapidly. In Part 3, you will find advice about which method of propagation is best for which plants. In this chapter, we describe the methods. As you'll see, many annuals and biennials readily produce seeds, which you can save and plant. By simply dividing perennials, you can get enough new plants to double the size of your garden in only a few years. And it is possible, even without experience, to propagate many shrubs and vines with little trouble.

Starting Plants from Seeds

YOU CAN PROPAGATE PLANTS either sexually by seeds or asexually by division, cuttings, layering, or grafting. Although planting seeds is the best way to start annuals, biennials, and certain perennials, seedlings of most cultivars of perennials or hybrid annuals are usually quite different from the parent in color, size, or growth habit — they don't "come true." If you plant every seed on a 'Peace' rose, for example, the results may yield interesting plants, but none will be exactly like the parent. Named cultivars of perennials, shrubs, trees, and vines are therefore almost always propagated asexually, a process often called cloning. In the next section, however, we talk about how to start seed of plants that do come true.

Where We Get Our Seeds

SAVING SEEDS. We save seeds only from the plants that we know will produce good offspring, such as English daisies *(Bellis perennis),* Canterbury bells *(Campanula medium),* delphiniums, pansies *(Viola × wittrockiana),* pinks *(Dianthus),* foxgloves *(Digitalis),* gloriosa daisies *(Rudbeckia hirta),* forget-me-nots *(Myosotis),* common rose mallows *(Hibiscus moscheutos),* hollyhocks *(Alcea rosea),* lupines *(Lupinus),* shasta daisies *(Leucanthemum × superbum),* sweet Williams *(Dianthus barbatus),* painted daisies *(Tanacetum coccineum),* lavateras, calendulas, and others. We buy the seed of special cultivars, such as 'Newport Pink' sweet William. If we grew only 'Newport Pink', we could safely save that seed and be sure of getting plants like the parent, but because we grow several cultivars of sweet William, we know that the seed of any one of them is likely to be a grand mixture of them all.

PURCHASING SEEDS. Fortunately, garden catalogs sell the seeds of outstanding cultivars of perennials, annuals, and biennials each year. We like shopping from the colorful catalogs that arrive almost daily in our mailbox in early winter. Studying them on a snowy day gives us a chance to plan the most perfect garden ever, though we invariably covet far more plants than we have space for.

It is important to order seeds early, before the choicest cultivars are sold out. When they arrive, sort the packages and store them in a cool, dry, dark closet until you are ready to plant. Read the directions carefully to see if any pre-planting care is necessary. Delphinium seeds, for instance, germinate better if they are kept cold in the refrigerator for three or four weeks before you plant them. Many shrubs and evergreens need a two- or three-month period of moist, cool storage (called *stratification*) in order to germinate well. Planting collected seeds directly in the soil as soon as they are ripe fulfills this requirement nicely. The seeds stay dormant and germinate the following spring.

LIKE FATHER, UNLIKE SON. Seeds from hybrids, such as this rose, do not produce plants exactly like their parents.

Outdoor Sowing

The easiest way to start the seeds of most hardy herbaceous and woody perennials is in an outdoor seedbed. You can safely plant most perennial seeds in late summer or fall, the same time that nature does, or you can save them over the winter and start them outside in a cold frame in early spring.

When you plant the seeds of some plants that ripen in the fall, they will lie dormant and not sprout until spring. Other seeds that ripen in summer, including common foxglove *(Digitalis purpurea)* and the biennial sweet William, may start to grow soon after planting. The extra months of growth enable them to bloom the following year. You can safely plant seeds of annuals like sweet peas *(Lathyrus odoratus),* calendula, and larkspur *(Consolida ajacis)* outside in late summer or early fall. They will also stay dormant through the winter and germinate in the spring.

Seed-Saving Savvy

1 To harvest your own seed, forego deadheading a few flowers so they form seeds (see seedhead at left of flower). The seeds are ripe when they turn brown.

2 Cut off the entire plant stem just as the seeds begin to drop, and let them dry a few days in a warm, airy place.

3 Shuck the stems from the seedhead, and let them dry a bit more on a newspaper or tight screen.

4 When the seeds are completely dry, place them in envelopes, labeled with the name of the plant, the date gathered, and any other relevant information. Store envelopes in a cool, dry location.

Starting Seeds Outdoors

1 Till or spade the bed thoroughly to a depth of 10 to 12 inches to provide loose soil for the roots to grow well, then rake smooth, removing all large sticks and stones. Mix in compost, dried manure, or both. (Four cubic feet, an average wheelbarrow level load, is about the right amount for 50 square feet.)

2 Follow the directions given on the packet for how deep to sow the seed.

3 Put chicken-wire netting or a window screen over the area to keep out seed-eating birds, and add a few moth-balls to discourage mice, voles, and ants. The seeds of most winter-hardy plants sprout better if they are shaded, so provide a cover of burlap, lath, or some other material. Leave it on until the seeds have germinated and the first small leaves have appeared.

4 After planting, keep the seed beds watered, but don't oversoak the soil. Usually it is best to water in the morning, so the surface of the soil will dry out quickly and diseases will be less likely to proliferate on the moist stems.

5 When the seedlings are well established and have developed their second set of leaves, remove any shade protection you have provided and thin the seedlings so they are 2 inches apart in each direction. We usually thin seedlings by snipping off the extras with scissors, which doesn't disturb the remaining plants as much as pulling.

6 Instead of snipping them out, you may instead transplant the extra seedlings to a new bed that has been thoroughly tilled and fertilized. Space them 2 inches apart.

7 Fertilize the plants with a weak solution of liquid fertilizer every week or two until mid-July. Then, move any plants that are large and healthy to their permanent location in the border, and transplant shrubs or vines to a separate bed for further growing. Mulch the plants lightly with shredded bark or a similar material.

Indoor Sowing

Although we prefer to plant perennial and biennial seeds outdoors, we always start a few indoors in mid-winter along with our annuals, because some plants, such as pansies *(Viola × wittrockiana)*, gloriosa daisies *(Rudbeckia hirta)*, and chrysanthemums, will bloom the same year if planted early enough. Over the years, we have planted seeds in hot beds (cold frames with heating cables in the bottom), a greenhouse, and sunny windows, but fluorescent grow lights have consistently given us the best results. It is easy to maintain the proper temperature and light conditions with grow lights, so the plants need less attention. Keep the soil at whatever temperature is recommended on the seed package; it's usually between 70° to 80°F. We like to use a nursery heating mat (the kind sold for seed starting) with a thermostat beneath the seed flats to provide the proper temperature evenly. Because we use a cool room for our growing, we cover the entire unit, lights and all, with a sheet of plastic at night to keep the seedlings warm. Marigolds and certain other plants will sprout in as little as two days with this method. By using a good seed-starting mix (see below) and watering the seedlings carefully, the major disease problems are nearly eliminated.

Seed-Starting Medium

It is possible to successfully start seeds outdoors in ordinary garden soil that has been finely tilled. When sowing seeds indoors, however, you will have better results and much less trouble with disease if you use a sterile, weed-free starting mix. Before commercial seed-starting mixes became available, we used either a vermiculite-and-perlite mix or soil sterilized by heat or chemicals. Now we strongly recommend using a commercial soilless medium, such as Pro-Mix. For extra insurance, most growers treat their tiny seedlings with a fungicide.

Don't use commercial potting soil. It is good for re-potting houseplants, but because it is usually not sterilized, it is likely to contain soil bacteria and possibly weed seeds. Some potting soils are also too heavy for starting seeds successfully.

Starting Seeds Indoors

1 Soak the seed-starting mix in your flats thoroughly with slightly warm water until it is completely moist. Spread the seeds over the top of the mix as sparsely as possible. Sowing them in rows will make them easier to transplant later. Although it is difficult not to spread seeds, especially the tiny ones, too thickly, they grow much better if they are not crowded.

2 Cover the seeds with a thin layer of fine vermiculite, unless your planting directions say to cover the flat with a sheet of glass or plastic. Vermiculite keeps the soil from crusting and helps discourage damping-off.

3 Label each flat with the name of the seeds and the day they were sown.

4 Leave the grow lights on 24 hours a day until the seedlings are well started. Water at least once each day, using a gentle spray that will not hurt the delicate seedlings. A bulb sprinkler, such as the type used for laundry, is ideal. The water should be at room temperature or slightly warmer to avoid chilling the seedlings. Try to give them enough, but not too much. Overwatering and cool temperatures are the primary causes of seedling failure.

5 In three or four weeks, once the seeds have sprouted and are growing well, gradually lower the heat to 65°F and leave the grow lights on for about 12 hours daily, or set the seedlings in a sunny window during the day. Apply a liquid fertilizer once a week, but at only half the strength recommended on the label.

6 As soon as the seedlings have developed their first set of true leaves, transplant them to flats or small pots that are filled with soilless mix. Space them 2 to 3 inches apart in flats, or one seedling to each pot. If you have a large number of seedlings you may prefer to transplant them into a prepared outdoor bed, as soon as it is warm enough.

Daylily Hybrids

CHOOSE TWO SUPERIOR PLANTS in the same genus—two daylilies, for example—for the parents. Just before the buds open, cover a flower from each plant with a small paper bag. After the flowers pop open, collect some of the pollen from one of the flowers. (Pollen is the yellow or brown dust on the stamens, the male parts of the flower.) Transfer this pollen to the sticky top of the pistil, the female part of the other flower. The pistil is usually a long green tube with an enlarged cap at the top end. Use a brush to collect and move the pollen, or pinch off one of the stamens and brush the pollen directly onto the pistil.

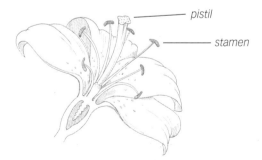

pistil

stamen

TAG THE FLOWER so you can identify the seed later, and record the names of both parents in a notebook. This step is important, because if you come up with something special, someone will want to know who the ancestors were.

Hybridizing Basics

HYBRIDIZERS TRY TO COMBINE the best qualities of two or more different species or cultivars of plants into outstanding new specimens. They work to improve size, color, vigor, disease resistance, hardiness, or fragrance. Although much plant breeding is done by universities and large nurseries, amateur horticulturists have also introduced many superior selections during the past century. Among their well-known successes are thousands of named cultivars of chrysanthemums, daylilies *(Hemerocallis),* hostas, marigolds, petunias, roses, and flowering shrubs.

Since seeds of hybrid plants don't often yield plants with qualities as desirable as those of the parents, we must buy seeds of most hybrid annual flowers and propagate our favorite perennials, shrubs, vines, and trees by cuttings, grafts, layers, or other asexual methods. The rest of this section describes those methods.

If you like to experiment, you may enjoy creating your own hybrids by controlling the pollination and collecting the seed from plants you choose. At left, you'll find directions for hybridizing daylilies. Use this advice to experiment with your favorite flowers.

Layering

LAYERING IS THE EASIEST WAY to start new plants if you want only a few, and some plants almost refuse to be started in any other way. Spreading plants, vines, and many rock plants and ground covers form new plants naturally by developing roots where their branches or canes touch the soil. Layering is a simple way to duplicate this natural rooting process with these as well as other types of plants, including most shrubs and many perennials. You can layer successfully anytime during the spring and early summer. Some plants, such as most vines, willows, hydrangea, spirea, and weigelia, will root over the summer. Roses, blueberries, and juneberries *(Amalanchier)* may not root until the next year, and it may be two or three years before layers of fruit trees form new roots. Young, vigorous plants root better than old ones.

Layering Techniques

1 With a hand trowel or garden fork, loosen the soil a few inches from a stem that is close to the ground. Bend the branch down, bury the center portion of the stem about ½ inch deep in the soil, and place a rock, bent wire, or other weight on it to hold it there. Roots should form where the stem is covered. With woody plants you can speed up the rooting process by cutting a bit of bark from the portion you bury and dusting rooting powder on it.

2 When you think roots may have formed, dig gently around the layered portion and feel to see if there is a good mass of them. When you find roots, firm the soil back, water it, and cut the newly rooted plant from its parent, but leave it in place to continue growing.

3 The following spring, carefully dig up the new plant and transplant it either to a protected nursery bed to grow larger or directly to the spot where you want it to grow. Care for it as you would any transplant, making sure to keep it well watered.

WHEN YOU NEED MORE VINES.
To start new vines, such as the clematis shown here, and other spreading plants, trail the stems along the ground and pile soil over them in spots about 2 feet apart in spring. After they have rooted, dig and separate the plants in the fall or following spring. Care for the young offspring as you would any transplants. Try this technique with various ivies, Virginia creeper (*Parthenocissus quinquefolia*), honeysuckles (*Lonicera*), and climbing hydrangea (*Hydrangea petiolaris*).

Divide and Conquer

EVEN WITH GENEROUS SPACING, most of your perennials will need dividing eventually. Dividing, or splitting a perennial clump into two or more plants, not only is the most common and usually the easiest way to propagate asexually, but also is often the best way to reduce clumps to a healthy size. It is a skill every gardener must learn early, even though at first most of us are hesitant to chop up our plants. Overgrown gardens appear messy and lose their charm, of course, but several other considerations make it even more important to divide plants that have become too large.

After your garden has grown a few years, you will be aware that some of the perennials, as they have gotten larger, aren't growing or blossoming well and, in fact, are beginning to deteriorate. As a plant expands, its outer parts may remain healthy, but the middle portion

Dividing Iris

1 For healthier, more attractive irises, keep clumps relatively small. Trim iris leaves and stems to make handling the divisions easier.

2 Once you have trimmed and cleaned away the leaves, it's easy to see the "doughnut-shaped" growth that indicates it's time to divide.

3 Use a sharp, square-bottomed spade to cut pie-shaped wedges from the large clump, and replant these as you would any transplant (see page 70).

usually becomes crowded and starved for nutrients and moisture. Sometimes called a "doughnut," a plant in such a condition is easily recognizable because the new, stronger roots and stems on the outside are visibly healthier than those in the interior. Shasta daisies *(Leucanthemum × superbum),* phlox, and chrysanthemums, for example, deteriorate in the center quite rapidly as they grow larger, and others, such as irises and coral bells *(Heuchera sanguinea),* push themselves out of the ground if they are too crowded.

Another important reason for division is to control growth. Certain plants spread rapidly by nature, and their clumps must be divided regularly to prevent them from crowding out their neighbors. Last, but not least, when you divide your plants you have a chance to get lots of new ones to expand your own plantings, share with friends, or donate to a community plant sale.

Get the Timing Right

Perennials vary a great deal in the timing of their need to be divided, but with a bit of experience, you will soon know when to take action. Most perennials need separation every three to six years, but some vigorous growers, such as bee balms *(Monarda),* lungworts *(Pulmonaria),* and yellow daisy *(Anthemis tinctoria),* may need to be divided nearly every spring. On the other hand, well-behaved plants, such as astilbes, gas plant *(Dictamnus albus),* peonies, hostas, and others, may thrive for many years in a clump without showing signs of deterioration or impinging on their neighbors.

Gardeners disagree about the best time of year to divide, but most, especially those who live in Zone 5 and cooler climates, divide plants in early spring. Since the plants are still partially dormant at that time, they suffer less shock and have a long growing season ahead to become well established in their new location. It is possible to split up plants in early fall in the North, if you do it early and cut back the foliage nearly to the ground first. If you do this, soak the plant heavily before digging, and water the planted divisions often so they won't dry out before new roots can form. Mulch them to help them survive over the winter.

Exceptions to Early Spring Division

❀ Divide leopard's banes *(Doronicum),* primroses, lungworts, and other early-blooming plants immediately after their flowers have faded.

❀ Divide peonies, irises, and Oriental poppies directly after their flowering period in midsummer. Peonies and irises may also be divided in fall (see page 123 for advice on dividing peonies).

In the warm areas of the country (Zone 6 and warmer), the general rule of thumb is to divide the spring-blossoming plants after they have bloomed, the summer bloomers in late summer or fall, and the fall bloomers in the spring.

There are gardeners who pay no attention to the seasons and divide plants successfully whenever the spirit moves them. At a small nursery near us, the owner sells perennials by chipping pieces off his established clumps whenever anyone wants a new plant, even if they are in full flower. Although such a practice seems somewhat risky, he has operated a successful business for years, and he credits his success to dividing the plants into pieces larger than is usually recommended and instructing his customers to plant them properly, shade them from the sun for a few days, and keep them well fed and watered.

Whenever you divide, if the weather is dry, soak the plant well before you begin the surgery. If possible, divide on a rainy or cloudy day or in the coolness and dimmer light of the evening, so the exposed plants won't dry out quickly. You'll find the steps for dividing overgrown iris on the facing page.

Dividing the Proceeds

Think of division as a simple form of pruning. It is as essential to the health of your perennials as pruning is to a hedge, fruit tree, or rose bush and, fortunately, is much easier. Make sure you have some healthy sprouts and good roots on each division. On dormant perennials, you will find buds or sprouts on the crowns. Leave two to four in each division as you split the clump apart. If you are dividing later, when the plant has live stems, cut back the tops by at least two-thirds so there will be less foliage for the roots to support. Don't worry about the way the plants look. New stems and foliage will begin to grow shortly.

For best results, you must first understand how the plant grows, because the method of division differs according to the plant's natural growth pattern. Most fall into one of the categories described below.

Methods of Division

A. COMPACT, SHALLOW-ROOTED PLANTS. Dig up the entire clump of shallow-rooted plants, like primroses (shown), and pull the various sections apart into smaller plants. Perform this operation carefully so the roots will not be injured.

B. PLANTS WITH CARROTLIKE ROOTS. Lupines (shown) and gas plant fall into this category. Carefully dig the entire plant in early spring, and cut apart each section with a knife so each division has both roots and sprouts. If you do it carefully, the new plants will recover quickly.

C. PLANTS WITH SUMMER DORMANCY. Some perennials become dormant for a short time after blooming and then resprout. A few, such as shasta daisies (shown), rebloom later in the summer. The best time to divide these plants is directly after blooming, when the tops have wilted. Cut back the tops and split the plants apart just as the new growth starts.

D. SOLID CLUMPS. Mountain bluet (*Centaurea montana*), daylilies (*Hemerocallis*) (shown), bleeding hearts (*Dicentra*), peonies, phlox, and similar plants fall into this category. When you simply want to make a healthy, overgrown clump smaller or to propagate one or two new plants, the easiest way is to cut away sections at the outside of the clump with a spade, thrusting the spade straight down. Chip off the outside plants carefully so you do not disturb the interior. The mother plant can then continue to bloom that year. If the center of the plant is looking sickly, however, dig up the entire clump and cut it into pieces or pry the different sections apart with a spading fork. Discard the weak or diseased parts; replant the good portions.

E. SHRUBS. Some shrubs, like lilacs (*Syringa*) (shown), spireas (*Spiraea*), and roses on their own roots (not grafted), may be divided when they are still dormant in the spring. Either split off a well-rooted offshoot from the perimeter or dig up the entire shrub and split the roots apart with clippers, a hatchet, or a saw. As with perennials, make sure there are good roots and tops on each division. Prune back the tops on each one and follow the directions for planting (see page 70). Keep in mind that your divisions will not be as well rooted as the plants you buy, so be sure to water them frequently and give them some liquid fertilizer to help compensate for surgery shock.

F. GROUNDCOVERS AND CREEPING PLANTS. To divide trailing groundcovers like lesser periwinkle (*Vinca minor*), sweet woodruff (*Galium odoratum*) (shown), and moss pink (*Phlox subulata*), dig up the plants and cut them apart nearly anytime, leaving roots and leaves on each division. Split off and dig the rooted offshoots of woody plants like creeping junipers, ivies (*Hedera*), and other groundcovers in the spring, when they are dormant. Cut back tops of offshoots by about two-thirds, so they won't grow faster than the roots can support them.

G. SPRING BULBS. It is time to divide your daffodils, crocosmias (shown), and other spring bulbs when they become too thick in the bed and the flowers are smaller and fewer. Dig the bulbs just after the foliage has died down, separate the mature ones, and replant them at the proper depth. If you want still more plants, plant the tiny bulblets, too, in prepared seed beds and leave them there for a year or two, allowing them to grow to blooming size before planting them in a permanent location.

H. SUMMER AND FALL BULBS. Split summer- and fall-blooming bulbs such as autumn crocuses (*Colchicum*) and magic lilies (*Lycoris*) in late spring or early summer, as their foliage dies. (See Part 3 for specific information.) Divide stored, tender summer-blooming bulbs, such as tuberous begonias, gladioli, and dahlias (shown), in spring. To separate gladiolus corms, peel off the papery covering and remove the old corm on the bottom. For even more plants, plant the tiny cormels in a seed bed. Separate dahlia tubers by cutting them apart where they join, making sure to have one or more eyes (buds) on each new piece. For the largest plants, leave three or more eyes on each new piece.

Caring for Divisions

Don't make your divisions too small, unless you want to create as many new plants as possible. Small plants need to be nursed carefully until they reach a healthy size; large divisions recover sooner, grow far better, and produce more blooms the following season. Unless your plants are huge, divide them into only two or three new sections. If you decide you must have a large number of new plants, grow the small plantlets in an out-of-the-way bed or in small pots for a season until they have developed good root systems. Then you can safely transfer them to their new location.

When moving new divisions, handle them with special care and, of course, never leave the roots exposed to air and sun. Keep them moist, replant them as soon as possible, and keep them well watered until they become established, as described in Chapter 4.

Starting Plants from Cuttings

YOUR GREAT GRANDMOTHER probably rooted geranium cuttings in sand or water near the kitchen stove, and a well-known story tells of the old gentleman whose newly cut poplar cane grew into a tree when thrust into the ground. Although layering and division are more efficient methods of creating husky new plants, cuttings will help you create a large quantity of additional plants, particularly when you don't want to disturb a valuable specimen by splitting it apart. There are three kinds of cuttings, including techniques for both woody and herbaceous plants:

❀ **Hardwood cuttings** are stems of woody plants taken when they are dormant, usually in late winter.

❀ **Softwood cuttings** are taken from new growth, usually in early summer.

❀ **Root cuttings** are pieces of root that, when planted, develop tops and additional roots. They are best made in spring.

Cuttings from Woody Plants

Some woody plants start very easily from cuttings, while others are much more stubborn about the reproduction process. Among those that start easily from either softwood or hardwood cuttings are the late-blooming lilacs (*Syringa × prestoniae* and others), mock oranges (*Philadelphus*), red-flowering currant (*Ribes sanguineum*), ivies (*Hedera*), hydrangeas, and weigelas. Flowering crabapples (*Malus*) and juneberries (*Amelanchier*) take much longer to root. Many deciduous shrubs and a few trees, such as poplars (*Populus*) and willows (*Salix*), root well from softwood cuttings, but most deciduous trees and evergreens resist starting life by that method. If you are interested in experimenting with cuttings, the plants listed below are good plants to start with. For a description of individual plants, see Part 3.

Perennials from Cuttings

Asters (*Aster*)
Avens (*Geum*)
Balloon flower (*Platycodon grandiflorus*)
Basket-of-gold (*Aurinia saxatilis*)
Beardtongues (*Penstemon*)
Bee balms (*Monarda*)
Bellflowers (*Campanula*)
Blanket flowers (*Gaillardia*)
Bleeding hearts (*Dicentra*)
Campions (*Lychnis*)
Candytuft (*Iberis sempervirens*)
Catchflies (*Silene*)
Catmint (*Nepeta × faassenii*)
Centaureas (*Centaurea*)

Chrysanthemums (*Chrysanthemum*)
Clematis (*Clematis*)
Delphiniums (*Delphinium*)
Eupatoriums (*Eupatorium*)
Evening primroses (*Oenothera*)
False sunflower (*Heliopsis helianthoides*)
Flaxes (*Linum*)
Forget-me-nots (*Myosotis*)
Gas plant (*Dictamnus albus*)
Gloriosa daisy (*Rudbeckia hirta*)
Lupines (*Lupinus*)
Mulleins (*Verbascum*)
Perennial lobelias (*Lobelia*)
Phlox (*Phlox*)

Pinks (*Dianthus*)
Purple rock cress (*Aubrieta × cultorum*)
Sages (*Salvia*)
Silvermound (*Artemisia schmidtiana*)
Sneezeweeds (*Helenium*)
Snow-in-summer
   (*Cerastium tomentosum*)
Soapworts (*Saponaria*)
Speedwells (*Veronica*)
Stonecrops (*Sedum*)
Sunflowers (*Helianthus*)
Tickseeds (*Coreopsis*)
Wall rock cress (*Arabis caucasica*)
Yarrows (*Achillea*)

Shrubs from Cuttings

Abelias (*Abelia*)
Bittersweets (*Celastrus*)
Bougainvilleas (*Bougainvillea*)
Boxwoods (*Buxus*)
Currants (*Ribes*)
Deutzias (*Deutzia*)

Elaeagnus (*Elaeagnus*)
Honeysuckles (*Lonicera*)
Hydrangeas (*Hydrangea*)
Mahonias (*Mahonia*)
Parthenocissus (*Parthenocissus*)
Pieris (*Pieris*)

Poplars (*Populus*)
Privets (*Ligustrum*)
Roses (*Rosa*)
Spireas (*Spiraea*)
Weigelas (*Weigela*)
Willows (*Salix*)

Hardwood Cuttings

Many woody plants, such as forsythia, hydrangea, and certain vines, start better from hardwood cuttings than from softwood. Some growers prefer that process, because they can be started outside in the ground in early spring, after being harvested in midwinter and stored until the time is right to plant outdoors.

1 Take the cuttings in midwinter, when the plant is still dormant. A cutting is usually able to produce roots no matter where you make the bottom cut, but the root formation tends to be faster and heavier if you snip about ¼ inch below a node (the joint where a leaf sprouts from the stem). Make the cutting at an angle, so there will be more surface to dust with rooting power and for root formation. Basal cuts on a slant also make it clear which end should be up, when planting.

2 Make the cuttings 6 to 10 inches long, and then clip off their tips to discourage top growth and encourage faster root development.

3 Bundle the cuttings so all the slanted cuts are at one end. If you're taking cuttings from more than one kind of plant, keep the bundles separate. Dust the bottom ends with rooting powder, such as Rootone or Hormodin. (Rooting powders are available from most garden stores.) Put some slightly moistened vermiculite in a plastic bag, and place the bundles in the bag. Tie the bag and store it vertically, with bottom the ends of cuttings down, in a cool, frost-free basement or root cellar.

4 By early spring, most of the cuttings probably will have formed calluses on their cut ends, where the roots will grow. If you didn't do it at storing time, dip these ends into a rooting powder. Stick the cuttings into a bed of a deep, sandy-soil mixture or a commercial product such as Pro-Mix, so that one-half to two-thirds of the bottom of each cutting is buried in the mix. Keep them moist. Most should start growing in a few weeks, but be patient, because they won't leaf out as soon as established plants, and some may take a long while to sprout leaves.

Cuttings from Softwood

If you are working with softwood, larger cuttings are more likely than small cuttings to develop a good root system quickly. It is easy to take large cuttings from a vigorous-growing shrub or a tall-growing perennial like phlox, but cuttings from low-growing plants—silvermound *(Artemisia schmidtiana)* and thymes, for instance—have to be shorter. Old-fashioned bleeding heart *(Dicentra spectabilis)* is best rooted from a sliplike portion—a side shoot with the tiny start of a leaf, rather than a stem with a single leaf. On daylilies *(Heme-rocallis),* look for a leafy sprout (proliferation) coming from the side of a flower stalk.

If you are serious about growing a large number of cuttings, you may want to invest in a mist system and a greenhouse where you can start many of them with little maintenance. Nursery and greenhouse supply companies sell this type of equipment in sizes ranging from hobby size to large commercial units.

SLIP CUTTING. Remove a side shoot from old-fashioned bleeding heart *(Dicentra spectabilis),* dip the end in rooting hormone, and stick the slip in Pro-Mix. Keep moist until roots develop.

Softwood Cuttings

The best time to take softwood cuttings from summer-blooming perennials is late spring; for spring and fall bloomers, and deciduous shrubs, early summer is best.

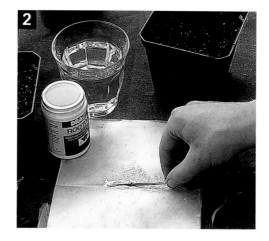

1 Choose a healthy, vigorous plant. Use hand pruners or a knife to cut off 4 to 8 inches of new top growth. Remove lower leaves from the portion of stem that will be buried; retain the rest.

2 Pour a little rooting hormone onto a piece of paper. Dip the base of each cutting about 1 to 2 inches into the powder. (Don't dip the stem into the hormone packaging or the remaining product may become contaminated.)

3 Stick the cuttings into a deep pot filled with Pro-Mix or a 1:1 mixture of fine perlite and fine vermiculite. Use a pencil or dibble to make a starter hole in the mix so that the coat of rooting hormone is not disturbed during planting.

4 Cover the pot with a bag or sheet of thin, clear plastic, such as plastic food wrap, and place it in a warm room or greenhouse out of direct sunlight. Never let the cuttings or the rooting mix dry out. Spray or sprinkle them with water several times a day, if necessary.

5 Roots should begin to form within two to six weeks. Check their progress by pulling very gently on the cutting to see if it has tightened into the mixture. As soon as the cuttings have rooted well, remove the plastic cover and water and feed them as you would new seedlings.

6 After a few more weeks, when the cuttings have developed a substantial root system and new leaves are starting to grow, transplant them to larger pots or a transplant bed.

Root Cuttings

Root cuttings are used primarily to obtain a large number of plants from a few parents, but the plants will be smaller and take longer to grow than those started by other means. We accidentally used this form of propagation once when we were trying to get rid of clumps of an old species of daylily, *Hemerocallis dumortieri*, which we had raised as foundation plants around a greenhouse. Even two years after we had carefully dug them out, hundreds of new plants kept springing from the tiny roots we had inadvertently cut off and left in

Starting Perennials from Root Cuttings

Early spring is the best time to take root cuttings. Keep the cuttings moist but not waterlogged. After they begin to grow, treat them just as you would seedlings. Once they have become well established, you can either plant them where they will grow permanently or cover them with leaves or other organic mulch for the winter and plant them out in the spring.

FINE-ROOTED PERENNIALS. These include phlox, yarrows, globe thistles *(Echinops)*, cushion spurge *(Euphorbia polychroma)*, blanket flowers *(Gaillardia)*, soapworts *(Saponaria)*, sages *(Salvia)*, and mulleins *(Verbascum)*. Cut the roots into pieces from 1½ to 2½ inches long. Scatter them horizontally over the surface of well-prepared, rich, sandy soil or starting mix. Cover them with ½ inch of sifted, light soil or starting mix.

FLESHY-ROOTED PERENNIALS. Baby's breaths *(Gypsophila)*, bear's breeches *(Acanthus)*, bee balms, old-fashioned bleeding heart *(Dicentra spectabilis)*, Oriental poppy *(Papaver orientale)*, and peonies fall into this category. Cut their roots into pieces from 1½ to 2½ inches long. (Peonies should be 3 inches long.) When taking the cuttings, be sure to lay them down with all the top ends facing the same way so you can plant them topside up. Set them vertically, about 3 inches apart, with the top of the root protruding about ¼ inch above the medium.

the ground. Although few choice perennials start as easily from root cuttings as those daylilies did, some species do very well. Huge numbers of bee balms (*Monarda*), flowering raspberry (*Rubus odoratus*), phlox, and yarrows (*Achillea*), for instance, can be produced in this manner.

With a spade, it is possible to slice off some of the outer roots from a parent plant without greatly disturbing it and, by cutting around the perimeter of the roots, to scoop up the root pieces for re-rooting. However, we usually dig up the entire plant and cut the roots into pieces from 1 to 3 inches long. If you want to save the parent plant, do not entirely dissect it; instead, leave about half of the roots intact and replant it. If saving the original is not important and creating a lot of plants is your goal, you can cut the entire root system of the plant into small pieces and start a large family.

Plants That Start Well from Root Cuttings

Baby's breaths (*Gypsophila*)
Blue bugloss (*Anchusa azurea*)
Butterfly weeds (*Asclepias*)
Evening primroses (*Oenothera*)
Gas plant (*Dictamnus albus*)
Globe thistles (*Echinops*)
Globeflowers (*Trollius*)
Japanese anemone (*Anemone × hybrida*)
Old-fashioned bleeding heart (*Dicentra spectabilis*)
Oriental poppy (*Papaver orientale*)
Phlox (*Phlox*)
Stokes' aster (*Stokesia laevis*)
Stonecrops (*Sedum*)
Yuccas (*Yucca*)

Grafting Techniques

GRAFTING IS THE PROCESS of transplanting a portion of one plant onto the stem of another to form a new plant. It is a precise surgical procedure commonly used for propagating named cultivars of fruit trees, hybrid tea roses, shrubs, and ornamental trees. We have a lilac (*Syringa*) with red, white, and pink blooms on it that we developed many years ago by grafting. It is an interesting novelty, but like most multiple grafts, some of the portions are more vigorous than others, so it requires regular pruning to keep the bush in balance.

It is not practical to start most plants by grafts, because easier methods of propagation work better, and most plants do better on their own roots. Nurserymen bud-graft hybrid tea roses on wild rose rootstocks to give them more vigor and put fruit and ornamental trees on a variety of rootstocks to propagate special cultivars that are difficult to start from cuttings or layers or to create dwarf and semidwarf trees.

Grafts are not usually practical for perennials, but the large, double, white- or pink-flowering cultivars of baby's breath are sometimes grafted onto seedlings of ordinary *Gypsophila paniculata*. The two parts are

DOUBLE YOUR MONEY. Some double-flowered baby's breath **(*Gypsophila paniculata*) cultivars are grafted onto ordinary species.**

joined in a cleft graft, covered with tape or wax, and planted with the union about an inch below soil surface. It's fun to try this interesting procedure, but don't expect perfect results every time. You may have noticed that grafted plants of baby's breath are expensive, which testifies to the difficulty of successful grafting. Most types of grafting are done in early spring, with the exception of bud-grafting, which take place in August.

CHAPTER 6

Coping with Garden Pests

FEW GARDENS STAY PROBLEM-FREE for long, but what would gardeners talk about if nothing went wrong? In humid or cool seasons, diseases can strike the best specimens the day before the big outdoor party. In hot, dry weather, ravaging insects threaten to devour every green thing in sight. Weeds can wrestle down the strongest of garden plants. A sudden wind or hailstorm can devastate an entire garden in a few minutes; an unexpected frost can ruin the display.

And then there are the animals. We speak kindly to bug-snacking toads and to the bats that consume thousands of insects each summer night. But surrounded by forest, we also host mice, rabbits, deer, and porcupines, which chew on everything, as well as skunks, woodchucks, and moles, which dig large holes. Even the birds we love so much often roost on the tall plants and break them off. And we've learned that wildlife is just as troublesome in our friends' city and suburban gardens.

Chemical Gardeners vs. Organic Gardeners

GARDENERS AND FARMERS have always known that raising plants means coping with nature's difficulties as well as with her beauty and bounty. If we are to have beautiful gardens, it is necessary to fight the bugs and diseases that strike the plants we enjoy and have toiled over. During the first half of the twentieth century, many people felt chemistry would solve all our pest problems, but by midcentury, this solution was beginning to seem less likely. The term "organic gardening" came into general use in the 1940s, and the organic movement began to boom in the 1960s after the appearance of Rachel Carson's famous book, *Silent Spring,* which discussed the worrisome problems of chemicals. Today a great many gardeners regard organic fertilizers and pesticides as their first choice and as much safer to use than chemicals.

Prevention First

Because the control of disease, insects, and weeds is difficult, aggravating, and expensive, ideally we try to prevent their occurrence from the outset. When we started our nursery many years ago, we were often careless about where we got our plants, since we wanted to offer a large variety in a short period of time. Consequently, we soon picked up a distressing assortment of insects, diseases, and weeds, some of which took years to eradicate before we could safely sell plants. We had to make the difficult decision then not to accept gift plants, no matter how tempting, and to buy stock only from certified pest-free sources.

Unless you are in the nursery business, you won't need to be as meticulous about not accepting gifts, but try to look each gift horse in the mouth. We can't repeat often enough that if you are suspicious about a plant's condition, wash all the soil off the roots and plant it in an isolated spot until you are satisfied that it is not harboring any weed roots or seeds, bugs, or blights that might infect your garden. We know one gardener who keeps a spot just for that purpose and moves all suspicious-looking specimens there as soon as any symptoms appear. He calls it his plant psychiatric ward.

We have found the following techniques helpful in avoiding garden problems:

❀ Keep your plants well-fed and cared for, so they'll be healthy, vigorous, and better able to resist problems.

❀ Leave plenty of space around each plant for proper air circulation. Overcrowding causes plant stress, and poor ventilation encourages disease.

❀ Avoid species particularly vulnerable to pests. Check in Part 3 for a detailed description of each plant you are considering and for information about its susceptibility to any troubles.

❀ Disease and insects often overwinter in old leaves and stalks, so cut the stems off herbaceous plants in late fall, leaving only about 2 inches of stubble, and remove the cuttings from the garden.

❀ Plant a few marigolds and ornamental onions *(Allium)* throughout the garden. Marigolds have been found to repel many insects and nematodes, and onion relatives discourage ants and Japanese beetles, among other pests.

❀ Try to inspect your plants daily. As soon as you see a problem, snip off the affected leaf or stem, and remove entirely any plant that looks hopelessly sick.

❀ Pick off the larger chewing bugs and drop them into a can of soapy water, or wash them off with soap (not detergent) and water.

❀ Fight back with natural enemies. Buy and distribute insects such as ladybugs and praying mantises, which eat aphids. Spread milky spore dust, which attacks the larvae (grubs) of chewing insects but does not harm the plants.

❀ Collect earwigs and slugs overnight by laying wide boards on the ground. Crush them or shake them into a pan of soapy water or kerosene in the morning.

❀ Use only sprays that are known to be the least toxic, such as insecticidal soaps, *Bacillus thuringiensis* (commonly called Bt), pyrethrin, neem, or horticultural oil.

Weighing the Options

Chemical pesticides can influence the ecology of your garden by their adverse effects on beneficial bugs, hummingbirds and other birds, and butterflies. Many of the sprays we were formerly told were "safe" have since been restricted or completely banned. Growers should consider that any product, chemical or organic, that was designed to kill bugs or weeds, check disease, or stimulate plant growth may not be completely safe for people, either. In other words, be cautious in using any pesticide. Always follow the directions, and store the product in a secure place.

Covering trees and shrubs with dormant oil spray before the leaves develop in the spring gives effective control of many insects that overwinter on woody plants. The oil also helps check the windborne spread of fungus spores, such as scab.

Pesticide companies frequently develop new products, so for an insect or disease problem that you can't control by recommended methods, check with your garden center or organic suppliers. Or, search the Internet to find the safest treatments now available.

Pesticides are sold in either powder or liquid form. Apply the powders with a hand duster, or, if the directions state, mix them with water and spray them or apply with a watering can. The "flit gun," a handheld

A GOLDEN HELPER. Marigolds have been found to repel many insects and nematodes, so let them work for you by finding places to fit them into your garden scheme.

The Problem May Not Be Disease or Insects

Insects and diseases cause many garden problems, but before you reach for the sprayer, consider whether your plant may be suffering instead from a physiological problem. Plants can be affected by a host of environmental hazards that are often mistaken for disease or insect troubles. They may look distressed because of too much or too little water, sun, fertilizer, or lime. They may be overcrowded, growing in compacted soil, or damaged from wind, frost, or hail. Or they may have had animal or mechanical damage. Here are some questions to investigate when you are troubleshooting a problem in your garden:

☐ Are clumps overgrown and in need of dividing?

☐ Are plants set too deep or too shallow?

☐ Have plants been damaged by frost?

☐ Is the soil too wet or too dry?

☐ Do plants need fertilizer or lime, or have they been given too much of one or the other?

☐ Have weed killers or pesticides been carelessly used?

☐ Has hot weather and/or drying winds caused wilting?

☐ Have animals such as moles, gophers, woodchucks, deer, or even domesticated pets damaged plants?

☐ Has there been damage from cultivators, mowers, or other equipment?

sprayer, is an excellent tool for pest control in a small garden because it is easily directed and uses a minimum amount of spray. If your garden is large, it will be more convenient to use a small tank sprayer or one that attaches to a hose.

If you use pesticides, organic or not, spray only the affected plants, and use only as much as is absolutely necessary. Never spray chemicals on plants that are in bloom, because bees may take the poisons back to their hive. Be sure to protect yourself with gloves, a hood, long pants, boots, eye protection, a mask, and an old long-sleeved shirt. When you are finished, wash your clothes and yourself thoroughly. Never buy chemicals in large amounts. They may subsequently be declared unsafe, and many products deteriorate rapidly and lose their effectiveness in storage, some in only a year or two. If you have small children or pets, be especially careful when using and storing pesticides and herbicides, even organic ones.

Organic Controls: What's What?

The interest in organic gardening has grown so rapidly in recent years that many manufacturers have introduced both organic fertilizers and excellent new organically based products that help gardeners control insects, diseases, and weeds. Keep in mind that any material that will eradicate pests is probably not completely safe, so as with chemical controls, use even these natural products according to the directions, and always with care. Store materials where children and pets can't reach them, and dispose of containers in a safe manner. Never dump unused products or the water used to clean sprayers into streams or storm drains.

INSECTICIDES

Bacillus popilliae (milky spore). A good, natural control for the larvae of Japanese beetle. It is safe and doesn't kill most beneficial insects, but it acts rather slowly. It doesn't kill adult insects.

Bacillus thuringiensis (Bt). Similar to *Bacillus popilliae* and used for much the same purposes.

Horticultural oil (summer oil). A safe control for many garden insects, both adults and larvae. Its viscosity is lighter than that of dormant oil, making it safe to use on growing plants.

Insecticidal soap. Similar to horticultural oil, insecticidal soap controls a wide variety of insects.

Diatomaceous earth. Skeletal remains of single-celled, fresh-water plants called *diatoms*. Its abrasive properties give good control against slugs and snails.

Neem. Pesticide made from neem seeds. Good for controlling insects, and also useful as a fungicide.

PROTECT YOUR VALUABLES. Neem is an effective and relatively safe pesticide. When spraying, take care not to hit beneficial creatures such as bees and spiders, because it will hurt them. Once the spray dries, neem is toxic only to insects that chew or suck on leaves that have been sprayed.

Pyrethrin. An organic spray made from the daisy *Chrysanthemum cinearaefolium*. Controls insects, but must be used frequently as the results are not long-lasting.

Garlic mixtures. Used against whiteflies, mites, aphids, and other pests.

Hot pepper wax. Made from cayenne pepper, hot pepper wax repels many insects, as well as animal invaders.

Teas. Made by stewing rhubarb or tobacco leaves in water. When sprayed on plants, these teas control many insects.

Row covers. If put over plants early, row covers keep moths from laying eggs that turn into leaf-eating larvae.

FUNGICIDES

Bordeaux mix. Mixture of powdered lime and copper sulfate used to check mildews and other leaf diseases.

Sulfur. Useful fungicide with little toxicity. Helps check mildew, rusts, and similar problems.

Fungicidal soap. Mixture of various compounds that control certain fungi.

Copper sulfate. Old-time fungicide used to control mildew on phlox, rust on hollyhocks, and some fungi.

Homebrews. Mixtures of vinegar and water or baking soda and water that check some kinds of fungi.

HERBICIDES

Nonselective weed killers. Scythe, BurnOut, and Finale are trade names of products that kill most vegetation. Most are potassium salts of fatty acids or a mixture of vinegar and lemon juices.

Selective herbicides. Corn gluten meal in products such as DynaWeed or WeedBan acts as a premergent, preventing the sprouting of weed seeds.

Clear plastic. Spread over an area for several weeks in summer, clear plastic will bake nearly all weeds to death and leave the soil fairly sterile.

Insect Invaders

THE LIST OF INSECTS that have a taste for plants may seem endless, but most of the millions of different kinds that share our planet will never become pests in the flower garden. Among the exceptions are voracious Japanese beetles, which are an overwhelming problem in some areas, and gypsy moths, which can devour practically everything when they fall from the tree leaves they have been consuming. In addition to the true insects, there are other chewing or sucking creatures, including spider mites, slugs, and snails, all of which may consider your garden a tasty opportunity.

Three general types of creatures may unexpectedly visit your garden: sucking pests, such as aphids and mites; chewing pests, such as caterpillars, beetles, and grasshoppers; and borers, which work in the interior of stems and roots.

Ants. These do not usually afflict the plants themselves, but they spread both aphids and scale by acting as farmers, moving these insects around plants to obtain their honeydew secretions. It is not pleasant, either, to dig into an anthill or to import the little creatures into the house on a freshly picked bouquet. To get rid of them, find their home and set out ant traps or jar covers containing a mix of borax and sugar syrup.

Aphids. These tiny insects suck the juices from plants, especially the new growth. Their sucking sometimes causes the leaves to curl. The damage is not as noticeable as when chewing insects are present, but aphids can greatly weaken a plant without being immediately obvious. Use insecticidal soap or summer oils, or wash them off with your garden hose. Beneficial insects offer good control (see page 104).

Beetles. Beetles, both beneficial and harmful, come in numerous shapes, sizes, and colors. The most common nuisances are the Asiatic garden beetle, blister beetle, flea beetle, and Japanese beetle. Both adults and larvae feed on plants. If you see leaf damage, but no insects,

beetles may be feeding at night. Control small numbers by using neem or by picking them off and dropping them into a jar of soapy water. Use milky spore to control large infestations of larvae.

Borers. Borers are larvae that spend the winter in old stalks and garden debris and in the summer live within growing plants. They are difficult to spot and even harder to reach with a spray. Iris borers are one common pest: Look for

small holes in any iris rhizomes (roots) you plant and cut them out. Stalk borers may bother delphiniums, lilies, peonies, phlox, and certain annuals, trees, and shrubs. Because they will die if their overwintering habitat is destroyed, the best control is to remove all dead plant tops and any other garden wastes in late fall, and cut borers out of the trunks of infected woody shrubs and trees.

Caterpillars. The larvae of various moths, butterflies, and sawflies are likely to

appear in a variety of sizes and colors. They are vigorous eaters, and the holes they make in leaves can be readily identified. Cutworms chew off small plants entirely at ground level. *Bacillus thuringiensis* will control them.

Earwigs. These evil-looking pests can be nearly as invasive in homes as in gardens and are difficult to eradicate from either. They appear on many kinds of plants and enjoy sneaking indoors by hiding in bunches of cut flowers. Birds don't seem to care for them. Spraying with an insecticide will provide

some relief, but the most effective method seems to be trapping. One trick is to invert a flowerpot filled with hay, held a bit off the ground by a short stake. Collect the earwigs gathered under the pot several times a day, and shake them into a can of soapy water or kerosene. They also gather under boards or sheets of cardboard, whereupon you can then crush or spray them.

Flies. Whiteflies, which may appear in white clouds around plants, are more of a problem in greenhouses than in outdoor beds. Usually they are brought into your garden on plants purchased from an infected nursery and are more of a nuisance  than a danger to your plants. Often they disappear by themselves outdoors, but if you have houseplants or grow plants in a greenhouse, they may cause a problem for years to come. Fuchsias are especially susceptible. Whiteflies are hard to control organically, but insecticidal soap sprays may provide some control.

Narcissus bulb flies can do serious damage to spring-flowering bulbs. They lay their eggs in the soil near bulbs on which the larvae then feed. Whenever bulb plants appear to be growing poorly, dig them up and inspect them. Discard any that show signs of being mushy. Insecticidal soap, horticultural oils, or hot pepper wax should give good control.

Grasshoppers. In late summer, hungry grasshoppers and locusts appear ready to chew on nearly anything in your garden. Ordinarily they are a problem only during years when there is a large infestation. Birds are often the best natural control.

Leafhoppers. If you notice that foliage has been eaten, look for these tiny, ⅛-inch bugs, which leap swiftly when disturbed. Most garden insecticides control them, but you will probably find that repeat applications are necessary.

TELL-TALE TRAILS. Leaf miner damage on a columbine.

Leaf miners. These minuscule insects feed on interior leaf tissue, leaving tiny trails, blotches, and blisters. Leaf miners sometimes afflict perennials and annuals, including chrysanthemums and columbines, as well as lilacs (*Syringa*) and birches (*Betula*). You can control small infestations by picking off and destroying the damaged leaves. If you have a problem with leaf miners, spray with an insecticide in the spring, when the adults emerge and lay their eggs.

Mealybugs. Mealybugs produce egg clusters that look like cotton and make them easily recognizable. They are a common pest in mild climates, but in the North they are usually confined to greenhouses. They feed on leaves and stems. Summer oils provide good control.

Midges. Galls, or abnormal growths on plants, are caused by these small flies, which are sometimes called gnats. The chrysanthemum gall midge is orange-colored and disfigures leaves, stems, and flower buds. Small infestations may be controlled by picking off the damaged parts. Use insecticidal soap to control larger infestations.

Millipedes and wireworms.
Millipedes, which are not
true insects, feed mostly on
decaying plant material,
although they sometimes feast on tender roots and
seedlings. Use diatomaceous earth to help control
them if you find they are causing damage. More of a
problem are wireworms, which eat not only seeds but
seedlings, tender roots, and bulbs, as well. They can be
especially troublesome in new gardens where sod
recently grew. Adding parasitic nematodes to the soil
may help control them if they appear in damaging
numbers.

Mites. Mites cause a blistered, rough appearance on
leaves and often prevent flowers from opening. They
are not true insects but have eight legs like a spider, so
they are commonly called spider mites. Because they
are very tiny, their damage may go unnoticed until it
becomes extensive. The two spotted spider mite and
the red spider mite are common, as is the cyclamen
mite, which can decimate plants. Use insecticidal soap,
pyrethrin, or neem to control them.

READING THE CLUES. Mite damage on a daylily.

Nematodes. These microscopic insects live in the soil.
Some nematodes are beneficial, feeding on a number of
garden pests and helping break down organic matter.
Pest species, on the other hand, feed on the roots and
leaves of a variety of garden plants and are a particular
menace in warm climates. Sometimes the only solution to a serious infestation of pest nematodes is to
sterilize the soil of a newly prepared bed with chemicals or steam before planting. One way of sterilizing the

soil is with solarization. Spread clear plastic over the
site during the summer months to bake the soil. For
general purposes, a few weeks of baking will kill weed
seeds, but for more complete soil sterilization, it is
better to allow all summer.

When adding new plants, buy only from certified
nurseries to reduce the likelihood of importing these
pests into your garden. Some gardeners report good
luck controlling pest nematodes by planting the old-
fashioned, tall, strong-smelling marigolds among the
plants. Others grow them as a cover crop and till them
into the soil. But if a garden is badly infested, the only
certain remedy is either to sterilize or to abandon the
planting and start over somewhere else.

Sawflies. The violet sawfly
eats holes in violet and
pansy leaves, most often at
night. Other sawflies attack
various plants, including trees such as mountain ashes
(Sorbus), apples *(Malus)*, poplars *(Populus)*, and willows
(Salix), so their highest concentrations are often found
in the vicinity of those trees. Most ordinary garden
insecticides control sawflies, but several sprayings may
be necessary.

Snails and slugs. Snails and
slugs are serious garden
pests that chew large holes
in plant leaves. They prefer
cool, moist places and usually feed at night. If slugs
are a problem in your area,
use mulches judiciously or
not at all, because these
pests like to hide and breed
beneath them. Remove rubbish and other breeding
places, and sprinkle alkaline materials, such as lime or
ashes, about the garden. Slugs can't crawl well over
rough material, so layers of diatomaceous earth, sand,
or gravel will discourage their wanderings. Diatomaceous earth is available from garden centers and mail-
order suppliers. Do not use the material sold for swimming pools, because it poses a respiratory hazard. Some
gardeners lay a board on the ground to attract slugs
seeking a cool place to hide during the day, then turn

the board over and crush them with another board or scrape them into a can of soapy water. Commercial slug bait may also help.

Tarnished plant bugs. These bugs are greenish yellow to brown with black, yellow, or brown markings and yellow triangles on the end of each front wing. The nymphs are pale yellow. They eat plant parts and inject a poison that deforms the plants. Insecticidal soap and horticultural oils are effective controls.

Thrips. These minute insects attack flowering plants by sucking sap from the leaves, which results in a silvery, mottled appearance. They are most active during hot, dry years. Pyrethrin, neem, and insecticidal soap can help control them.

Weevils. Both adult weevils and their larvae attack hollyhocks (*Alcea rosea*), primroses, and some other plants, but they are not usually a serious problem. Adult weevils vary in size and have pronounced snouts. All-purpose garden dusts and sprays control serious infestations well.

Beneficial Insects

In the world of insects, some are very useful. Here are some insects that are the gardener's friends.

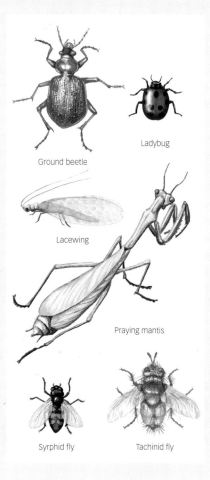

Ground beetle

Ladybug

Lacewing

Praying mantis

Syrphid fly

Tachinid fly

GROUND BEETLES. The backs of these large insects are ridged lengthwise. They are iridescent brown or dull black and can run rapidly but can't fly. Both adult beetles and the larvae eat caterpillars of all kinds.

LACEWINGS. These pale green flies with lacy, netted wings lay their eggs on the ends of stalks attached to leaves and stems. When they hatch, the hungry larvae at first consume each other, but because there are so many, others go on to consume aphids and mealybugs in large numbers.

LADYBUGS. These are often offered for sale in garden magazines and mail-order catalogs, but those you import often "fly away," as the well-known children's poem says, and do not stick around long enough to do much good where you want them. They are well known for their appetite for aphids, so be careful not to spray and harm the ones you already have in residence. Their bright orange-red color and dark spots add a bit of cheeriness to the garden, and they are rumored to bring good luck.

PRAYING MANTIS. The huge size and unusual appearance of this creature make it appear more of a foe than a friend, but it is an impressive consumer of aphids and other insects, so welcome it and its large, brown egg clusters, which appear in the fall. Although mantises don't survive well in cold climates, they are welcome additions in warmer regions, where they are needed most. Look for offers of them in the classified columns of garden magazines.

SYRPHID FLIES. Also called hover flies, these tiny insects visit flowers for their honey, and you can see them hovering over blooms with rapidly vibrating wings. Their larvae feed on aphids, so don't harm them.

TACHINID FLIES. Looking very much like houseflies, tachinid flies have iridescent, black-gray wings and attach their eggs to other insects; the larvae subsequently consume their hosts. One strain was introduced into North America to help control the gypsy moth.

Animal Scoundrels

WE ONCE RECEIVED a frantic phone call from a neighbor. She had spent the entire previous day planting tulips and carefully placing ¼ cup of bonemeal in each hole. The next morning not a single bulb was still in the ground. It was clear that a dog, skunk, fox, or coyote looking for dinner got the scent of the bonemeal and dug up each one, searching for the bone. We suggested that when she reset the bulbs she drop a mothball in with each one to confuse the wily creatures.

Wild animals aren't the only critters that can devastate flower beds. Our neighbors' pigs and cattle have tramped through ours more than once with disastrous results. Pet dogs, goats, sheep, and ponies can wreck a garden in short order, too. Even cats seeking a cool place to nap on a hot day can crush small plants. We wish we could give you a surefire method of coping with animals in the garden, but after years of trying, we can report only partial success. Wild animals are far more crafty than their civilized cousins, because the less intelligent of their species were destroyed long ago, and by the selection process the smart ones have become more skilled at their mischief with each generation. Compared to the bugs we are accustomed to fighting, they seem like monsters.

When the snow disappears in the spring, our lawn and garden are often riddled with mole tunnels and mounds, looking as though a miniature bulldozer had been working there all winter. Gardeners formerly used chemicals to kill the grubs that attracted moles (and skunks) to lawns and flower beds, but those products are now restricted. Some organic pesticides use scents offensive to the moles to drive them to another area. Gardeners may also have good luck fighting grubs by spreading beneficial nematodes and milky spore dust on their lawns. Hunting cats can also be a great help in catching moles and chipmunks and, if they are really aggressive, can also keep rabbits at bay. Moles don't eat plants, but their burrows are unsightly, and they let air into the roots, which dries them out. Mice, voles, and chipmunks also use these underground passageways, and they do eat roots and bulbs.

Growers use flashing lights, radios, noisemakers, human hair and urine, rotten eggs, mothballs, bloodmeal, and other foul smells, including chemical ones, to deter animals but get only mixed results because the hungry animals discover over time that these tactics pose no real threat. Although strong, tight fences, including electric ones, offer the best security and are fine around a vegetable garden or orchard, they spoil the appearance of a flower garden that is intended primarily for beauty. A dog is good protection if it is smart enough to frighten off the pillagers without killing deer or getting involved with skunks or porcupines. Guns, traps, and poisons are either illegal or unwise in many locations, so deer, woodchucks, rabbits, and even the cute little bud-eating chipmunks often gain the upper hand.

The list of possible pests and hazards to the plants in your yard can appear distressing, but, as we said before, most of them will never trouble you. If they do, try to regard these surprises that appear each season as challenges rather than disasters.

A TASTY SNACK. This gray squirrel casually collected stem after stem of a dahlia plant, retreating to a safe place and devouring what was apparently a very satisfying feast.

When Diseases Are the Problem

FORTUNATELY MOST PERENNIALS, annuals, ornamental grasses, and shrubs are not as vulnerable to disease as vegetables and fruits, but they are by no means immune. Diseases can be caused by fungi, bacteria, or viruses that spread from plant to plant by wind, by insects such as aphids and leafhoppers, by additions of infected soil and compost, and by contaminated tools such as trowels and spades.

If you need to use fungicides on your plants, consult the package labels to be sure they are formulated for the particular disease you hope to control.

Anthracnose or leaf spot. These diseases usually show up as the dying back of new growth and as leaf spots with slightly raised borders. Though not common on perennials, they occasionally hit chrysanthemums, delphiniums, and monkshoods *(Aconitum)* and often appear on annuals and shrubs, especially during wet seasons. Most fungicides give effective control. Besides anthracnose, a variety of other diseases can cause leaf spots. Fungicides may help control them if fungi are the cause (sometimes bacteria are to blame), but the best remedy usually is to remove the infected part immediately and destroy it.

Blight. There are many kinds of blights. Especially prevalent in damp weather, they appear as spots or lesions that disfigure the leaves, sometimes issuing a gummy substance. Botrytis, sometimes called gray mold, is common in greenhouses but can also attack chrysanthemums, lilies, primroses, and other plants in the garden. Anemones, Japanese spurge *(Pachysandra terminalis),* lupines *(Lupinus),* and poppies *(Papaver)* may suffer from blight. Suspect the disease, also, when peony buds wither and do not open. To help prevent its spread, remove and destroy diseased parts as soon as you notice them. Use a fungicide to control epidemics.

Canker. Although uncommon on perennials, bleeding canker can affect peonies, tulips, and others, as well as shrubs. Remove the oozing portion and destroy it.

Club root. This fungus disease affects members of the cabbage family, including the ornamental kinds, as well as sweet alyssum *(Lobularia maritima),* honesty *(Lunaria annua),* and certain perennials. Roots develop gall-like swellings and growth is stunted. Club root is most prevalent in acidic soils, so applying lime to the soil helps discourage it. If the disease does appear, choose a new spot for susceptible plants and avoid planting them in the same spot year after year.

Mildew. Garden phlox *(Phlox paniculata)* is often a target of this fungal disease, which covers the leaves and blossoms with a whitish powder. It can also hit bee balms *(Monarda),* chrysanthemums, delphiniums, and red-flowering currant *(Ribes sanguineum),* among others. Buy only disease-free plants, give them a site with good air circulation, and never allow foliage to become so dense that air movement is impeded and sunlight blocked out. Sulfur dusts have long been used for mildew problems, but some of the newer fungicides work better.

Mold. Some strains of mold are also called botrytis. These fungi grow on leaves and stems. Plants that are overcrowded and growing where air circulation is poor are especially susceptible. Most molds, such as those that grow on decaying organic matter, are harmless, however. Those affecting living plants may be gray, white, dark colored, or, in the case of lawn grasses, even pink. Fungicides help but sometimes fail to completely control a bad infestation. If the problem persists, it is best to destroy the plants.

THE CULPRIT. Anthracnose caused this hollyhock to die back and become disfigured.

CROWN ROT STRIKES IRIS. The affected plant must be eradicated and the soil sterilized in order to avoid spread of the disease.

Mosaic. Symptoms of this and similar viruses are yellow spots on the leaves, which tend to give them a mottled effect. Another sign may be a dwarfing of both the plant and its blooms. Even if only a few leaves show symptoms, the entire plant will eventually become infected and die. This ailment is primarily spread by aphids, and it affects chrysanthemums, pinks *(Dianthus),* delphiniums, irises, lilies, primroses, and others. Mosaic diseases are not completely understood and there is no effective remedy, so the best control is to quickly remove and destroy any plant that shows signs of infestation before the condition spreads.

Rot. This condition looks like its name and manifests on stems, leaves, roots, and occasionally even flowers. Crown rot sometimes appears on bugleweeds *(Ajuga),* delphiniums, monkshoods, irises, lilies, and some of the spring bulbs. The only sure way to wipe out the disease is to destroy the affected plants and sterilize the soil where they grew. However, fungicides can help keep it under control. To avoid most of the common root and bulb problems that appear in soggy soil, plant in soil that is well drained, if possible.

Rust. Rusts look like their name and so are easy to identify, but they are not easy to control. In weather conditions that encourage them, such as rainy or humid seasons, they can disfigure an entire planting. Various rusts strike chrysanthemums, pinks, hollyhocks *(Alcea rosea),* and mint relatives, including bee

Good Garden Hygiene

Fireblight, some rots, and certain other bacterial diseases deadly to plants are often spread by tools, especially pruning tools. It is important to sterilize your tools if your plants have these diseases. Mix 1 part chlorine bleach to 9 parts water, and dip your tool in this solution before moving on to the next plant. Don't mix more than you need, because the active ingredient, chlorine, evaporates quite quickly.

Getting rid of diseased plants can be a problem. Burning them is the best option. If you can't burn, take the diseased plants to a landfill that will accept them. Do not compost them, because most compost piles don't heat up enough to kill the disease organisms.

balms. Plant only disease-free stock, and destroy any badly infected plants as soon as you notice them. Sulfur dusts and other fungicides provide partial control if applied at the first sign.

Scab. This fungus shows up on plant leaves as spots with white centers. Pansies and violets are fairly susceptible. Spray regularly with a fungicide and remove the infected parts to keep the problem in check.

Viral disease. There are many viral diseases in addition to mosaic (see above), including some of the so-called "diebacks." They are spread by close contact with an infected plant and by sucking insects. To date there is no effective treatment, so the best prevention is, whenever possible, to plant virus-free plants. Plants infected with a virus have discolored leaves, and their growth is often stunted. Deterioration may be fairly rapid or, with trees and shrubs, could take place over several years. Remove any suspicious-looking plant as soon as you notice virus-related symptoms, and destroy it before it infects others in your garden.

Wilt. Wilting may be caused by lack of moisture in the soil, or it can be the result of one of the serious wilt diseases that suddenly cut off the water supply to a plant part or sometimes an entire plant. The two most common wilts, fusarium and verticillium, affect many perennials, annuals, shrubs, and trees. Pruning off the affected part, which may be the entire plant, is the only treatment. Since the disease may remain in the soil for months or longer, it is best not to grow annuals or perennials on land used the previous two or three years for raising potatoes, tomatoes, strawberries, roses, or other plants that are especially susceptible to wilt.

The Fine Art of Weed Control

WEEDS, IN SPITE OF THEIR BAD REPUTATION, have a worthwhile purpose. Nature abhors barren earth as much as it does a vacuum and quickly works to cover any naked soil. Weeds protect the soil from erosion, and by dying and providing organic matter, they work to make it productive once more. Although this system benefits us all, we often wish, as we're on our knees in the garden, that weeds didn't do their jobs quite so enthusiastically.

If you garden in a city or well-groomed suburb, the weeds in your garden will be far fewer and easier to control than in a rural area, where every breeze seems to be full of weed seeds. If you live in the country and take advantage of rural resources by using raw farm manure or compost that is not fully decomposed or by spreading straw and hay for mulch, you may also be adding thousands of ambitious weed seeds to your garden soil.

Know Your Enemies

Even experienced gardeners sometimes have trouble differentiating a plant from a weed. One grower told us that if a plant looks especially healthy and vigorous she assumes it must be a weed, but she waits a few weeks before pulling it up, just to be sure. Whether you garden in the city or country, the seashore or the mountains, you will find weed species that are common to all areas as well as those restricted to a particular locale. It is worthwhile to learn to identify the most common weeds early in your gardening experience and find out how they grow and reproduce, so you will be better able to control them.

Weeds are classified as either broadleaf or grass. Broad-leaved weeds range from low-growing, creepy invaders such as wild speedwells *(Veronica)*, chickweed *(Stellaria media)*, and purslane *(Portulaca oleracea)* to tall monsters like burdock *(Arctium lappa)* and bull thistle *(Cirsium vulgare)*. Grasses make wonderful lawns, and some are truly ornamental, but most are not welcome in the garden. Two of the worst weeds we face are quack grass *(Agropyron repens)* and crabgrasses *(Digitaria)*; you probably battle them too, no matter where you live. In the Northeast, quack grass is known as witch grass, but our Canadian friends call it twitch grass. More colorful adjectives often precede the words in both countries.

Both grasses and broad-leaved weeds may be either annuals or perennials. Perennial weeds such as quack grass live for years and may spread over many acres by sending up new plants from their far-reaching rhizomes and by scattering seeds. In only a few months one tiny horsetail *(Equisetum)* plant (which produces spores rather than seeds) growing in lightweight soil can spread its roots and spores 40 feet in every direction and create a new plant every few inches. Perennials like goldenrods *(Solidago)*, dandelion *(Taraxacum officinale)*, and thistles *(Cirsium)* reproduce rapidly by scattering seeds, as do annual weeds such as the vigorous lamb's-quarters *(Chenopodium album)*, kochia *(Kochia scoparia)*, purslane, and crabgrasses. Scientists tell us it is possible for a single tiny common groundsel *(Senecio vulgaris)* to produce one billion seeds a year. No wonder a gardener's work is never finished!

Weed Control

Controlling weeds is an exercise in persistence. If you attack weeds for a few minutes each day, or even twice a week, they are unlikely to get a foothold and grow out of control. Deep, rich, loose garden soil makes it easy to pull sprouting weeds before they become well anchored, and a mulch discourages the germination and establishment of seeds scattered by plants in the area or blown in from afar.

The battle with weeds, as with bugs, will never be completely won, and each of us gardeners has a sneaking suspicion that, without our efforts, weeds would take over the world. We recommend controlling them by hand whenever it is feasible. Take advantage of kneeling pads and stools and some of the new hand-cultivating tools. We're told that weeding is good therapy, and much cheaper than an analyst. Some gardeners even claim to derive great pleasure from wolfing down a meal of dandelion greens or lamb's-quarters, like cannibals eating their enemies.

Gardeners who prefer a chemical approach rely on commercial herbicides for weed control. In the past fifty years or so a great many weed killers have been developed, ostensibly to solve all our weed problems. But, like insecticides, many were found to be dangerous to people or the environment and are now prohibited or restricted. Even some of the so-called "safe" herbicides often cause more problems than they solve.

If you decide to use herbicides for weed control, it is important to understand how they work. They act in either a selective or nonselective manner. The selective types kill only certain weeds or grasses and are commonly used on lawns and farm crops. The nonselective kinds destroy all vegetation and are sprayed on driveways and paths, under fences, on rights-of-way, and to "clean up" areas before planting. The most common herbicides, both selective and nonselective, work in one of the following ways.

Foliar Herbicides. When sprayed on foliage, the chemical is absorbed by the plant. Among the chemical herbicides that kill plant life in this way is Roundup, effective on most growing plants and considered relatively safe to use; it deactivates as soon as it touches the soil. Vinegar (5% acetic acid concentration) is a safe organic spot spray, effective on a variety of weeds.

Soil-activated Herbicides. These weed killers work on the roots and, when sprinkled or sprayed on the soil, kill established plants. Preemergent herbicides prevent the sprouting of seeds already in the soil, as well as any new seeds that blow in during the time that the chemicals remain active. They are also effective in suppressing the growth of seeds brought in with manure or mulch and prevent the germination of seeds self-sown by perennials and biennials.

Some herbicides, such as Scythe and Burnout, have now been developed especially for organic growers. Ask your farm store or garden center about the products now available that you can feel comfortable using. With any herbicide, follow the directions carefully. An herbicide's effectiveness may depend on the growth stage of the plant, the type of soil, the rainfall, and the air temperature on the day you apply it.

We often dream of the day our plantings will be free of quack grass, purslane, and dandelions, but when we think more logically, we realize that, like bugs, all these nuisances will be around much longer than we will. As we continue in the struggle to keep them a safe distance from our flower gardens, we can't help but admire their tenacity at what they do best — serving as groundcovers for bare earth.

Do Look Gift Horses in the Mouth

If you are just beginning to garden and need more plants, you can take advantage of other gardeners' surpluses. Most people are ready to share their extras, and you can find more by attending neighborhood plant sales. Be careful, however, that you don't pick up invasive species, and check any newcomer to your garden to see that it is not harboring weeds, diseases, or bugs that could create problems. It is a good idea to carefully wash off the soil from the roots of any doubtful gift plants before planting them.

Aggressive plants, like the gooseneck loosestrife (*Lysimachia clethroides*) shown here, need not be completely banished from your garden, if you plant them where their spread does not impose on other plants and you are willing to keep them in check.

7 Caring for Your Garden

ONE PURIST WE KNOW stalks his beds like Sherlock Holmes, looking for anything out of place. When he discovers a weed, insect, or disease, he's ready to do battle before it can prolifer-

ate. He snips off the lupine blossoms the very day after they are past their prime, rescues the frail astilbe from its aggressive bee balm neighbor, and notes in his little book that a

large clump of peonies needs dividing right after blooming. When we compliment his meticulous beds, he invariably points out some small detail that isn't quite perfect.

Everyone approaches gardening chores differently, but we, like most gardeners, love our time in the garden, even when it's hard to fit the necessary horticultural chores into our busy lives. We've come to recognize, however, that it's important to occasionally stop clipping and weeding and take time to appreciate our handiwork. Happy gardeners notice the flowers as well as the weeds and see the butterflies as well as the slugs.

The Joy of Awakening

WITHOUT THE RESPITE that winter affords, many northern gardeners would lose interest in an avocation as intensive as gardening. But each spring our vigor is renewed, along with the unrealistic hope that this year both our gardens and the weather will be perfect. By the time the snow has melted and the crocuses and snowdrops (Galanthus) have faded, any disappointments from the previous season are forgotten, and we are eager to dig in the soil once more. Early spring is a perfect time to be outdoors: The days are not yet too hot, the evenings are long, and the black flies and mosquitoes are still asleep. In the South, however, the "down time" for growers is the heat of summer, when gardens, lawns, and gardeners all rest for a spell. Then, when the days cool in the fall, it is time to return to the garden with enthusiasm and renewed vigor.

The Uncovering

The first spring job in the North is to remove any mulch covering the perennials and roses. Especially in cold regions, it is useful to remove mulch in two stages. First push away the mulch from the crowns of the plants, and a week or two later, clear away the rest. The advantage of this system is that if hard frost threatens, you can easily cover the plants again. At any rate, take the mulch away on a cloudy day so any tender sprouts starting beneath the mulch can gradually adjust to daylight before bright spring sunshine can burn them.

Vigorous weeds always seem to appear first and grow faster than cultivated plants, so, armed with a trowel, clippers, and dandelion digger, get ready to deal with them as soon as they show up. For light spring jobs, we've found that a plastic laundry basket is more convenient than a garden cart for carrying tools, moving plants, and transporting weeds to the compost pile.

In addition to eliminating the weeds, it is usually necessary to reset a few primroses and other shallow-rooted plants that frosts have popped out of the ground. Occasionally some young plants, such as newly planted daylilies (Hemerocallis), sink deeper into the soil over the winter and must be raised up a few inches to be in a position to grow well.

STRENGTH IN NUMBERS. Relatively uniform, tulips [ABOVE] make the greatest impact when planted in masses of the same color.

Assessing Casualties

When everything has sprouted, look for empty spots. Some years every plant survives, but other springs you may need to consult the labels or your garden plan to discover which plants have died over the winter and make a note to replace them. Don't be too hasty in your judgment. Some perennials, such as balloon flower *(Platycodon grandiflorus)* and crocosmias, are notoriously late in making their spring appearance.

Losing choice plants is tough, but gardeners must expect it to happen occasionally. Even if you do everything right and the winter has been mild, certain perennials are naturally short-lived. There may also be casualties among experimental plants, but when one succumbs for no apparent reason, we suspect it may have died out of pure cussedness. A cynic once told us that the secret of successful gardening is to pretend you don't care whether a plant lives or dies, because it will usually live just to outwit you.

Moving and Dividing

Early spring is a good time to move any plants that were blooming in the wrong place the previous year (see page 69) and to divide clumps that are too large (see page 86). Only the spring bloomers and a few others, such as irises, peonies, and Oriental poppies *(Papaver orientale),* are safe from this springtime shuffle, since they prefer to be moved during the period just after they have blossomed.

Choose a rainy or cloudy day, or the cool of the evening, for transplanting. If the soil is dry, water the plant thoroughly before you uproot it so the soil will stick firmly to the roots. Dig it up carefully in order to keep the entire root ball intact, and follow the rules for planting (see page 70). When you give it its first watering after planting, add a small amount of liquid fertilizer to the water. Be generous with water until you're sure the plant is well established. If you notice it is wilting, shade it from the sun for a few days with a basket, cardboard box, paper bag, or white sheet.

Planting and Transplanting

As the days get warmer, set out the perennial and shrub plants you couldn't resist in the garden catalogs last winter and the treasures you have discovered at local nurseries. This is also the time to transplant any perennial and biennial seedlings you started earlier or bought at a greenhouse and, after frosts are over, put in the annuals. If you are planting in an established bed, get your new plants off to a good start by spading compost or dried manure into the soil where you will add the newcomers, as described in Chapter 3.

Be sure you harden off any seedlings grown indoors or in a hot bed or bought from a greenhouse before you expose them to the harsh outside world. Help them adjust to the outdoor conditions gradually by setting them outside for two or three warm days in a sheltered, shady place and taking them in again before it cools off each night. Be sure to keep them watered throughout the day.

Spring is also the time to plant the bulb-type plants: dahlias (see next page), tuberous begonias, gladioli, cannas, and other tender summer and fall bloomers. These may be the same bulbs you carefully dug, dried, and stored last fall or some you have just purchased from a catalog or garden center. It doesn't take many to furnish a riot of color for the garden and armfuls of glorious bouquets. Wait to plant these tender summer bulbs until you are sure frosts will be over by the time they come through the ground, and follow the planting directions that come with the bulbs.

SHOP NOW. Purchase plants at your local garden center.

Planting Dahlia Tubers

THE PLANTING DEPTH for dahlias depends on the type you are plant-ing. For those growing to 4 feet or more, dig a hole about 12 inches deep. Set shorter-growing dahlias 6 to 10 inches deep, again depending on their height at maturity.

Put a handful of complete organic plant food in the hole, then cover it with a thin layer of soil. If you dug dahlia tubers in the fall and have over-wintered them, use a sharp knife to divide the clump into individual tubers, each with at least two healthy sprouts (see photo, page 89). Place one of the tubers on the soil at the bottom of the hole, taking care to position it with the sprouts on top. Cover with about 3 inches of soil. As the sprouts grow and develop foliage, begin to fill in around the plant stem, gradually adding soil until it is level with the surrounding soil. Keep the plant well watered during the growing season. Provide sturdy stakes for tall-growing dahlias early in the season (see pages 116–117 for advice on staking).

Spring Bulb Care

As soon as the foliage of daffodils and other spring bulbs has turned yellow or brown, clip it off. Some-times daffodils stay green for what seems an abnor-mally long time, so we like to set started annuals among them to hide their discoloring foliage. If the bulbs are becoming overgrown, this is a good time to divide them, too.

Although wild species tulips, those in the Greigii, Kaufmanniana, and Fosteriana groups, and other perennial tulips bloom for several years without being dug and stored for the summer, most tulips and hya-cinths are likely to be short lived when they are left in the ground. Some gardeners therefore treat them like annuals, discarding the old bulbs and planting a new crop each fall. You can save them, however, by fertiliz-ing them lightly when they appear in the spring. Then, after they have bloomed and their leaves have died, dig and dry the bulbs, store them in a cool, dark place, and replant them in early fall.

Declining tulip foliage can spoil the appearance of a garden for several weeks, so to avoid this eyesore, dig up the bulbs just after they have finished blooming, lay them out in a temporary bare bed and cover the roots with a 2-inch layer of good soil, leaving the foliage ex-posed. This treatment makes it possible for the energy in the leaves to return to the bulbs. After the leaves are completely dead, cut off the bulbs, dry them in a shed or airy garage for a few days, and store them in a paper bag in a cool, dry place until time for fall planting.

A TEMPORARY HOME. Place tulip bulbs in a temporary bed, about 2 inches deep, until their foliage dies completely.

Early Summer Chores

AFTER THE FLOWERS have faded on spring-blooming shrubs like azaleas, spireas, and lilacs (Syringa), snip the blossoms off, both for appearance and so the plants won't produce an abundance of seeds. Heavy seed production saps the shrub's energy and prevents it from blooming well the following spring. If you need to prune flowering shrubs for cosmetic reasons or to curb their growth, this is also the correct time to do so.

Soil Cultivation and Nourishment

If you use mulch, earthworms will have worked beneath it to keep the soil loose and aerated, but if you didn't add mulch, the soil in your bed may have hardened. Early summer is a good time to aerate it with a garden spading fork or small hoe and to carefully cultivate around the plants.

After the garden cleanup is done, it is feeding time. Scratch a cup of manure or compost into the soil between each plant, or use an organic or chemical commercial fertilizer or a similar plant food at the rate of one level tablespoon of 5-10-10 for each medium-sized clump. Adjust the amount accordingly for smaller or larger plants. Nutrients in the soil need replacement often because they are continually depleted by plant growth, evaporation, and leaching.

Be careful not to overfeed plants. Too much fertilizer is likely to stimulate lush foliage growth but result in fewer blooms. Discontinue feeding after mid-July because perennials, shrubs, and vines need to stop growing and harden up their new growth before freezing nights begin. See Chapter 3 for more information about choosing and using fertilizers.

After the soil is fertilized and the spring plant-moving and dividing chores are finished, it is a good time to replenish the garden mulch if you didn't do it the previous fall. Apply 1 to 2 inches of shredded bark or other good mulch material after a hard rain, when the soil is well soaked. Tough weeds will still be able to penetrate the mulch, but you can easily pull them out.

To further aid weed control, before mulching, apply an organic preemergent to keep wind-blown seeds, like those of dandelions, from sprouting.

A CLEAN CUT. Prune faded lilac blooms right at the blossom base.

For an Extra Boost

If growth appears to be weak, we give our plants a solution of liquid fertilizer once or twice during the early summer, in addition to the annual feeding. After a few seasons of gardening, you'll know better what your own plants need and how to adjust their feeding schedules. One of our favorite summer tonics is manure tea. Near our garden, we keep a burlap bag full of manure from a nearby farmer in a large covered plastic garbage can filled with water. As we remove "tea," we add more water. This liquid solution gives plants a good balance of fast-acting nutrients.

Staking

Staking is one garden chore that is easy to forget, but it is important to tackle the job early, before plants start to flop over. No one enjoys having to use artificial supports in the garden, but some flowers are naturally weak and can bend or break in a wind or rainstorm, or even if a bird alights on them. In an informal garden protected from the wind, it may be necessary to stake only plants with large, heavy blooms, such as peonies and tall-growing delphiniums, hollyhocks *(Alcea rosea),* and golden glow *(Rudbeckia laciniata* var. *hortensia).* But if your garden is more formal or in a windy spot, you may also need to stake lilies, lupines *(Lupinus),* foxgloves *(Digitalis),* and other flowers of medium height.

Bamboo, wood, plastic, and metal supports of various sizes and plant ties are all available commercially. Pieces of cloth torn into strips can also be used for tying and staking. To make homemade ties as inconspicuous as possible, some gardeners rub them in soil or dye them green. Don't use ordinary string or wire, as it will cut into the plant stems.

The trick to effective and inconspicuous staking is timing. Do it early, as soon as stems are sturdy enough, but before flower buds form and plants actually need it. This way stakes and ties will be hidden by new foliage as it grows and the form of the plant will appear to be natural, rather than as if it were staked.

Sturdy plants such as monkshoods *(Aconitum)* and foxgloves need only one stake per clump at a height about three-quarters that of the mature plant. Loop the tie around the entire clump and secure it by wrapping it around the stake two or three times.

You may need to stake clumps of plants that have tall, weak stems and relatively heavy blossoms, such as hollyhocks and delphiniums, more carefully. It may even be necessary to stake each stem separately. Put in several tall stakes early and tie the stalks to them at increasingly higher intervals as they grow. The developing foliage will intertwine with the support and make it less visible. Or you can use the 4-foot-tall, three-sided metal "tomato" fences to support such tall, clumpy plants. Their greatest advantages are the ease of installation and the fact that the growing plant effectively hides the wires. Friends of ours who live near a windswept lake are even more efficient. They built a rustic rail fence at the back of their border, so they could tie their giant Pacific hybrid delphiniums to it.

Peonies and large-flowering chrysanthemums, gladioli, and exhibition dahlias often need support, not because of their height, but because their blossoms are extraordinarily heavy. Ring-type supports on wire stakes are suitable for these plants and are available at garden centers and in catalogs, or you can make your own by welding or soldering a heavy ring such as a wreath hoop to metal garden stakes. The ring supports the stems yet allows the foliage and blossoms to bend over it naturally. Once the plants have stopped blooming, you can remove the ring supports, since the foliage itself does not need staking.

STAKE OUT

A. Delphinium stems are relatively weak and their blossoms are often quite heavy, so staking is inevitable if you want to get the maximum enjoyment out of every flower. Here, the stem is tied to a tall bamboo stake with flexible plastic plant tape, which is available at garden centers on a roll and is quite inexpensive. The middle of an 8-inch length of tape is wrapped first around the plant stem, crossed, and then tied to the stake, creating a figure eight. This method allows some flex, so that the stem has room to develop and move without being tightly choked. Trim the ends, if necessary.

B. This simple stake-and-string technique is inexpensive and also inconspicuous, if done in early spring. The plant clump will grow up through the support, hiding it completely when full grown. Drive bamboo, wood, or metal stakes into the ground around the plant, then crisscross twine around the perimeter, as well as diagonally from corner to corner. Use more stakes for larger clumps, if necessary.

C. Tomato supports, composed of two or three graduated rings, make easy-to-apply supports for many floppy perennials.

D. Often called "peony supports," these plastic-coated, circular metal supports feature crosswise divisions through which large plants grow, naturally keeping a symmetrical shape. They are useful not only for peonies but also for other tall-growing plants, such as shasta daisies, garden phlox, and fall asters.

E. For especially striking specimens, you may wish to use a single stake, like this sturdy, plastic-coated one, that can be slipped around the stem, even after it is nearly full-grown. A boon for plants that you may have neglected to stake earlier!

Summer Care

AFTER YOUR GARDEN IS GROWING WELL, it must not be left unattended. As the saying goes, "The frequent footsteps of the gardener are the best fertilizer." Summer grooming is similar to tidying up a room, only much more fun. Most jobs are obvious. Remove the weeds as soon as they appear, for example, and cut off any broken, dead, or injured stems as well as all diseased or insect-damaged leaves.

Pest and Disease Alert

During warm, humid summer days and nights, diseases and insects are likely to proliferate in your garden, so watch for them during regular garden inspections. At one time gardeners were urged to spray early and often to prevent any possible troubles, but most now prefer not to spread pesticides without good reason. (For more on pest control, please refer to Chapter 6.)

Deadheading

Our most frequent summer activity is deadheading the perennials and annuals. This aggressive verb, which means snipping or pinching off the faded flowers of plants, seems to be peculiar to gardeners, since it only recently appeared in dictionaries. The deadheading habit has become so established in us that more than once we've found ourselves in the embarrassing position of deadheading while visiting a friend's garden.

Unless you want to save seeds from your plants, pick off the faded flowers not only for appearance's sake but also to prevent seeds from forming. The process of developing seeds weakens a plant and sometimes even shortens its life. It also causes the plant to stop bloom-

A LITTLE BIT OF ENCOURAGEMENT. Many plants, including delphinium, will provide continued blooms if they are regularly deadheaded. As soon as the blossoms begin to fade, prune the stem back to a point where you see new growth developing.

ing, so if you want to enjoy your garden to its fullest, keep the flowers coming as long as possible by regular deadheading.

There are other reasons for the practice. Certain biennials, such as sweet William *(Dianthus barbatus)*, common foxglove *(Digitalis purpurea)*, and forget-me-nots *(Myosotis)*, produce an abundance of seeds in order to perpetuate themselves, and these can grow into aggressive weeds. Also, some plants, if allowed to procreate, produce vigorous, but inferior, seedlings that crowd out their hybrid parents. All around the countryside we notice border phlox *(Phlox paniculata)* blooms of a dull magenta color that have taken over the beds of their brightly colored hybrid predecessors.

Cutting Back for Even More Bloom

In climates with a long growing season, cutting back lupines, phlox, yellow daisy *(Anthemis tinctoria)*, and delphiniums to a few inches from the ground directly after blooming can often encourage a second flowering in late summer.

Pinching and Thinning

Home gardeners sometimes wonder why their plants and blooms aren't as impressive as the magnificent specimens shown in garden catalogs. The secret is often not a magic fertilizer or mystical incantation but simple pinching or thinning, which you can do as well as the professionals.

FOR BUSHIER PERENNIALS.
To grow the low, cushion chrysan-themums as compact and bushy as those at the florist's, pinch the ends of all the new sprouts once a week in early summer. This pinching will stimulate the growth of side branches, make the plants produce more blooms, and prevent them from becoming tall and leggy.

FOR BETTER-BEHAVED PLANTS.
Shrubs and small trees usually benefit from some light pruning in the summer. Clip off any branches that are trailing on the ground, blocking path-ways, or spoiling the symmetry of the plant, as well as those that are dis-figured by disease or insect damage.

FOR BETTER-LOOKING SHRUBS.
Remove the faded blooms of roses and other shrubs. Not only will your plants be more attractive, but many will also continue to put out new growth and bloom, in the same way perennials do.

FOR LARGER BLOSSOMS. If you want to grow giant-sized roses, "football" chrysanthemums, dahlias, and certain other flowers, snip or pinch off most of the flower buds. The remaining flowers will be bigger. To get giant-sized peony blossoms, for example, pick off all of the small side buds on a stem as they appear in early summer. The plant's energy will then be forced into the one fat bud at the end of each stem. Later, you may want to repeat this procedure on your large-blooming common rose mallow (*Hibiscus moscheutos*) and zinnias (*Zinnia elegans*). The results will be well worth your trouble, just as when you thin carrots.

Watering

At one time or another, unless you live in Camelot, where it rains every night and the clouds disappear in the morning, your garden is likely to need extra water. New plants and seedlings without a heavy root system require extra moisture, and in a dry climate or during a drought period you may need to irrigate the entire garden frequently. Don't provide water unless there is good reason, however, because the plants become dependent on it and fail to develop the deep roots they need for good growth.

During a dry spell, a heavy soaking about twice a week is more beneficial than a light daily watering. Water moves through soil slowly, and a short shower or watering is not likely to reach the roots before it evaporates. At least 1 inch of water, from either rain or irrigation, is the minimum amount necessary to provide sufficient moisture to soak through mulch and soil and reach the roots. A rain gauge is a helpful piece of garden equipment, but judging how much is the right amount of water for your garden is often a matter of "by guess and by gosh." If plants are wilting or growing slowly in early to midsummer, however, they probably need more water. The optimum for most plants is about 1 inch a week either from rain or by watering.

Because moisture evaporates rapidly in the heat of the day, do not water when the sun is high unless your plants are obviously wilting. Some gardeners feel that the best time to water is early morning, because the sun will quickly dry any moisture on the leaves, whereas watering in the evening keeps the foliage wet all night and can encourage mildew and other diseases. In general, we prefer evening irrigation because less evaporation takes place at that time and the results last longer, but we are careful not to water plants that are susceptible to mildew at that time.

If hand watering, with either a hose or a watering can, doesn't appeal to you, you can choose from a variety of irrigation systems in kit forms that are easy to install. These include drip systems, misters, and soaker hoses, with timers to make them automatic. We prefer a soaker hose to a lawn sprinkler, because the water goes directly into the soil rather than onto the foliage or into the air. Water from lawn sprinklers falls like a light shower and may never reach the soil under plants with heavy, umbrella-like foliage. Although we use other means of watering occasionally, we like hand watering best because it gives us a chance to inspect each plant for any troubles that might be developing.

Signal Plants

Lupines (*Lupinus*) serve as a good watering indicator before and during their blooming period because, even though they have very deep roots, they are particularly sensitive to lack of moisture. You might want to plant a clump as signal plants; when they begin to wilt, the garden needs watering. Cinquefoil (*Potentilla*) shrubs are also very sensitive to lack of moisture, so water them at the first sign of wilting, as they will die if they get too dry.

Summer Transplanting

There are gardeners who like to move things about and there are those who never disturb a plant no matter how out of place it may look. Years ago we gardened for a lady who moved her furniture so often her husband was never sure where he would sleep at night, and she frequently rearranged her flower border with the same energy. She employed another part-time gardener, and since we worked on different days and didn't see each other, we never knew where any perennial might be growing the next time we appeared. The poor plants never had a chance to adjust and grow to perfection.

For your sake and the sake of the plants, a weekly shuffling of the garden is not recommended, but occasionally a perennial does need moving, even in the summer. You can transplant many herbaceous plants safely even when they are in bloom if you are careful.

Fall Chores

IN MILD CLIMATES, gardeners can continue to enjoy their plantings, divide plants, prune, and set out new plants late in the fall, and in some areas such chores go on all winter. Northern growers, however, know they are about to face a winter of unfriendly weather and possibly other surprises, so the garden must be prepared.

Gardeners disagree about how to treat plants in the fall and debate about how much to cut down perennials, how heavy to mulch, and whether or not to fertilize at that time. We feel it makes sense to let the plants die down naturally as much as possible, so that all the nutrients in the leaves and stems can return to the roots to be stored for the winter. After a light frost or two, we cut the tops off of most perennials but leave them on the lower-growing, bushy ones like bellflowers *(Campanula),* sweet William *(Dianthus barbatus),* Virginia bluebells *(Mertensia pulmonarioides),* and all the perennials that stay evergreen through the winter. We cut back the blooming stalks (scapes) on daylilies *(Hemerocallis)* but leave the foliage for a mulch. (The dead leaves are easy to rake away in the spring.) When we cut back other perennials, we leave about 4 inches of old stems to catch and hold the winter snow for additional insulation. If your garden will not be protected by snow, you may want to cut back the stems to about 2 inches from the ground and mulch any tender plants.

If you grow ornamental grasses or perennials that hold their attractive dried blooms into the early winter, don't cut those back, since you can enjoy their color for a few more months.

In early fall, we dig the frost-tender plants: gladioli, dahlias, cannas, tuberous begonias, and others. Many will stand a light frost, but be sure to get them out of the ground before it starts to freeze. Dry the entire plant by hanging it in a warm airy place, then cut off the roots and dry them a bit more. Store gladioli, begonias, and cannas in a dry, cool, frost-free place until spring planting, but inspect them from time to time to make sure they do not dry out. Don't let them get too wet, either, or they will rot. Label everything if keeping the different cultivars or colors separate is important to you.

OVERWINTERING DAHLIAS. Once the first light frost hits, dig up tender plants like these dahlias, rinse off the soil, and hang them to dry before storing in a cool, dry place until spring.

Fall Planting

Fall is the time to plant more spring-blooming bulbs
and to locate and plant the tulip bulbs we so carefully
dug and stored last spring. (See page 114.) It is also the
season to pull out and compost the now-dead annuals
that brightened the summer. Give the plot a final weeding, and you'll have less work the next spring.

We like to put a sprinkling of dried manure or compost over the area for the plant roots to absorb during
the winter, working it into the soil or quickly covering
it with the new mulch we have acquired.

Fall mulch protects the roots of dormant plants during the winter months, and in regions where frequent
thaws and frosts are common, it keeps shallow-rooted
perennials from being heaved out of the ground. We
have found that tucking a 3- to 6-inch layer of leaves,
or a thinner layer of finer organic material, around
plants each fall will help prevent winter losses and keep
weed seeds from sprouting in the spring.

Protecting Tender Plants

Like gardeners everywhere, we are frequently tempted
to grow plants that are intended for a climate milder
than ours. As extra insurance, we cover them with several thicknesses of evergreen boughs in the fall. If you
don't live in evergreen country, use other insulating
materials such as straw, salt hay, or the foam blankets
sold in garden stores. Wait until after a few frosts before
you insulate the plants, so you are sure they are completely dormant. Otherwise, they may continue to
grow under the warm cover and have their new growth
killed when the cold finally penetrates it. If you have
newly planted shrubs or vines, it is a good idea to mulch
them, too, to give them some welcome protection for
their first winter.

When the garden is finally put to bed, it is time for
us gardeners to pause, sit down with our whole weight,
and, like the garden, take a rest. A garden is never
finished, but the final fall euphoria is the closest we
come to feeling that it is. By late January we will have
forgotten about weeds and bugs and be ready, once
again, to make plans for spring.

Dividing Peonies

Although peonies may be divided right after they bloom in early summer, many gardeners prefer to take on this task in fall.

1 Cut straight all around the peony plant with a spade or garden fork before tipping the plant out of the ground. If the plant is old, the roots may be as much as 3 or 4 feet long, but don't worry if you break some of them.

2 Use a strong spray of water to wash some of the soil off the root system so that you can see what you're doing. If you can't divide and replant the peonies immediately, place them in a cool, shady spot and cover them with a damp cloth so they don't dry out.

3 Use pruning shears or a large, sharp knife to cut the divisions apart. Be sure there are three or more "eyes" (the pinkish-white sprouts) in each division.

4 Dig a large hole, amend the soil, then heap it up in the middle so that, when the division is in place, the point where the sprouts emerge from the root is only an inch below the surface. Planting peonies too deep is the most common cause of failure. Cover root with soil; water well.

1"

A Flower Gardener's Calendar

A MONTH-BY-MONTH GARDEN CALENDAR would not work for all the planting zones of the United States and Canada, but the cycle of garden chores is rather similar no matter where you live. We've put together a list of some of these chores, with suggestions of when to do each one grouped within seasons. Although spring arrives in each zone at various times, as does the first fall frost, you'll soon recognize the clues that indicate when early spring or late summer occurs in your area. You'll also notice that the exact dates differ from year to year even in the same locality. You may want to customize this checklist by adding tasks that are specific to your garden when you find the best time to get them underway. And don't let the length of the "to-do" list overwhelm you! Many of these suggestions may not apply to your own situation, but we hope whatever is appropriate will help jog your memory and organize your garden year.

Early Spring

☐ If you didn't do so during the winter, clean, sharpen, and oil your pruning tools, hoes, and shovels.

☐ Inspect all plants for winter damage. Prune out dead and damaged wood on shrubs. Reset any plants that frost-heaved out of the ground.

☐ Prune later-flowering shrubs (including roses and broad-leaved evergreens such as rhododendrons) while they are still dormant or just emerging from dormancy. (Take care not to remove flower buds.)

☐ Prune vines.

☐ Retrieve hardwood cuttings from storage and prepare to set them in a plant "nursery" outdoors.

☐ Consider replacing unwanted shrubs.

☐ In cold climates, start indoors the seeds of plants (herbs and flowers) that you plan to plant out later. Refer to seed catalogs and garden references for suggested planting dates; you don't want seedlings to outgrow their indoor homes and become leggy before being moved to the garden.

☐ Order bedding plants from your local nursery or your favorite mail-order suppliers.

☐ Uncover perennial plants and clean up last year's dead plant material and any debris blown in over winter.

☐ Move existing plants that you want in a new location.

☐ Begin perennial-border rejuvenation project.

☐ Cut back overwintered ornamental grasses.

☐ Watch for fall-planted bulbs to emerge. Try to remove any winter mulch before the new growth appears, so that you don't damage young foliage.

☐ Fertilize summer-blooming bulbs.

☐ Carry out soil improvement measures: Test your soil, if you didn't do so in the fall, and add appropriate amendments to adjust the pH and nutrients needed by your plants.

☐ Spread compost and add mulch in gardens if the layer is getting thin.

Midspring

☐ Remove winter covers from bush, climbing, and tree roses, as well as lavender and other plants that are marginally hardy in your area.

☐ Stake floppy rose growth and tie climbers.

☐ Plant containerized roses.

☐ Plant balled-and-burlapped shrubs.

☐ Plant new vines.

☐ Plant new groundcover plants.

☐ Plant newly purchased container-grown perennials. Be sure to label everything you plant.

☐ Divide overgrown perennial clumps.

☐ Stake tall-growing perennial plants, such as peonies and delphiniums, before they reach 12 inches.

☐ Pick the lateral buds off peonies to promote larger blooms on the terminal buds.

☐ Take cuttings from the tips of chrysanthemums and delphiniums to start new plants.

☐ Begin weeding.

☐ Watch for pests and diseases.

☐ Water and fertilize newly planted shrubs and herbaceous plants.

☐ Feed any flowering shrubs that you transplanted last season.

☐ Replace any plant labels that have deteriorated.

Late Spring

☐ Make a list of bulbs to order for fall planting.

☐ Cut off daffodil foliage as soon as it yellows and dies back. After the foliage yellows but before it disappears, divide bulbs if they are too crowded.

☐ After the foliage yellows but before it disappears, dig up tulip bulbs and store them in a cool closet for fall replanting, or give them a temporary home in the garden for later storage (see page 114).

☐ Use shallow-rooted annuals to fill spots where bulbs grew and to hide the dying foliage of bulbs and spring-blooming perennials.

☐ Mark the spots where bulbs are growing if you wish to move them later or if you plant annuals over them.

☐ Set out flowering annuals and herbs. Check with your Cooperative Extension Service for the average last frost date in your region, so that you don't get started too soon.

☐ Deadhead perennials as blooms fade. This will direct strength to the roots rather than to seed formation, as well as improve the appearance of your garden and avoid unwanted self-sowing.

☐ Shear early flowering perennials, such as moss phlox (*Phlox subulata*) and mountain bluet (*Centaurea montana*).

☐ Pinch back fall-flowering perennials, such as asters and chrysanthemums.

☐ Plant or transplant perennials.

☐ Take cuttings from perennials you wish to propagate.

☐ Weed perennial beds. Vigilance against young, newly sprouting weeds will mean much less weeding later in the season when they have become entrenched.

☐ Keep new groundcovers well watered. Pull weeds in the area, so that young plants don't have to compete for space to grow.

☐ Prune lilacs and other spring-flowering shrubs immediately after blossoms fade.

☐ Fertilize and water newly planted shrubs, if natural rainfall is not sufficient.

☐ Be watchful for any insect or disease problems and take steps to control them, if necessary.

Early Summer

☐ Mulch around perennials. Be sure to leave 2 to 3 inches around the base of the plant free of mulch to prevent rotting.

☐ Deadhead perennials as blooms fade. This will encourage healthier growth and also prevent unwanted self-sowing.

☐ Cut back delphiniums after blossom to encourage a fall bloom.

☐ Pinch back chrysanthemums and other perennials to induce compact growth and larger blooms.

☐ Stake tall-growing perennials that will need support, if you haven't already done so.

☐ Deadhead annuals, and if necessary, plant more.

☐ Water and weed new groundcover area.

☐ Water newly planted shrubs frequently.

☐ Water all gardens regularly and often if weather is dry. As a rule of thumb, most garden plants and lawns need about 1 inch of water each week.

☐ Fight weeds: Hand pull; keep weeds from spreading seeds; use preemergent organic herbicide to prevent sprouting of new weeds; mulch.

☐ Control insects: Hand pick; use beneficial insects to control pests or spray insecticides.

☐ Deter disease: Remove infected parts or entire plants; plant healthy, disease-resistant plants; spray or dust with fungicide, if necessary.

☐ Take softwood cuttings from woody plants you wish to propagate.

☐ Order spring-blooming bulbs for fall planting.

Midsummer

☐ Deadhead perennials as blooms fade. This is particularly important for perennials that tend to spread by self-sowing. Some plants will offer a second blooming period if cut back at this time.

☐ Divide Oriental poppy (Papaver orientale) after tops have died down and new sprouts have started.

☐ Cut back perennials that go dormant early, such as old-fashioned bleeding heart (Dicentra spectabilis) and leopard's banes (Doronicum).

☐ Check staked perennials to see if they need to be secured or tied.

☐ If you transplant perennials now, be sure to cut them back, water them well, and mulch thickly to conserve water and protect them against weeds.

☐ Deadhead annuals, to encourage continued bloom.

☐ Start seeds for fall-blooming annuals, such as ornamental kale and cabbage.

☐ If you have climbing and rambling roses, continue to prune them lightly and tie them to their support as they grow.

☐ Check all trellised plants and tie them to supports, as needed.

☐ Water new groundcovers and weed them to encourage spreading.

☐ Continue to water newly planted shrubs.

☐ Water all areas of the garden if weather turns dry. Monitor rainfall—most plants need about 1 inch per week for healthy growth.

☐ Keep up with weeding all gardens and foundation plantings.

☐ Be watchful for any disease or insect problems and take steps to control them, if necessary.

☐ Apply fertilizer to perennials and annuals if plants are actively growing. Do not fertilize in hot weather.

☐ Check mulch and add more, as needed, to suppress weeds and conserve moisture. Keep mulch 2 to 3 inches away from the base of plants, to avoid rotting.

☐ If you will be away on vacation during the next few weeks, arrange to have someone water your plants, particularly those in containers.

Late Summer

☐ Deadhead late-blooming perennials as their flowers fade.

☐ Check all staked perennials to be sure they are still secure.

☐ Cut back spent perennials, such as shasta daisies *(Leucanthemum × superbum),* and dead daylily stalks. This not only keeps your garden looking neater, but also helps control perennials that spread by self-sowing.

☐ Divide perennials, such as poppies, that bloomed earlier in the season and replant them or give them to friends.

☐ Deadhead flowering ornamental grasses before they sow their seeds, except for those you wish to leave in place to enjoy over the winter.

☐ Deadhead annuals, and pull out those that have stopped blooming.

☐ Cut annual and perennial flowers and ornamental grasses suitable for dried flower arrangements and hang them in a dry, airy location.

☐ Set out fall-blooming plants, such as chrysanthemums or ornamental kales and cabbages, either directly in the ground or in containers.

☐ Continue to train climbing and rambling roses, clipping and tying them as needed.

☐ Continue weeding, but to discourage tender, late-season growth, discontinue fertilizing.

☐ Watch for any disease or insect problems and control them, if necessary.

☐ If you plan to create a new garden next spring, choose the location now, mark the area, and begin to prepare the soil (including testing and adding compost and lime or sulfur).

Early and Midfall

□ Cut down perennials for neatness, disease control, and to prevent self-seeding. Leave a few inches of stem to hold snow for winter protection in northern areas.

□ Divide overgrown clumps of perennials and dig and discard (or give away) any you no longer want.

□ Plant or transplant perennials.

□ Renew mulch around plants.

□ As soon as leaves fall, rake them up. Use them to mulch perennials or add them to the compost pile.

□ After two or three fall frosts, fertilize perennial beds.

□ Plant spring-blooming bulbs, including tulips, daffodils, hyacinths, crocuses, and minor bulbs.

□ Fertilize established plantings of bulbs.

□ Dig summer bulbs such as dahlias and gladioli; dry and store for winter.

□ In cold climates, prepare roses for winter.

□ In mild climates, begin perennial border rejuvenation projects.

□ In mild climates, prune vines.

□ Continue watering and insect and disease control as long as necessary.

□ Prepare the soil for any new plantings you are planning for next spring.

□ Clip dried hydrangea blooms for winter bouquets.

Late Fall

☐ Drain and hang up hoses. Turn off water to outside spigots.
☐ Turn the present compost pile and start a new one.
☐ Apply compost to flower beds.
☐ Do final weeding in all flower beds.
☐ Clean, sharpen, and oil pruning tools, hoes, and shovels for easier digging and cutting next summer.
☐ Clean all other tools, and oil them to prevent rust.
☐ Take notes on projects you want to undertake first next year.

☐ Begin to study garden and nursery catalogs and review your favorite gardening books, so that you can plan what to order for next year.
☐ Check fertilizers, peat moss, seed-starting mix, vermiculite, perlite, potting soil, and pesticides. Make a list of which garden supplies are running low, so you can order them in late winter when garden stores are restocked.
☐ Check your supply of flats, pots, stakes, labels, and marking pens, and order necessary items as soon as catalogs arrive.

Early Winter

☐ As soon as the ground freezes lightly, cover tender perennials with evergreen boughs. Don't do this too early, or you'll provide an inviting winter home for hungry rodents.
☐ If you start your own plants, order seeds by early January, before seed companies run out of your favorites.

☐ Sharpen hoes, shovels, and clippers, and put them in their wintering-over spots.
☐ Take hardwood cuttings of any shrubs and vines you want to propagate; label and store them upside down in vermiculite for spring planting.
☐ Read garden books, and sketch out designs and ideas for new plantings.

Late Winter

☐ In warm climates, prune dormant roses.
☐ Remove dead and damaged wood from roses and other shrubs.
☐ Mow or cut down ornamental grass areas and rake.
☐ Order plants and seeds, if you haven't done so already. Inspect new tools and equipment in hardware stores and garden centers. Buy peat moss, fertilizers, and organic pesticides as new supplies arrive in stores.
☐ Start perennial and biennial seeds indoors under grow lights. Consult catalogs and garden reference books for the optimal planting time before the last frost in your area.

☐ Begin your garden journal, and resolve to record all routine and unusual events such as weather, new plants, unexpected happenings, plans for future development, and other notes related to your gardens.
☐ Line up hired help, if necessary, to handle spring chores. Landscape workers are busiest during this season and may be booked well in advance.

PART TWO

A Gallery of Gardens

When most of us hear the words "flower garden," we envision a border where an ever-changing panorama of attractive flowers blooms throughout the spring, summer, and fall. This beautiful image can be expanded to include many other kinds of gardens. One of the joys about gardening, we've found, is the chance to experiment with plants and do something different with them. You probably won't want to start a collection entirely of poisonous plants like one we visited at the Montreal Botanical Garden, or one that attracts rabbits, but there are endless other possibilities. You might create a spectacular water garden; collect many cultivars of a single species; build a rock garden to showcase alpine plants; or transform a barren field into an extravaganza of wildflowers. Your location might suggest a seaside bed if you live near the ocean, a woodland border if you are near a forest, or a hillside planting if your home is adjacent to a steep slope. On the pages that follow, we hope you will find practical tips, new ideas, and inspiration to create gardens that will give you perennial pleasure.

Rock cress (*Arabis procurrens*)

Down the Garden Path

Variegated blue lilyturf
(*Liriope muscari* 'Variegata')

THE PHRASE "TO LEAD HER DOWN THE GARDEN PATH" has special meaning for gardeners. Rather than being devious, our purpose is completely innocent—to show someone a new bloom, perhaps, or to enlist suggestions for improving the garden layout. A pathway makes an ideal setting for flowering plants, whether you use a modest row of chrysanthemums to line a short, straight walkway from porch to garage or construct an elaborate winding pathway through meadow and woods bordered by shrubs, trees,

annuals, bulbs, and herbaceous perennials. Planted paths can add character to your landscape by dividing a lawn or large garden into interesting smaller plots. A path is not only aesthetically pleasing, but, from a practical point of view, also makes it easier to haul along a garden cart.

Your path may be as simple as a strip of mown grass, or it can be lined with crushed rock, pebbles, gravel, wood chips, bark nuggets, flagstones, stepping-stones, slate, or elaborately designed bricks. Some are even paved with asphalt or concrete. Investigate the choices thoroughly before deciding what best fits your needs, because the

appearance, construction, and maintenance of each type of surface is quite different. A poorly paved pathway may crack in climates where frosts go deep; flagstones, bricks, and slate should be laid on a base of gravel or coarse sand to provide proper drainage and prevent heaving if you live where the ground freezes and thaws. Although they can help keep your feet dry, stepping-stones often sink and become covered with grass, and gravel or crushed rock tends to become weedy.

If you use crushed rock or a similar material, install an edging to border it so plant roots will not infringe on the path. An edging is useful on any path

with loose materials, in fact, to keep them and garden mulches separate from each other. When the pathway is lined with flagstones or stepping-stones, you may want to use grass between them, or plant fragrant herbs that stand moderate traffic well, such as thymes or Roman chamomile (*Chamaemelum nobile*). Make the walking area wide enough, a minimum of 3 to 4 feet, so it will invite strollers to walk and the path won't disappear as the plants bordering it grow larger. If you are constructing a winding path, clothesline or rope will work well to define its edges at planning time.

The width of the plantings on each side of a path depends on many variables. If the walkway winds through a cottage garden or herb bed, it will already be surrounded by extensive plantings. But if you are digging a new garden on each side of the path, the size should depend on the plant material you intend to use and the time you have for maintenance. For primroses (*Primula*) and other compact plants, 2 to 3 feet would be adequate, but for ferns, hostas, and other large specimens, a minimum of 4 feet is necessary. Try not to make the bed wider than you can easily reach across to tend the plants.

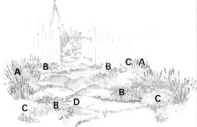

Plant Key

A | Lavenders (*Lavandula*)
B | Pinks (*Dianthus*)
C | Silvermound (*Artemisia schmidtiana*)
D | Thymes (*Thymus*)

Good Pathway Plants

Astilbes (*Astilbe*)
Big blue lilyturf (*Liriope muscari*)
Cranesbills (*Geranium*)
Daylilies (*Hemerocallis*)
Heart-leaved bergenia
  (*Bergenia cordifolia*)
Hostas, smaller cultivars (*Hosta*)

'King Edward' yarrow
  (*Achillea × lewisii* 'King Edward')
Lavenders (*Lavandula*)
Pansies and violets (*Viola*)
Rock cresses (*Arabis*)
Sea thrift (*Armeria maritima*)
Silvermound (*Artemisia schmidtiana*)
Thymes (*Thymus*)

Goldmoss stonecrop *(Sedum acre)*

Primrose *(Primula 'Peter Klein')*

Pansy *(Viola* 'Sorbet Yellow Delight')

As in any planting, your choice of plants for lining the path will be dictated by your climatic, soil, and light conditions. Spring bulbs, rock plants, groundcovers, and other low growers make good choices for sunny paths; a woodsy lane looks great with wildflowers, hostas, ferns, and other shade-loving foliage plants. One of the most charming garden paths we've ever had the pleasure to walk along meandered beside a small brook and ascended a hillside. Colorful primroses of every shape and size were tucked into narrow beds bordering it. Another of our favorite paths winds through a friend's backyard to her vegetable garden and is bordered by lavender and other fragrant and edible herbs.

There are no hard rules for choosing plants, but neither tall-growing herbaceous species, such as delphiniums, nor sprawlers, such as Oriental poppy *(Papaver orientale),* are good choices. As in any border, a mass of similar plants is more effective than a hodgepodge of colors. Keep in mind that attractive foliage plants can be as eyecatching as flowers and require less maintenance.

Annuals are colorful throughout the season, although most need frequent deadheading, and the work of planting them each spring may be time-consuming. Sweet alyssum *(Lobularia maritima),* rocket candytuft *(Iberis amara),* impatiens, and petunias are favorite pathside annuals, as are geraniums *(Pelargonium),* a tender peren-

nial. Beware of planting rows of one kind of plant spaced regularly, since inevitably a few will not survive and you'll be left with gaps. To avoid this problem, you can always grow extras in another location to use as replacements. Some gardeners change the plantings throughout the year, using daffodils and other bulbs in spring, annuals for summer bloom, and chrysanthemums or flowering cabbage and kale *(Brassica oleracea)* in autumn.

If your area is very open, you might want a few shrubs or large rocks as a background for bulbs and herbaceous plants. Select evergreen or flowering shrubs such as cinquefoils *(Potentilla)* that will not grow too large and over-hang the path and its flower border, unless you are prepared to prune them back severely forevermore. In northern areas, if the path is to be shoveled in the winter, use tough shrubs that will not easily be crushed by snow.

When the path is long, upright-growing shrubs, such as pyramidal American arborvitae *(Thuja occidentalis* 'Pyramidalis') or yews *(Taxus),* might be ideal along it, as would statues or standing stones to guide the stroller along. A garden path has added impact when it leads to a destination or spot of interest. In a flat or formal garden, a sundial, gazebo, or statue could be a fine focal point; in a more natural setting, the path might lead to another garden, to a small pool, or simply to a bench where you can sit and enjoy the beauty.

Spirea (*Spirea thunbergii* 'Ogon')

A Fantastic Foundation Garden

THERE WAS A TIME WHEN NO ONE would think of buying anything but tightly clipped evergreens for foundation plants around the home. No more. Flowering shrubs, bulbs, perennials, annuals, and even vegetables are now among the happy alternatives. Not only are they far less expensive than shrubbery and easier to bring home and plant, but they disappear underground for the winter, like Persephone. In the North and in mountainous regions, tons of snow and ice either slide or must be shoveled from rooftops every winter, and the weight of either can devastate evergreens and flowering shrubs. Although we have built structures to cover

Hollyhock (*Alcea rosea*)

the few shrubs we have, we now grow mostly herbaceous perennials around our house and avoid the problem altogether. Even where heavy snows are not a problem, perennials, annuals, and vines are popular as foundation plants because they add such interesting foliage textures and a changing variety of colorful blooms to an otherwise green landscape.

Choose plants that are appropriate to the style of your house. A few evergreens, both conifers and broad-leaved types, furnish badly needed color when the landscape is brown, but flowering shrubs and herbaceous plants make it worth a second look the rest of the year. Hollyhocks (*Alcea rosea*) seem to belong next to a shingled country cottage, for instance, and a clematis vine with plantings of peonies, daylilies (*Hemerocallis*), and monkshoods (*Aconitum*) looks natural with a Cape bungalow. Our neighbors have a narrow perennial bed bordering the front of their white clapboard New England home, which provides them and all passersby with a frequent change of blooms, from the

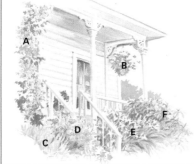

Plant Key

A | Clematis *(Clematis)*

B | Fuchsias *(Fuchsia)*

C | Peonies *(Paeonia)*

D | 'Anthony Waterer' spirea *(Spiraea japonica)*

E | Daylilies *(Hemerocallis)*

F | Rhododendrons *(Rhododendron)*

earliest spring bulbs to late-fall chrysanthemums and cannas.

The best plants to use near a house or other building are those that will develop into good-sized plants but not spread too much. Since they are always on display, they should have attractive foliage and look nice even when not in bloom. We use several colors and heights of daylilies for this purpose, as well as large clumps of pink peonies, which people often mistake for rhododendrons when they bloom. Their foliage overlaps the lawn, making it easy to mow beneath it.

Sun-loving plants won't do well in areas that receive only a few hours of direct sunlight, even if exposed to skylight the rest of the day. For such lightly shaded spots use columbines *(Aquilegia)*, fringed bleeding heart *(Dicentra eximia)*, ferns, hostas, daylilies, monkshoods, and globe flowers *(Trollius)*. For the difficult area on the north side of a building and other spots that get little direct sunlight, try ferns, hostas, impatiens, the tawny daylily *(Hemerocallis fulva)*, or beds of lily-of-the-valley *(Convallaria majalis)*. Certain shrubs, such as azaleas and other broad-leaved evergreens, clipped hemlocks *(Tsuga),* and Canadian yew *(Taxus canadensis),* also work well. (For a list of shade-loving perennials, see page 154.)

Certain plants, such as delphiniums, lupines *(Lupinus)*, old-fashioned bleeding heart *(Dicentra spectabilis)*, and Oriental poppy *(Papaver orientale)*, are attractive when they are in bloom but look sad after their blossoming period is finished and the foliage has faded. If you use them, do so sparingly, and tuck in tall-growing annuals or brightly colored geraniums *(Pelargonium)* to camouflage their messy post-bloom foliage.

If your home is white, brown, gray, or another neutral shade, you will not need to be fussy about choosing flowering plants of the proper color; but if it is red, blue, yellow, or an unusual tone, select plants that will have blooms of compatible colors. Foliage plants or those with pale or white blossoms may be your best option. Flowering vines, such as clematis and honeysuckles *(Lonicera)*, can break up the expanse of wide walls.

If you choose to use perennials entirely, you might plant a traditional design, positioning large clumps of massive perennials just as you would evergreens or flowering shrubs. Use taller specimens to soften the corners and mark each side of the front doorway, and use lower-growing plants beneath the windows. Other alternatives are to plant a narrow perennial border, a kitchen garden, or a cottage garden near the building.

Always leave space enough to walk between the plantings and the structure. Otherwise, leafy plants will block air circulation and allow moisture to build up on the wall behind them, rotting wooden siding and causing the paint to deteriorate quickly. Dense growth close to the house can also encourage the development of carpenter ant or termite colonies. Brick houses and concrete and stone foundations attract heat that may make nearby plants wilt in the sun, unless there is

Good Flowering Foundation Plants

PERENNIALS
Blanket flowers *(Gaillardia)*
Chrysanthemums *(Chrysanthemum)*
Daylilies *(Hemerocallis)*
Evening primroses *(Oenothera)*
Gas plant *(Dictamnus albus)*
Gloriosa daisy *(Rudbeckia hirta)*
Hollyhock *(Alcea rosea)*
Hostas *(Hosta)*
Lavenders *(Lavandula)*
Peonies *(Paeonia)*
Phlox *(Phlox)*

BULBS
Spring Bulbs
Crocuses *(Crocus)*
Daffodils *(Narcissus)*
Glory-of-the-snows *(Chionodoxa)*
Hyacinths *(Hyacinthus)*
Lily-of-the-valley
    (Convallaria majalis)
Netted iris *(Iris reticulata)*
Snowdrops *(Galanthus)*
Tulips *(Tulipa)*

Summer Bulbs and Bulb-type Plants
Anemones *(Anemone)*
Dahlias *(Dahlia)*
Gladioli *(Gladiolus)*
Irises *(Iris)*
Lilies *(Lilium)*
Ornamental onions *(Allium)*

Fall-blooming Bulbs
Autumn crocuses *(Colchicum)*
Fall-blooming crocuses *(Crocus)*
Magic lilies *(Lycoris)*

SHRUBS
Dwarf deciduous shrubs
Northern bayberry *(Myrica pensylvanica)*
Lowbush blueberry
    (Vaccinium angustifolium)
Cotoneasters *(Cotoneaster)*
Daphnes *(Daphne)*
Euonymus *(Euonymus)*
Flowering quinces *(Chaenomeles)*
Firethorns *(Pyracantha)*
Roses *(Rosa)*
Spireas *(Spiraea)*
Weigelas *Weigela)*

Tall shrubs for corners and entrances
Lilacs *(Syringa)*
Rhododendrons *(Rhododendron)*
Viburnums *(Viburnum)*

Broad-leaved evergreens
Azaleas *(Rhododendron)*
Mountain laurels *(Kalmia)*
Rhododendrons *(Rhododendron)*

VINES
American bittersweet *(Celastrus scandens)*
Clematis *(Clematis)*
Climbing roses *(Rosa)*
Honeysuckles *(Lonicera)*
Japanese wisteria *(Wisteria floribunda)*

room for air to circulate behind them. Set plants outside the drip line of any overhanging roof so they will get the benefit of rainfall but not be directly beneath the drip.

As for any planting, provide good topsoil and proper drainage. Mulch the area around the plants with bark, wood chips, or another attractive material. This will prevent rain from splashing dirt on the house, help control weeds, and conserve the soil's fertility. Before you plant, consider laying down landscape fabric, a weed-blocking material

that is available at most garden supply stores. When placed under the mulch, it allows moisture to penetrate but effectively suppresses weeds.

If your plants get considerable runoff from the roof, it will tend to wash out the lime and nutrients from the soil quickly, so apply additional fertilizer every spring. Also, add liquid fertilizer during the early part of the summer if the plant foliage begins to look pale or yellow or if growth is stunted. Apply a sprinkling of lime every few years if your soil tends to be acidic.

New England aster
(Aster novae-angliae)

Wildflower Extravaganza: Meadow and Woodland

To design a garden of wildflowers might seem to be a contradictory exercise, since such plants thrive when uncultivated, unfertilized, and unmulched. It is difficult to improve on nature and her methods, so the goal of a wildflower gardener is primarily to make such a planting look attractive and unaffected. We know of one successful garden on a hillside near a lake where wildflowers

Snow trillium (Trillium grandiflorum)

bloom continuously, beginning in the spring with a luxurious carpet of bloodroot (Sanguinaria canadensis) and spring beauty (Claytonia virginica), continuing with colorful lady's slippers (Cypripedium) and other wild orchids, followed by summer flowers such as oxeye daisy (Leucanthemum vulgare) and Queen Anne's lace (Daucus carota var. carota), and topped off in late autumn with deep purple asters and fringed gentian (Gentiana crinita). It took many years for the couple who established this plot to achieve an unstudied, natural appearance there. Considerable expertise was required as well, because each wildflower is particular about its home and is happy only when living in its favorite type of soil with the right amount of sunlight.

When the term "wildflower" is applied to a garden, it suggests that only native and naturalized plants are included, but garden perennials with a natural, uncultivated appearance are also welcome. Yarrows (Achillea), various daisies, meadow rues (Thalictrum), gayfeathers (Liatris), bellflowers (Campanula), and pinks (Dianthus) fit nicely into such plantings, whereas the more refined peonies and hybrid delphiniums appear out of place, as do plants with large or double blooms.

Since the most desirable wildflowers are fussy about where they grow, it is imperative to select plants according to the soil, light, and moisture conditions of the garden or be prepared to modify your conditions to match those that the various species demand. Blue flag (Iris versicolor), jewelweed (Impatiens pallida), marsh marigold (Caltha palustris), and cattails (Typha) grow only in sunny, moist locations, for example. By looking to see what flourishes locally in the wild areas in your locale and in soil, light, and moisture conditions similar to yours, you will be able to create a natural-looking garden without a great

deal of work or discouragement. Some wild plants are very particular about soil, needing quite acidic conditions. Most also like well-drained soil that contains an adequate amount of moisture for good growth. Many forest wildflowers, such as wild orchids, fringed bleeding heart *(Dicentra eximia),* and trilliums, need the same conditions found under deciduous trees in the woodland—bright full sun in early spring but medium to heavy shade during the summer months.

Although it is possible to create a new environment for wild plants, it is easier, and the results will be better, if you choose plants for the conditions that already exist. Rather than trying to drain a marshy area, for instance, use aquatic, semi-aquatic, or bog plants that prefer such a spot. If the area is so heavily shaded by dense trees that few wildflowers will grow, ferns and other foliage plants will be the best option. In a hot, sandy location, choose drought-tolerant plants such as cacti and yuccas.

Garden catalogs and stores offer mixed wildflower seeds for various climates in different sections of North

Plant Key

A | Joe-Pye weed *(Eupatorium maculatum)*

B | Black-eyed Susan *(Rudbeckia fulgida)*

C | Blue lobelia *(Lobelia siphilitica)*

D | Bee balm *(Monarda didyma)*

Off to a Good Start

In spite of alluring ads that promise wonderful wildflower meadows by the mere scattering of seed over an open field, the result of such a sowing of most species is likely to be unsuccessful. Nature tosses seeds generously over hayfields and some will thrive, but your chances of creating a beautiful spot are far better if you prepare the soil first. Wildflower fields don't need to be cultivated and fertilized endlessly like a perennial border, but if the seed is to germinate and start well, it is best to plant it in soil that has been tilled to a depth of several inches.

You will achieve the best results if you get rid of all the weed roots and seeds in the top layer of soil. An easy way is to cover the area with clear plastic during the hot summer months. The weeds will die and the seeds that germinate will be burned by the heat that is generated. Nevertheless, you can't expect a weed-free planting, because some seeds lie dormant for years waiting for the right opportunity to grow, and in some locations, weed seeds will continue to blow in from great distances. We know, because we struggle continually with dandelion *(Taraxacum officinale)* and goldenrod *(Solidago)* seedlings. An annual mowing every year in late summer, after the annuals drop their seeds, will help keep the meadow from growing up to weeds, hay, and brush.

Wildflower Garden Plants

FOR SPRING SUNSHINE AND SUMMER SHADE

Canada wild ginger (*Asarum canadense*)
Dutchman's breeches
    (*Dicentra cucullaria*)
False Solomon's seal (*Smilacina racemosa*)
Foam flower (*Tiarella cordifolia*)
Glory-of-the-snows (*Chionodoxa*)
Grecian windflower (*Anemone blanda*)
Jack-in-the-pulpits (*Arisaema*)
Lesser periwinkle (*Vinca minor*)
Partridgeberry (*Mitchella repens*)
Snowdrops (*Galanthus*)
Spring beauty (*Claytonia virginica*)
Spring snowflake (*Leucojum vernum*)
Squirrel corn (*Dicentra canadensis*)
Star flower (*Trientalis borealis*)
Trilliums (*Trillium*)
Trout lilies (*Erythronium*)

FOR A MEADOW GARDEN

Bee balm (*Monarda didyma*)
Black-eyed Susan (*Rudbeckia fulgida*)
Blue lobelia (*Lobelia siphilitica*)
Columbines (*Aquilegia*)
Gentians (*Gentiana*)
New England aster (*Aster novae-angliae*)
New York aster (*A. novi-belgii*)
Oxeye daisy (*Leucanthemum vulgare*)
Tickseeds (*Coreopsis*)
Wild blue flax (*Linum lewisii*)
Wild lupine (*Lupinus perennis*)
Wood lily (*Lilium philadelphicum*)

FOR SUN OR LIGHT SHADE

American pennyroyal
    (*Hedeoma pulegioides*)
Anemones (*Anemone*)
Bearberry (*Arctostaphylos uva-ursi*)
Black cohosh (*Cimicifuga racemosa*)
Blue false indigo (*Baptisia australis*)
Butterfly weed (*Asclepias tuberosa*)
Hepatica (*Hepatica nobilis*)
Mallows (*Malva*)
Moonseeds (*Menispermum*)
Sea lavender (*Limonium latifolium*)
Shooting star (*Dodecatheon meadia*)
Small-flowered agrimony
    (*Agrimonia parviflora*)

FOR MOIST SOIL

Baneberries (*Actaea*)
Bloodroot (*Sanguinaria canadensis*)

Bluet (*Hedyotis caerulea*)
Bottle gentian (*Gentiana andrewsii*)
Bouncing bet (*Saponaria officinalis*)
Bunchberry (*Cornus canadensis*)
Canada lily (*Lilium canadense*)
Canada wild ginger (*Asarum canadense*)
Goldthread (*Coptis trifolia*)
Jack-in-the-pulpit (*Arisaema triphyllum*)
Lady's slippers (*Cypripedium*)
Spring beauty (*Claytonia virginica*)
Trilliums (*Trillium*)
Turtlehead (*Chelone glabra*)
Virginia spiderwort
    (*Tradescantia virginiana*)
Wintergreen (*Gaultheria procumbens*)
Wood anemone (*Anemone quinquefolia*)

FOR LIGHT TO MODERATE SHADE

Asters (*Aster*)
Bee balm (*Monarda didyma*)
Bellflowers (*Campanula*)
Coltsfoot (*Tussilago farfara*)
Dwarf larkspur (*Delphinium tricorne*)
Evening primrose (*Oenothera biennis*)
Marsh marigold (*Caltha palustris*)
Mayapple (*Podophyllum peltatum*)
Milkweeds (*Asclepias*)
Pearly everlasting
    (*Anaphalis margaritacea*)
Perennial lobelias (*Lobelia*)
Queen Anne's lace
    (*Daucus carota* var. *carota*)
Speedwells (*Veronica*)
Spring forget-me-not (*Myosotis verna*)
Violets (*Viola*)
Wild geranium (*Geranium maculatum*)
Wild lupine (*Lupinus perennis*)
Yarrows (*Achillea*)

FOR SWAMPY, WET SOIL

Blue flag (*Iris versicolor*)
Cattail (*Typha latifolia*)
Jewelweed (*Impatiens pallida*)
Marsh marigold (*Caltha palustris*)
Yellow adder's tongue
    (*Erythronium americanum*)

FOR ACID SOIL

Bearberry (*Arctostaphylos uva-ursi*)
Bunchberry (*Cornus canadensis*)
Lady's slippers (*Cypripedium*)
Trailing arbutus (*Epigaea repens*)
Wintergreen (*Gaultheria procumbens*)

America. Usually the packets contain perennial, biennial, and annual seeds and may also include grasses. The mixtures may be formulated for either a sunny field or a shady spot. You can also gather seeds from wild plants along country roadsides after they have finished blooming. Collect them when they are completely ripe and either plant them at once or dry, store, and plant them in the spring. (See page 79 for advice on collecting seed.) We are gradually covering a hillside near us with lupines (*Lupinus*) and black-eyed Susan (*Rudbeckia fulgida*) planted from seeds we have collected. The plants are all acclimated to our area and grow rapidly. We don't cultivate the soil but plant them as nature does, by scattering them as soon as the seed is ripe.

A Meadow of Wildflowers

Meadow wildflowers such as asters, black-eyed Susan, buttercups (*Ranunculus*), and oxeye daisy are easier to grow than woodland species. Most like full sun and thrive even in poor soil. Unfortunately, as gardeners know well, some grow so prolifically that they become rampant weeds. An open landscape such as a meadow or hillside that is a bother to keep mowed is a good spot for a wildflower planting. By judicious mowing once a year, you can enjoy a wild and semi-wild blooming area and, at the same time, greatly cut down on the maintenance chores and costs of mowing frequently.

Spring is the best time to plant most commercial seed mixtures, although you can also sow them in the fall where winters are not severe. A good method of sowing the seeds over a large area is to mix them thoroughly with sand to help you spread them more evenly. Scatter the mix by flinging it outward by hand, and then rake it into the soil. If the weather is dry, you may need to sprinkle it heavily twice a week during the germination period, which may take as long as six weeks.

The annuals in your planting will bloom the first year. If well adapted to your area, they will then drop seeds, which will sprout and provide new plants next year. The perennials should continue to live and thrive for years.

Woodland Wildflowers

One wildflower gardener in our community announces in church each spring when his collection of pink-and-white showy lady's slipper *(Cypripedium reginae)* is in bloom, so we can go to view his large, beautiful display at its peak. Although he is very modest, we all know it is his skill and care that make the plantings flourish so well. In his small backyard, he has successfully duplicated the various conditions that each of his woodland flowers loves.

You won't need to be a specialist to grow woodland wildflowers, but study-ing a good book about them and providing the environment each requires will help ensure your success. Most need at least partial shade and deep, rich soil. Each, too, has its own preference in regard to moisture conditions and soil pH. Flowering times can vary as much as two to three weeks from year to year, depending on the temperature and amount of sunlight.

You can grow woodland wildflowers from seed but are likely to have better luck buying plants from one of the many wildflower nurseries and gardens where they grow plants under ideal conditions. Never dig plants from the wild or buy from someone who does, as they may be endangered species.

Since most woodland wildflowers bloom for only a short time and then die down, you must plant a few of many different species in order to enjoy blossoms throughout the spring and summer. It may be best to establish your wildflower garden in a place where it can be enjoyed at its peak but not be highly visible at a time when the blooms are scarce. We know a couple who have made numerous pathways through their deciduous forest and planted a variety of wildflowers along the borders of each path. During different times of the year, they invite visitors to walk along whichever path is in its blooming period.

The soil in most woodlands is likely to be loose and shouldn't need much preparation, so spot planting usually works well. Wildflowers don't require the care or fertile soil that cultivated flowers do, but it may be necessary to remove unwanted plants occasionally if they intrude. In addition to reading books on wildflower identification and culture (see ideas for further reading on page 350), you may want to visit displays of wildflowers at a botanical garden, arboretum, or nature center.

Plant Key

A | Jack-in-the-pulpits *(Arisaema)*
B | Trout lilies *(Erythronium)*
C | Horned violet *(Viola cornuta)*
D | Wild gingers *(Asarum)*

Heath (*Erica carnea* 'Springwood Pink')

A Rock Garden to Love

WHEN A LADY FROM A LARGE CITY moved to our small town many years ago and announced she was starting a rock garden, a lot of spirited discussion took place among our neighbors as to how large a crop of stones the woman planned to grow. Rocks were something our ancestors had spent several generations removing from the fields, so making a garden with them was unimaginable. Since then, our local population has become more enlightened about rock gardens, but some still wonder at the wisdom of spending a great deal of time and money to haul back the rocks that the original settlers dragged away.

Carpathian harebell (*Campanula carpatica* 'Suzie')

The beauty of rocks in the landscape is now widely recognized, and gardeners use them as foils and focal points in traditional beds, as well as in rock gardens. If your property has a slope dotted with weathered rock formations, it may be an ideal spot for a rockery, as rock gardens are sometimes called. Some gardeners dig the earth away from a ledge to expose more stone surface as background for such a bed. It is not necessary to have a slope for the planting, since you can create one on a flat location with just a few loads of topsoil and a pile of rocks. In very different locations, in Florida and in England, for instance, we have seen very attractive rockeries built on what was originally level ground. Some people plant their rock gardens in the crevices of a retaining wall.

Whatever your terrain, this specialized form of gardening can be fascinating and addictive. Purists feel that a rock garden should contain only plants under 12 inches tall that grow naturally on rocky slopes in poor soil above the timberline, but most rock gardeners use

Basket-of-gold (*Aurinia saxatilis*)

a wide variety of low-growing perennials, annuals, bulbs, and shrubbery. Since the term "rock garden plant" usually refers to species that grow in temperate areas rather than subtropical desert spots, it is those species that we describe here.

If you want a beautiful overall effect, your rock garden must be designed, rather than aimlessly constructed. Yet even though it may have been years in the planning and execution, the garden should look as if it evolved naturally. Because rock gardens must be planted and cared for by hand, it is best to start with a small area, unless you have a lot of time or help. If you have a perfect spot, you may not need to do more than choose plants, locate paths, and create level outcroppings as kneeling places. You can find plants that will be at home either in a sunny or shady spot.

When you must bring in rocks and soil, more planning and work is involved. If you buy rocks from a stone yard, choose kinds that are compatible with the landscape, and avoid those that are highly colored or polished. When building a mound, set the rocks in the lowest front part first and work upward, burying more than half of each rock firmly so that it will be well anchored but still look natural. Allow plenty of space for the plants, and leave room to walk and kneel as you care for them. After the rocks are in place, let the soil settle around them for several days before planting. Check the construction frequently in the early stages by viewing it from a distance as well as close up, to be sure the positioning of the stones is aesthetically pleasing.

Although many rock plants do not require fertile soil, the soil should be at least 8 inches deep and have excellent drainage so that water pockets will not

Plant Key

A | California poppy (*Eschscholtzia californica*)
B | Blue fescue (*Festuca* 'Siskiyou Blue')
C | Stonecrops (*Sedum*)
D | Rock roses (*Helianthemum* 'Wisley White')
E | English daisies (*Bellis perennis*)

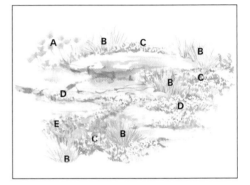

Traditional Rock Garden Plants

PERENNIALS

Alpine toadflax (*Linaria alpina*)
Anemones (*Anemone*)
Asters (*Aster*)
Avens (*Geum*)
Baby's breaths (*Gypsophila*)
Basket-of-gold (*Aurinia saxatilis*)
Bellflowers (*Campanula*)
Bishop's hats (*Epimedium*)
Blanket flowers (*Gaillardia*)
Bloody cranesbill (*Geranium sanguineum*)
Blue fescue (*Festuca glauca*)
Bugleweeds (*Ajuga*)
Buttercups (*Ranunculus*)
Campions (*Lychnis*)
Columbines (*Aquilegia*)
Coral bells (*Heuchera sanguinea*)
Cupid's dart (*Catananche caerulea*)
Daylilies, dwarf cultivars (*Hemerocallis*)
Dropwort (*Filipendula vulgaris*)
English daisy (*Bellis perennis*)
Flaxes (*Linum*)
Forget-me-nots (*Myosotis*)
Fringed bleeding heart (*Dicentra eximia*)
Heart-leaved bergenia
    (*Bergenia cordifolia*)
Hens-and-chicks (*Sempervivum*)
Hostas (*Hosta*)
Irises, dwarf species (*Iris*)
Jacob's ladder (*Polemonium caeruleum*)
Lady's mantle (*Alchemilla mollis*)
Lamb's ears (*Stachys byzantina*)
Lebanon stonecress
    (*Aethionema cordifolium*)
Moss campion (*Silene schafta*)
Moss phlox (*Phlox subulata*)
Northern bedstraw (*Galium boreale*)
Perennial candytuft (*Iberis sempervirens*)
Pinks (*Dianthus*)
Plumbago (*Ceratostigma plumbaginoides*)
Prickly pears (*Opuntia*)
Primroses (*Primula*)
Purple rock cress (*Aubrieta* × *cultorum*)
Sandworts (*Arenaria*)
Saxifrage (*Saxifraga umbrosa*)
Sea lavender (*Limonium latifolium*)
Siberian bugloss (*Brunnera macrophylla*)
Siberian dragon's head
    (*Dracocephalum ruyschiana*)
Silvermound (*Artemisia schmidtiana*)
Snow-in-summer (*Cerastium tomentosum*)
Soapworts (*Saponaria*)

Speedwells (*Veronica*)
Spurges (*Euphorbia*)
Stonecrops (*Sedum*)
Sun roses (*Helianthemum*)
Sweet woodruff (*Galium odoratum*)
Thymes (*Thymus*)
Tunic flower (*Petrorhagia saxifraga*)
Violets (*Viola*)
Virginia bluebells
    (*Mertensia pulmonarioides*)
Wall rock cress (*Arabis caucasica*)
Wild gingers (*Asarum*)
Woolly yarrow (*Achillea tomentosa*)
Yellow corydalis (*Corydalis lutea*)

ANNUALS

Alpine poppy (*Papaver alpinum*)
California poppy (*Eschscholtzia
    californica*)
Dusty miller (*Centaurea cineraria*)
Marigolds, dwarf cultivars (*Tagetes*)
Rocket candytuft (*Iberis amara*)
Sweet alyssum (*Lobularia maritima*)
Verbenas (*Verbena*)

FOR LIGHT SHADE

Alpine poppy (*Papaver alpinum*)
Bugleweeds (*Ajuga*)
Common primrose (*Primula vulgaris*)
Crested iris (*Iris cristata*)
European wood anemone
    (*Anemone nemorosa*)
Hostas, dwarf cultivars (*Hosta*)
Jacob's ladder (*Polemonium caeruleum*)
Japanese painted fern
    (*Athyrium niponicum*)
Mazus (*Mazus reptans*)
Sharp-leaved hepatica
    (*Hepatica acutiloba*)
Shooting star (*Dodecatheon meadia*)
Wall fern (*Polypodium vulgare*)

FOR SUNNY SPOTS

Alpine aster (*Aster alpinus*)
Alpine catchfly (*Silene quadrifida*)
Alpine columbine (*Aquilegia alpina*)
Alpine forget-me-not (*Myosotis alpestris*)
Alpine pasque flower (*Pulsatilla alpina*)
Alpine pink (*Dianthus alpinus*)
Alpine poppy (*Papaver alpinum*)
Alpine sunflower (*Tetraneuris grandiflora*)
Edelweiss (*Leontopodium alpinum*)
Wall rock cress (*Arabis caucasica*)

form. To accomplish this, spread a layer of crushed rock between the rocks before putting in the topsoil, and if the soil is heavy, mix in some sand and peat moss to lighten it. Alpine plants prefer a light, sandy soil, but for other plants mix a little manure, leaf mold, or compost into the soil. Think of each planting pocket as if it were a container.

Choosing Plants

A rock gardener has a wide variety of plants from which to choose, but it may be a challenge to find the perfect species for your site and to combine them aesthetically. The alpines, particularly, are not easy to grow because they are fussy about soil and climate conditions, so you may want to choose some of the compact, low-growing perennials that are not as picky. To achieve pleasing combinations, consider not only plant colors and mature heights but also their form. Are they rounded, like cranesbills (*Geranium*); spiky, like irises; or spreading, like moss pink (*Phlox subulata*)? Plants that cascade easily over rocks, such as thymes, may be especially good choices.

For the best effect, the size of the plants should fit the scale of the garden itself. Obviously, tiny plants are the ideal choice for a small space, while taller perennials, dwarf evergreens, and low-growing shrubs such as spreading cotoneaster are more appropriate on a long, wide hillside. Because so many perennial plants well suited to a rock garden bloom only in spring, you may want to consider strategic placement of some summer-blooming heathers (*Calluna vulgaris*), heaths (*Erica*), and other perennials, as well as some annuals for color in the rest of the growing season.

Select plants that are best for your garden's climate and light conditions, whether it is a cool, north-facing hillside or a dry, south-facing sunny slope. If you live where winters are long and the growing season short, you may be able to establish a garden of true alpine plants native to the European mountain ranges or the White Mountains, Appalachians, Rockies, or other high elevations. Most alpine plants are small and compact with rugged root systems that enable them to live in poor soil under severe weather conditions. To thrive, they need cool summers and perfect drainage. Although most rock plants do well in poor soil and are not fussy about other conditions as long as drainage is good, some need acidic conditions, and others prefer more alkaline soil. At the nursery or garden center, the tags containing information about the plants should indicate their needs.

Certain nurseries specialize entirely in alpine and rock garden species and seeds, and their catalogs can be good sources for planting ideas. The North American Rock Garden Society is also a valuable resource, since its members, as in other plant societies, swap seeds, plants, and ideas. For further inspiration, visit the beautiful rockeries in botanical gardens.

Caring for Rock Plants

Your rock garden perennials could be compared to a collection of potted plants, and they will grow best if you tend them accordingly. In the spring, check each plant. Reset any that were heaved out by frost, cut back the dead portions, and remove any that have died. Scatter some manure, compost, or complete organic fertilizer over the bed. To ensure that water will not collect in the "pots" and drown the plantings, loosen the soil in each pocket occasionally with a small garden fork. Spread a mulch of stone chips or coarse gravel around the plants to divert moisture from their crowns and prevent weed growth.

Housekeeping chores include cutting back any leggy plants after flower-

BEAUTY IN STONE. A variety of rock plants flourish in this natural setting.

ing, clipping off dead portions, and dividing any plant that has overgrown its space. Check for diseases and insects, as in any other bed. Slugs may be especially pesky because they enjoy shelter among the rocks. Never allow weeds to grow in nooks and crannies, not just for appearance's sake but, more important, because they can quickly crowd out good plants. Whether it is weeds or vigorous plants that take over, an unkempt rockery is a sad sight. Just a short period of daily care will prevent the need for a future overhaul.

Because only a small amount of soil is available for the plant roots, check them regularly to see if watering is necessary. Winter weather can be hard on rock garden plants because they are more exposed to cold winds and dehydration than plants grown in a level bed. Alpines on their native mountaintops have become toughened, but they are also accustomed to a heavy snow cover. If you don't get snow, a winter mulch can protect tender plants. In particularly exposed regions, it is a good idea to cover the entire bed with evergreen branches or straw just after the ground starts to freeze in the fall.

Water in a Rock Garden

A waterfall or stream is a natural addition to a rockery, providing both musical sounds and a cooling effect. Most of us are not lucky enough to have a small natural stream running among our rocks, but you can build your own by installing a small, submersible, circulating pump designed especially for fountains and waterfalls. These pumps require little electricity; some can even be powered by solar cells. The best systems make everything appear as natural as possible. Especially effective in the right location is a series of short waterfalls that drop from one rock-formed pool to the next below it, then finally to the bottom pool, from which the water is circulated back to the top. If you have no rock formations suitable for running water, garden supply catalogs offer pools as well as complete waterfall units.

Mock orange *(Philadelphus)*

Don't Forget to Smell the Flowers

Sweet autumn clematis
(Clematis terniflora)

DURING THE BUSY SUMMER SEASON we need to remind ourselves to stop occasionally and enjoy our garden, so we post the small, familiar sign: "Don't Forget to Smell the Flowers." No reminder is necessary to sniff our old-fashioned lilacs *(Syringa),* regal lilies *(Lilium regale),* or the rugosa roses *(Rosa rugosa),* but sometimes we need to get so close to a delicately scented flower that our noses become covered with yellow pollen. Once we had to administer first aid to a young visitor who didn't notice a bee hard at work within the bloom he was examining.

The scented garden is often one of the most popular in public botanical gardens. Planted entirely with perennials, annuals, herbs, and shrubs chosen for their aromatic characteristics, these gardens are filled with delicious floral and foliage scents blown by the breeze. In most backyard gardens, generally, fragrant plants are interspersed with unscented specimens, but it can be fun to create a garden dominated by plants with pleasant aromas. If you place it near the windows or doorways that you frequently use, you can enjoy the fragrance indoors as well as out. As an added bonus, you can cut, dry, and use many fragrant flowers in potpourri.

When you're choosing plants for fragrance, you'll find that many old-fashioned flower species and cultivars are more fragrant than their hybrids, since breeders, in search of larger and double blooms or more unusual colors, have often sacrificed the original fragrance. Many carnations and pinks *(Dianthus),* for example, no longer have the rich, spicy scent of their forebears, and the original lemon daylily *(Hemerocallis lilioasphodelus)* is sweeter than most of its descendants. Many modern roses, too, lack the wonderful perfume of the old cultivars.

You may want to avoid plants with scents that don't appeal to you. Gas plant *(Dictamnus albus),* for instance, has a pungent medicinal odor that some people find offensive. Ornamental onions *(Allium)* and common valerian *(Valeriana officinalis)* also have distinctive scents that are beloved by some but distasteful to others. Even garden phlox has both lovers and detractors when it comes to aroma. On the other hand, few of us dislike the fragrance of sweet peas *(Lathyrus odoratus),* lily-of-the-valley *(Convallaria majalis),* mock oranges *(Philadelphus),* or cinnamon rose *(Rosa cinnamomea* var. *plena).*

When designing a scented garden, keep in mind that many highly fragrant plants placed in a small area can produce a confusion of aromas, and the totality may not be pleasant. Allow at least 10 feet between the different fragrances by planting unscented flowers between the aromatic ones that bloom at the same time. A pathway winding through a scented garden gives

Plant Key

A | 'Hyperion' daylilies *(Hemerocallis* 'Hyperion')
B | Roses *(Rosa)*
C | Lily-of-the-valley *(Convallaria majalis)*
D | Stock *(Matthiola incana)*
E | Mock oranges *(Philadelphus)*

accessibility to the plants, especially foliage plants like rosemary *(Rosmarinus officinalis)* and lavenders, which release their fragrance when you brush against them.

You can construct a delightfully fragrant mixed border by combining perennials with scented shrubs like mock oranges *(Philadelphus)* and shrub roses, annuals like sweet peas and flowering tobaccos *(Nicotiana),* and bulbs like hyacinths and lilies, all of which have exquisite scents. Vines like sweet autumn clematis *(Clematis terniflora)* and Carolina jasmine *(Gelsemium sempervirens)* have fragrant flowers, and many herbs have aromatic foliage (see the list).

Don't expect the fragrance of such a garden to be obvious throughout the season, because many scents are so light that they are noticeable only in the evening or on cloudy days with no wind. Nevertheless, you can fully enjoy the garden anytime because most fragrant flowers are also attractive, and the herbs have many other uses.

Flowering tobacco *(Nicotiana sylvestris)*

Fragrant Plants

HERBS WITH FRAGRANT FOLIAGE
Basils *(Ocimum)*
French tarragon *(Artemisia dracunculus)*
Lavenders *(Lavandula)*
Lemon balm *(Melissa officinalis)*
Lemon verbena *(Aloysia triphylla)*
Mints *(Mentha)*
Rosemary *(Rosmarinus officinalis)*
Sages *(Salvia)*
Sweet woodruff *(Galium odoratum)*
Thymes *(Thymus)*

SHRUBS WITH SCENTED FLOWERS
Abelias, several species *(Abelia)*
Butterfly bushes *(Buddleia)*
Carolina allspice *(Calycanthus floridus)*
Daphnes *(Daphne)*
Deutzias *(Deutzia)*
Gardenias *(Gardenia)*
Koreanspice viburnum
    (Viburnum carlesii)
Lilacs *(Syringa)*
Magnolias *(Magnolia)*
Mock oranges *(Philadelphus)*
Rhododendrons and azaleas,
    some species *(Rhododendron)*
Roses, many species and cultivars *(Rosa)*
Sweet pepperbush *(Clethra alnifolia)*

PERENNIALS AND BULBS WITH FRAGRANT FLOWERS
August lily *(Hosta plantaginea)*
Bearded irises *(Iris)*
Bee balms *(Monarda)*
Common valerian *(Valeriana officinalis)*
Daffodils, some species and cultivars
    (Narcissus)
Daylilies, some species and cultivars,
    such as 'Hyperion' *(Hemerocallis)*
Evening primroses, some species
    (Oenothera)
Hyacinth *(Hyacinthus orientalis)*
Lilies, several species *(Lilium)*
Lily-of-the-valley *(Convallaria majalis)*
Magic lilies *(Lycoris)*
Pansies and violets, some species and
    cultivars *(Viola)*
Peonies, some cultivars, including
    'Avalanche', 'Monsieur Jules Elie',
    and 'Sarah Bernhardt' *(Paeonia)*
Pinks *(Dianthus)*
Primroses, some species and cultivars
    (Primula)
Sweet rocket *(Hesperis matronalis)*
Waterlily, many cultivars
    (Nymphaea odorata)

ANNUALS WITH FRAGRANT FLOWERS
Calendula *(Calendula officinalis)*
Floss flower *(Ageratum houstonianum)*
Flowering tobaccos, several species
    (Nicotiana)
Heliotrope *(Heliotropium arborescens)*
Marigolds *(Tagetes)*
Nasturtium *(Tropaeolum majus)*
Pansy *(Viola × wittrockiana)*
Petunias *(Petunia)*
Snapdragon *(Antirrhinum majus)*
Stock *(Matthiola incana)*
Sweet alyssum *(Lobularia maritima)*
Sweet pea *(Lathyrus odoratus)*
Sweet sultan *(Amberboa moschata)*
Virginia stock *(Malcomia maritima)*

VINES WITH FRAGRANT FLOWERS
American wisteria *(Wisteria frutescens)*
Carolina jasmine *(Gelsemium
    sempervirens)*
Goldflame honeysuckle
    (Lonicera × heckrottii)
Moonflower *(Ipomoea alba)*
Silver vine *(Actindia polygama)*
Sweet autumn clematis
    (Clematis terniflora)

Showy evening primrose
(*Oenothera speciosa* 'Siskiyou')

Great Gardening on a Hillside

WHEN WE WERE STARTING OUR FIRST perennial bed, an experienced local horticulturist dropped by and remarked that it would be difficult to create a worthwhile garden on our uneven backyard lawn. She advised that we bring in several loads of topsoil to do it right. Since neither our time nor budget would allow that, we worked with what we had and have not been sorry. There is no doubt that many of the world's greatest formal gardens are on level ground, but our sloping country border makes no pretense to being either formal or great. We have found that an informal hillside garden has a character of its own.

Whether your hillside is a gentle slope or a near precipice, and whether it is sunny, shaded, wet, or dry, it's possible to make it more colorful and attractive with well-chosen plants. A hillside, even more than a garden on the level, is in full view, so whatever vegetation you place on it will be plainly visible. In addition to the aesthetic effect, however, there may be practical reasons for planting on an incline, if your slope is eroding, for instance, or so steep it is difficult and perhaps even dangerous to mow.

Paths may be an important feature on a wide slope if you are going to be able to work there or have visitors wander about inspecting your plants. You might design a route that meanders over the slope with switchbacks, to allow viewing the garden from many angles. If the garden is narrow, design a more direct path to the top. Use natural materials such as gravel or wood chips or perhaps a series of stepping-stones. On a steep slope where paths would erode badly and would be difficult to navigate, it will probably be necessary

Black-eyed Susan (*Rudbeckia fulgida*)

to omit them entirely and cover the area with a heavily rooted groundcover such as English ivy *(Hedera helix)*, Boston ivy *(Parthenocissus tricuspidata)*, or Virginia creeper *(P. quinquefolia)*. If the slope is dangerously steep, you might be able to convert it into narrow terraces held in place by retaining walls of stone or rot-resistant wood timbers.

Preparing the Slope

When poison ivy *(Toxicodendron radicans)*, thistles *(Cirsium)*, wild brambles *(Rubus)*, sumacs *(Rhus)*, or other brush covers the slope, you may need to hire a professional with a heavy-duty brush trimmer to clean the area before planting. Then, as the roots resprout, you can keep the hillside clear for planting by spraying an organic herbicide, such as Scythe or Burnout.

If your slope has just recently been graded and is completely naked, it is easy to prepare it. Do the work as soon as possible so it won't erode and so the birds won't plant it with seeds of junky plants you don't want. Depending on the condition of the soil, you may want to cover the slope with topsoil first to get plants off to a better start. Spread some manure, compost, or a commercial complete fertilizer and till or rake

Chrysanthemums (Chrysanthemum)

it in. Then, to prevent steep slopes from eroding, place a weed-blocking fabric over the area and cut holes in the material to set in the plants. (Although you can grow bulbs on a slope, this method is not useful for them.) For continual bloom, plant clumps of rugged perennials such as daylilies, astilbe, phlox, or similar plants.

To get your slope in really top condition, after preparing the soil as above, seed it with an *annual* grain such as oats. Sow the grain thickly so it will crowd out any sprouting weed seeds, and let it grow throughout the summer undisturbed. It will freeze and become a strawlike mulch, and in the spring you can set the new plants into loose, fertile soil. To prevent new weeds from starting, apply an organic preemergent herbicide two to three weeks after the new plants are in and growing.

Choosing Plants

The design and plants you choose should depend on the light and soil conditions, the angle of the slope, and your own inclinations. A rocky, gravelly hillside with stone outcroppings might be ideal for conversion to an attractive rock garden. It is usually more prudent to feature any existing rock formations such as outcroppings or crevices, rather than attempting to conceal or remove them. (See pages 142–45 for rock garden suggestions.)

To dispense with fussy gardening, however, plant either groundcovers or clumps of other easy-care plants. A few years ago we planted a variety of colorful daylilies 3 feet apart on a slope and mulched between them with wood chips. The plants have become more beautiful each summer and have spread enough that the mulch is no longer visible. The slope is as low-maintenance as an attractive garden can be.

If you use groundcovers and have plenty of space, consider planting seve-

Bee balm (Monarda)

ral different kinds, both for aesthetic interest and to ensure against choosing a kind that might not do well. Let each one cover a good-sized area so that interesting patches result, rather than mixing various kinds together. (See Gardening with Groundcovers on page 205.) Separate them by metal or plastic vertical edgings or paths to ensure that the effect won't be lost by intermingling. Spring-flowering bulbs such as crocuses, daffodils, and grape hyacinths *(Muscari)*, are attractive when planted among such groundcovers.

Many garden perennials are suitable for planting on sunny slopes if the soil is rich and deep. If the soil is poor, choose only rugged kinds with vigorous root systems that hold the slope well and prevent erosion. Plants with foliage that will stay in good condition throughout the growing season are best. As we mentioned, our favorite perennials for this purpose are the vigorous cultivars of daylilies, which

bloom over a long period and, even when they are not in bloom, have foliage that remains attractive if it is healthy. Others that do well on sunny slopes are yarrows *(Achillea)*, bee balms *(Monarda)*, chrysanthemums, yellow daisy *(Anthemis tinctoria)*, moss pink *(Phlox subulata)*, evening primroses *(Oenothera)*, black-eyed Susan *(Rudbeckia fulgida)*, stonecrops *(Sedum)*, shasta daisy *(Leucanthemum × superbum)*, Siberian iris *(Iris sibirica)*, and many ornamental grasses.

You may want to experiment with various species of shrubs in your location before planting large amounts of any one species. Heathers *(Calluna vulgaris)*, heaths *(Erica)*, dwarf hemlocks *(Tsuga)*, yews *(Taxus)*, lowbush blueberries *(Vaccinium angustifolium)*, and azaleas *(Rhododendron)* all need acidic soil to grow well. For less acidic soils in light to moderate shade, use some of the plants recommended in the list for shade gardens on page 154.

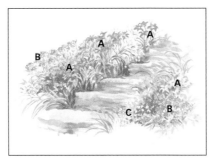

Plant Key

A | Daylilies *(Hemerocallis)*

B | Japanese spirea *(Spiraea japonica)*

C | Cinquefoils *(Potentilla)*

Highway crews often plant daylilies, crown vetch *(Coronilla varia)*, vigorous-growing grasses, and perennial wildflowers on sunny slopes bordering roads in many areas of the country. Lupines *(Lupinus)* have been naturalized on roadside banks all over our area. When they are in bloom, people drive for miles to photograph the masses of lavender, purple, and pink.

Groundcovers for Hillsides

FOR LIGHT TO MEDIUM SHADE

Bugleweeds *(Ajuga)*

Fringed bleeding heart *(Dicentra eximia)*

Lesser periwinkle *(Vinca minor)*

Lily-of-the-valley *(Convallaria majalis)*

Pachysandras *(Pachysandra)*

Sweet woodruff *(Galium odoratum)*

Wild gingers *(Asarum)*

FOR FULL SUN

Daylilies *(Hemerocallis)*

Moss pink *(Phlox subulata)*

Showy evening primrose
   (Oenothera speciosa)

Snow-in-summer
   (Cerastium tomentosum)

Speedwells *(Veronica)*

Thymes *(Thymus)*

Woolly yarrow *(Achillea tomentosa)*

For more suggestions, see page 207.

Creeping Jacob's ladder *(Polemonium reptans)*

Gardening in a Shady Nook

A SHADE GARDEN OFFERS REFRESHING RELIEF on a hot summer day and a completely different assortment of plants from those that grow in a sun-drenched border. When trees and shrubs provide the shade, they also furnish protective shelter to a wide range of birds and small animals, further enhancing the garden with sound and motion.

Mountain laurel *(Kalmia latifolia)*

The term "shade" encompasses many different light conditions. Shade can range from the dense darkness of a pine forest, where only plants like Indian pipe *(Monotropa uniflora)* will grow, to the light-dappled shade under birch *(Betula)* trees, which allow a great deal of sunlight to filter through. It may also connote an area that gets strong skylight but no sun, such as the north side of a building. The intensity of light and shade also differs at various latitudes and at different times of the growing season. In the North, for instance, the northeast side of a building might get an abundance of sun in early June, but as the sun rises more toward the southeast and sets earlier in August, that same location may get little or no sunlight. Another factor that affects the amount of light in a garden is the growth of nearby trees. We have met many gardeners who were puzzled because a garden that once bloomed prolifically ceased to grow well. When we checked it out, the culprit was the gradually increasing shade from growing trees, as well as their encroaching roots, which were stealing moisture and nutrients from the flowers.

If you are not already familiar with light conditions in your prospective garden spot, observe that area for one entire growing season to determine the quality of shade at various times of the day and year. If deciduous trees are the shade source, note whether the light is dappled when they are in full leaf, as it is under birches, locusts *(Robinia),* and poplars *(Populus),* or dense, as under an oak *(Quercus)* or a maple *(Acer).* If the light appears too diminished for the proper growth of most plants, cutting off a few lower limbs from the offending trees sometimes allows more light to enter from the sides.

The amount of moisture a shady spot receives will also affect what you can grow there. The soil under pine

trees is usually dry because the tree acts as an umbrella and falling rain seldom reaches the base. It is just as likely, however, for a shaded spot to be excessively moist. If you hope to grow plants where the soil is soggy for most of the summer, you must drain it, build it up by adding topsoil, or plant only specimens that do well in both moist and shade conditions, such as hostas and royal fern *(Osmunda regalis)*.

Where the soil is thin and tree roots completely fill the area, even strong plants may not survive such competition. If you run into roots when you dig, add a thick layer of topsoil or plant only shallow-rooted groundcovers, such as lesser periwinkle *(Vinca minor)*, pachysandras, and woodland plants that normally grow in such conditions.

To grow plants successfully in the shade, you obviously need those that are appropriate to the type of shade you have, although soil type and climate are also determining factors. Most plants need at least a few hours of direct sun, as well as filtered light or full skylight (in other words, light shade) for the rest of the day. Many can also grow where they get little or no sunshine but have an abundance of filtered light (medium or dappled shade). Only a few plants can thrive in the darkness of an evergreen forest (dense shade), although lesser periwinkle, pachysandras, trailing arbutus *(Epigaea repens)*, and moneywort *(Lysimachia nummularia)* are worth a try in the slightly open areas where small amounts of light filter through the trees to ground level.

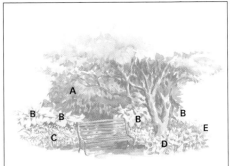

Plant Key

A | Mountain laurel *(Kalmia latifolia)*

B | Hostas *(Hosta)*

C | Sweet woodruff *(Gallium odoratum)*

D | Painted trillium *(Trillium undulatum)*

E | Virginia bluebells *(Mertensia pulmonarioides)*

Flowering Plants for Shady Places

The lists below are meant only as a guide for choosing plants. Those listed in one group will often thrive in other shade conditions.

Spring Flowers

FOR LIGHT SHADE (OR SUN)

Coral bells (*Heuchera*)

Moss pink (*Phlox subulata*)

Navelworts (*Omphalodes*)

Pansies and violets (*Viola*)

Sweet alyssum (*Lobularia maritima*)

FOR LIGHT TO MEDIUM SHADE

Bergenias (*Bergenia*)

Bishop's hats (*Epimedium*)

Forget-me-nots (*Myosotis*)

Fringed bleeding heart (*Dicentra eximia*)

Leopard's banes (*Doronicum*)

Lungworts (*Pulmonaria*)

Solomon's seals (*Polygonatum*)

FOR MEDIUM TO DENSE SHADE

Pachysandras (*Pachysandra*)

Sweet woodruff (*Galium odoratum*)

Trilliums (*Trillium*)

Virginia bluebells
    (*Mertensia pulmonarioides*)

Early Summer Flowers

FOR LIGHT SHADE (OR SUN)

Begonias (*Begonia*)

Blue false indigo (*Baptisia australis*)

Columbines (*Aquilegia*)

Coral bells (*Heuchera*)

Dead nettles (*Lamium*)

Gladwyn iris (*Iris foetidissima*)

Globeflowers (*Trollius*)

Impatiens (*Impatiens walleriana*)

Purple rock cress (*Aubrieta × cultorum*)

FOR LIGHT TO MEDIUM SHADE

Creeping Jacob's ladder
    (*Polemonium reptans*)

Crested iris (*Iris cristata*)

Foam flowers (*Tiarella*)

Fringed bleeding heart (*Dicentra eximia*)

Perennial candytuft (*Iberis sempervirens*)

Siberian bugloss (*Brunnera macrophylla*)

Violets (*Viola*)

Wild blue phlox (*Phlox divaricata*)

FOR MEDIUM TO DENSE SHADE

Lesser periwinkle (*Vinca*)

Lily-of-the-valley (*Convallaria majalis*)

Primroses (*Primula*)

Rodger's flower (*Rodgersia*)

Sandworts (*Arenaria*)

Summer Flowers

FOR LIGHT SHADE (OR SUN)

Astilbes (*Astilbe*)

Astilboides (*Astilboides tabularis*)

Bellflowers (*Campanula*)

Clematis (*Clematis*)

Coral bells (*Heuchera*)

Cranesbills (*Geranium*)

Daylilies (*Hemerocallis*)

Edging lobelia (*Lobelia erinus*)

Flowering tobaccos (*Nicotiana*)

Foxgloves (*Digitalis*)

Gas plant (*Dictamnus albus*)

Goat's beards (*Aruncus dioicus*)

Lady's mantle (*Alchemilla mollis*)

Lamb's ears (*Stachys byzantina*)

Ligularias (*Ligularia*)

Lilies, many kinds, including
    L. canadense, L. martagon, and
    Aurelian and Oriental hybrids
    (*Lilium*)

Pearly everlastings (*Anaphalis*)

Saxifrages (*Saxifraga*)

Speedwells (*Veronica*)

Spurges (*Euphorbia*)

FOR LIGHT TO MEDIUM SHADE

Bee balms (*Monarda*)

Bugbanes (*Cimicifuga*)

Bugleweeds (*Ajuga*)

Cardinal flower (*Lobelia cardinalis*)

Corydalis (*Corydalis*)

Foxgloves (*Digitalis*)

Himalayan fleeceflower
    (*Persicaria affinis*)

Meadow rues (*Thalictrum*)

Monkshoods (*Aconitum*)

Sweet rocket (*Hesperis matronalis*)

FOR MEDIUM TO DENSE SHADE

Hostas (*Hosta*)

Lilyturfs (*Liriope*)

Fall Flowers

FOR LIGHT SHADE (OR SUN)

Asters (*Aster*)

Autumn monkshood
    (*Aconitum autumnale*)

Common rose mallow
    (*Hibiscus moscheutos*)

Coral bells (*Heuchera*)

Daylilies (*Hemerocallis*)

Japanese anemone (*Anemone × hybrida*)

Stonecrops (*Sedum*)

Turtleheads (*Chelone*)

FOR LIGHT TO MEDIUM SHADE

Gentians (*Gentiana*)

Hellebores (*Helleborus*)

Himalayan fleeceflower
    (*Persicaria affinis*)

Groundcovers

Barren strawberry (*Waldsteinia ternata*)

Bishop's hats (*Epimedium*)

Box huckleberry (*Gaylussacia brachycera*)

Dwarf wintercreeper
    (*Euonymus fortunei* 'Minimus')

European wild ginger
    (*Asarum europaeum*)

Impatiens (*Impatiens walleriana*)

Mazus (*Mazus reptans*)

'Saishu Jima' hosta (*Hosta* 'Saishu Jima')

Shrubs

Azaleas and rhododendrons
    (*Rhododendron*)

Burning bush (*Euonymus alatus*)

Honeysuckles (*Lonicera*)

Japanese pieris (*Pieris japonica*)

Leucothoes (*Leucothoe*)

Mountain laurel (*Kalmia latifolia*)

Red chokeberry (*Aronia arbutifolia*)

Red osier dogwood (*Cornus stolonifera*)

Smoke bush (*Cotinus coggygria*)

Viburnums (*Viburnum*)

Winterberry (*Ilex verticillata*)

Witch hazels (*Hamamelis*)

Yews (*Taxus*)

We have a light shade situation in our backyard where the house and a dense evergreen hedge keep the sun out of a small corner of the garden for much of the day, although abundant skylight is still available. Many sun-loving perennials can grow there, but since they get only a bit of afternoon sun, they tend to bloom later and for a longer period than those in full sun. This shaded corner gives us the opportunity to grow beautiful primroses, hostas, and maidenhair ferns *(Adiantum)*, which do not enjoy full sun.

In light shade, it is possible to have continuous bloom beginning with a carpet of early spring bulbs, such as snowdrops *(Galanthus)*, Siberian squill *(Scilla siberica)*, grape hyacinths *(Muscari)*, and daffodils, and continuing into the late spring with primroses, lily-of-the-valley *(Convallaria majalis)*, violets, and similar species. Plants like fringed bleeding heart *(Dicentra eximia)* blossom throughout the growing season. The tall, vigorous martagon lilies *(Lilium martagon)* and their hybrids are

MADE FOR THE SHADE. This shady garden features plants with a variety of textures.

just some of the lilies that will grow in light shade. Meadow rues *(Thalictrum)* and black cohosh *(Cimicifuga racemosa)* are well worth planting, too. Cultivars of autumn snakeroot *(Cimicifuga simplex)* with deep purple foliage, such as 'Black Negligee', 'Brunette', and 'Hillside Black Beauty', are also good plants for light shade. Clumps of astilbes and

hostas are ideal midheight plants. The various cultivars of European wood anemone *(Anemone nemorosa)* are good choices to try, as are hellebores and saxifrages. Long-blooming annuals, like impatiens and begonias, can add color when perennial blossoms are scarce.

It is difficult to grow a conventional flower garden in the medium-to-heavy shade of trees or on the north side of a tall house, although many garden plants do flourish there. Foliage plants are especially pleasing when combined to show off their textures and colors. Large hosta leaves, for example, contrast pleasantly with the delicate, lacy greenery of ferns. A woodland garden can also be ideal for such a spot. In fact, although the name suggests a forested area, a woodland garden will flourish even in the shadow of city buildings if the right soil and moisture conditions exist. (See the list of medium-to-dense shade plants opposite.)

The colors of plants in a shade garden may in actuality appear quite different from those you had carefully planned on paper, because our perception of color differs according to the quality of light that is present. In general, white and pastel blooms provide a

Hosta *(Hosta* 'Tall Boy'*)*

bright, glowing quality in a garden that gets little sun. More vivid colors may appear dim or, in certain shade situations, shine brilliantly and clash so much that they must be shifted from one spot to another.

In a shady planting, as in a rock garden, natural features like running water, old stumps, stones, and pools add greatly to the atmosphere. If the area is large, you might construct pathways through it bordered by plantings of ajuga, hosta, pachysandra, ferns, ivy, or wildflowers. Use informal, natural path materials such as pea stone, coarse wood chips, or even bare earth. You may also want to create a welcoming focal point by adding a bench or other garden seat.

Planting and Caring for Your Shade Garden

Because so many shade-loving plants grow best in somewhat acidic soil, test your soil before planting. Add lime only if the pH is below 5.5 in spots where you plan to grow cultivated garden plants rather than acid-loving wildflowers and ferns. Allow more space for each plant in the shade than you would in full sun, so that the foliage has room to spread out and absorb all the available light.

Plants in woodland locations must compete with trees for nutrients, so be sure to fertilize them each spring, feeding them a bit more heavily than you would those in a conventional garden. Check plants growing under trees each spring to see if fallen leaves or needles need to be cleaned away so they will not smother the plants. In addition, throughout the growing season, make sure that the plants are getting the moisture they need, especially if they are under a canopy of trees or sheltered from wind-driven rains by buildings, walls, or solid fences.

Ferns for Shady Spots

In the evolution of plant life, ferns are a notch below seed-producing plants. Rather than bearing seeds and fruit, they reproduce by spores, usually located on the underside of their leaves (fronds). The following are excellent choices for a woodland garden.

Adiantum (Maidenhair ferns). Among the most beautiful ferns, these lacy plants are not difficult to grow. They like an area that gets only a little morning sun and a bit of skylight during the day. Often abundant in the rich, moist, well-drained, leaf-mulched soil of maple woods, they do not require an acid soil. *A. pedatum,* a native and the most recommended, has horizontal, near-circular fronds and grows to a height of about 20 inches. Zones 2–8.

Asplenium. Walking fern *(A. rhizophyllus),* a less common creeping fern, is found growing near rocks where the soil is moist and relatively alkaline. Growing only 5–12 inches tall, it is useful in moist rock gardens. Zones 3–8.

Athyrium (Lady ferns). Among this large group of ferns, **lady fern *(A. filix-femina)*** is the best known. It is not fussy about soil pH and grows in sun or shade. It needs adequate moisture, however, or the leaves become brown. Grows to a height of 30–36 inches. Zones 3–8. **Japanese painted fern *(A. niponicum)*** is a colorful import, with 2-foot fronds of gray-green and wine red. It needs moisture, lots of organic matter, and partial shade to grow to its best color and vigor. Zones 5–8.

Botrychium. There are several common varieties of **rattlesnake fern *(B. virginianum),*** all of which grow from 12–24 inches tall. It likes moist, moderately acid soil and sun or shade. It is unique because it produces seeds in small clusters on the fronds. Its foliage emerges in early spring. Zones 3–8.

Cystopteris. Bladder fern *(C. bulbifera)* grows from 24–36 inches tall and produces small bulblets along the stem at the base of the leaves. It likes moist soil, is not particular about acidity, and grows into a dainty, attractive plant. Zones 3–8.

Dryopteris (Wood ferns). A very large genus with many attractive choices, these shade-loving ferns are not particular about soil. **Crested wood fern *(D. cristata)*** grows to 30 inches. Its dark green, leathery fronds are evergreen in the warmer parts of the country. Zones 3–8. *D. erythrosora* has coppery-colored fronds in spring that become dark green and shiny with age. Needs moist soil. Zones 6–9. **Marginal shield fern *(D. marginalis)*** is evergreen and grows to 2 feet; it is used in floral displays. Zones 3–8. **Toothed wood fern *(D. spinulosa)*** is semi-evergreen, very attractive, and often collected for florist use because it is so long lasting. It is also outstanding in the landscape; 20–28 inches. Zones 2–8. **Goldie's wood fern *(D. goldiana)*** likes moist soils and cool spots; 4–5 feet. Zones 6–8.

Matteuccia. Ostrich fern *(M. struthiopteris)* is a massive, vigorously spreading fern that grows up to 5 feet tall and likes moist, rich soil and shade. It should not be planted too deep. Zones 2–8.

Onoclea. Sensitive fern *(O. sensibilis)* is a hardy plant, which grows fast enough to become weedy, especially in moist locations. It thrives in sun or light shade, is very tender to fall frosts, and reaches a height of 12–30 inches. It produces interesting spore-bearing fronds that are widely used in dried flower arrangements. Zones 2–8.

Osmunda (Flowering ferns). Cinnamon fern *(O. cinnamomea)* grows 2–5 feet tall with spores borne on cinnamon-like sticks in the center of the fronds. Likes

A. Cinnamon fern *(Osmunda cinnamomea),* B. Japanese painted fern *(Athurium niponicum),* C. *Dryopteris erythrosora,*
D. Ostrich fern *(Matteuccia struthiopteris),* E. Maidenhair fern *(Adiantum pedatum).*

moist places in sun or shade. The newly emerged frond tops are the edible spring treat known as fiddleheads. **Interrupted fern *(O. claytoniana),*** another impressive specimen, is happy in moist spots. It grows in sun but seems to be at its massive best in light shade. It gets 3–4 feet tall or more, with spores growing about midway along its large fronds. **Royal fern *(O. regalis)*** grows in very moist places, sometimes even in water, and likes sun or light shade and somewhat acid soil. Grows up to 6 feet tall but is usually shorter. Zones 3–9.

Polypodium. **Common polypody *(P. virginianum)*** is a small evergreen fern, 6–12 inches tall. It grows in both sun and shade, and in either acid or alkaline soil. It is an especially good plant for rock gardens, where it will develop into a thick mass. Zones 3–8.

Polystichum* (Shield ferns). Christmas fern *(P. acrostichoides), a beautiful evergreen for all seasons, resembles the houseplant Boston fern *(Nephrolepis exaltata* 'Bostoniensis'). It likes the shade of deciduous woods and moist soil rich in leaf mold, but can be grown in the sun if kept well watered; 1–3 feet tall. Zones 2–8.

Thelypteris. **New York fern *(T. noveboracensis)*** has feathery, evergreen foliage. It likes moist soil and shade; 2 feet tall. Zones 2–8.

Woodsia* (Woodsias). Blunt-lobed woodsia *(W. obtusa) is a small fern, 1–2 feet tall. It likes moist, shady places. Since it thrives in difficult spots with little soil, it is useful in shady parts of a rock garden and as an edging. Zones 4–7. **Rusty woodsia *(W. ilvensis)*** is only 6 inches tall with dark brown new growth and makes a good groundcover. Zones 3–8.

Woodwardia* (Chain ferns).** **Netted chain fern *(W. areolata) likes acid, swampy soil and partial shade. It grows to 12 inches tall. Zones 4–9. **Virginia chain fern *(W. virginica)*** is much taller (to 60 inches) and likes wet soil. Zones 4–9.

Zinnias (*Zinnia elegans*)

Successful Seashore Plantings

IF YOU LIVE OR VACATION NEAR THE SHORE, you know that raising most plants there is not easy. Strong winds, glaring sun, sandy soil, and salt spray present a constant challenge to gardeners from New Brunswick to Key West on the Atlantic and from British Columbia to southern California on the Pacific. Nevertheless, spectacular flower borders flourish on each coast, nestled near sand dunes, alongside sea walls, and around homes and cottages. The ocean light intensifies colors and makes blossoms more vivid, especially if they are near clear blue water.

Spurge (*Euphorbia longifolia*)

If you have a choice of locations, place your flower bed where it is away from the salt-loaded splashes of the highest tides and protected from the effects of wind. Wind not only breaks fragile plants and bends sturdy ones but also rapidly dries out all growing things, a condition that is aggravated by the bright, glaring sunlight typical of coastal sites. Because of the glare, many plant species that demand full sun inland do better in light shade when grown near the shore. Buildings, hedgerows, walls of brick or stone, and board fences are all effective as wind-

breaks and shade providers. The barrier does not need to be high in many locations, because even a low wall provides some protection, but before you build walls or change the contour of land in any way, check local and state environmental laws, which are often more stringent in seashore areas.

Any trees or shrubs you choose to plant should, of course, be salt-tolerant. Some species are sensitive to salt spray on their foliage and others are killed outright by salt water on their roots. Among those that are fairly resistant to both salt spray and salt on their roots

are arrowwood viburnum *(Viburnum dentatum)*, Austrian pine *(Pinus nigra)*, amur and California privets *(Ligustrum amurense* and *L. ovalifolium)*, shore pine *(Pinus contorta)*, Colorado spruce *(Picea pungens)*, mountain pieris *(Pieris floribunda)*, common lilac *(Syringa vulgaris)*, Russian olive *(Elaeagnus angustifolia)*, and junipers. On the other hand, red pine *(Pinus resinosa)*, white pine *(Pinus strobus)*, Canadian hemlock *(Tsuga canadensis)*, Scots pine *(Pinus sylvestris)*, yews *(Taxus)*, arborvitae *(Thuja)*, and most other hedge-type evergreens are extremely susceptible to salt spray on their foliage.

The soil along the shore may be sandy, clay, or rocky, but it is likely to be poor in quality, so it will be necessary to enrich it if you want to raise most plants. By sending a soil sample to your state soil-testing laboratory for analysis, you can find out exactly what amendments it needs. Otherwise, mix generous amounts of compost, topsoil, peat moss, manure, or, better still, all of these into the soil before planting. Seaweed, too, is exceptionally good for conditioning and enriching soil; best of all, it contains no weeds, is disease-free, and can be composted, used as a mulch, or tilled directly into the soil. Like manure, it provides humus and nutrients, and it is even richer in trace elements. Before using seaweed or salt hay, however, be sure to wash off the salt and other debris.

You will probably find it necessary to water seaside plants frequently during hot, dry spells and to wash residual salt off the plants after a high wind. If the ground is covered with salt water after flooding, leave sprinklers running for several hours to leach the salt away.

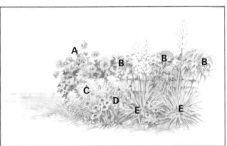

Plant Key

A | Common rose mallows *(Hibiscus moscheutos)*

B | Virginia creepers *(Parthenocissus quinquefolia)*

C | Spurges *(Euphorbia)*

D | Blanket flowers *(Gaillardia)*

E | Yuccas *(Yucca)*

A built-in sprinkler or trickle irrigation system can save you a lot of time if you garden in an area where the summer weather is particularly hot and dry. Mulch around your plants with marsh hay, seaweed, wood chips, shredded bark, cocoa hulls, or whatever organic material is available. Not only can mulch help protect the soil against moisture loss and erosion, but it will cut down on weeding chores, as well.

Sea lavender (*Limonium latifolium*)

When selecting plants, try to find those that will be blooming when you are in residence, and observe what is doing well around your neighborhood. Choose vigorous ones that will thrive in sandy soil, full sun, wind, and salt-laden air. If possible, purchase them from garden centers and catalogs that have experience with seaside plantings. Although salt spray sometimes acts as fungicide, avoid plants that are extremely fungus-susceptible, because seaside fog encourages disease. For nearly maintenance-free gardening, if you are planting in sand, choose the native species that thrive along the shore, such as American bittersweet (*Celastrus scandens*), bayberries (*Myrica*), beach plum (*Prunus maritima*), common rose mallow (*Hibiscus moscheutos*), goldenrods (*Solidago*), rugosa rose (*Rosa rugosa*), trumpet vines (*Campsis*), and yuccas.

Dependable Seashore Plants

PERENNIALS

American turk's cap lily
  (*Lilium superbum*)
✳ Asters (*Aster*)
Astilbes (*Astilbe*)
Baby's breaths (*Gypsophila*)
Beach wormwood (*Artemisia stelleriana*)
Bee balm (*Monarda didyma*)
Blanket flowers (*Gaillardia*)
Blue bugloss (*Anchusa azurea*)
Blue false indigo (*Baptisia australis*)
Bugbanes (*Cimicifuga*)
Bugleweeds (*Ajuga*)
Butterfly weed (*Asclepias tuberosa*)
Chrysanthemums (*Chrysanthemum*)
Columbines (*Aquilegia*)
Common rose mallow
  (*Hibiscus moscheutos*)
Coral bells (*Heuchera sanguinea*)
Cupid's dart (*Catanache caerulea*)
Daylilies (*Hemerocallis*)
Delphiniums (*Delphinium*)
Fleabanes (*Erigeron*)
Foxgloves (*Digitalis*)
Globe thistles (*Echinops*)
Hens-and-chicks (*Sempervivum*)
Hollyhock (*Alcea rosea*)
Hostas (*Hosta*)
Lamb's ears (*Stachys byzantina*)
Leopard's bane (*Doronicum orientale*)
✳ Orange coneflowers (*Rudbeckia*)
Oriental poppy (*Papaver orientale*)
Perennial candytuft (*Iberis sempervirens*)
Phlox (*Phlox*)
Pinks (*Dianthus*)
Rose campion (*Lychnis coronaria*)
Sea hollies (*Eryngium*)
✳ Sea lavender (*Limonium latifolium*)
Sea thrift (*Armeria maritima*)
Silky beach pea (*Lathyrus littoralis*)
Spike lilyturf (*Liriope spicata*)
✳ Spurges (*Euphorbia*)
✳ Stonecrops (*Sedum*)
Tickseeds (*Coreopsis*)
Torch lilies (*Kniphofia*)
Tufted pansy (*Viola cornuta*)
Wall rock cress (*Arabis caucasica*)
✳ Woolly yarrow (*Achillea tomentosa*)
✳ Yellow daisy (*Anthemis tinctoria*)
✳ Yuccas (*Yucca*)

ANNUALS

China aster (*Callistephus chinensis*)
Cosmos (*Cosmos*)
Petunias (*Petunia*)
Sages (*Salvia*)
Sweet alyssum (*Lobularia maritima*)
Zinnias (*Zinnia*)

GRASSES

American beach grass
  (*Ammophila breviligulata*)
European dune grass
  (*Ammophila arenaria*)
Fountain grass (*Pennisetum alopecuroides*)
Lyme grass (*Leymus arenarius*)
✳ Salt meadow cord grass
  (*Spartina patens*)
✳ Switch grass (*Panicum virgatum*)

SHRUBS AND VINES

See also the shrubs and trees mentioned for their salt-tolerance on page 159.
American bittersweet
  (*Celastrus scandens*)
American highbush cranberry
  (*Viburnum trilobum*)
Autumn olive (*Elaeagnus umbellata*)
✳ Beach plum (*Prunus maritima*)
Border privet (*Ligustrum obtusifolium*)
Grapes (*Vitex*)
Honeysuckles (*Lonicera*)
Inkberry (*Ilex glabra*)
Northern bayberry (*Myrica pensylvanica*)
Rugosa rose (*Rosa rugosa*)
Russian olive (*Elaeagnus angustifolia*)
✳ Scotch broom (*Cytisus scoparius*)
Sea buckthorn (*Hippophae rhamnoides*)
✳ Sea lavender (*Limonium latifolium*)
Shadbush (*Amelanchier canadensis*)
Shore juniper (*Juniperus conferta*)
Trumpet vine (*Campsis radicans*)
✳ Virginia creeper
  (*Parthenocissus quinquefolia*)

✳ = Particularly effective in dry locations

Sweet alyssum (*Lobularia maritima* 'Snow Crystals')

Common foxglove
(*Digitalis purpurea*)

The Charm of a Cottage Garden

The term "cottage garden" evokes an image of annual and perennial flowers, bulbs, fruits, berries, herbs, vegetables, and shrubs in a variety of colors, sizes, and shapes, all tucked into a small front yard that leads to a Thomas Kinkade–style storybook cottage with a thatched roof. Fortunately, cottage gardens can also look lovely around more modern homes.

Although cottage gardens exist all over the world, the British have elevated them to an art form. The skill of these inveterate gardeners makes what could be an unsightly hodgepodge a beautiful and productive display instead. Cottage gardens are usually small but they can approach an acre in size. Such plantings are not as common in North America, where we are conditioned to the sight of well-groomed lawns in front of our homes and where, in some suburbs, zoning regulations forbid anything so unconventional. Nevertheless, in front and backyards in many places, colorful, charming American cottage gardens thrive. It is convenient and fun to grow a variety of plants in a small space near the house, and the bonus is that there is no lawn to mow.

The basic requirement for this sort of garden is a sunny spot with well-defined boundaries, such as walls, fences, hedges, or buildings. The soil should be rich and deeply tilled to encourage plant roots to grow downward rather than outward. Pathways that meander through each section help you reach all parts easily, and plants fill every nook and cranny. Usually such a garden comprises the entire front or backyard, and sometimes both.

Although you should grow whatever appeals to you, the plants in a bona fide cottage garden are traditionally old-fashioned and informal, including native species and near-wild cultivars that are the very antithesis of modern hybrids. Vintage plants like hollyhocks *(Alcea rosea),* primroses,

Anemone clematis (*Clematis montana*)

and pansies *(Viola × wittrockiana)* are ideal. A clump of staked Pacific hybrid delphiniums or a group of hybrid tea roses would be considered "flora non grata," but their predecessors, larkspur *(Consolida ajacis)* and species roses, would be very much at home. Many old-fashioned cottage garden flowers have a delicious fragrance, unlike most of their modern descendants.

Woodland forget-me-not
(Mysotis sylvatica 'Ultramarine'*)*

No firm rules exist for designing such a plot, but the underlying concept is that no symmetrical rows of plants or careful arrangement of colors should spoil the patchwork effect. Nevertheless, an eye for the harmonious arrangement of colors and heights will make the garden more attractive. Let lavenders, lamb's ears *(Stachys byzantina)*, onions, lettuce, and lupines *(Lupinus)* enjoy each other's company in a conglomeration of diverse little plots. Set annual bedding plants amid vegetables, herbs, and perennials, and put berry plants in clumps instead of orderly rows. On the walls, use espaliered fruit trees or grape vines. If you wish, plant dwarf fruit trees and small fruits such as gooseberries *(Ribes uva-crispa)*, currants *(R. rubrum* and *R. nigrum)*, and blueberries *(Vaccinium)*, all ideal inhabitants of a cottage garden. (Since fruit trees and grapevines may need spraying, separate them from any edibles,

Plant Key

A | Clematis *(Clematis)*

B | Roses *(Rosa)*

C | Lilies *(Lilium)*

D | Painted daisies *(Tanacetum coccineum)*

E | Snapdragons *(Antirrhinum majus)*

F | Canterbury bells *(Campanula medium)*

G | Mealycup sages *(Salvia farinacea)*

H | Pansies *(Viola × wittrockiana)*

Columbine (*Aquilegia* 'Carol Ann')

Suggested Cottage Garden Plants

These old-fashioned plants are special favorites among cottage gardeners, but you will also want to include your own beloved plants. It is even permissible to sneak in a hybrid now and then if the spirit moves you.

PERENNIALS
Bee balm *(Monarda didyma)*
Black-eyed-Susan *(Rudbeckia fulgida)*
Canterbury bells *(Campanula medium)*
Clary sage *(Salvia sclarea)*
Clematis *(Clematis)*
Columbines *(Aquilegia)*
Daylilies *(Hemerocallis)*
Forget-me-nots *(Myosotis)*
Foxgloves *(Digitalis)*
Fringed bleeding heart *(Dicentra eximia)*
Hollyhock *(Alcea rosea)*
Lily-of-the-valley *(Convallaria majalis)*
Lupines *(Lupinus)*
Mountain bluet *(Centaurea montana)*
Pansies and violets *(Viola)*
Peonies *(Paeonia)*
Phlox *(Phlox)*
Pinks *(Dianthus)*
Poppies *(Papaver)*
Primroses *(Primula)*
Sunflowers *(Helianthus)*
Sweet rocket *(Hesperis matronalis)*
Wallflowers *(Erysimum)*
Yellow daisy *(Anthemis tinctoria)*

HEIRLOOM SHRUBS
Blueberries *(Vaccinium)*
Elderberries *(Sambucus)*
Honeysuckles *(Lonicera)*
Lilacs *(Syringa)*

Mock oranges *(Philadelphus)*
Rhododendrons and azaleas
   (Rhododendron)
Roses *(Rosa)*
Viburnums *(Viburnum)*

ANNUALS
Including most bedding plants, especially those that look good all season
Annual phlox *(Phlox drummondii)*
Bachelor's buttons *(Centaurea cyanus)*
Calendulas *(Calendula)*
China aster *(Callistephus chinensis)*
Cosmos *(Cosmos)*
Flowering tobaccos *(Nicotiana)*
Geraniums *(Pelargonium)*
Impatiens *(Impatiens)*
Marigolds *(Tagetes)*
Nasturtium *(Tropaeolum majus)*
Poppies *(Papaver)*
Sages *(Salvia)*
Snapdragon *(Antirrhinum majus)*
Spider flower *(Cleome hassleriana)*

SUMMER BULB-TYPE PLANTS
Cannas *(Canna)*
Dahlias *(Dahlia)*
Gladioli *(Gladiolus)*
Irises *(Iris)*
Lilies *(Lilium)*, especially
   'Enchantment', *L. candidum*,
   L. regale, and *L. lancifolium*

such as herbs, berries, and leafy vegetables. Even most organic pesticides have some degree of toxicity.) Although the plantings may appear crowded, each plant must have enough space to get the sun, moisture, and fertility it needs to thrive.

As you would guess, the ornaments most at home in a cottage garden are natural-looking objects. It would be appropriate to have an arbor to hold a rambling rose or grapevine, as well as strawberry jars, hanging baskets, a beehive, a swinging gate, and furniture of weathered wood or stone. The pathways should be natural looking, constructed of wooden blocks, flagstone, or similar earthy materials.

The charm of your cottage garden will be due primarily to the frequent attention it receives with hoe and trowel. Not a garden for the dilettante, it is a project for the true amateur in the best meaning of that word: one who loves a pursuit but is not a professional practitioner of it. Cottage gardeners must be dedicated and have enough time and energy to devote to their passion, since cultivating, feeding, and weeding must all be done by hand, and you may occasionally find it necessary to move plants to get the effect you want. Old-fashioned plants usually do not require as much spraying and fussy

care as new hybrids, but they still need adequate water and nutrient renewal. Such plants tend to grow more profusely than hybrids, too, so division and deadheading may take more time than in other gardens. Although demanding, this care will reward you with abundant, colorful blooms, from the earliest spring snowdrops *(Galanthus)* and daffodils to the last fragrant roses of summer. No matter where you grow a cottage garden, it will feel like home.

Waterlily *(Nymphaea* 'Mrs. George T. Hitchcock')

The Magic Spell
of Water Gardening

AFTER TRYING UNSUCCESSFULLY to drain a small swamp near his home, a friend of ours read an article about water gardens and subsequently hired a bulldozer to dig a shallow pool there. Now he's developing a small garden reminiscent of Claude Monet's at Giverny, with pink, red, and white waterlilies and other water plants, which all of his friends love to visit.

Waterlily *(Nymphaea* 'Texas Dawn')

Water gardening is a fascinating hobby. Although the term may include simply growing plants around a pond, a bona fide water garden will contain aquatic plants like waterlilies *(Nymphaea)* that grow entirely in water and often also marginals (semi-aquatics) — moisture-loving shrubs and perennials, such as pitcher plants *(Sarracenia),* that inhabit bogs or swamps. In addition to the aesthetic value a beautiful water garden adds to your property, it is likely to attract not only fascinating frogs but also birds, bees, bats, butterflies, dragonflies, turtles, and salamanders.

One of the nice things about gardening with water is that usually you need to put in only minimal work after the initial construction and planting is complete, as long as you maintain the ecological balance of the area. There is no hoeing or cultivating, little weeding, and, of course, no watering.

For several years, we had a small pool filled with red and white waterlilies in our backyard. It was much enjoyed both by us and by a friendly green frog who spent a lot of time sitting on the pads, catching insects and being photographed by visitors. We made our garden by sinking a plastic pool into the ground, filling it with water, and placing a few pots in it, each containing a lily planted in soil. Water trickled in slowly through a camouflaged inlet pipe, and the small amount of overflow spilled onto the lawn. It could not have been more simple or carefree, which was its undoing. We became so accustomed to ignoring it that during a dry spell one summer we forgot to check the water inflow. It had stopped, and we lost all the plants.

When constructing an in-ground water garden, most people do not use a plastic pool, since it is not durable. Instead, use a flexible pond liner made of PVC, EPDM, or rubber, available in many sizes from pool suppliers. After

excavating a hole the size you want, put down an underlayment to protect the pond liner from stones or other sharp objects in the soil. The underlayment may be a 2-inch layer of fine mulch or peat moss, a 1-inch layer of sand, or a commercial geotextile material. Place the liner above the underlayment and use sod, rocks, bricks, or other weights to fasten it around the edges. Instead of a flexible liner, you might choose a preformed rigid liner. These come in many shapes and sizes but are more expensive. They are also not as satisfactory as flexible liners in northern climates because frost heaving tends to crack them, as it does concrete pools unless they are carefully constructed.

Hardy waterlilies need at least four hours of full sunlight daily, and tropi-

cals at least 6 hours, so if you plan to grow them, select a sunny spot for your pool. Also, locate the pool away from trees, so that leaves or needles don't fall into the water and contaminate it.

A pool does not need to have fresh water running through it all the time, but it is a good idea to install plumbing so you can add water whenever evaporation makes it necessary. Also, since the pool will need cleaning occasionally, a drain and plug will save you the trouble of pumping out the water.

The pool should be from 15 inches to 3 feet deep, depending on what you wish to grow. Aquatic plants are grown in the pool inside containers, each type requiring a different planting depth. Pool builders often create a ledge about 9 inches deep around the perimeter of

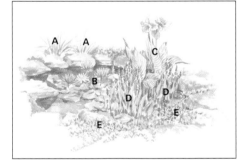

Plant Key

A | Blue flag *(Iris versicolor)*

B | Waterlilies *(Nymphaea)*

C | Cannas *(Canna)*

D | Pickerel weed *(Pontederia cordata)*

E | Creeping Jenny *(Lysimachia nummularia)*

the pool where they can set plants like irises that live in shallow water.

A successful pond will need a pump and filtration system. Get some expert advice and do a little research before you decide to invest either in one of the submersible or external pumps or in a filtration system, since dozens of types are on the market and the size you use is crucial to its effectiveness. Whatever electrical devices you install, for safety's sake you should use a GFCI (ground fault circuit interrupter) to avoid electrocution. The sound of running water adds greatly to the appeal of a pool, so you may want to design a waterfall, fountain, or other attraction, which, with the help of a pump, will provide a pleasant, melodious sound. "Bubblers" and "gushers" will also produce the happy sound of running water with little disturbance to the pool.

You may not need to construct a special pool to grow aquatic plants if you already have a shallow pond or slow-moving stream. (Note that waterlilies cannot survive in fast-moving water.) If you have a naturally wet area, like our friend's, you may be able to scoop out part of it to create a pond. In a soil-bottom pond, you can plant waterlilies directly in the muddy soil at the bottom, provided the water is not more than 2 feet in depth. Most ponds constructed for irrigation, raising fish, or fire protection are much too deep and often too cold for successful waterlily culture.

If you would like to grow water plants but haven't enough space to build a pool, you can create a charming, small, inexpensive water garden in a half-whiskey barrel, old tub, or any other watertight container that you can enjoy on the deck or terrace. Many suppliers sell kits that contain instructions and everything you need to set up such a garden.

Aquatic Plants

The term "aquatic" refers to all plants that live in water. They are usually categorized as follows:

- **Submerged plants,** rooted in soil, with leaves floating on the water surface
- **Oxygenating plants,** rooted in soil with their plant parts submerged
- **Floating plants,** not rooted in soil and floating freely
- **Marginals or bog plants,** growing in wet soil or shallow water

The most showy and colorful water plants are members of the *Nymphaeaceae* family, which includes waterlilies, pond lilies *(Nuphar),* and similar plants. Both hardy and tropical waterlily species are available, and they have been widely hybridized. The hardy types grow year-round in Zones 3 to 11 but die back in winter in the North. You must treat the spectacular tropicals as annuals in Zones 3 to 8 or take them

Aquatic Plants

SUBMERGED PLANTS WITH FLOATING LEAVES

American lotus *(Nelumbo lutea).* Bluish green leaves and yellow flowers. Zones 4–11.

Golden club *(Orontium aquaticum).* Slender yellow spike blooms. Long oval leaves. Grows best in shallow water. Zones 6–11.

Pickerel weed *(Pontederia cordata).* Tall, spiky, deep blue flowers. Plant in 8-inch pots set in no more than 6 inches of water. Zones 5–11.

Sacred lotus *(N. nucifera).* Large, sometimes double pink or white flowers. Many hybrids. Zones 5–11.

Water clover *(Marsilea mutica).* Large leaves resemble a four-leaf clover. Matlike plant that helps fight algae. Zones 9–11.

Waterlilies *(Nymphaea).* Fragrant waterlily *(N. odorata)* has white, waxy blooms. White waterlily *(N. tuberosa)* is a native species with no fragrance. Marliac hybrids have red, pink, yellow, lavender, red, or apricot blooms. Zones 3–8.

FLOATING PLANTS

Duckweeds *(Lemna).* Aquatic stemless floating plants, often used as food for fish. In a stream or pond, can sometimes cover the water with a green scum during the summer; should be used with caution. Zones 4–9.

Water lettuce *(Pistia stratiotes).* A tropical floating plant that needs no pot or soil. Fish lay their eggs in its roots. Zones 7–11.

OXYGENATING PLANTS

Brazilian waterweed *(Egeria densa).* Partly submerged plant with many stems, sometimes up to 3 feet long. White flowers on the surface. Zones 6–11.

Canadian pondweed *(Elodea canadensis).* Green submerged leaves just below surface. White flowers form just above the water surface. Zones 6–11.

Fanwort *(Cabomba caroliniana).* Green submerged leaves, white or purple-pink flowers in summer on surface. Zones 6–11.

Water canna *(Thalia dealbata).* Grows to 6 feet, with large leaves and small violet flowers on tall stalks. Zones 7–11.

Yellow flag *(Iris pseudacorus)*

indoors in winter. The plants range in size from the giant waterlilies *(Victoria)*, with flowers that are 15 inches in diameter, to tiny pygmy cultivars that are only 1½ to 2 inches wide. Of the fifty or so cultivars and species of waterlilies available today, the Marliac hybrids are among the best for home growers.

The fragrant flowers of hardy waterlilies and certain tropical types do not stay open around-the-clock but usually unfurl on a summer day at 8 A.M. and close about ten hours later at 6 P.M.; some of the tropical types, however, are night bloomers. The length of the daily bloom depends on the amount of light and the temperature. One of the fascinating things about these unusual plants is the slow, hour-long unfolding, one by one, of the petals each day. When they close, the same process is repeated in reverse. You may also notice that the color of certain cultivars changes considerably from day to day.

Another spectacular water plant is the heat-loving lotus *(Nelumbo),* which offers both miniatures and full-size plants that grow 2 to 5 feet above the water surface. They provide large, colorful blooms and a delightful scent.

Floating plants that are blown by breezes around the water surface are lovely additions to a pool, and they also provide shade to suppress the growth of algae. Among the best are duckweeds *(Lemna)* and water lettuce *(Pistia stratiotes).* Water lettuce and water spinach *(Ipomoea aquatica)* are prohibited in some states because they are invasive, as is the water hyacinth *(Eichhornia crassipes).* Check with your local Cooperative Extension Service before adding them to your collection.

Submerged oxygenating plants are valuable to any pond because they absorb the carbon dioxide from bacteria and fish and produce oxygen. Experts recommend planting one for every square foot of surface water. The hardy Canadian pondweed *(Elodea canadensis)* is a good example.

Many of the marginal or bog plants that grow in shallow water or in very moist soil are familiar to many of us — cattails *(Typha),* sweet flag *(Acorus calamus),* yellow flag *(Iris pseudacorus),* and others that provide vertical beauty in a water garden.

Putting in the Plants

To keep the water in a lined garden pool somewhat clear, set your plants in containers filled with soil, rather than planting them in soil at the bottom. The size of the container should correspond to plant size. A 10-inch pot is suitable for small pygmy waterlilies, for example, but the huge tropical types need at least a bushel-size tub, and a lotus needs eight gallons of soil.

Place only one plant in each container. Water plants are heavy feeders, so the soil mix should contain somewhat heavy, fertile garden soil. (Commercial potting mix is too light for water gardens.) The soil should be supplemented with a commercial fertilizer, such as 1 cup of high-analysis lawn fertilizer (10-10-10) for each 4 gallons of soil. In addition, slow-release fertilizer tablets, available from water garden suppliers, may be placed in the soil at the base of the container for future use by the plant. See the package directions for the recommended amount.

Winter Care

Hardy water plants will survive even a northern winter as long as their roots remain below ice level. If your pool is likely to freeze almost or completely solid, remove the containers and store them in a cool root cellar or basement until spring. Tropical waterlilies require a completely frost-free environment, so take them inside unless no frost is likely. Never let the stored plants dry out during the winter. Follow the directions that come with any of the water plants that you buy.

Waterlilies grow from rhizomes. Plant them in the container so that the crown is barely exposed. Then cover the top of the soil with pea-sized gravel or coarse sand to keep it from clouding the water. Thoroughly water the pot before you submerge it. Otherwise, it may float back to the surface. For best results, lower the containers carefully so that the rims are 4 to 8 inches under the surface of the water. Adjust the height, if necessary, by placing rocks, bricks, concrete blocks, or plastic crates under the containers. Space them from 4 to 8 feet apart, according to the size of the mature plants. A hardy waterlily needs at least 12 square feet of water surface when mature, and a tropical type or a lotus needs even more. The pygmy

Cardinal flower *(Lobelia cardinalis)*

cultivars take up only about 4 square feet. Foliage over the entire garden should cover no more than 70 percent of the water surface; a good proportion is 50 percent waterlilies and 20 percent other aquatic plants.

Set out hardy water plants in early spring, but wait to put tropical types outside until the water temperature is a minimum of 70°F. Don't be alarmed if leaves stay submerged for the first few days before they float to the surface.

Getting Fishy

Goldfish and koi (carp) are the types of fish most often kept in an ornamental pool. They add beauty and motion and can help balance the pond's ecosystem, but they also add to the maintenance duties since they need feeding regularly and produce a great deal of waste. With the help of the experts from whom you buy the fish, calculate the number per pool carefully, since fish grow rapidly and too many can ruin the ecosystem. We have a friend whose entire pond edge was ruined because, as his fish multiplied, they began to consume the roots of the surrounding bushes and the shore itself fell into the pond.

On the other hand, some underwater scavengers are welcome. Japanese black snails, which you can order from most pool suppliers, devour pond debris and are worthwhile additions. Stock one per square foot of pond surface, unless your pond has more than 100 square feet, in which case, stock one for every two square feet. Don't keep ducks or geese near a pond or pool if you raise water plants, because they will rapidly wreck the plantings.

Water Garden Care

Although a water garden generally requires less care than one planted in soil, it should not be neglected. Remove any unsightly yellow foliage as it appears. If your plants are not thriving, bury

soluble fertilizer tablets around their roots every two weeks. Hardy waterlilies growing in the soil bottom of a shallow pond can be left undisturbed, but you should divide those in containers every two to five years. If the plants become too large, their flowers will become fewer and smaller, but when given proper care they may live for fifty years or more.

Too much algae, besides being unsightly, competes for pond nutrients that the plants should use. There is likely to be an initial algae "bloom" six to eight weeks after you plant, before the ecosystem of the pool becomes balanced, but soon the plants should begin to shade and discourage algae. The oxygenating plants you use help prevent algae growth, and snails also consume it.

To clean debris from the surface of the pond, use a pool skimmer. You may also want a mechanical filter, which removes debris into a catch bag that you need to empty periodically. If debris accumulates on the base of the pool, clean it in the spring.

Like their soil counterparts, aquatic plants can be affected by pests. Waterlily aphids *(Rhopalosiphum nymphaeae)* are the most common insects. You can usually control them by hosing them off into the water or by using one of the organic pesticides recommended by water garden suppliers. Japanese beetles, leaf-eating beetles, and larvae such as cutworms may also feed on the plants, but these can be controlled by pyrethrin. Never use any chlorinated hydrocarbon insecticides as pest control in ponds, especially if you have fish or frogs there. In hot, humid weather, a fungal disease sometimes develops on the leaves of waterlilies if conditions in the pond are crowded. It can be controlled by a careful, limited application of a fungicide, but be careful not to spill any into the water.

Bog Gardens

If you have a damp area that you would like to beautify, you'll discover that the plant life that can grow in such places is unique and endlessly fascinating. If the area is quite swampy, you can sometimes scoop out a portion of it to make a small, year-round pond. If it is dug to a depth of 1½ to 2 feet, with a greater depth in the middle, you will be able to raise the hardy waterlilies as well as plants that grow upright with their roots submerged in water. Use part of the earth moved from the bottom to build small low islands or hummocks where moisture-loving ferns, mosses, pitcher plants, and other bog plants can grow.

Creating a bog in a spot where no heavy amount of moisture exists can be difficult, unless there is adequate rainfall that will drain into the area or you find an underground spring while digging. Bog gardens that receive moisture only from rainfall can suffer badly during droughts, and such spots may become very acidic. Also, there may be a real shortage of nutrients, so it will be necessary to add fertilizer annually. Some bog plants, like the pitcher plant, however, are carnivorous and get their nourishment by capturing insects.

Some plants can become pests in earth-bottom ponds. When ordering, check on their invasiveness and hardiness in your area.

A Wet/Dry Garden

If you own land that fluctuates between being covered with water during prolonged rains and drying out during hot or arid spells, then you have a swale — a landscaping challenge, since most common garden perennials and wildflowers won't tolerate these conditions. The plants listed below, however, can stand considerable moisture as well as dryness for short periods. You will be most successful if you use native plants as much as possible. If you want to convert a boggy area into a wet/dry garden, add rocks or gravel to make the spot less wet during part of the year.

Marginal or Bog Plants

Arrowheads (*Sagittaria*)
Blue flag (*Iris versicolor*)
Cattails (*Typha*)
Common pitcher plant
    (*Sarracenia purpurea*)
Giant reed (*Arundo donax*)
Golden club (*Orontium aquaticum*)
Green arrow arum (*Peltandra virginica*)
Lotus (*Nelumbo lutea*)
Pickerel weed (*Pontederia cordata*)
Pond lilies (*Nuphar*)
Royal fern (*Osmunda regalis*)
Sweet flag (*Acorus calamus*)
Water clovers (*Marsilea*)
Yellow flag (*Iris pseudacorus*)

Pitcher plant (*Sarracenia* 'Judith Hindle')

Plants for a Wet/Dry Garden

Bee balm (*Monarda didyma*)
Blue lobelia (*Lobelia siphilitica*)
Boltonia (*Boltonia asteroides*)
Boneset (*Eupatorium perfoliatum*)
Bottle gentian (*Gentiana andrewsii*)
Cardinal flower (*Lobelia cardinalis*)
Cattail (*Typha latifolia*)
Cinnamon fern (*Osmunda cinnamomea*)
Common rose mallow
    (*Hibiscus moscheutos*)
Culver's root (*Veronicastrum virginicum*)
Duck potato (*Sagittaria latifolia*)
Forget-me-nots (*Myosotis*)
Hostas (*Hosta*)
Joe-Pye weeds (*Eupatorium purpureum*
    and *E. maculatum*)
Lance-leaved goldenrod
    (*Solidago graminifolia*)
Marsh marigold (*Caltha palustris*)

Meadow beauty (*Rhexia virginica*)
Meadow phlox (*Phlox maculata*)
New England aster
    (*Aster novae-angliae*)
Pickerel weed (*Pontederia cordata*)
Ragged robin (*Lychnis flos-cuculi*)
Royal fern (*Osmunda regalis*)
Sensitive fern (*Onoclea sensibilis*)
Siberian iris (*Iris sibirica*)
Swamp buttercup
    (*Ranunculus septentrionalis*)
Swamp candle
    (*Lysimachia terrestris*)
Swamp milkweed
    (*Asclepias incarnata*)
Virginia bluebells
    (*Mertensia pulmonarioides*)
Zebra grass
    (*Miscanthus sinensis* 'Strictus')

English lavender (Lavandula angustifolia)

The Multifaceted Herb Garden

THE FIRST YEAR WE HAD AN HERB GARDEN it was a great success. Each little plant flourished and, by fall, had filled the spot we had allotted to it. By the middle of the next summer, however, it was clear that we had a problem. The spearmint (Mentha spicata), sweet woodruff (Galium odoratum), and thymes were running wild and crowding out more restrained plants like rosemary (Rosmarinus officinalis) and common sage (Salvia officinalis). The garden had to be completely revamped. We learned the hard way that when certain invasive herbs are happy with their bed and board, you must severely discipline them and keep them in their place, or some of your choice herbs will disappear in a mass of green.

But herb gardens can be attractive indefinitely. Thanks to their varied growth habits and foliage, it's possible to use herbs to design an aesthetically pleasing garden, though most gardeners usually grow them more for culinary, medicinal, or aromatic purposes than for their beauty. People who enjoy cooking grow the herbs used for flavoring and savoring, such as sweet basil (Ocimum basilicum) for pesto, French tarragon (Artemisia dracunculus) for

butter or vinegar, and mints (Mentha) for tea. Others concentrate on plants for medicinal tonics and salves. Still others specialize in fragrant herbs. We have a friend who, each summer, fills a large potpourri jar with dried lavender and other aromatics and later makes gift sachets for her friends.

A culinary herb garden wouldn't be complete without the annual herbs we all enjoy. Sow directly in the garden, or, for an earlier harvest, start seedlings indoors or purchase plants. Note that parsley, a biennial, and several favorite tender perennial herbs, such as bay laurel (Laurus nobilis), sweet marjoram (Origanum majorana), garlic, and rosemary, are usually treated as annuals in the North.

Learning about the lore, history, and uses of herbs adds immensely to the fun of cultivating them. If you have an older home, for example, you might want to research the plants in common use when it was built and feature them in a border. Or you might design a bed using herbs mentioned in the Bible. We enjoyed visiting Caprilands in Coventry, Connecticut, a mecca for

herb lovers, where gardens feature such historical themes as the medieval and colonial periods, and visitors may also find a bride's garden, a saints' garden, a Shakespeare garden, plots with only silver- or gold-colored plants, a bed filled completely with fragrant geraniums, and a cutting garden for dried bouquets and wreaths.

Designing and Planting Your Herb Garden

Herbs are so versatile that most are at home almost anywhere in the landscape—along pathways, on terraces, as groundcovers, in rock gardens, in vegetable beds, in flower borders, and in containers. For many gardeners, however, herbs give the most pleasure when planted in a well-designed bed all their own. It may be as informal as a tiny plot outside a country cottage or as formal and elaborate as the classic medieval gardens formed into knots, wheels, butterflies, stained-glass windows, or other geometric designs. In a sunny corner outside a kitchen door, you might plant a small salad garden of culinary perennial and annual herbs, along with a few radishes, cherry tomatoes, lettuce, and scallions. An open hillside might lend itself to a series of small, circular, terraced plots, each with a different type of herb.

The ideal site for most herbs is in the sun, although a few, such as the mints, watercress (*Nasturtium officinale*), and lemon balm (*Melissa officinalis*), also grow well in light shade. Some thrive in almost any type of soil, but most prefer it to be well drained, with a pH that is from neutral to slightly alkaline. In a small, informal bed, you don't need to plan much more than the arrangement and proper spacing for the plants you have chosen. Consider the ultimate size of each plant, and arrange the bed so the small species, such as parsley

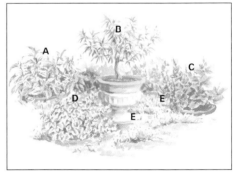

Plant Key

A | Peppermint *(Mentha × piperita)*

B | Lemon verbena *(Aloysia triphylla)*

C | Spearmint *(Mentha spicata)*

D | Pineapple mint *(Mentha suaveolens* 'Variegata'*)*

E | Roman chamomile *(Chamaemelum nobile)*

(*Petroselinum crispum*) and the thymes, are not crowded by lovage (*Levisticum officinale*), comfrey (*Symphytum officinale*), or other tall growers.

If you choose to make a large, more ornamental bed, plan it first on graph paper. To attain symmetry and balance, arrange the different species in a way that is orderly, with colors and sizes that balance each other. Edgings are essential to confine the plants, and pathways, which are integral to the design of a large, geometric-type garden, should be in place before planting begins. Paths of pebbles, brick, flagstone, or mown grass form the skeleton of a formal herb bed. The paths should be wide enough that you can move about and work in each area. If you use sundials, birdbaths, or statuary, install them, too, before setting in the plants.

Garlic chives (*Allium tuberosum*)

It is fun to arrange the many different forms and colors of herb foliage in interesting patterns. You can surround gray-leaved wormwoods (*Artemisia*) or pale lavenders with purple basil, for instance, or set some curly parsley around clumps of erect chives (*Allium schoenoprasum*). Blooming times are not especially important, because most herb flowers are rather inconspicuous. Compact, low-growing plants, such as chives and parsley, are useful to separate various groupings and for edging paths, and you may want to reserve spots for some low-growing, flowering annuals, like nasturtiums (*Tropaeolum majus*), marigolds, or sweet alyssum (*Lobularia maritima*), to add color.

We grow our annual herbs and a few of the perennial kinds from seed each spring. We buy most of the perennials, though, because different strains of French tarragon, lavender, oregano, mints, and others vary a great deal in flavor. When you buy herbs, taste or smell each plant before choosing it for your garden. Lemon verbena (*Aloysia triphylla*), rosemary, and most other tender herbs start easily from cuttings or layers if you want to expand your plantings. Most perennial herbs, once established, are hardy and will live for years, but in northern zones, pot up tender herbs in fall and grow them as houseplants during the winter.

Prepare the soil as you would for any flower or vegetable garden, mixing in manure or compost. Most herbs, except for annuals, don't need as much fertilizer as other plants, however, and overfeeding will encourage rapid spreading. Smooth the surface and, with your design in hand, outline the spaces for each herb with white flour or lime. Whether your garden is formal or informal, keep any invasive species under control by planting each one in a separate soil "pocket." These might be large, bottomless, plastic pots or clay tiles, such as chimney liners, sunk into the garden. After planting, spread a mulch around each plant to help prevent erosion and to keep the plants clean. It is annoying to find herbs that you intend to use in a salad or potpourri spattered with dirt from the latest rainstorm.

Favorite Herbs

PERENNIAL HERBS

Bay laurel (*Laurus nobilis*). Slow-growing, sun-loving, evergreen shrub with aromatic leaves frequently used to flavor soups and stews. It is a tender perennial; bring indoors in winter in cold climates. Difficult to propagate. To 10 feet in warm climates. Zones 8–10.

Chamomile, Roman (*Chamaemelum nobile*). Tea made from the blossoms is a soothing tranquilizer or tonic. Grows easily from seed or divisions. To 10 inches, with a spreading growth habit. Zones 6–9.

Chives (*Allium schoenoprasum*). Small onionlike plants useful in salads, soups, and egg dishes. White-flowering garlic chives (*Allium tuberosum*) are especially attractive for a flower garden. Easily grown from plants or seeds. 2 feet. Zones 2–9.

Costmary (*Tanacetum balsamita*). Fragrant, mint-flavored leaves were pressed and used as bookmarks in Bibles during colonial days. Useful as a garnish, in tea, and for potpourri. Propagate by root division. Likes a sunny spot and ordinary garden soil. 2–3 feet. Zones 3–8.

Garden sage (*Salvia officinalis*). White, woolly leaves. Different varieties have different-colored flowers. Propagate by division, cuttings, or seeds. Zones 3–8.

Horehound (*Marrubium vulgare*). Dried or fresh leaves used for candy, cough syrup, and tea. Grown from seed, cuttings, or division. Needs full sun and dry, sandy soil. 1–2 feet. Zones 3–8.

Hyssop (*Hyssopus officinalis*). An ancient, hardy herb used as a purifying tea and for medicine; said to cure ailments from head lice to shortness of breath. Started by seed or division. Prefers full sun and well-drained, alkaline soil. To 3 feet. Zones 6–9.

Lemon balm (*Melissa officinalis*). Lemon-scented leaves, either dried or fresh, used for tea, jelly, or flavoring.

Common rue *(Ruta graveolens)*

Attracts bees. Start from cuttings or division. Plant in sun or light shade and well-drained soil. 1–3 feet. Zones 3–7.

Lemon verbena *(Aloysia triphylla)*. Tender, aromatic perennial that cannot stand frost; bring indoors in winter in northern climates. May lose its leaves in the fall, but they promptly return. May be used for culinary purposes but most often enjoyed for its fragrance. To 10 inches. Zones 8–11.

Lovage *(Levisticum officinale)*. Celery-flavored leaves and stalks used in soups and salads. Grows well from seed. Grows best in partial shade and moist, fertile soil. 4–6 feet. Zones 3–8.

Mints *(Mentha)*. Peppermint *(M. × piperita)* and spearmint *(M. spicata)* are the most popular, but apple mint *(M. suaveolens)*, lemon mint *(M. × piperita* f. *citrata)*, and others are also widely grown. Used medicinally as well as in teas, jelly, and salads and as flavoring for candy and ice cream. You can grow some mints from seed, but you are better off buying small plants to be sure you get the scent and flavor you want. To 3 feet. Zones 2–7.

Oregano *(Origanum vulgare)*. A perennial, sometimes known as wild marjoram, used in soups, salads, meat

dishes, and pizza, especially in Italian and Mexican cuisines. *O. vulgare* is easily grown from seed, cuttings, or division. Because there are many species, taste the plants before you buy. Grows in full sun and ordinary garden soil. 1 foot. Zones 5–9.

Rosemary *(Rosmarinus officinalis)*. Used as both an aromatic and a flavoring herb, in sauces, soups, teas, and especially as flavoring for lamb. Tender in the North, so must spend the winter indoors; can be grown as a bonsai. Thrives with moisture, but needs well-drained, alkaline soil. Start from seed, cuttings, or layers. To 6 feet in warm climates, but much shorter elsewhere. Zones 8–10.

Rue *(Ruta graveolens)*. A bitter medicinal herb used for thousands of years as an antidote to all kinds of poisons. Often worn as a potion to ward off fevers and fleas; used as a disinfectant as well. Easily grown from seed, but ancient Greeks believed that if you stole it from a neighbor's garden, it had more power. Plant in alkaline soil, in sun or partial shade. 2–3 feet. Zones 5–9.

Sweet cicely *(Myrrhis odorata)*. Anise-flavored leaves used in soups and salads. Propagated by seed, but not easily; grows in rich soil in a shady spot. 2–3 feet. Zones 3–7.

Sweet woodruff *(Galium odoratum)*. Fragrant herb sometimes used to flavor May wine or soda. Makes a ground-covering carpet. Likes shade and slightly acidic soil. 8 inches. Zones 4–8.

Thymes *(Thymus)*. A mainstay of many gardens, often as a groundcover or rock garden plant or between stones on terraces or in paths. Most species and cultivars have ornamental, culinary, and aromatic qualities. Easily grown from divisions, seeds, or cuttings. To 1 foot. Species vary in hardiness; most grow in Zones 3–8.

Lemon thyme *(Thymus × citriodorus* 'Doone Valley')

ANNUAL HERBS

Anise *(Pimpinella anisum)*. A culinary and medicinal herb used for thousands of years. Leaves are used to flavor food, the flowers in certain alcoholic beverages, and the seeds in perfumes and soaps. 2 feet.

Basil *(Ocimum basilicum)*. Comes in different colors and flavors, with white or purple flowers. The ornamental leaves go well with tomatoes, particularly in pesto. Pinch the top when it is growing to make it branch and produce more leaves. 1–2 feet.

Borage *(Borago officinalis)*. Attractive blue, purple, or white flowers. Both flowers and leaves are used as flavorings. 3 feet.

Chamomile, German *(Matricaria recutita)*. Medicinal qualities similar to those of the perennial Roman chamomile; taller than the Roman herb. To 30 inches.

Dill *(Anethum graveolens)*. Both the feathery leaves and the seeds of this tall herb are used as flavorings. 2–4 feet, depending on variety.

Parsley, curly *(Petroselinum crispum)* and Italian *(P. crispum* var. *neapolitanum)*. Biennials usually treated as annuals. Used as a garnish and in salads, soups, and many other dishes. Grown easily from seed, but slow to germinate. Prefer full sun or light shade and moist, rich soil. 1 foot.

Summer savory *(Satureja hortensis)*. Bushy stems and fragrant pink or purplish flowers. Leaves are used for flavoring food, particularly lentils, limas, and other beans. 18 inches.

St. John's wort
(Hypericum cerastioides)

Outdoor Gardening in Containers

IF YOUR GARDENING PLOT is a paved courtyard, balcony, patio, or deck or on the roof of a high-rise apartment building, containers are your saving grace. Even if you have plenty of bare earth around your home, it can be fun to brighten up the exterior with window boxes and a collection of potted plants.

At our small nursery, we have grown and sold plants in containers for many years, so we have become very familiar with this type of gardening. We've found that plants in pots and planters are like pets, needing almost daily watering and careful feeding, as well as more protection than those growing in the ground. But there are many advantages, too, and as gardeners have come to appreciate them, container gardens increase in popularity every year.

One of the most obvious advantages of using containers instead of planting directly in the ground is that unless the planters or pots are permanently installed, they are portable gardens. You can rearrange the display to show blossoms at their best and even create continuous bloom throughout the season, just as public gardens do, by growing your plants in an out-of-the-way spot

Alpine aster *(Aster alpinus)*

and then moving them into the garden area as they bloom. By rotating the pots, it is possible to enjoy bulbs like daffodils, hyacinths, and tulips in spring, followed by a multitude of summer bloomers, both annual and perennial. And in fall, you can enjoy asters, cannas, chrysanthemums, Japanese anemones *(Anemone × hybrida),* and stonecrops *(Sedum).* You can also move the plants, if necessary, to spots with more or less favorable sunlight conditions during the year or to a place that is sheltered from torrential rains or damaging windstorms.

Growing Oriental lilies in the garden can be tricky because they need perfect drainage, which is difficult to get without building a high raised bed, but containers make it easy to grow these spectacular flowers. Even in close quarters, it is easy to have a wide variety of plants that prefer different conditions. You can regulate the moisture, soil fertility, and acidity to suit each individual plant, whereas in a garden bed it would be difficult to grow, for example, acid-loving hollies *(Ilex)* next to an alkaline-loving clematis vine.

Also, because the foliage of container-grown plants covers most of the soil surface, soil-borne diseases and insects are not as easily spread. Weeds are less likely to be a problem in pots if you use sterile soil, and invasive plants, such as bee balms *(Monarda didyma)* and mints *(Mentha),* are easily controlled. Except for watering, most plants in containers require less care than those in a bed, and they can be set at any level, making this type of gardening ideal for people who have trouble stooping or bending.

Houseplants may come first to mind when you think of container growing, but it is possible to grow almost any plant in a container, including perennials, herbs, spring bulbs, ferns, annuals, shrubs, and even good-sized trees and vines. Rock-garden plants grow well in the sides of strawberry pots. Tender plants, such as bay laurel *(Laurus nobilis),* camellias, Chinese hibiscus *(Hibiscus rosa-sinensis),* and Norfolk Island pine *(Araucaria heterophylla),* can spend the summer outside and the winter in a sunroom or cool greenhouse. Where climates are milder, of course, plants can survive outdoors year-round in tubs and ornamental urns.

The Perfect Pot

Only your imagination limits what can serve as a container. We have grown plants in hollow stumps, iron kettles, the center of an old gristmill stone, and a concrete tub originally used for watering cattle, as well as in window boxes and clay, wood, and plastic hanging pots. Old whiskey barrels, cut-off hot

WHIMSICAL TOUCHES. Group plant containers with other favorite garden objects.

Plant Key

A | Yellow daisy *(Anthemis tinctoria)*

B | Mealycup sage *(Salvia farinacea)*

C | Blue oat grass *(Helictotrichon sempervirens)*

D | Edging lobelia *(Lobelia erinus)*

E | Sweet alyssum *(Lobularia maritima)*

F | Lavenders *(Lavandula)*

G | Petunias *(Petunia)*

water tanks, stone urns, and planters of wood fiber, concrete, brick, ceramic, stone, clay, fiberglass, metal, or glass offer equally appropriate possibilities.

Plastic pots, although often not as beautiful as clay, wood, or stone, have real advantages. They are easy to clean, and the soil in them does not dry out as fast as in clay pots. They take less space in storage, plus they are lightweight, which becomes an asset when you need to rearrange the terrace furniture, turn the pots so plants don't lean toward the light, or move them into a greenhouse or root cellar for the winter. They are available in an array of colors and sizes. Some look very natural; you can fit less attractive ones inside baskets or other more decorative containers.

Choose containers that are large enough to allow your plants to grow comfortably for at least one year. After that, you can repot in bigger containers, if necessary. Many perennials and dwarf shrubs have large root systems, so a 10-inch pot is the minimum for all except the tiniest kinds. Be certain that the planter you use has large drainage holes, so the soil won't become waterlogged during a heavy rain.

BRIGHT SPOTS. Use container plantings to bring color to an area.

Give Your Plants a Good Home

Since the amount of soil in a container is limited and the roots cannot search further for nutrients, the soil must be of particularly good quality. Not only is commercial potting mixture more convenient than garden soil, but if you buy it sterilized, it is free from diseases, insects, and weed seeds. Soilless mixes of peat and perlite or vermiculite are also good choices and weigh less than garden soil. Try to use a growing medium that comes in a sealed plastic bag, rather than from an unsterilized, open pile at the garden center. Left in the open, the mixture is likely to pick up weed seeds and disease spores.

If you need a great deal of potting mixture, you can make your own by mixing one-third part each (by volume) of peat moss or compost, rich loamy soil, and either perlite, sand, or vermiculite. Whether you make your own mixture or buy it, dump it into a clean wheelbarrow or other large container. Then, blend in 4 quarts of dried manure and 2 quarts of bonemeal, plus a complete, organic, slow-release fertilizer, following package directions. Mix thoroughly. Add lime only if needed by the plants you intend to grow. If you use a commercial potting mix and the pH is not listed on the label, you can check its acidity level with a soil test kit, as described in Chapter 3.

Before potting your plants, place a thin layer of coarse gravel, pebbles, or broken clay pot fragments at the bottom of each container so the potting mixture won't plug the drainage holes. Put enough potting mix into the container that you can position the rootball of the plant at its original depth and the surface is within an inch of the top to allow room for watering. Firm the potting mixture, leaving no air to dry out the roots, and then add a thin layer of mulch. Water thoroughly. To save the back-breaking job of moving a large pot filled with potting mixture and plant, position the pot where you plan to keep it, and do the filling and planting job on the spot.

WALL FLOWERS. Even blank walls can be brightened with touches of color.

Ongoing Care

Water is crucial to the health of container plants, and daily watering is likely to be necessary. Whether you use a watering can or hose, do not pour water haphazardly over the plants. Since the foliage may act as an umbrella, most of the water may never reach the potting mixture. Instead, place the water directly on the mix. A light rain may be diverted in the same way, so don't depend on rain for moisture. If you water with a hose, use low pressure so the force of the stream will not damage the plant or wash out the soil. An automatic watering system can eliminate this chore, but you may not want to clutter the area with an array of hoses and feeder tubs. If you decide to set one up, however, you can partially conceal the equipment.

Since frequent watering is likely to leach away nutrients rapidly, add small amounts of dry or liquid fertilizer every three or four weeks, in addition to the slow-release fertilizer you applied when you planted. Lime may also be depleted quickly in containers, leaving the potting mixture too acidic to permit the nutrients to be absorbed by the plants; if you have container plants that are not flourishing, test the pH of the potting mixture and add lime if necessary. Also, depending on their location, you may need to turn the pots weekly so the plants do not grow one-sided as they lean toward the light.

Wintering Over Perennial Container Plants

In cold climates, perennials and shrubs from warmer zones need to be taken indoors before frosts begin and wintered in a warm greenhouse, frost-free basement, or garage. Container-grown winter-hardy perennials, on the other hand, can stay safely outdoors with no protection as long as they are not permitted to dry out. Where there is little or no snow cover, however, the soil is likely to freeze solid in the pots, which can desiccate plant roots. Even hardy plants cannot survive this treatment, and those on a paved terrace or deck or in an elevated planter, where they can't draw moisture from the ground, are particularly vulnerable.

Marigolds *(Tagetes)*

One way to protect plants in movable pots is to store them in a *cool* greenhouse or deep cold frame for the winter. Temperate plants need a dormant period, so don't try to overwinter them in a warm greenhouse. You can also pack the pots close together in a sheltered place on the ground outside, so they can absorb heat and moisture from the soil. After a few hard frosts, cover pots with evergreen boughs or a foam insulating blanket available from garden supply stores.

If you have only a few pots and a convenient place, burying them for the winter also gives good protection. Each fall we sink several pots of perennials and herbs into our vegetable garden after they have spent the summer on our backyard deck. In the spring, it's important to tip the pots on their sides so water won't collect in them during thaws and drown the plants when the drainage holes are still frozen.

It probably will be necessary to repot many container-grown plants each spring and, if clumps are large, divide them at the same time so they will not become rootbound. Use new potting mix, compost, and additional slow-release fertilizer as you repot.

Geraniums for the Winter Windowsill

Boisterously colorful geraniums *(Pelargonium)* do beautifully wintered indoors on a windowsill, if you have a good southern exposure. Pinch them occasionally, so they don't become leggy, and turn them once a week to encourage them to grow evenly; apply a liquid fertilizer each month.

You can also winter them over in a frost-free basement or garage. Cut them back to 5 inches, so they won't drop leaves all over the area. Don't let them dry out, but keep the soil only slightly moist or they will rot.

Container Favorites (Mix and Match as You Like)

Million bells (*Calibrachoa* 'Terra Cotta') and petunias

Choosing Plants

When selecting plants for your containers, consider where you would like to place them and estimate the amount of available sunlight. Consider, too, the size of the plant so that it will be in proportion to the container size. Choose plants that appeal to you, combining colors, forms, and foliage textures in interesting ways. The mobility of containers makes this easy. If there is space, you might use a few evergreen shrubs, ornamental grasses, and other foliage plants to set off your blooming annuals and perennials. Combine small plants such as coral bells (*Heuchera*), primroses, and 'Stella de Oro' daylily (*Hemerocallis*) with annuals and geraniums for a long season of bloom. On elevated surfaces, include plants that droop over the edge of the containers, such as trailing nasturtiums (*Tropaeolum majus*), edging lobelia (*Lobelia erinus*), and 'Cascade' petunias. Don't hesitate to try new and unusual plants. Most plants will thrive in containers as long as they have enough good potting mix, adequate water, and the light they need.

For a list of plants that bloom over a long season, see pages 32–33.

ANNUALS

Cosmos (*Cosmos*)
Edging lobelia (*Lobelia erinus*)
Marigolds (*Tagetes*)
Nasturtium (*Tropaeolum majus*)
Petunias (*Petunia*)
Sages (*Salvia*)
Sweet alyssum (*Lobularia maritima*)
Zinnias (*Zinnia*)
Also, many herbs

ORNAMENTAL GRASSES

Blue oat grass (*Helictrichon sempervirens*)
Japanese blood grass (*Imperata cylindrica*)
'Karl Foerster' feather reed grass
    (*Calamagrostis* × *acutiflora*
    'Karl Foerster')

SHRUBS

Cotoneasters (*Cotoneaster*)
Daphnes (*Daphne*)
Heather (*Calluna vulgaris*)
Heaths (*Erica*)
Hollies (*Ilex*)
Hypericums (*Hypericum*)
Lavenders (*Lavandula*)
Pieris (*Pieris*)
Roses (*Rosa*)
Spireas (*Spiraea*)
Viburnums (*Viburnum*)
Weigelas (*Weigela*)

EARLY-FLOWERING PERENNIALS

Columbines (*Aquilegia*)
Daffodils (*Narcissus*) and other
    spring bulbs
Fringed bleeding heart (*Dicentra eximia*)
Leopard's banes (*Doronicum*)
Mountain bluet (*Centaurea montana*)
Pansies and violets (*Viola*)
Primroses (*Primula*)

SUMMER-FLOWERING PERENNIALS

Baby's breaths (*Gypsophila*)
Beardtongues (*Penstemon*)
Bee balms (*Monarda*)
Blanket flowers (*Gaillardia*)
Coral bells (*Heuchera*)
Cranesbills (*Geranium*)
Daylilies (*Hemerocallis*)
Evening primroses (*Oenothera*)
Gayfeathers (*Liatris*)
Lilies (*Lilium*)
Monkshoods (*Aconitum*)
Orange coneflowers (*Rudbeckia*)
Painted daisy (*Tanacetum coccineum*)
Phlox (*Phlox*)
Pinks (*Dianthus*)
Shasta daisy (*Leucanthemum* × *superbum*)
Torch lilies (*Kniphofia*)
Yarrows (*Achillea*)
Yellow daisy (*Anthemis tinctoria*)

FALL-FLOWERING PERENNIALS

Asters (*Aster*)
Autumn monkshood
    (*Aconitum autumnale*)
Chrysanthemums (*Chrysanthemum*)
Japanese anemone (*Anemone* × *hybrida*)

Nasturtium (*Tropaeolum majus* 'Alaska')

Yellow daylilies *(Hemerocallis),* purple phlox *(Phlox paniculata),* and white-flowering tobaccos *(Nicotiana)*

A Deckside Garden

Rose-scented geranium *(Pelargonium capitatum)*

ONE OF THE BEST HOME IMPROVEMENTS we have made recently was to build a small deck on the back of our old country home, overlooking our garden. In the spring, while the grass is still wet and the garden soil mushy, we eat lunch there in the sun, enjoying the hundreds of daffodils waving in the breeze. In summer and fall, we relish the ever-changing blooms in the perennial bed. It is one of the few places where we actually stop and relax, and where our elderly friends can safely enjoy viewing the flowers.

The deck would appear sterile and lifeless, though, without the surrounding plantings both in the ground and in containers around it. Some years, we plant cascading purple petunias in the containers, and other years, pink or fuchsia-colored geraniums *(Pelargonium)*. Our Chinese hibiscus *(Hibiscus rosa-sinensis)* tree and other houseplants occasionally spend the summer out there, too. Some decks have built-in tubs and "window box" planters, which the owners fill with new plants each season.

We wanted a small, nice-looking flower bed surrounding our deck, so we planted a narrow border of hybrid daylilies *(Hemerocallis)*. They fulfill all of our qualifications: easy care, attractive foliage that hides the short deck supports throughout the season, and beautiful blooms over several weeks at the height of the summer. We can mow easily beneath their drooping foliage, so no trimming is necessary. We know gardeners with a shady deck who use hostas with a variety of different foliage colors in the same way.

An in-ground flower bed around the deck provides color and life. Since the deck is a transition spot from indoors to outdoors, the eye moves from any flowering plants on the deck to compatible ones surrounding it. Likewise,

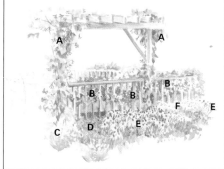

Plant Key

A | Honeysuckles *(Lonicera)*

B | Petunias *(Petunia)*

C | Evening primroses *(Oenothera)*

D | Bachelor's buttons *(Centaurea cyanus)*

E | Golden glow *(Rudbeckia laciniata)*

F | Shasta daisy *(Leucanthemum × superbum)*

as you approach from outdoors, the adjacent plantings should connect, rather than clash, with those on the deck. One year we were startled to find that our bright red daylilies, when they began to bloom, fairly screamed at the fuchsia geraniums in tubs on the deck.

A mixed bed of annuals and perennials can make a head-turning vista. On a nearby rural dirt road we enjoy the charm of an old farmhouse painted yellow and with an attractive deck surrounded by blue and golden perennials and annuals blooming throughout the season — bachelor's buttons *(Centaurea cyanus)*, blue delphiniums, evening primroses *(Oenothera)*, yellow daisies *(Anthemis tinctoria)*, and golden glow *(Rudbeckia laciniata* var. *hortensia)*.

When planning a deckside garden, take into account the deck's size and height and the colors of both your deck and your home, so the plantings will be in the right proportion and the shades of the flowers will not clash with those of the building. Around a deck that is only 2 to 4 feet from the ground, low-growing shrubbery is ideal. If the deck is higher, you might use taller shrubs to soften any visible supports, latticework, or empty space beneath the deck flooring. If it is far above the ground, then tall evergreen or deciduous shrubs make good concealers. Vines such as clematis, wisterias, honeysuckles *(Lonicera)*, and climbing roses also work well. If you prefer herbaceous plants, astilbes, delphiniums, globe thistles *(Echinops)*,

Goldflame honeysuckle *(Lonicera × heckrottii)*

Adam's needle *(Yucca filamentosa)*

hollyhocks *(Alcea rosea),* Culver's root *(Veronicastrum virginicum),* sunflowers *(Helianthus),* and yuccas are good landscaping possibilities.

If you want privacy or shade, however, tall shrubs or trees planted near the deck may be the answer. We appreciate the shade from afternoon summer sun provided by a nearby maple tree on the southwestern corner of our deck. Another solution would be to build a pergola over part of the deck and let vines grow over it. Many vines, both flowering and evergreen, are available and can provide either light or heavy shade. Avoid planting overly vigorous types such as Virginia creeper *(Parthenocissus quinquefolia)* and hops *(Humulus lupulus),* however, or you may spend most of the summer trying to control them. Fragrant flowering vines are beautiful, and grapes *(Vitis)* or kiwi *(Actinidia)* hanging from above can make you feel like you are lounging in an Italian trattoria. If the deck is high above the ground, you might plant such shade-giving vines in large tubs on the deck floor.

Most landscapes are properly contoured when a deck is built, but if you find that the earth slopes even slightly toward the deck instead of away from it, correct the angle before you till the

new flower bed, so no water will run toward the house foundation. Also, leave enough room between the bed and the deck that you can walk there easily. When we were painting our deck brown last summer, we found we had barely enough space to set the paint bucket, and some of the foliage became brown before its time. If there is a concrete foundation in the vicinity of the flowers and shrubs, keep the plantings apart from it, since concrete attracts heat and you may find plants near it wilting from heat exhaustion.

Planting on the deck itself is similar to decorating a terrace or patio. We have neighbors who didn't want a railing around their high deck, so they surrounded its perimeter with tubs and planters to keep their guests from wandering over the edge. They fill the containers with plants that bloom over a long season — geraniums, petunias, impatiens, and other annuals — as well as plants that flow over the deck's edge, such as vinca vine *(Vinca major* 'Variegata'), ivies *(Hedera),* and edging lobelia *(Lobelia erinus).* For a deck that is partly covered, hanging baskets filled with 'Cascade' petunias, trailing nasturtiums, or other vining plants can add a nice, decorative touch. Potted compact shrubs, such as dwarf evergreens, are

Japanese wisteria *(Wisteria floribunda)*

especially attractive in early spring and late fall when color is scarce.

The nice thing about landscaping on a deck is that you can change the plants every year, and even every season if you are so inclined. It is a perfect spot for displaying corn stalks and pumpkins in the autumn and decorating evergreens with red ribbons at Christmastime, while your deckside flower garden is fast asleep.

Fritillary on butterfly weed *(Asclepias tuberosa)*

Tiger swallowtail on Brazilian vervain
(Verbena bonariensis)

A Bed for Butterflies

MOST OF US CULTIVATE OUR FLOWER BEDS without concern for butterflies and are delighted with whatever beautiful *Lepidoptera* drop by. Long ago, however, we visited a garden planted specifically to attract them at the Bok Tower Gardens at Iron Mountain, Florida, and we have never forgotten the sight of thousands of beautiful butterflies feeding in the same small area. People who have seen the monarchs congregate in their Central American wintering grounds report a similar sense of awe.

Tickseed *(Coreopsis* 'Limerock Ruby'*)*

The metamorphosis of a butterfly from egg to caterpillar to chrysalis to, finally, a butterfly with wings is the stuff poetry is made of. A garden designed to attract butterflies should provide food for the feeding stages of these transformations — leaves for the caterpillar and nectar for the winged butterfly. See our suggestions on the facing page for which plants are the best choices for specific butterflies at their caterpillar and butterfly stages.

Caterpillars can be very picky eaters, and some kinds feed on only one type of plant. These larvae particularly favor native "weedy" plants such as milkweeds *(Asclepias),* upon which mon-archs choose to lay their eggs. Queen Anne's lace *(Daucus carota* var. *carota)* is preferred by swallowtail caterpillars, and painted lady larvae haunt thistles *(Cirsium).* These plants would probably not be welcome in a cultivated garden, so you could consider growing them in a separate area or situating your garden near a meadow or other natural area.

Adult butterflies feed on the nectar of flowers and are attracted to gardens with masses of brightly colored blooms. If you want to attract different types of butterflies, grow a diversity of plants (see our list). The old-fashioned species have more nectar than modern hybrids, and butterflies like nectar that is easily accessible to their long tongues. A flowering hedge of butterfly bushes *(Buddleia)* or a wall covered with honeysuckles *(Lonicera)* will provide food and shelter at the different levels that various species prefer.

Butterflies need moisture, and your butterfly garden should include shallow water where they can drink but not drown, such as a mud puddle. To create "puddling" spots, place shallow containers filled with moist sand in several

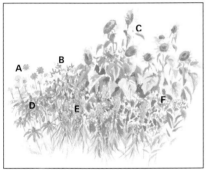

Plant Key

A | Globe thistle *(Echinops)*
B | Black-eyed Susan *(Rudbeckia fulgida)*
C | Sunflowers *(Helianthus)*
D | Purple coneflower *(Echinacea purpurea)*
E | Gayfeathers *(Liatris)*
F | Butterfly weed *(Asclepias tuberosa)*

Butterfly Plants

TO ATTRACT ADULTS

Asters *(Aster)*: especially buckeyes, clouded sulphurs, pearl crescents, and spring azurs

Bee balms *(Monarda)*

Black-eyed Susans *(Rudbeckia)*: especially pearl crescents

Butterfly bushes *(Buddleia)*: especially tiger swallowtails

Butterfly weed *(Asclepias tuberosa)*: especially black swallowtails, checkered whites, spring azurs, and tiger swallowtails

Cosmos *(Cosmos)*: especially monarchs

Flowering tobaccos *(Nicotiana)*

Foxgloves *(Digitalis)*

Gayfeathers *(Liatris)*

Globe centaurea *(Centaurea macrocephala)*

Globe thistles *(Echinops)*: especially black swallowtails, gulf fritillaries, and pearl crescents

Honeysuckles *(Lonicera)*: especially tiger swallowtails

Impatiens *(Impatiens)*: especially gulf fritillaries

Lantanas *(Lantana)*: especially gulf fritillaries

Lilacs *(Syringa)*: especially monarchs and tiger swallowtails

Lilies *(Lilium)*

Lupines *(Lupinus)*

Milkweeds *(Asclepias)*: especially monarchs

Mistflower *(Eupatorium coelestinum)*

Orange coneflowers *(Rudbeckia)*

Phlox *(Phlox)*

Pinks *(Dianthus)*

Purple coneflower *(Echinacea purpurea)*

Sunflowers *(Helianthus)*

Sweet alyssum *(Lobularia maritima)*

Sweet rocket *(Hesperis matronalis)*

Tickseeds *(Coreopsis)*: especially buckeyes

TO ATTRACT LARVAE

Asters *(Aster)*: especially pearl crescents

Bermuda grass *(Cynodon dactylon)*

Clovers *(Trifolium)*: especially clouded sulphurs

Lupines *(Lupinus)*

Mallows *(Malva)*

Milkweeds *(Asclepias)*: especially monarchs

Parsley *(Petroselinum crispum)*

Plantains *(Plantago)*

St. Augustine grass *(Stenotaphrum secundatum)*

Snapdragons *(Antirrhinum)*: especially buckeyes

Viburnums *(Viburnum)*: especially spring azurs

spots in the garden, and remember to keep them filled with water. Butterflies also need minerals and enjoy rotting bananas and other fruit and, if you can find it, animal scat. Place flat rocks in different areas of the garden, too, for butterfly sunbathing. The sunlight's warmth helps them keep their body temperature at the level necessary to function properly, and they thrive on at least six hours of sunlight per day.

You can find butterfly feeders at your garden center, and butterflies, in chrysalis form, are available from butterfly supply stores. Some gardeners use salt blocks, sold in farm stores, to attract males that, during the mating season, like to gather around sources of sodium. As in a hummingbird garden (see page 184), avoid using pesticides of any kind, even organic ones, because they are likely to poison the butterflies as well as the insects you are trying to discourage.

To begin butterfly gardening, invest in a good identification book. Learn to recognize the different species that frequent your area and understand their habits, so you will be better able to provide the habitat they like. Don't be discouraged if the butterflies don't flock to your garden every year. There will be years when they have had a bad winter and are scarce, or they may just locate in another area for a season.

Trumpet vine (*Campsis* × *tagliabuana* 'Madame Galen')

A Five-Star Garden for Hummingbirds

Bee balm (*Monarda didyma*)

WE GARDENERS MAY RATE PLANTS for their visual appeal, but hummingbirds are more interested in them as cuisine. A yard that offers a lush menu of nectar and insects will get a top rating from the winged world. Fortunately, it is easy to develop such a garden, because nectar is secreted by a great many of the colorful flowers we all love. Many flowers attract both hummingbirds and butterflies, which is nice if you want to attract both.

In late spring, everything comes to a halt when we hear the unmistakable whirring of that first ruby-throated hummingbird newly returned to our New England garden after spending the winter in Central America. It seems a miracle to us that these tiny visitors, weighing an eighth of an ounce or less, with wings that beat seventy-five times each second and propel them at speeds of 30 miles per hour, should choose our simple yard for their summer vacation.

No matter where you live, some of the 16 species of hummingbirds may find you. East of the Mississippi, it will be mostly the ruby-throated, but many others, including the black-chinned, broad-tailed, and rufous, can be found in western mountains. In the Southwest and along the Pacific coast, you'll find Anna's, calliope, Costa's, and others. All of them are attracted to flowers by sight rather than scent. Their favorite blooms are in brilliant shades of red, pink, and orange, and they particularly like those with tubular shapes, such as fuchsia. Color triggers such an automatic response in these birds that they will curiously inspect even a red umbrella, orange shirt, or red-handled hoe. In a shady spot, bright orange colors appeal most to them, and in desert locations where flowers, leaves, and grass are scarce, they are attracted to green.

Obviously, the flowers in a garden for hummingbirds should bloom in

their favorite colors and produce good amounts of nectar. To provide a constant food supply, choose perennial species with blossoming seasons that overlap, and supplement the perennials with red-hued annuals, such as cosmos, geraniums *(Pelargonium)*, petunias, sages *(Salvia)*, scarlet runner bean *(Phaseolus coccineus)*, and snapdragon *(Antirrhinum majus)*, which provide nectar throughout the summer. Include flowering shrubs and vines that attract hummingbirds, as well. You can't have too many blooms, because the birds need a great deal of nectar to satisfy their voracious appetites.

Plant Key

A | Hollyhock *(Alcea rosea)*

B | Lupines *(Lupinus)*

C | Columbines *(Aquilegia)*

D | Pinks *(Dianthus)*

Plant several early-flowering species to attract the birds in spring and encourage them to stay for the summer. Nature plans the return of the hummingbirds from their winter home to coincide with the blooming of early nectar-producing flowers in the spring, but in some years, cool, wet weather delays blossoming.

You can help ensure the birds' survival by providing artificial nectar in a hummingbird feeder. Bring to a boil a solution of 1 part white sugar to 4 parts water. After it has cooled, pour it into the feeder and the hummingbirds will quickly find it. Do not use honey or other sweeteners because they develop bacteria easily in warm weather, and do not use red dye to color the sugar solution. Clean the feeder with soap and water and rinse thoroughly before refilling. Daily cleaning may be necessary in warm weather and every three or four days when the weather is cool. Disinfect with chlorine bleach at least once a week.

Although the sweet syrup provides energy, it doesn't offer much nourishment. For that, hummingbirds need nectar from your flowers, as well as tiny spiders, aphids, and other small insects. Avoid using insecticides or other chemicals in the garden that might diminish the birds' food supply or poison them.

Begonia (*Begonia* 'Dragon Wings')

Torch lilies (*Kniphofia*)

Hummingbird Attracters

Choose red, pink, or orange varieties of the following plants.

PERENNIALS

Bearded irises (*Iris*)
Beardtongues (*Penstemon*)
Bee balm (*Monarda didyma*)
Bellflowers (*Campanula*)
Betonies (*Stachys*)
Border phlox (*Phlox paniculata*)
Butterfly weeds (*Asclepias*)
Campions (*Lychnis*)
Cardinal flower (*Lobelia cardinalis*)
Columbines (*Aquilegia*)
Common sage (*Salvia officinalis*)
Coral bells (*Heuchera sanguinea*)
Daylilies (*Hemerocallis*)
Delphiniums (*Delphinium*)
Foxgloves (*Digitalis*)
Hollyhock (*Alcea rosea*)
Lilies (*Lilium*)
Lupines (*Lupinus*)
Pinks (*Dianthus*)
Poppies (*Papaver*)
Soapworts (*Saponaria*)
Torch lily (*Kniphofia uvaria*)

ANNUALS AND BEDDING PLANTS

Begonias (*Begonia*)
Common morning glory
    (*Ipomoea purpurea*)
Flowering tobacco (*Nicotiana alata*)
Fuchsias (*Fuchsia*)
Geraniums (*Pelargonium*)
Lantana (*Lantana camara*)
Nasturtium (*Tropaeolum majus*)
Petunias (*Petunia*)
Scarlet runner bean (*Phaseolus coccineus*)
Scarlet sage (*Salvia splendens*)

SHRUBS AND VINES

Beautybush (*Kolkwitzia amabilis*)
Butterfly bush (*Buddleia davidii*)
Cotoneasters (*Cotoneaster*)
Flowering quinces (*Chaenomeles*)
Lilacs (*Syringa*)
Pea shrubs (*Caragana*)
Red-flowering currant (*Ribes sanguineum*)
Rhododendrons and azaleas
    (*Rhododendron*)
Tatarian honeysuckle (*Lonicera tatarica*)
Trumpet honeysuckle (*L. sempervirens*)
Trumpet vine (*Campsis radicans*)
Weigela (*Weigela florida*)

Hosta *(Hosta sieboldiana* 'Elegans')

A Garden for Plant Collectors

Aunt Molly had enough salt and pepper shakers to fill all the shelves in her large dining room from floor to ceiling. We always enjoyed her display because each set obviously meant so much to her, either because of its beauty and uniqueness or because it reminded her of some special person or place.

Just as she collected salt and pepper shakers and other individuals amass coins, stamps, buttons, or rare books, still others accumulate plants. Most specialize in only one or two genera or species,

Daylily *(Hemerocallis* 'My Sweet Love')

but they grow many cultivars of the plant group they have chosen. A collection might range from a few different species of a single wildflower genus, such as native orchids, to many hundreds of irises, roses, peonies, lilies, or another plant group.

Most serious plant collectors belong to whatever national society promotes the use, increased knowledge, and continued development of their favorite plant or plant group. You'll find societies for most popular plants, including cacti, daffodils, daylilies *(Hemerocallis),* delphiniums, ferns, herbs, hostas, irises, lilies, peonies, pinks *(Dianthus),* primroses, rock garden plants, roses, and wildflowers. Society members receive a magazine or newsletter several times a year, attend meetings with other enthusiasts, and tour public and private gardens where they can view new introductions as well as old favorites. At these gatherings they often swap information, seeds, and plants. (See the list of plant societies on page 351.)

Many people who collect a specific plant did not begin growing it with that intent. Instead, they were initially attracted by its beauty or special characteristics, and when their interest grew, along with the plants, it developed into an engrossing hobby. If you decide to specialize, select a species that

Plant Key

A | Lenten rose *(Helleborus × hybridus)*
B | Fragrant hellebore *(Helleborus odorus)*

will do well in your location. We know a man who started a huge collection of chrysanthemums in our county one year but had to give it up when he realized that the short growing season and hard winters made it too difficult to grow his favorite plant successfully.

Luckily, wherever you live, you have a wide range of plants from which to select, and if you live in a unique area, you may have an opportunity to grow special kinds that are denied to gardeners in some other parts of the country. For example, in a mountainous region, alpine plants might be a perfect choice; in a coastal area, seashore plants; and in a desert location, cacti or other succulents. Likewise, a woodland location might be the perfect spot for ferns or native flower species, while a wetland provides an opportunity to cultivate unusual water plants.

Just as you might proudly display your tintypes, seashells, or miniature boats in various ways, you also have a choice of how to show off your collection of plants. Some collectors plant them in neat rows, arranged scientifically as if they were in a plant nursery. This kind of grouping is easy to care for and less likely to become mixed or mislabeled. Others prefer to blend their collection into the landscape using attractive garden beds or borders. Often they plant their species with annuals, shrubs, or trees that not only complement the primary collection, but also provide color when it is not in bloom.

However you place your plants, it is best not to plant your collection haphazardly. The small differences among many cultivars may appear indistinguishable to the casual observer, and unless you grow similar cultivars next

to each other, the subtle differences are hard to recognize. Otherwise, visitors may doubt your claim to possess 120 different cultivars of Siberian iris *(Iris sibirica)* or be skeptical when you announce that the triploid bloom of a certain daylily is actually eight millimeters larger than the diploid.

When you have a collection, labeling each plant becomes extremely important, not only for displaying your selections, but also so you can be sure of the name if you sell or swap plants, use them in breeding new hybrids, or exhibit them in shows. Small green or white plastic garden markers inscribed with permanent ink are easy to read without stooping, but we have found that alu-

minum labels, embossed with a ball-point pen and wired to a metal stake, last much longer. When ordering new plants, accurate records are necessary, too, or you may buy something you already own. Keep a written planting record in a safe place. Labels may be pulled out and read by visitors, then lost or put back with the wrong plant.

When working with our own daylily collection, we found one discouraging aspect of amassing a plant collection to be the confusion over plant names. Sometimes the same cultivar may have several different names, and it is not unusual to find that the same name is used for different kinds. Over the years, we have bought many plants that were incorrectly labeled and, unfortunately, did not find out about the mistake for many years. Most nurseries are honest, but sometimes in their spring rush,

employees are careless and mistakes happen. Buy only from firms that you have found trustworthy, and report any errors to the company as soon as a flower blooms. If mistakes continue, report the erring firm to your plant society so that others can be alerted.

A plant collection can be a rewarding hobby. We enjoy our 500 cultivars of daylilies and eagerly await the first flower of each newly acquired hybrid. Like many other collectors, we enjoy cross-pollinating our best blooms to see what new surprises the seedlings will produce, always hoping to come up with a spectacular new daylily cultivar, possibly even a blue one.

Plant specialists may gain rewards beyond the fun of growing. In addition to developing new cultivars, hobby gardeners also add to the sum of scientific horticultural knowledge. A cousin of

COLLECTORS' FAVORITES. With their many species and cultivars, several plant genera are endlessly fascinating because of the many variations in form, color, and size they offer, and they naturally invite collecting. The plants featured above are just some of the many possibilities.

A. Lenten rose (*Helleborus* × *hybridus*)

B. Bearded iris (*Iris* 'Spirit World')

C. Japanese primrose (*Primula japonica*)

D. Chinese tree peony (*Paeonia suffruticosa* 'Big Deep Purple')

E. *Epimedium* × *youngianum*

ours who collects wildflowers discovered a native orchid that had not previously been identified, and it now bears his name in botanical treatises. Such recognition was gratifying, but we're sure that the many beautiful photos he has taken, as well as the pleasure his avocation brought him over the years, have meant much more to him.

Bleeding heart *(Dicentra spectabilis)*

Create a Child's Garden

DURING THE THIRTY YEARS we led a 4-H club, gardening was one of the most popular projects. The boys and girls always displayed their prize vegetables and flowers at the county fair or local field day with great pride. Although competition undoubtedly stimulated the care they gave their gardens, the sense of accomplishing something on their own, often for the first time, was a great confidence builder, and for some of them, growing plants became an intriguing pastime and a lifelong hobby.

Chinese lantern *(Physalis alkekengi)*

As soon as a child is old enough to know you don't eat the daisies and disciplined enough to pull weeds rather than flowers, it is time to give him or her a small space for a private plot. We have friends whose 5-year-old son loves growing things, and if they show any inclination, even 3-year-olds can have fun digging in the dirt. One of the greatest gifts you can give children is love for the earth and its living things, but if gardening is made to seem a series of chores at an early age, their first gardening experience is likely to be their last. One man told us that in seeking a wife, he always asked each candidate if she liked to garden. If the answer was

yes, he immediately struck her from his list. He remembered his mother's stern discipline in the garden and wanted no more of it!

To encourage a sense of accomplishment, let the garden belong exclusively to the child, even though you may need to lend a helping hand. Perhaps provide a sign, such as "Shaun's Garden" or "Karen's Plot," to stimulate pride of ownership. We know of a couple who allotted their son a high-fenced-in area, hidden from the rest of the yard, for his very own "secret" garden. Keep a child's garden small so that when other diversions appear, as they will, the weeds will not get out of hand. Narrow raised beds, with mulched paths between them, can make it clear where to walk and where the plants are to grow. And even if a plastic or ceramic ornament may not appeal to you, it may help your child better enjoy his or her garden.

Involve the child in the project from the start, first in studying pictures and selecting what to plant, and then in preparing the bed and planting seeds and seedlings. Provide some child-size, well-made, sturdy tools — a watering

can, hoe, shovel, wheelbarrow, and other tools that are easy to handle. Depending on the child's age, he or she will probably be capable of doing much of the watering, weeding, fertilizing, deadheading, and, especially, the fun part—gathering the bouquets and harvesting the vegetables.

Since the young are impatient and likely to lose enthusiasm if they cannot see results quickly, a garden that combines a few bulbs, annuals, vegetables, and perennials may be ideal. Most children have such a short attention span that work periods of 10 to 15 minutes may be just about right to accomplish one task, such as watering or weeding.

Children are not likely to be very impressed by garden design, so forget about careful arrangement and disciplined rows. Most find a patch of dandelions as beautiful as a clump of cultivated globeflowers *(Trollius)*. Above all, the garden should be fun—a place of pleasure rather than beauty, where it is all right to get dirty and play, to pick the zinnias, open the pea pods, and behead the dandelions.

Encourage children to grow vegetables they like to eat, and be sure to include flowers with bright colors or pleasing fragrances that are fun to pick. Give them seeds that are large and easy to handle, such as beans, peas, and

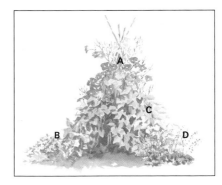

Plant Key

A | Morning glories *(Ipomoea)*

B | Pansies *(Viola × wittrockiana)*

C | Scarlet runner beans *(Phaseolus coccineus)*

D | Coral bells *(Heuchera)*

pelleted carrots. Nasturtium *(Tropae-olum majus)* seeds are large and easy to plant, and they produce colorful, fragrant flowers quickly. Some flowering beans grow fast, too, and may stimulate memories of *Jack and the Beanstalk.* Children might enjoy growing catnip *(Nepeta cataria)* for their feline pets or mints for their tea parties. Spring bulbs are perennial favorites for children as they wait for the dead-looking, egg-shaped balls they planted in the fall to push their green tips through the earth and become sunny yellow daffodils or bright red tulips.

Hens-and-chicks *(Sempervivum tectorum)*

Your child, grandkid, or little friend next door is likely to be intrigued by flowers with interesting features, such as the Canterbury bells *(Campanula medium),* the rich fragrance of lily-of-the-valley *(Convallaria majalis),* the red valentines of old-fashioned bleeding heart *(Dicentra spectabilis),* or the smiling faces of pansies *(Viola × wittrock-iana).* They may also like to examine the fascinating growing habits of hens-and-chicks *(Sempervivum)* or the silver dollars of honesty *(Lunaria annua),* also called money plant. Corn can bring up images of the corn dodger who lived in shocks of corn. Most children like to grow huge vegetables, and "Peter Peter, Pumpkin Eater" is a good inspiration. Who can grow the biggest pumpkin, and make the best jack o'lantern? Very young children enjoy plants that have stories and songs attached to them, especially ones connected to songs or nursery rhymes:

> *Lavender's blue, dilly-dilly,*
> *lavender's green.*
> *When I am king, dilly-dilly,*
> *you shall be queen.*

If the garden stimulates the imagination, it is doing its job. A distinguished adult friend of ours swears that, as a child, he once saw a small elf dressed entirely in green, dancing about in the family garden. His story is so convincing that we believe him. Children are much more attuned to nature than adults and more ready to accept magic and miracles.

The perennial and biennial plants listed at right are among those worth choosing for your child's first garden, because they are easy to grow and each has something about it that will be especially intriguing to a youngster.

Annuals are important, too. We remember being excited when the four o'clocks *(Mirabilis jalapa)* opened on time in the afternoon and wondering if their name should change to five o'clocks with daylight savings time. Sweet peas *(Lathyrus odoratus)* are a bit hard to grow but can give children many happy, scented memories. Showy marigolds, calendulas, and asters make great bouquets to share with neighbors and grandparents.

Plants for a Child's Garden

Butterfly weed *(Asclepias tuberosa).* Notice the way that it attracts butterflies.

Canterbury bells *(Campanula medium).* Cartoon characters often ring these "bells."

Chinese lantern *(Physalis alkekengi).* These dried orange flowers can decorate a Halloween party.

Coral bells *(Heuchera sanguinea).* More bells to pretend ringing. White ones are fun, too.

'Coronation Gold' yarrow *(Achillea 'Coronation Gold').* The rich golden color can signify great wealth.

Daylilies *(Hemerocallis).* Children can be intrigued with a plant that delivers a fresh flower every day.

Gas plant *(Dictamnus albus).* What other plant can produce gas that can be lit like a torch on a warm summer night?

Hens-and-chicks *(Sempervivum).* Watch these multiply.

Hollyhock *(Alcea rosea).* Something to look way up to.

Honesty or money plant *(Lunaria annua).* Peel the cover off of the seedpod to find a silvery coin.

Lily-of-the-valley *(Convallaria majalis).* There can be delight in finding that such a tiny flower has such a powerful smell. Note, however, that all parts of this plant are poisonous.

Old-fashioned bleeding hearts *(Dicentra).* Not only are the heart-shaped blooms appealing, but taking one apart and finding all the interesting objects inside is an intriguing project for both boys and girls.

Pansy *(Viola × wittrockiana).* Imagine things about the many faces: savage pirate, laughing clown, cross teacher.

Honesty, also known as money plant *(Lunaria annua)*

Pinks (*Dianthus* 'Blue Pigmy')

An Island of Flowers

IN THE MIDST OF A MOWED LAWN in Tasha Tudor's landscape is an enchanting fairy ring, encircled on the outer rim by lacy pinks *(Dianthus)* that enclose a mound of blue bellflowers *(Campanula)*. Her planting, illustrated in the book *Tasha Tudor's Garden* (Houghton Mifflin, 1994), is completely in character for this nineteenth-century-like artist and gardener — informal, whimsical, and so lovely it lifts your spirits just to think of it.

An "island" garden is an ideal spot to indulge your own garden fantasy. It may be large or small, with a square, circular, oval, or irregular shape, and raised, sunken, or planted on level ground, in sun or in shade. The style might be formal or informal, and it could either stand alone or surround a statue, small pool, fountain, special tree, or other feature. You could arrange the plants in an intact block or separate them with paths into "pie pieces," like the pattern of a wheel. With a bit of imagination, the island could be your most creative garden bed.

Since it will be seen from all directions, like a flower arrangement on a dinner table, an island bed needs to

Bellflower (*Campanula* 'Kent Belle')

be approached differently than a bed backed by a hedge, fence, wall, or building. Before you plant, try to visualize the bed from every direction. Put tall growers in the center and medium and low growers around the edges. As in any border, however, it would look artificial to layer the plants to resemble a pyramid, so let a few of the larger plants grow near the outer edge, as long as they do not hide those behind. It is usually best not to use plants that need lots of staking in such a garden, because the stakes are likely to be visible.

Unless the island bed is large, small to medium-size plants look best, with the possible exception of a pyramidal evergreen or large shrub as the focal

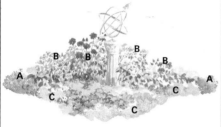

Plant Key

A | Sweet alyssum
(*Lobularia maritima* 'Royal Carpet')

B | Hybrid tea roses

C | Lady's mantle (*Alchemilla mollis*)

point. You could also use an unusual stone, vine-covered post, or other striking object as an eye-catching feature.

Our own island planting in the backyard is a circle, slightly sunken, over the spot where an aboveground swimming pool once stood. Unlike the typical island arrangement that we've described, daylilies surround the circumference, and in the center, within a walk-in bed of low-growing annuals that we plant every spring, is a sundial on a short post. The annuals are a "secret garden," not visible until you reach the interior. It is not especially elegant, but this informal planting is attractive from both inside and out, and the greenery looks nice even when the daylilies are not blooming.

Island beds are the ideal settings for plants that might not fit well in a border garden, such as a collection of spring bulbs. When the tulips, daffodils, grape hyacinths *(Muscari),* Siberian squill *(Scilla siberica),* and similar plants have died back in late spring, you can fill the space for the rest of the summer with annuals or tender bulb plants, such as gladioli and dahlias.

Some gardeners simply let the bed lie dormant and covered with grass that they mow for the rest of the season. If you take this approach, fertilize the bulbs lightly in the spring.

Rock-garden enthusiasts often use islands for their plantings. We have neighbors who built a mound of soil and rocks in the middle of their sunny back lawn and filled it with a magnificent collection of alpine plants. They do not have a model train running up and around the plants, but it would be a perfect spot for a garden-train enthusiast to play.

Hybrid tea roses also show to perfection in an island bed. There they are easy to view, and the setup is perfect for sniffing each individual rose as you stroll around the perimeter. Roses fit well in formal, rectangular or round beds or in informal, irregular-shaped islands. They are effective all by themselves or combined with other small shrubs, perennials, and annuals.

If your lawn is large, it may be just the spot for a series of formal or semiformal island gardens of the same size and shape. In this type of planting,

Daffodil *(Narcissus)* with grape hyacinths *(Muscari)*

each individual bed usually contains plants of the same species, but you can use a mixture of cultivars. They may be all roses, perennials, annuals, geraniums, or similar plants, either all one color or a carefully color-coordinated mix. Sometimes brightly hued foliage plants, such as coleus or caladiums, are featured. If you are ambitious or have help caring for your garden, you might fill the beds first with tulips, then with annuals, and finally with fall chrysanthemums for an all-season display.

An informal design allows you more freedom than a formal bed, since the island plot is not limited to a particular shape or size, and you may fill it with a wide range of plant materials such as wildflowers, shrubs, annuals, grasses, herbs, and even vegetables, as well as perennials. Such a bed is possible even on an uneven lawn.

Finally, keep the rest of your grounds in mind when you plan. Although an island, by definition, is set apart from its surroundings, it looks best when connected in size, shape, and proportion to the rest of the setting. Carefully planted, it can be the most stunning feature of your landscape.

Scented cranesbill *(Geranium macrorrhizum)*

Morning glory *(Ipomoea nil* 'Chocolate')

An Island with a Purpose

Whether your mailbox is a standard aluminum fixture on a post or a custom-made ornamental box on a pedestal, it will be enhanced with an island planting of shrubs, flowering vines, perennials, and/or annuals, with the post or pole as the focal point. Unless you can tend to it regularly, however, choose plants that need little watering, deadheading, spraying, or other care, since it will probably be near the entrance of your property and may be at some distance from the house.

Evergreens provide attractive greenery all winter but might suffer if they will be exposed to road salt and snow plowing where you live. Deciduous shrubs, such as daphnes, spireas, and cinquefoils *(Potentilla),* are all good choices for summer blooms that will make the entrance to your property friendly and welcoming. Lightweight vines are ideal for climbing your mailbox post or lamppost, too. Some good choices are mandevilla, a tender perennial that is treated like an annual in colder zones; morning glories *(Ipomoea);* and climbing roses. None of these would run rampant and interfere with mail delivery or keep you from raising your flag. Large annuals like cosmos and spider flower *(Cleome hassleriana),* as well as shorter types like impatiens, nasturtium *(Tropaeolum majus),* and geraniums *(Pelargonium),* are ideal for all-summer bloom. If you use perennials, choose those with attractive foliage for the times when they aren't in bloom. A few daylilies *(Hemerocallis)* or hostas surrounding the post will dress it up considerably.

Blue false indigo *(Baptisia australis)*

True Blue, the Zenith of Gardens

IF DIAMONDS, CAVIAR, AND CHAMPAGNE were a dime a dozen, they would probably not be as beloved and coveted as they are. For many gardeners, true-blue flowers fall in the same category. Because they are not easy to come by, they have long been sought after by sophisticated gardeners, and a bed dressed in shades of blue, with touches of white, is often considered preeminent among gardens.

Mealycup sage *(Salvia farinacea)*

Long ago, when we were gardeners-in-training, one of the leading horticulturists in our community hired us to work in her gardens. Of the several she had, her favorite was a small blue-and-white garden enclosed by a low stone wall, overlooking a view of mountains. In summer it was spectacular, bursting with blue delphiniums, blue annuals, white phlox, snow-in-summer *(Cerastium tomentosum),* and other flowers. Of all the gardens we tended, this unusual and beautiful bed was the one we showed most often to friends.

The palette of blues ranges along numerous shades, from light blue to the deep, clear blue of the fabled Himalayan poppy *(Meconopsis betonicifolia)* and the near-purple hues of many bellflowers *(Campanula).* Many common blue flowers are actually lavender-blue, which is fine as long as you are not a purist. Hybridizers keep trying but have been unable to come up with a truly blue daylily *(Hemerocallis)* or rose.

A blue-and-white garden seems to look best set in a small, intimate space, rather than in a large, open area where brighter colors, like reds and oranges, combined with white, might be more appropriate. Blue, by itself, no matter how beautiful, can be a little monotonous, since it is a cool color and needs lightening. By simply adding white to the garden, the blue colors and textures become spectacular. One of our favorite combinations has always been the blue shades of delphinium combined with the early whites of 'Miss Lingard' meadow phlox *(Phlox maculata* 'Miss Lingard') and Madonna lilies *(Lilium candidum).* Masses of white are not necessary, since only a small number of white blooms will intensify the blues to an impressive degree.

In most perennial beds, there are already enough common plants in blue shades to give a blue-slanted gardener a good start. We were surprised to find

so many in ours: delphiniums, balloon flower *(Platycodon grandiflorus),* mountain bluet *(Centaurea montana),* globe thistles *(Echinops),* monkshoods *(Aconitum),* speedwells *(Veronica),* bellflowers, and blue-flowering clematis cultivars. For somewhat shaded areas, hostas—not only the lavender-blue-flowering types but also those with blue-tinged foliage—can be an excellent choice.

In Zone 5 and warmer areas, you have a wider palette of blue, including perennial flax *(Linum perenne)* and Miss Wilmott's ghost *(Eryngium giganteum).* Gentian sage *(Salvia patens)* has exceptionally vivid blue flowers; though it is a tender perennial, it can be grown in cool zones by treating it as an annual or by taking it indoors for the winter. Some of our favorite blue-flowering shrubs include blue spirea *(Caryopteris × clandonensis)* and blue-flowering cultivars of French hydrangea *(Hydrangea macrophylla).*

Many beautiful blue annuals are available to complement your perennials and come to the rescue when the perennial blooms are scarce. From tall statice *(Limonium sinuatum)* and mealy-cup sage *(Salvia farinacea)* to the shorter edging lobelia *(Lobelia erinus),* China aster *(Callistephus chinensis),* and floss flower *(Ageratum houstonianum),* you can find proper heights to keep your garden singing the blues all summer. (See our list on the next page.)

If you want the blue season to start early, spring bulbs are beautiful beginnings. The "minor" bulbs we consider heartwarming include blue and white

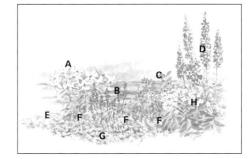

Plant Key

A | Madonna lily *(Lilium candidum)*

B | Speedwell *(Veronica austriaca* ssp. *teucrium)*

C | Balloon flower *(Platycodon grandiflorus)*

D | Delphiniums *(Delphinium)*

E | Snow-in-summer *(Cerastium tomentosum)*

F | Jacob's ladder *(Polemonium caeruleum)*

G | Carpathian bellflower *(Campanula carpatica)*

H | 'Miss Lingard' phlox
   (Phlox maculata 'Miss Lingard')

crocus, Siberian squill (*Scilla siberica*), Spanish bluebell (*Hyacinthoides hispanica*), grape hyacinths (*Muscari*), and glory-of-the-snows (*Chionodoxa*). Blue Dutch hyacinths, bluish tulips, Virginia bluebells (*Mertensia pulmonarioides*), lungworts (*Pulmonaria*), and forget-me-nots (*Myosotis*) will all fill the spring garden with different shades of blue.

Blue corydalis (*Corydalis flexuosa* 'China Blue')

Some plants in the following lists have many different cultivars, including blues and whites. Check to determine which are most appropriate for your garden.

Blue-Flowering Plants
Perennial bloom times: A = Spring, B = Early Summer, C = Summer, D = Autumn

SHORT PERENNIALS (to 1 foot)

Blue corydalis (*Corydalis flexuosa*) B

Carpathian bellflower (*Campanula carpatica*) B, C

Forget-me-nots (*Myosotis*) A

Lungworts (*Pulmonaria*) A

Plumbago (*Ceratostigma plumbaginoides*) D

Violets (*Viola*) A, B

MEDIUM-HEIGHT PERENNIALS (12–30 inches)

Balloon flower (*Platycodon grandiflorus*) C

Bellflowers (*Campanula*) B, C

Blue sage (*Salvia × sylvestris*) C, D

Blue stars (*Amsonia*) B

Columbines (*Aquilegia*) B

Cranesbills (*Geranium*) C

Irises (*Iris*) B, C

Jacob's ladder (*Polemonium caeruleum*) C

Lavenders (*Lavandula*) C

Lupines (*Lupinus*) B

Mountain bluet (*Centaurea montana*) B

Perennial flax (*Linum perenne*) B

Speedwells (*Veronica*) B, C

Spiderworts (*Tradescantia*) C

Stokes' aster (*Stokesia laevis*) C

Virginia bluebells (*Mertensia pulmonarioides*) A

TALL PERENNIALS (30 inches or more)

Asters (*Aster*) C, D

Blue bugloss (*Anchusa azurea*) C

Blue false indigo (*Baptisia australis*) B

Globe thistles (*Echinops*) C

Hostas, blue-leaved cultivars (*Hosta*) C

Monkshoods (*Aconitum*) C, D

ANNUALS

Bachelor's buttons (*Centaurea cyanus*)

Blue lace flower (*Trachymene caerulea*)

China aster (*Callistephus chinensis*)

Edging lobelia (*Lobelia erinus*)

Floss flower (*Ageratum houstonianum*)

Mealycup sage (*Salvia farinacea*)

Morning glory (*Ipomoea tricolor*)

Petunias (*Petunia*)

Sapphire flower (*Browallia speciosa*)

Statice (*Limonium sinuatum*)

White-Flowering Plants
Perennial bloom times: A = Spring, B = Early Summer, C = Summer, D = Autumn

SHORT PERENNIALS (to 1 foot)

Astilbes (*Astilbe*) C

Coral bells (*Heuchera*) B, C

Fringed bleeding heart (*Dicentra eximia*) B, C

Pinks (*Dianthus*) B, C

Sea thrift (*Armeria maritima*) A

Snow-in-summer (*Cerastium tomentosum*) B, C

MEDIUM-HEIGHT PERENNIALS (12–30 inches)

Astilbes (*Astilbe*) C

Balloon flower (*Platycodon grandiflorus*) C

Bellflowers (*Campanula*) B, C

Cranesbills (*Geranium*) B, C

Daylilies (*Hemerocallis*) C

Gas plant (*Dictamnus albus*) C

Irises (*Iris*) B, C

Old-fashioned bleeding heart (*Dicentra spectabilis*) A, B

Peonies (*Paeonia*) B

Shasta daisy (*Leucanthemum × superbum*) C

Snowdrop anemone (*Anemone sylvestris*) B

Spiderworts (*Tradescantia*) C

Spike gayfeather (*Liatris spicata*) C

TALL (30 inches or more)

Anemones (*Anemone*) D

Common foxglove (*Digitalis purpurea*) C

Delphiniums (*Delphinium*) B, C

Goat's beard (*Aruncus dioicus*) C

Phlox (*Phlox*) B, C

ANNUALS

Annual baby's breath (*Gypsophila elegans*)

China aster (*Callistephus chinensis*)

Common garden verbena (*Verbena × hybrida*)

Cosmos (*Cosmos bipinnatus*)

Dahlias (*Dahlia*)

Flowering tobaccos (*Nicotiana*)

Geraniums (*Pelargonium*)

Impatiens (*Impatiens walleriana*)

Lavatera (*Lavatera trimestris*)

Morning glories (*Ipomoea*)

Petunias (*Petunia*)

Sages (*Salvia*)

Snapdragon (*Antirrhinum majus*)

Sweet alyssum (*Lobularia maritima*)

Wax begonia (*Begonia* Semperflorens hybrids)

Zinnias (*Zinnia*)

Speedwell *(Veronica)*

A Take-It-Easy Garden

Summer snowflake *(Leucojum aestivum)*

CUSTOMERS AT OUR NURSERY have often asked, "What looks nice all year and requires no care whatsoever?" Except for recommending a birdbath, flagpole, or plastic flowers, we have never been able to provide a satisfactory answer. The best we can do is suggest plants that thrive with a minimum of care. Easy-care plantings are ideal for anyone who wants an attractive border without the maintenance that most gardens require, perhaps because of a demanding job, advancing years, a physical handicap, or simply because you're able to be in your garden only on weekends.

The design of your garden can determine the amount of labor required nearly as much as the kinds of plants you choose. Formal, symmetrical beds with sheared hedge borders are certain to appear in disarray if anything grows out of place or gets weedy, while an informal or partially wild planting can look good even if it's not tended for a couple of weeks. Any garden needing a large amount of hand weeding, like a rock garden, is not a good choice if you want to avoid time-consuming care.

Most neglected gardens suffer primarily because they are too large for their owners to easily maintain, so the first rule of easy-care gardening is to keep it small. When you design a flower border, keep it relatively narrow so you can reach most of the plants from the front or back without having to pick your way among them.

To make gardening easier, separate any vigorous, fast-spreading kinds from less active plants by edgings, paths, or other solid barriers that they cannot cross. When you plant, leave more space between the different clumps than you ordinarily would, so they won't need dividing as often. If you live where you know that frequent watering will be necessary, simplify the process by installing sprinklers in the bed at planting time and equipping them with a timer valve.

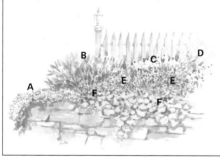

Plant Key

A | Stonecrops (Sedum)

B | Peonies (Paeonia)

C | Gloriosa daisy (Rudbeckia hirta)

D | 'Miss Lingard' phlox
(Phlox maculata 'Miss Lingard')

E | Cranesbills (Geranium)

F | Nasturtium (Tropaeolum majus)

Gardens for the Physically Challenged

We will never forget the day many years ago when we discovered one of our favorite octogenarian friends lying flat on her side beside her garden, bracing herself with one hand and pulling weeds with the other. She was crippled with arthritis of the hip but had always been a dedicated gardener and had no intention of giving up her favorite pastime.

Gardening chores are made much easier these days with ergonomic tools such as trowels and pruners with comfortable grips, long-handled weed pullers, and shears with a long reach for cutting flowers. Some shears also hold the cutting, rather than letting it drop on the ground. Lightweight spades and other tools designed to require little leverage pressure are also available. Garden centers and catalogs often sell these and other labor-saving devices.

If you or a family member are confined to a wheelchair or for some other reason find it difficult to bend over, large pots or boxes set on a railing or other raised surface will make it easier to do the chores and smell the flowers. Be sure the plants are set at the proper height for tending from a wheelchair and that there is plenty of space between tables or rows for a wheelchair to fit easily. Narrow, raised planters made of brick, concrete, or stone, built to the height that is best for the gardener, are better than pots for most plants. If the soil in these planters reaches to the ground, there is increased space for roots, and plants are less prone to winterkill because they do not run out of moisture as easily. For further information, check out Internet websites on gardening for the physically challenged.

As much as possible, choose plants that will stay compact and attractive for years without needing division or constant cutting back. Many plants fit this category, but it is difficult to compile a foolproof list, since some that are ideal in one section of the country may expand much more rapidly under other climatic conditions. Look for the following characteristics:

❀ No need for division oftener than every 3 to 4 years
❀ Disease and insect resistance
❀ Hardiness in your climate, needing no extra protection for winter
❀ Sturdy stems that don't need staking
❀ Long blossoming period (fewer different plants will be needed to keep your garden filled with bloom)
❀ Foliage that remains attractive throughout the season
❀ Does not spread rapidly, either by seed or runners

Consider groundcovers to help you dispense with some gardening chores. Heaths *(Erica)*, heather *(Calluna vulgaris)*, and daylilies *(Hemerocallis)* can cover sunny areas beautifully, and periwinkles *(Vinca)* and pachysandras are good choices for shady spots. Spreading shrubs such as cotoneasters, creeping juniper *(Juniperus horizontalis)*, and bristlecone pine *(Pinus aristata)* are also attractive covers.

Controlling the Weeds

After you've chosen easy-care plants, the next important step is to find ways to cut down on weeding chores, the most time-consuming duty in the garden. The following techniques may help. (See Chapter 6 for more on weeds and how to restrict their growth.)

❀ Prepare the soil well before planting, removing all perennial weed clumps and roots. If you have very heavy sod, remove it altogether, because otherwise you will constantly

Easy-Care Plants

PERENNIALS
Astilbes, dwarf cultivars *(Astilbe)*
Baby's breaths *(Gypsophila)*
Balloon flower
      (Platycodon grandiflorus)
Bleeding hearts *(Dicentra)*
Cardinal flower *(Lobelia cardinalis)*
Coral bells *(Heuchera)*
Cranesbills *(Geranium)*
Daylilies *(Hemerocallis)*
Gas plant *(Dictamnus albus)*
Gayfeathers *(Liatris)*
Globeflowers *(Trollius)*
Hostas *(Hosta)*
Lungworts *(Pulmonaria)*
Monkshoods *(Aconitum)*
Orange coneflowers *(Rudbeckia)*
Peonies *(Paeonia)*
Perennial candytuft
      (Iberis sempervirens)
Phlox *(Phlox)*
Speedwells *(Veronica)*
Stonecrops *(Sedum)*
Turtleheads *(Chelone)*

Yarrows *(Achillea)*
Yuccas *(Yucca)*

BULBS
Crocuses *(Crocus)*
Daffodils *(Narcissus)*
Fritillaries *(Fritillaria)*
Glory-of-the-snows *(Chionodoxa)*
Grape hyacinths *(Muscari)*
Lilies, especially Asiatic *(Lilium)*
Ornamental onions *(Allium)*
Snowflakes *(Leucojum)*

ANNUALS
Calendula *(Calendula officinalis)*
Cosmos *(Cosmos)*
Floss flower *(Ageratum houstonianum)*
Impatiens *(Impatiens)*
Lavateras *(Lavatera)*
Marigolds *(Tagetes)*
Nasturtium *(Tropaeolum majus)*
Zinnias *(Zinnia)*

Zinnia *(Zinnia elegans)*

be fighting weeds. Removal of the sod will take some of the topsoil with it, so you will need to replace it with good soil. Make sure the purchased soil is weed-free, as well.

❀ Insert a vertical edging (plastic, aluminum, or steel) in the soil around the bed to prevent adjacent grass roots from creeping into the area.

❀ Examine each new plant you add to the garden to be sure no weeds are clinging to the clump. Most nurseries carefully keep out weeds, but look over newly purchased plants anyway, as well as gifts from other gardeners. If you are in doubt about a plant's "cleanliness," carefully wash off the soil before setting it in the ground.

❀ Use organic herbicides to prevent the sprouting of weed seeds that may subsequently blow in.

❀ After planting, carefully spread a generous layer of mulch between the plants to prevent new weeds from getting a foothold. The mulch will also hold moisture so waterings won't need to be as frequent.

❀ Avoid the use of fresh farm manure for fertilizer and hay for mulch, because they are likely to contain weed seeds. Use dried manure or commercial dry or liquid organic fertilizers instead. These are weed-free, and only one feeding per year should be necessary.

❀ Pave pathways with bricks or crushed stone rather than trying to maintain them as grass.

Viburnum
(*Viburnum sieboldii*)

Tea viburnum (*Viburnum setigerum*
'Aurantiacum')

A Shrub Garden

Rhododendrons (*Rhododendron*)

FROM THE GOLDEN FORSYTHIA BLOOMS that spell spring to the flaming foliage of burning bush *(Euonymus alatus)* in fall, we greatly enjoy our ever-changing shrubs. A planting of shrubs, both deciduous and evergreen, can be a spectacular addition to the landscaping of your property, and as beautiful as any other garden. It can also act as a screen to block out noise, provide privacy, or divide one part of the property from another. If you spend only a few weeks at a vacation home, if your gardening hours are limited, or if it is physically difficult for you to hoe, weed, stake, and divide plants, a shrub border may be the perfect solution to your gardening dilemma.

Shrubs are less demanding than perennials and annuals, and some will even thrive with no attention at all. You can find a wide range of mature sizes, leaf textures, and bloom and foliage colors, no matter where you live.

A shrub border is not the same as a hedge. Most common hedges consist of plants the same size, set in a single, straight row. In a shrub border, on the other hand, there is a variety of plants usually set in an irregular shape with curving contours. Typically, tall plants compose the back tier, with lower ones

in front of them and low, spreading plants set in the foreground.

The shrubs can be entirely evergreen, all deciduous, or, better yet, a mixture. Tall, slender evergreens in the background make for fine eye-catchers and form a backdrop for the spreading ones in front. They provide year-round structure and winter greenery, as well. Deciduous shrubs change the scene periodically with their interesting foliage. Many flower only in the spring or early summer, so include a few that come later such as shrub roses, butter-

fly bushes *(Buddleia)*, blue spirea *(Cary-opteris × clandonensis)*, hydrangeas, and rose-of-Sharon *(Hibiscus syriacus)*. Some spring- and summer-flowering shrubs produce small fruits that add color later in the season, among them dogwoods *(Cornus)*, crabapple *(Malus)*, rugosa rose *(Rosa rugosa)*, and viburnums. Don't neglect, either, those with foliage that changes to brilliant colors in the fall (see the list on the next page). Consider also including a few shrubs with foliage that is yellow, white, gray, silver, blue, variegated, or even multicolored.

Not only do the colors of the leaves vary, but the shapes and textures can be very different as well. For example, a smoke bush *(Cotinus coggygria)* from the Netherlands, 'Young Lady', grows leaves in puffs at the ends of the limbs, resembling a green poodle, and in fall they turn a rich orange-red.

Designing the Border

To lay out a shrub border, first draw a design to scale, indicating the placement of the plants you want to include. Shrubs are a long-term project and are

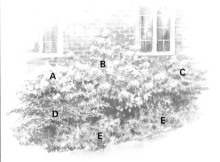

Plant Key

A | White rugosa rose *(Rosa rugosa* var. *alba)*

B | PeeGee hydrangea *(Hydrangea paniculata* 'Grandiflora')

C | Burning bush *(Euonymus alatus)*

D | Rockspray cotoneaster *(Cotoneaster horizontalis)*

E | Mistflower *(Eupatorium coelestinum)*

more expensive than perennials and annuals, so choose carefully. It is not easy to safely move a large, mature shrub. To define the borders of the bed, lay down a hose, rope, or clothesline to mark a graceful, curving edge. Get rid of the grass where you will be planting by tilling or with an organic herbicide. Then, after you have the perfect design and the ground is bare, drive in stakes with labels for each species in the spots where you want them to grow. Place low-growers at the front of the curving areas in groups of three or five. You may want to space out the flowering shrubs so there will be a few of the same plants blooming along the row at the same time. As you visualize the mature size of the shrubs, you will probably move the stakes around a few times before planting them. You don't have to do all the planting at once. Set in the background plants first since they will take longer to mature, and keep your planting plan in a safe place so you can follow it in subsequent years.

Plant the shrubs as described in Chapter 4, adding organic matter to enrich the soil before planting. After they are installed, water thoroughly and spread an attractive mulch over the area to check weed growth, conserve water, and help the appearance. Unless you are starting with full-grown specimens, the planting will likely look a bit sparse in the beginning. If you want, you can fill in the spaces with bedding plants for the first years. As the shrubs grow, feed them, prune them to keep them in shape, and remove any broken or damaged branches. Shovel off any heavy loads of winter snow that might crush them, being careful not to break the brittle branches.

Many of the shrubs listed here come in a variety of cultivars. Some of them vary widely in size, bloom color, and foliage. Check out the various kinds

carefully when ordering to get the ones that best fit your landscaping needs.

Be careful not to plant too many single-season shrubs like spireas, lilacs (*Syringa*), and mock oranges (*Philadelphus*). Beautiful as they are, they bloom for only a week or two and offer little interest the rest of the year. You may want to choose mostly those species that bloom for a longer season, produce ornamental fruits, or have colorful, interesting fall foliage.

Climbing hydrangea (*Hydrangea petiolaris*)

Favorite Flowering Shrubs

DWARF SHRUBS

'Hummingbird' sweet pepperbush (*Clethra alnifolia* 'Hummingbird')

Dwarf flowering almond (*Prunus glandulosa*)

Garland flower (*Daphne cneorum*)

Heather (*Calluna vulgaris*)

Winter creeper (*Euonymus fortunei*)

MEDIUM-TO-TALL SHRUBS

Abelias (*Abelia*)

Deutzias (*Deutzia*)

Dogwoods (*Cornus*)

Elderberries (*Sambucus*)

Flowering quinces (*Chaenomeles*)

Honeysuckles (*Lonicera*)

Hydrangeas (*Hydrangea*)

Japanese kerria (*Kerria japonica*)

Juneberries (*Amelanchier*)

Lilacs (*Syringa*)

Mock oranges (*Philadelphus*)

Roses (*Rosa*)

Shrubby cinquefoil (*Potentilla fruticosa*)

Snowberries (*Symphoricarpos*)

Spireas (*Spiraea*)

Star magnolia (*Magnolia stellata*)

Ural false spirea (*Sorbaria sorbifolia*)

Viburnums (*Viburnum*)

Virginia sweetspire (*Itea virginica*)

Weigelas (*Weigela*)

BROAD-LEAVED EVERGREENS

Azaleas and rhododendrons (*Rhododendron*)

Dwarf mountain laurel (*Kalmia latifolia* f. *myrtifolia*)

SHRUBS WITH ORNAMENTAL FOLIAGE, BERRIES, OR TWIGS

Cherry plum (*Prunus cerasifera*). 'Thundercloud' and other cultivars have purple leaves.

Chokeberries (*Aronia*). Great fall color; red or black fruits.

Cotoneasters (*Cotoneaster*). Ornamental berries in late summer and fall.

Dogwoods (*Cornus*). Twigs and autumn leaves in different shades of red, brown, and yellow.

Elaeagnus (*Elaeagnus*). Gray-green or variegated foliage.

Elderberries (*Sambucus*). Foliage comes in a variety of colors; showy flowers.

Emerald 'n Gold euonymus (*Euonymus fortunei* 'Emerald 'n Gold'). Green leaves with wide yellow margins.

Firethorns (*Pyracantha*). Bright orange, red, or yellow berries in fall.

Heather (*Calluna vulgaris*). Foliage in various colors.

Purple-leaved sand cherry (*Prunus* × *cistena*). Dark foliage.

Smoke bush (*Cotinus coggygria*). 'Royal Purple' and other cultivars have deep purple foliage.

Spireas (*Spiraea*). 'Gold Flame' and other cultivars have golden yellow leaves.

Moss phlox (*Phlox sublata* 'White Delight')

Gardening with Groundcovers

WE HAVE A STEEP HILLSIDE NEAR A BROOK in deciduous woods that washed badly each year during heavy rains and when snow was melting. There had been so much erosion that many of the large tree roots were exposed. We planted dozens of divisions of lesser periwinkle *(Vinca minor)* over the area, and after a few years, the earth was covered with a deep carpet of green. It has been very effective at holding the soil and catching the leaves that drop, which, we hope, now are slowly building a new soil layer. In the spring, bright blue flowers cover the plants, and the hillside has now become our favorite picnic spot.

Lesser periwinkle (*Vinca minor*)

Spotted dead nettle (*Lamium maculatum* 'White Nancy')

Once upon a time, the word *ground-cover* referred almost exclusively to English ivy *(Hedera helix),* Japanese spurge *(Pachysandra terminalis),* or lesser periwinkle *(Vinca minor).* Gardeners, however, have since transformed the definition to include a long list of low-growing, spreading plants less than 2 feet tall — evergreen and deciduous, herbaceous and woody, perennial and annual. Some, like the dreaded bishop's weed *(Aegopodium podagraria),* spread like wildfire, while others, like hostas, form tidy clumps. The best choices for your garden are those that make an attractive covering over a long season, successfully suppress weeds, and are not overly invasive.

Both gardeners and nongardeners choose groundcovers to avoid mowing a lawn, to cover banks that are difficult to mow, to suppress weeds, and to halt erosion — all valid reasons. But groundcovers can also be the foundation of the most interesting and beautiful garden areas in your landscape.

Start out by choosing the proper plants for your soil, light conditions,

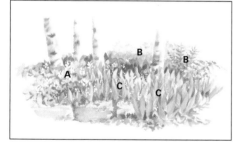

Plant Key

A | Dead nettles *(Lamium)*

B | Ferns (various)

C | Lily-of-the-valley *(Convallaria majus)*

and climate. A newcomer to our northern region recently told us she intended to cover her newly acquired hillside with an assortment of heathers *(Calluna vulgaris)*. We agreed they would be lovely but reluctantly advised against the investment of her time and money. Her windy, cold, partially shaded hill has fairly alkaline soil, and heathers would be most unhappy there, since they prefer acidic soil and, in cold climates, a sunny, sheltered spot.

She will undoubtedly find some other lovely plantings for her slope, since there are so many groundcovers available. Whether it is hot or cool, wet or dry, sunny or shady, you can find the ideal plants for your spot (see the list). But choose carefully, because changing a plot of vigorous groundcovers after they are well established is not an easy task. Before you plant, make sure your choices will stay in your area; you don't want to introduce a new unwelcome weed (see page 12). If possible, study groundcover displays at local nurseries,

arboreta, public gardens, or those of friends, before you plant your own.

If your space is small, it is best to use only one species or cultivar, but if you are working with a large area, a mass of a single kind of plant can get boring. By planting sizable patches of different coverings, you can create an eyecatching garden. Use plants of various forms and textures that make a tapestry of colorful flowers or green, silver, or variegated foliage, just as an artist might paint a picture by interweaving patterns of color. You may want to stick with only one species of plant but use various cultivars to provide variety. If there is danger that one species or cultivar might crowd out another, use an edging between the plant types you wish to keep separate.

When you plant woody specimens, such as junipers, cotoneasters, or other low-growing shrubs, you can dig individual holes for each with a successful outcome. But before planting herbaceous groundcovers, like bugleweeds

(*Ajuga*) or pachysandras, in heavy sod, first remove all other vegetation, either by tilling the area or by spraying an organic herbicide such as Scythe or Burnout. When you have gotten rid of all the weeds and grass, prepare the soil by tilling or digging. Then proceed to plant as you would in any garden (see Chapter 4). In a woodland area without heavy sod, this preparation shouldn't be necessary.

The distance that you set the plants apart depends on the type of plants and the speed with which they spread, so ask for advice at the nursery where you buy them. Mulch is important in a new planting of groundcovers, both to retain moisture and to keep weeds at a minimum. Until plants cover the entire area, which will take a few years, you may need to pull some weeds, but after that, most plantings should remain relatively work-free.

It can be effective to plant groundcovers as a carpet for flowering bulbs. Spring bulbs can be especially striking when they are combined with low-growing groundcovers. We will never forget the breathtaking sight of a large bed of daffodils underplanted with a carpet of glorious blue forget-me-nots (*Myosotis*) at Longwood Gardens in Pennsylvania. We have also seen beds of grape hyacinths (*Muscari*) used in a similar way with tulips at Keukenhof Gardens in the Netherlands. Tulips in bloom are also beautiful in combination with greenery like dwarf hostas, which hide the bulbs' yellowing foliage as it dies. Some of the so-called "minor" spring bulbs, such as bright blue Siberian squill (*Scilla siberica*) and glory-of-the-snows (*Chionodoxa*), can become groundcovers by naturalizing. Since they disappear late in the spring, however, they must be interplanted with later-blooming plants for all-season beauty. Summer lilies are striking rising out of a carpet of greenery. An area of groundcover is also a perfect place to plant fall-blooming bulbs that have their foliage only early in the summer. When their blooms rise again in the autumn, fall crocus (*Crocus speciosus*), meadow saffron (*Colchicum autumnale*), and magic lilies (*Lycoris*) appreciate the background that a low, green groundcover supplies.

Good Groundcovers

FOR SUNNY SPOTS
Common juniper (*Juniperus communis*)
Creeping juniper (*J. horizontalis*)
English ivy (*Hedera helix*)
Goldmoss stonecrop (*Sedum acre*)
Mazus (*Mazus reptans*)
Moss pink (*Phlox subulata*)
Spike lilyturf (*Liriope spicata*)
Virginia creeper
 (*Parthenocissus quinquefolia*)
Wall rock cress (*Arabis caucasica*)
Woolly yarrow (*Achillea tomentosa*)

FOR SLIGHTLY MOIST SHADE
Blue flag (*Iris versicolor*)
Bog arum (*Calla palustris*)
Canadian yew (*Taxus canadensis*)
Ferns (see pages 156–57)
Fringed bleeding heart (*Dicentra eximia*)
Hostas (*Hosta*)
Japanese pachysandra
 (*Pachysandra terminalis*)
Lesser periwinkle (*Vinca minor*)
Lily-of-the-valley (*Convallaria majalis*)
Sedges (*Carex*)
Snowy wood rush (*Luzula nivea*)
Spotted dead nettle (*Lamium maculatum*)
Swamp pink (*Helonias bullata*)
Tawny daylily (*Hemerocallis fulva*)
Turtleheads (*Chelone*)
Wild bee balm (*Monarda fistulosa*)

Bugleweed
(*Ajuga* 'Chocolate Chip')

Shrub rose *(Rosa* 'Bonica'*)*

The Romance of a Rose Garden

WHENEVER YOU VISIT A LARGE ROSE GARDEN in an arboretum, park, or private estate, you may feel as inspired as we do. The extraordinary colors of each perfectly shaped flower, the carefully pruned bushes, and the absence of any bugs or disease all make us want to hurry to start our own beautiful bed of roses.

Hybrid tea rose *(Rosa* 'Perfect Moment'*)*

A rose garden on home ground, fortunately, does not have to rival in size and perfection those in public places or need a staff of gardeners to keep it looking magazine-picture-perfect. You can get just as much enjoyment from fewer than a dozen plants in a bed at the side of the house or an informal island garden in the back lawn. Some rose lovers design small, formal plantings with statuary and fountains. If you happen to live in a cold climate, your rose bed may consist entirely of the hardy, rugged shrub roses, some of which, we think, rival the hybrid teas in beauty and fragrance.

Roses don't, of course, need a separate bed of their own. Single specimens can fit well in mixed borders, and the miniatures are well suited for a rock garden or container. Roses combine well with other plants, particularly if the rose is a type that blooms only once during the summer. We have found that annuals, bulbs, evergreen shrubs, vines like clematis, and many other plants are excellent companions. They can be right at home in a cottage garden or at the edge of a cutting garden. The climbers will cover arbors, pillars, and walls. They may also encircle lamp-posts, look stunning against a building or hedge, frame the front entrance to a home, mount trellises, or cascade dramatically over a fence.

Roses' names alone beg you to grow them: 'Apricot Nectar', 'Ballerina', 'Carefree Delight', 'Climbing Iceberg', 'Garden Party', 'Laura Ashley', 'Little Bo Peep', 'Maiden's Blush', 'Pink Bells', 'Pleasure', 'Raspberry Ice', and thousands more. They fill entire catalogs and abound in garden centers in every color (except black and true blue) and numerous sizes and forms.

Fortunately, you do not have to be a rose expert to grow beautiful roses. Years ago, a dairy farmer in our town became interested in hybrid tea roses and began growing them in front of

his barn. He added a few each year, and finally word began to spread that they were worth a look. Farmers in those days didn't care to waste either land or time being a "posy grower," as they called him, so he was considered a bit odd. In spite of a bad location and little encouragement, he stuck to his project, continuing to add a few more each year, until he had a magnificent display and crowds of visitors.

There is no doubt that any rose garden is a traffic stopper. It is not, however, a project for an absentee gardener, since roses need plenty of tending if they are going to succeed. You must feed, water, mulch, disbud, deadhead, prune, and, very likely, even spray them occasionally. When you give them the proper care, though, they will reward you many times over.

The key to growing roses successfully is to understand their individual needs and tend them accordingly. Although it may be tempting to buy a rose simply because it is beautiful and you like it, find out first if it will grow successfully in your climate. We have found that it is difficult to grow hybrid tea roses in the cold zones of the North, but it is possible if you protect them carefully over the winter, just as our farmer friend did. Because many roses are susceptible to diseases and as attractive to insects as they are to us, look for disease-resistant selections if you don't like to spray.

A narrow border is an effective way to arrange roses, both for ease of working with them and for better viewing and sniffing their fragrance. Find out the mature size of each bush before

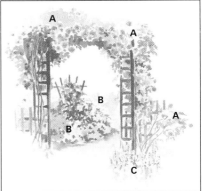

Plant Key

A | Climbing roses
B | Hybrid tea roses
C | Lamb's ears (*Stachys byzantina*)

Climbing rose (*Rosa* 'Seven Sisters')

planting so you'll be able to give it the space it needs. You may want to group different cultivars together and blend colors according to your taste. If the bed is in a location backed by a hedge, wall, or other structure, climbing roses are a good choice for the rear of the garden. If your climate is hospitable to tree roses, intersperse an occasional one amid the others, for a stunning effect. For advice on planting and caring for roses, see Part 3, page 323.

Roses in Cold Climates

Many roses need special care to survive the winter in Zone 5 and cooler areas. Just after fall frosts have begun, carefully bend the bush over and pin it or weight it down. If the canes are so large that they will not bend easily, carefully loosen the soil on one side of the plant and dig a shallow hole large enough to hold the plant. Then bend the entire plant over into the hole, burying it completely. If it is difficult to cover the entire plant easily, bury part of it and mound soil over the remaining stems. Cover it entirely with mulch or an insulation blanket, and as extra insurance, spread a layer of evergreen branches over the mulch. Uncover the plant only after the frosts are over in the spring. Do this on a cloudy day, to prevent sunburn on the new shoots. Wait until spring to prune, when you can also cut off any winter injury.

Northern gardeners find that growing shrub roses that come on their own roots, rather than those that have been grafted, are the best bet for them. Most are hardy in Zone 3 and some will even survive in Zone 2.

Shrub roses are generally the most pest-resistant, too. We particularly enjoy our rugosa roses (*Rosa rugosa*) and their hybrids, such as 'Hansa' and 'Pink

A Rose by Any Classification

The different classes of roses can be confusing to a newcomer to the rose world. The American Rose Society recognizes 35 different classifications and divides them into three categories: species roses; old garden roses (OGR), which existed before 1867; and modern roses, those introduced after that date.

SPECIES ROSES
These "wild" roses usually have single petals and grow on shrubs ranging from 2–20 feet tall. Most are fragrant and bloom only once a season, in early summer.

OLD GARDEN ROSES
These include alba, Bourbon, centifolia (the "cabbage rose"), damask, hybrid China, hybrid perpetual, moss, Noisette, tea, and others. Many have strong fragrances, and some species bloom only once in early summer.

MODERN ROSES
Hybrid tea. The most elegant rose; when first introduced in 1867, it ushered in the era of modern roses. Blooms commonly one to a long stem, sometimes with side buds. Bloom cycles every 6–7 weeks.

Grandiflora. Similar to hybrid tea, but bears smaller blooms in clusters.

Floribunda. Large clusters of colorful, short-stemmed flowers. Blooms continually, all season long.

Polyantha. Compact, sturdy shrub rose that bears large clusters of small flowers.

Miniature. Flower form and foliage like hybrid tea and floribunda roses, but scaled down. Usually 15–30 inches tall, except for micro-minis, which grow only 6–8 inches tall.

Large-flowered climbers and hybrid wichurana. Long, arching canes with great variety of blooms in different forms and colors. Train these vigorous types to grow along fences and up trellises and arbors. Rambler roses are similar but have smaller blooms and are hardier.

Shrub roses. Large, spreading, easy-to-grow bushes produce many blooms. Height and width from 5–15 feet. Many are very hardy and vigorous, and some of the newer kinds can compare quite favorably with the tea roses in bloom quality. This class includes David Austin's English roses and the Canadian Explorer hybrids.

Grootendorst', which bloom throughout the summer with little care. Their thorny canes make them ideal for an impenetrable hedge, and they produce large, colorful hips in the fall.

Climbing Roses

Climbing roses on an arbor or trellis enhance any garden. The climbers have long, relatively pliable canes, but they are unable to cling to a wall or trellis like ivy or twine like wisteria, so you must fasten them to their support. Many climbers are derived from hybrid tea roses, so they may need winter protection in cool climates. Some of the rambler roses are grown on their own roots, however, and are more winter hardy. As fall frosts begin in cool planting zones, take the tender kinds off their supports, lay them on the ground, and cover them as described on the facing page.

Tree Roses

Most tree roses ("standards") are hybrid tea roses grafted on the tall, straight stem of another rose. They grow up to 6 feet tall and need staking. Since the tops are extremely vulnerable to low temperatures, the usual practice for overwintering them in cool climates is to dig a trench on one side of the plant near the stem, loosen the roots on the other side, carefully bend over the entire tree, and bury it completely in soil and mulch. In the spring, after danger of frost has passed, dig it up carefully. Prune it then, if necessary.

For the Serious Rose Grower

Rosarians, as rose hobbyists are called, often specialize in a certain group of roses, such as fragrant, antique, or All-America Selections. If you get addicted, or you simply want more information about roses to get started on this fascinating hobby, you may want to become involved with a rose society. The American Rose Society rates roses according to their performance and has established a network of consulting rosarians who offer free advice to any gardener needing assistance. Their website offers technical information as well as some inspirational photographs. (For contact information, see page 351.)

Hardy, Vigorous, Disease-Resistant, Easy-Care Roses

HYBRID RUGOSAS
'Belle Poitevine' (pink)
'Jens Munk' (pink)
'Pink Grootendorst' (pink)
'F. J. Grootendorst' (red)
'Hansa' (red)
'Sir Thomas Lipton' (white)

HYBRID KORDESII
'William Baffin' (deep pink)

FLORIBUNDA
'Betty Prior' (pink)

SHRUB
'Carefree Delight' (pink)

EGLANTERIA
'Magnifica' (purple-crimson)

HYBRID FOETIDA
'Harison's Yellow' (yellow)

Hybrid tea rose *(Rosa* 'Opening Night'*)*

Climbing rose *(Rosa* 'William Baffin'*)*

PART THREE

A Feast of Flowers

 The directory that follows contains more than 350 plants, all readily available throughout North America. You will find species-by-species information on each plant's characteristics, where it likes best to grow, and how to care for it, as well as advice about pests and diseases that might affect it and suggestions for how to propagate it. Please note that plants may grow to different heights and bloom at different times than are listed, depending on the climatic conditions that exist.

For each plant we also offer a range of USDA hardiness zones where it can grow. Use these zones only as a guide. You may find that even though you live in Zone 5, you have a Zone 6 garden because you are near a large lake or the ocean. On the other hand, high elevations or frost pockets may very well put you in Zone 4. With reliable snow cover in Zone 3 or 4, you may be able to grow perennials that are ordinarily hardy only up to Zones 5 and 6, because the snow acts as insulation. And, wherever you live, weather variables may cause your zone to change considerably from year to year.

Abelia × grandiflora

Abelia (a-BEE-lee-a)
Abelias

Plant type: Shrub
Bloom time: Summer
Best location: Sun or light shade; fertile, well-drained soil
Diseases: Root rot, anthracnose, powdery mildew, cercospora leaf spot
Garden pests: No serious problems
Good garden companions: Underplant with wild bee balm *(Monarda fistulosa)*
Propagation: Softwood cuttings in early summer
Zones: 6–9, unless indicated otherwise below

This deciduous or evergreen shrub from Asia and Mexico and attractive foliage and funnel-shaped blooms over a long season. It is useful for borders, foundations, specimens.

GROWER'S CHOICE

Chinese abelia *(A. chinensis),* is deciduous, spreading, 5 feet tall. Zones 7–9.
'Edward Goucher', a hybrid, is semi-evergreen, with lilac-pink flowers.
Glossy abelia *(A. × grandiflora),* with fragrant, pink-tinged white flowers, grows up to 10 feet tall. Its cultivar 'Francis Mason' has golden leaves with green markings on 5-foot-tall plants; 'Goldsport' has all-yellow foliage.

Achillea (a-KIL-ee-a)
Yarrows

Plant type: Perennial
Bloom time: All summer
Best location: Sun; well-drained soil
Diseases: Crown gall, mildew, rust
Garden pests: Relatively pest-free
Good garden companions: Shasta daisy *(Leucanthemum × superbum),* monkshoods *(Aconitum)*
Propagation: Root cuttings. Easy to divide clumps in either spring or fall. Start species from seed or root cuttings.
Zones: Varies (see below)

Yarrow has fernlike, fragrant foliage. It forms nice spots of color in a flower border, but most species need frequent division so the garden doesn't become filled with them. Species range in size from tiny, creeping rock garden plants to 4-foot giants. Easy to grow, they are useful in gardens with poor, dry soil.

GROWER'S CHOICE

A. ageratifolia, with white flowers, is a good rock garden plant. 6 inches tall. Zones 2–8.
'Coronation Gold', a hybrid, is one of the best yarrows, with large, golden flowerheads that can be dried so successfully that winter bouquets look nearly as fresh as summer ones; blooms over a long period. 3 feet tall. Zones 3–8.
'Fire King' yarrow *(A. millefolium* 'Fire King')* has rosy pink flowers. 2 feet tall. Zones 3–9.
'Gold Plate' fern-leaved yarrow *(A. filipendulina* 'Gold Plate')* is similar to 'Coronation Gold' but taller, with larger flowers. 4–5 feet tall. Zones 3–9.
'Moonshine', a pale yellow hybrid, is particularly recommended for cutting. 18–25 inches tall. Zones 3–7.
'The Pearl' sneezewort *(A. ptarmica* 'The Pearl')* gets its common name from the fact that the roots were once dried and used as snuff. Its small, double, pure white blooms are excellent in arrangements and for drying. 2 feet tall. Zones 3–8.
'Taygetea', another hybrid, has attractive, silvery green foliage and light yellow flowers. Zones 3–8.
Woolly yarrow *(A. tomentosa),* with bright yellow blooms, is another good rock garden plant. 6 inches tall. Zones 2–8.

Achillea filipendulina 'Gold Plate'

Aconitum carmichaelii 'Arendsii'

Aconitum (a-koh-NEE-tum)
Monkshoods

Plant type: Perennial
Bloom time: Midsummer
Best location: Sun or partial shade; moist soil
Diseases: Crown rot, mildew, mosaic, wilt
Garden pests: The plants, being poisonous, have few insect troubles.
Good garden companions: Globe thistles (*Echinops*), 'Miss Lingard' meadow phlox (*Phlox maculata* 'Miss Lingard')
Propagation: Easily divided at any time of the year, but early spring or fall is best. Seeds take a long time to germinate and grow.
Zones: 3–8

Like delphiniums, these tall, magnificent plants add class to the border with their stately blue or purple flowers. They are not as brittle as delphiniums and so need less staking. Once established, they thrive for years without needing division. They are useful in a semi-wild garden, in a lightly shaded border, or as tall foundation plants between windows. Each individual blossom looks like a little hood; people like to lift the hood and see the two "monkeys on sticks" inside. Monkshoods are poisonous if ingested, so take care when very small or very curious children are around the plants.

GROWER'S CHOICE

A. × *cammarum* 'Bicolor' has blue-and-white flowers in mid- to late summer. 3–4 feet tall.
Autumn monkshood (*A. autumnale*) blooms in early September.
Azure monkshood (*A. carmichaelii*) has dark blue flowers in late summer and early fall. 3–4 feet tall. 'Arendsii' is a sturdy-stemmed cultivar, with blue blossoms from early fall.
Common monkshood (*A. napellus*) bears dark blue flowers in mid- to late summer. 3–4 feet tall.
'Ivorine', a hybrid, has white flowers and blooms in early summer. About 3 feet tall.
Wolf's bane (*A. lycoctonum* subsp. *vulparia*) has pale yellow flowers and blooms for most of the summer. 3–5 feet tall.

Aethionema
(ee-thee-oh-NEE-ma)
Stone cresses

Plant type: Perennial
Bloom time: Late spring to early summer
Best location: Sun; dry, sandy, alkaline soil
Diseases: Few problems
Garden pests: Aphids and spider mites
Good garden companions: Lamb's ears (*Stachys byzantina*)
Propagation: Seed; cuttings in midsummer
Zones: 5–8

Stone cresses have evergreen or semi-evergreen foliage and bear attractive, sometimes fragrant pink, red, or white flowers, similar to those of candytufts (*Iberis*). They are ideal rock garden plants. Cut back the plants after blooming.

Aethionema grandiflorum

GROWER'S CHOICE

Persian stone cress (*A. grandiflorum*) has rose-pink blooms and bluish leaves. 8–12 inches tall.

'Warley Rose' is a fine hybrid with numerous pink flowers. 6 inches tall.

Agapanthus africanus

(a-ga-PAN-thus af-rih-KAY-nus)

Lily-of-the-Nile,
African blue lily

Plant type: Perennial; treated as annual
in the North

Bloom time: Mid- to late summer

Best location: Full sun; fertile,
well-drained soil

Diseases: Occasional rots

Garden pests: Snails and slugs

Good garden companions: 'Coronation
Gold' yarrow (*Achillea* 'Coronation Gold')

Propagation: Divide in spring

Zones: Most 9–10

This tuberous-rooted perennial bears
sword-shaped leaves and 2- to 3-foot-
tall stalks of funnel-shaped, bright blue
or white flowers. Later, the flowerheads
become decorative seedheads. Where
hardy, grow in the border; in the North,
grow them in large tubs and move
them inside for the winter.

GROWER'S CHOICE

Headbourne Hybrids are the hardiest
types. Zones 7–9.

Agapanthus africanus

Ajuga reptans

Ajuga (a-JOO-ga)
Bugleweeds

Plant type: Perennial

Bloom time: Early spring

Best location: Light shade for best leaf
color; not fussy about soil conditions

Diseases: Crown rot, various leaf spots

Garden pests: Few problems

Good garden companions: Variegated
hostas

Propagation: Seed; division (easy any time
during the growing season)

Zones: 3–8

Excellent, low-growing groundcovers
with attractive foliage and blooms, but
unless used carefully, they can crowd out
your other garden plants. Ideal for spots
where they can be confined, such as in
rock gardens, in the space between a wall
and path, beneath roadside trees, or in
other places where it is difficult to mow
or where other plants do poorly. After
blooming, cut down the messy flower
stalks with lawnmower set high.

Ajuga 'Chocolate chip'

GROWER'S CHOICE

Carpet bugleweed (*A. reptans*) is a
spreader that comes in many cultivars,
all with 3- to 6-inch-tall flower spikes.
'Alba' has white flowers; 'Burgundy Glow'
has violet-blue flowers and foliage that
changes color as it ages throughout the
season, starting out wine red, then
becoming creamy white, then dark pink;
'Chocolate Chip' has brown leaves and
blue flowers and is only 4 inches tall.
Pyramidal bugleweed (*A. pyramidalis*)
has dark green leaves and blue, white, or
pink flowers; 10 inches tall. Unlike other
bugleweeds, this species does not spread,
so is the best choice for a border planting.

Alcea rosea

(al-SEE-a RO-see-a)

syn. *Althaea rosea*

Hollyhock

Plant type: Biennial or perennial

Bloom time: Midsummer to fall

Best location: Full sun; deep, rich soil

Diseases: Crown rot, leaf spot, mildew, rust, wilt

Garden pests: Aphids, borers, Japanese beetles, nematodes, slugs

Good garden companions: White border phlox *(Phlox paniculata)*, baby's breath *(Gypsophila paniculata)*

Propagation: Seed (often self-sows, assuring a continuous supply of plants)

Zones: 3–8

These tall-growing flowers are prized because they are so stately and bloom over a long period in a wide range of colors. They are biennial in warm climates and short-lived perennials in Zones 3 and 4. They are ideal against a building, fence, or hedge, since they need protection from wind; otherwise, they require staking. They have been favorites in cottage gardens for generations and were one of the few flowers grown around American farmhouses a century ago.

Alcea rosea

GROWER'S CHOICE

The old-fashioned, single-flowered hollyhocks are slightly hardier and often taller than the double hybrids, but the latter are showier, and their ruffled, roselike blooms come in many shades. 'Chater's Double' is one of the most popular cultivars and comes in a range of colors. All types are 4–8 feet or more tall.

Alchemilla (al-keh-MIL-a)

Lady's mantles

Plant type: Perennial

Bloom time: Early summer

Best location: Sun or light shade; nearly any soil except wet

Diseases: Snails and slugs

Garden pests: Few problems

Good garden companions: Catmint *(Nepeta × faassenii),* blue-flowered cranesbills *(Geranium)*

Propagation: Cuttings in summer; seed sown in spring or fall

Zones: 3–7

Alchemilla mollis

These attractive foliage plants have tiny, chartreuse blooms that last a remarkably long time after cutting. They are a good groundcover.

GROWER'S CHOICE

Alpine lady's mantle *(A. alpina)* is mat-forming, with deeply lobed, gray leaves and yellowish flowers. To 6 inches tall.

Common lady's mantle *(A. mollis)* has clusters of long-lasting, yellow-green flowers over rounded leaves. 2 feet tall.

Allium christophii

Allium (A-lee-um)
Ornamental onions

Plant type: Bulb	
Bloom time: Spring and early summer	
Best location: Full sun; rich, well-drained soil. Plant at a depth equal to 2–3 times the height of the bulb.	
Diseases: Rot, leaf spot	
Garden pests: Onion fly and thrips	
Good garden companions: Pink-flowering annuals, white-flowered yarrows (*Achillea*)	
Propagation: Divide clumps in early spring. May be grown from seed, but many species take a long time to germinate.	
Zones: 4–9 for most species	

These easy-to-grow plants are members of the same family as garlic, leeks, onion, and shallots. Flowers usually grow in round umbels. Leaves have strong odor when crushed. Good in borders, small species in rock gardens.

GROWER'S CHOICE

A. cyaneum has tiny blue flowers in summer. 6 inches tall.

A. zebdanense produces white flowers in spring. 10–18 inches tall.

Blue globe onion *(A. caeruleum)* has blue flowers in early summer. 18 inches tall.

Chinese chives *(A. tuberosum)*, also called garlic chives, have fragrant, white flowers in late summer. 12–20 inches.

Chives *(A. schoenoprasum)* are usually grown as a culinary herb, but with their attractive lavender-pink flowers, they make a nice edging plant. 1–2 feet tall.

Lily leek *(A. moly)* bears bright yellow flowers in early summer. 10 inches tall.

Naples onion *(A. neapolitanum)* has white flowers in spring. 15 inches tall.

Ostrowsky onion *(A. oreophilum,* formerly *A. ostrowskianum)* bears rose-purple flowers in early summer. 9 inches tall.

Rosenbach onion *(A. rosenbachianum)* has rosy purple flowers that are good for drying. 30 inches tall. Zones 3–9.

Stars of Persia *(A. christophii)* bears 8-inch-wide, pinkish-purple flowers in early summer. 12–24 inches. Zones 5–8.

Amaranthus
(a-ma-RAN-thus)
Amaranths

Plant type: Tender perennial grown as an annual	
Bloom time: Summer to early fall	
Best location: Sun; moderately rich soil	
Diseases: Leaf spot, rust, root rot, yellows	
Garden pests: Few problems	
Good garden companions: Mealycup sage (*Salvia farinacea*)	
Propagation: Seed	
Zones: 10–11	

GROWER'S CHOICE

Joseph's coat *(A. tricolor)* produces bushy, 3- to 4-foot-tall plants topped with insignificant flowers and brightly colored foliage, from crimson and purple to yellow, pink, or bronze, varying by cultivar.

Love-lies-bleeding *(A. caudatus)* has long, drooping, tassel-like spikes of tiny crimson or red flowers on bushy, 3- to 4-foot-tall plants. The flowers of 'Viridis' are bright green fading to cream.

Amaranthus caudatus

Amsonia hubrectii

Anaphalis (a-NAH-fa-lis)
Pearly everlastings

Plant type: Perennial
Bloom time: Mid to late summer
Best location: Full sun or partial shade; well-drained, moist soil
Diseases: Rust, stem rot, leaf spot
Garden pests: Few problems
Good garden companions: Azure monkshood (*Aconitum carmichaelii*)
Propagation: Seed; division in early spring
Zones: 3–8

Pearly everlastings grow so well, even in partial shade, that plants spread quickly. Their clusters of white flowers make them useful in rock gardens and wildflower plantings. Use them to separate drifts of brightly colored flowers in the border. To use as a dried flower, pick just before the flowers open fully, then tie in a bunch and allow to dry naturally, or dye with food coloring or florist dye before drying.

Anaphalis margaritacea

GROWER'S CHOICE

Common pearly everlasting *(A. margaritacea)* is a native wildflower with small yellow flowers surrounded with white bracts. About 2 feet tall.
Three-veined everlasting *(A. triplinervis)* has similar blooms over mounds of woolly gray-green leaves. To 3 feet.

Amsonia (am-SO-nee-a)
Blue stars

Plant type: Perennial
Bloom time: Spring and early summer
Best location: Light shade to full sun; moist, well-drained soil
Diseases: Leaf spot, rust
Garden pests: Few problems
Good garden companions: Yellow daisies (*Anthemis*) and early-blooming irises
Propagation: Seed; division of large clumps in early spring
Zones: Varies (see below)

These easy-to-grow, light blue flowers are fine in either a sunny border or a semi-shaded wildflower garden.

GROWER'S CHOICE

A. hubrectii has clear blue flowers; bright yellow fall foliage. 3 feet tall. Zones 5–9.
Blue milkweed *(A. ciliata)* has dark blue flowers and slender, threadlike leaves. 1–3 feet tall. Zones 5–9.
Willow blue star *(A. tabernaemontana)* bears pale blue flowers; yellow foliage in fall. 2 feet tall. Zones 3–9.

Anchusa (an-KOO-sa)
Alkanets

Plant type: Perennial or biennial
Bloom time: June and July
Best location: Full sun; deep, well-drained, fertile, light soil
Diseases: Mosaic, rust, mildew
Garden pests: Leafhoppers, grubs, cutworms
Good garden companions: Lady's mantle (*Alchemilla mollis*)
Propagation: Seed (plants often self sow); division or root cuttings in early spring
Zones: 3–8

The beautiful blue shades of alkanets' forget-me-not-type flowers are greatly prized in flower gardens, though the plants tend to be short-lived. Attractive to bees. Deadhead to encourage a second bloom.

GROWER'S CHOICE

A. azurea 'Loddon Royalist', sturdy stems need no staking. 3 feet tall.

Cape bugloss *(A. capensis)*, biennial usually grown as annual, has bright blue blooms all summer; good in rock gardens; has pink or white cultivars. 8 inches.
'Dropmore' blue bugloss *(A. azurea 'Dropmore')*, an excellent cultivar, has rich blue flowers. 2–3 feet tall.

Anchusa azurea 'Loddon Royalist'

Androsace (an-DROSS-a-see)
Rock jasmines

Plant type: Perennial

Bloom time: Early summer to fall

Best location: Sun; poor, sandy, slightly alkaline soil

Diseases: Rust, leaf spot, downy mildew

Garden pests: Aphids

Good garden companions: *A. sarmentosa* with alpine columbine (*Aquilegia alpina*)

Propagation: Separate the rosettes and replant in spring or early summer. Water from below to keep the neck and foliage dry to prevent disease.

Zones: 5–7

These attractive alpine plants resemble primroses and grow well in the parts of North America with dry weather and cold winters. They do especially well in a sunny rock garden.

GROWER'S CHOICE

A. ciliata bears deep pink flowers in spring and early summer. 1 inch tall.

A. lanuginosa is a trailing, mat-forming plant with silver-gray foliage and pink-lilac blooms in mid- to late summer. 2–4 inches tall.

A. sarmentosa has rosettes of light green leaves and attractive, rosy pink flowers in late spring and early summer. 2–4 inches tall.

Androsace ciliata

Anemone blanda

Anemone (a-NEM-oh-nee)
Anemones, windflowers

Plant type: Perennial with fibrous or bulb-type roots (tubers or rhizomes)

Bloom time: Various times for different species

Best location: Light shade, except for Japanese and grape-leaved anemones, which prefer full sun; all like moist loam that's rich in leaf mold or compost.

Garden pests: Blister beetle, caterpillars, slugs

Diseases: Leaf spot, collar rot, viruses, downy mildew

Good garden companions: Grecian windflower goes well with red tulips; other species with ferns or hostas

Propagation: Division in early spring (best method); root cuttings; seed

Zones: Varies (see below)

These popular plants produce saucer- or cup-shaped flowers in white or shades of pink, red, yellow, or purple. Some species, such as the meadow anemone (*A. canadensis*), are ideal for wildflower gardens and rockeries, since these spots are their natural settings.

GROWER'S CHOICE

Alpine columbine (*A. alpina*) has 18-inch blue flowers in late spring. Zones 4–7.

A. multifida, a native of North America, has yellow flowers in summer and is exceptionally hardy. 1 foot tall. Zones 2–6.

Grape-leaved anemone (*A. vitifolia*) blooms in fall, even after light frosts, with white flowers. 3 feet tall. Zones 5–8.

Grecian windflower (*A. blanda*) blooms in early spring, with pink, blue, or white, daisylike flowers. 6 inches tall. Zones 4–8.

Japanese anemones (*A.* × *hybrida* and *A. hupehensis* var. *japonica*) are fall bloomers, coming even after light frosts, with white, pink, or rosy red flowers. 2–4 feet tall. Zones 4–8.

Meadow anemone (*A. canadensis*) is a native plant good for meadows or light-shaded woodland gardens, with white-and-gold blooms in early summer. 2 feet tall. Zones 3–8.

Snowdrop anemone (*A. sylvestris*) bears 1- to 3-inch-wide white flowers in spring. 1 foot tall. Zones 4–8.

Anthemis tinctoria
(AN-them-iss tink-TOR-ee-a)

Yellow daisy,
golden marguerite

Plant type: Perennial

Bloom time: Summer

Best location: Full sun; ordinary garden soil

Diseases: Rare

Garden pests: Rare

Good garden companions: Pink lavateras; yarrows (*Achillea*)

Propagation: Named cultivars by division in spring; others by seed or division

Zones: 3–7

These bright-flowering beauties have aromatic, fernlike foliage and bear an abundance of medium-sized daisies for many weeks in summer, ranging in color from bright yellow to creamy white and in height from 1–3 feet. Yellow daisies often spread so rapidly, both by seed and underground stems, that they require frequent division to keep them in control.

Try to keep the flowers picked so they won't go to seed and start new plants; seedlings usually are not as attractive as the named cultivars and are even more weedy. May be short-lived.

GROWER'S CHOICE

'**Kelwayi**' has exceptionally large, lemon-colored flowers. 2 feet tall.

'**Moonlight**' has light yellow flowers and blooms over a long season. 30 inches tall.

Antirrhinum majus 'Double Azalea Apricot'

Antirrhinum majus
(an-tee-REE-num MAH-juss)

Snapdragon

Plant type: Short-lived perennial, usually grown as an annual

Bloom time: Summer

Best location: Full sun to light shade; well-drained, fertile garden soil

Diseases: Blight, leaf spot, root rot, rust, downy mildew

Garden pests: Leaf miners

Good garden companions: Western mugwort (*Artemisia ludoviciana*), white phlox

Propagation: Seed

Upright spikes of aromatic flowers in a wide range of bright and pastel colors; grow from a few inches to 6 feet tall.

GROWER'S CHOICE

'**Black Prince**', with crimson flowers and bronze foliage. 18 inches tall.

A. majus 'Black Prince'

'**Double Azalea Apricot**', with fragrant, frilly double flowers. 30–36 inches tall.

'**Madam Butterfly**', with double flowers in many colors. 3 feet tall.

Aquilegia (a-kwi-LEE-gee-a)
Columbines

Plant type: Perennial

Bloom time: Spring and early summer

Best location: Sun or light shade; good garden soil

Diseases: Crown rot, leaf spot, mosaic, root rot, rust

Garden pests: Borers, leaf miners, caterpillars

Good garden companions: White-flowering kinds go well with bright red plants such as geraniums (*Pelargonium*); colored columbine is good with willow blue star (*Amsonia tabernaemontana*); red-and-yellow wild columbine is lovely with blue phlox (*Phlox divaricata*).

Propagation: Natives by seed; hybrids by division or seed. (It is best to buy seed, rather than save your own, because the flowers will usually be better.) Plan to be patient: The seeds of some species germinate irregularly, over a period of several months, and seedlings require at least a year's growth before blooming.

Zones: 3–8, unless indicated otherwise

These bell-shaped flowers are treasures for the garden, whether you choose the wild species, found frequently in rocky pastures and along roadsides, or the new, brilliantly colored, large-flowering hybrids. Some of these have flowers as large as daffodils, with long, showy spurs. All of the hybrids make excellent border plants and cut flowers, but unlike their wild ancestors, they need to be replaced every three or four years because they are short-lived. The natives fit well into a wildflower or rock garden. Growing in compact clumps, they dance gaily in a light breeze. Most get 20 to 30 inches tall.

GROWER'S CHOICE

Eastern wild columbine (*A. canadensis*), a native, bears red-and-yellow flowers with short spurs. 2 feet tall.

European columbine (*A. vulgaris*) has blue, purple, white, or pink flowers. 3 feet tall. Zones 3–9.

Fan columbine (*A. flabellata*) has purple-blue flowers over handsome, blue-green leaves. 12 inches tall. Needs moist soil and light shade. Zones 3–9.

Aquilegia chrysantha

Golden columbine (*A. chrysantha*) blooms later than the others, with long-spurred yellow flowers. 3 feet tall.

Rocky Mountain columbine (*A. caerulea*) has white petals and long blue spurs. 4 feet tall.

Arabis caucasica

Arabis (A-ra-bis)
Rock cresses

Plant type: Perennial

Bloom time: Early spring

Best location: Full sun; good, loose garden soil

Diseases: Clubroot, rust, leaf spots, mildew

Garden pests: Aphids, midges

Good garden companions: Spring bulbs of all sorts; 'Flore Pleno' wall rock cress with *Primula auricula* in varied colors

Propagation: Seed; division in spring; cuttings

Zones: 5–8; colder areas where good snow cover is present or when mulched over winter

As its name suggests, this plant is excellent in the rock garden, where its pure white to purple flowers reach well above the foliage, completely covering it; the plants form a dense mass. Cut off dead flowers after blooming.

GROWER'S CHOICE

A. procurrens is a free-blooming species with white flowers and glossy green leaves; its cultivar 'Variegata' has green leaves edged in creamy white. 2–3 inches tall.

'Spring Charm' fringed rock cress (*A. blepharophylla* 'Spring Charm') has rosy purple, fragrant flowers and green leaves. 4–8 inches tall.

Wall rock cress (*A. caucasica*) is a vigorous groundcover with gray-green leaves and sweetly scented, single white flowers. 6–10 inches tall. The cultivar 'Flore Pleno' has double white blooms; others come in pink and rose shades.

Arisaema triphyllum

(a-riss-EE-ma tri-FIL-um)

Jack-in-the-pulpit

Plant type: Bulb (tuber)

Bloom time: Late spring to early summer

Best location: Moderate shade; moist, slightly acidic soil

Diseases: Rust, leaf blight, anthracnose

Garden pests: Weevils, slugs, snails

Good garden companions: Turtleheads (*Chelone*), trilliums, false Solomon's seal (*Smilacina racemosa*)

Propagation: Divide the bulb offshoots in fall or plant seed.

Zones: 3–9

The curious bloom is composed of an upright, trumpet-shaped, green or purple-and-green spathe capped with a hood (the pulpit). Inside, the flowers are borne on a narrow, upright structure known as a spadix (or the "Jack"). The spathe eventually falls off, and the flowers on the spadix develop into red berries in summer. 6–24 inches tall. Good in shady wildflower gardens and woodland plantings. Set the tuber so its base is 2–3 inches below the soil surface.

Arisaema triphyllum

Armeria maritima 'Rubrifolia'

Armeria (ar-MEER-ee-a)

Thrifts

Plant type: Perennial

Bloom time: Late spring into summer

Best location: Sun; sandy soil

Diseases: None

Garden pests: None

Good garden companions: Soapworts (*Saponaria*), blue crested iris (*Iris cristata*)

Propagation: Divide clumps in spring every 3 years; sow seed in fall and protect over winter in a cold frame.

Zones: Varies (see below)

Thrifts produce grasslike clumps of foliage that is mostly evergreen, except in severe climates. They are good choices for a seaside or rock garden.

GROWER'S CHOICE

'Bee's Ruby', a hybrid, has bright pink flowers. 1 foot tall. Zones 6–8.

Plantain thrift (*A. pseudarmeria*) is taller than the others, with white or pink-toned flowers on 18-inch stems. Zones 6–8.

Sea thrift (*A. maritima*) is the most popular species, with white, red, or pink blooms, depending on the cultivar; usually to 8 inches tall. 'Laucheana', one of the best selections, has crimson flowers; to 1 foot tall. 'Rubrifolia' has purple-pink flowers. Zones 3–9.

Artemisia (ar-teh-MI-zee-a)
Wormwoods

Plant type:	Perennial
Bloom time:	Grown primarily for foliage
Best location:	Full sun; fertile, well-drained soil
Diseases:	Rust, mildew
Garden pests:	Quite free of pests
Good garden companions:	Bright pink and red perennials (for example, 'Powis Castle' with red astilbes)
Propagation:	Division in spring or fall (easy); cuttings; seed
Zones:	Varies (see below)

Most wormwoods have inconspicuous flowers, so you'll grow them for their silvery white, silky-textured foliage, which is sometimes fragrant. An occasional trim keeps them bushy and looking good.

GROWER'S CHOICE

'Powis Castle', a hybrid, has lacy, silvery white leaves on handsome, shrubby plants. 2 to 3 feet tall. Zones 5–8.

'Silver Brocade' beach wormwood (*A. stelleriana* 'Silver Brocade'), a compact, creeping selection with woolly white foliage, is widely used in seashore plantings. 6–8 inches tall. Zones 3–7.
'Silver King' artemisia (*A. ludoviciana* var. *albula* 'Silver King') is a spreader but superb for bouquets and drying, with silvery white foliage. 3 feet tall. Zones 4–9.
Silvermound (*A. schmidtiana*) is one of the most popular choices for flower borders because of its strikingly beautiful mounds of feathery, silvery foliage. 12–18 inches tall. Zones 3–8.
Southernwood (*A. abrotanum*) has aromatic, lacy, gray-green leaves on a shrubby plant that makes a good background for colorful flowers. About 4 feet tall. Zones 5–8.
White mugwort (*A. lactiflora*), unlike the other species, is grown for its feathery, white, late-summer-to-fall flowers. To 4 feet tall. Zones 5–8.
Wormwood (*A. absinthium*) is a fast-spreading or very invasive perennial with sharp-scented, silvery gray foliage often planted to repel wild animals in gardens and poultry yards. To 3 feet. Zones 3–8.

Arum italicum

Arum (AIR-rum)
Lords-and-ladies

Plant type:	Bulb (tuber)
Bloom time:	Spring
Best location:	Sun or light shade; rich, moist soil. Plant 2–3 inches deep.
Diseases:	None
Garden pests:	Quite free of pests
Good garden companions:	Ferns
Propagation:	Divide clumps of tubers in spring, or plant seed in the fall.
Zones:	Varies (see below)

GROWER'S CHOICE

Black calla (*A. pictum*) has purple-hooded spathes. About 10 inches tall. Zones 7–9.
Italian arum (*A. italicum*) has arrow-shaped leaves and 1-foot-tall, greenish white, hooded spathes in spring, followed by red berries. The leaves wither and die after blooming, leaving the berries visible during the summer until new leaves appear in the fall. It is one of the hardiest species and grows well in Zones 6–9. 'Marmoratum' has interesting cream-veined foliage.

Artemisia lactiflora

Aruncus (a-RUN-kus)
Goat's beards

Plant type: Perennial
Bloom time: Early summer
Best location: Prefer light shade and moist soil; will grow in full sun and average soil.
Diseases: Seldom troubled
Garden pests: Tarnished plant bug
Good garden companions: Lady's mantle (*Alchemilla mollis*)
Propagation: Division in early spring or fall (easy); seed. The plant is dioecious, with male and female blossoms on separate plants, so don't be surprised when you don't find seeds on some of the plants.
Zones: 4–8

These handsome perennials bear plumes of snow-white blossoms held well above the leaves. The tallest ones make good single specimens or background plants in the border, and they are also useful in wild or semi-wild gardens. Their bloom period is rather short.

GROWER'S CHOICE

Common goat's beard (*A. dioicus*) reaches up to 7 feet when in bloom. 'Kneiffii' is an improved cultivar with finer leaves that grows 2–4 feet tall.
Dwarf goat's beard (*A. aethusifolius*) is more compact and has more open flower clusters. To 1 foot tall.

Aruncus dioicus

Asarum (a-SAH-rum)
Wild gingers

Plant type: Perennial
Bloom time: Spring
Best location: Light to full shade; humus-rich, well-drained, slightly acidic soil
Diseases: Rust
Garden pests: Snails and slugs
Good garden companions: Other shade-loving plants, such as ferns and hostas
Propagation: Divide in early spring; sow fresh seed in summer.
Zones: Varies (see below)

Wild gingers are low-growing, with bell-shaped, brownish purple flowers and ginger-scented roots. They make fine groundcovers for shady gardens.

GROWER'S CHOICE

Canadian wild ginger (*A. canadense*) has light green, kidney-shaped, deciduous

Asarum europaeum

leaves over bell-shaped, purple-to-brown flowers. To 6 inches tall. Zones 2–8.
European wild ginger (*A. europaeum*) is a slower-spreading evergreen species, with shiny leaves over bell-shaped, purple-to-brown flowers. 3 inches tall. Zones 4–8.

Asclepias (a-SKLay-pee-us)
Milkweeds

Plant type: Perennial
Bloom time: Midsummer to early fall
Best location: Sun; most prefer dry soil (except for swamp milkweed)
Diseases: Leaf spot, mosaic, rust
Garden pests: Aphids, caterpillars, scale
Good garden companions: Wild bergamot (*Monarda fistulosa*), gloriosa daisy (*Rudbeckia hirta*), delphiniums
Propagation: Seed. Since milkweeds are difficult to transplant, plant the seed in pots and let them become well established before moving them to the garden.
Zones: Varies (see below)

Dense clusters of blooms are followed by elongated pods that enclose silky-haired seeds. Milkweeds start to grow late in spring, so it's a good idea to mark their place in the garden so that you don't accidentally damage their underground sprouts when you cultivate earlier. They have long roots and are difficult to divide or transplant.

GROWER'S CHOICE

Bloodflower (*A. curassavica*) bears red-and-orange flowers. It is evergreen where hardy and grown as an annual elsewhere. 3 feet tall. Zones 8–10.
Butterfly weed (*A. tuberosa*), true to its name, attracts butterflies. The flowers range from bright orange-red through clear orange to yellow flowers. 2–3 feet tall. Zones 3–7.
Swamp milkweed (*A. incarnata*) has pink flowers. Unlike the other species, swamp milkweed prefers evenly moist soil. 3–4 feet tall. Zones 3–8.

Asclepias tuberosa

Aster novae-angliae 'September Ruby'

Aster (AS-ter)
Asters

Plant type: Perennial (for annual asters, see *Callistephus chinensis*)	
Bloom time: Late summer and fall	
Best location: Light shade to full sun; fertile garden soil	
Diseases: Leaf spot, mildew, rust, wilt	
Garden pests: Japanese beetles, lacebugs, nematodes	
Good garden companions: 'Autumn Joy' sedum (*Sedum* 'Autumn Joy'), goldenrods (*Solidago*), common sneezeweed (*Helenium autumnale*), dahlias	
Propagation: Division in early spring; seed	
Zones: Varies (see below)	

Because perennial asters bloom at the end of the summer when flowers are few, they would be appreciated even if they weren't particularly beautiful. The hundreds of species and cultivars range in height from a few inches to nearly 6 feet. Colors range from lavender, purple, and deep blue to pink, red, rose, and white. Many bloom too late for the short growing season of the far northern states. Asters need little special care beyond regular division, but pinching back several times in early summer will help develop more compact, bushy plants.

Although in England all asters are called Michaelmas daisies, in North America the term is commonly applied only to such old standbys as the New England and New York asters. Both are worth planting in wildflower gardens and borders. The new hybrids of both species, with their brilliant colors and larger blooms, are ideal for any perennial border. We can mention only a few of the many outstanding cultivars here. Visit a nursery, if possible, and buy only those that you are sure will do well in your climate.

GROWER'S CHOICE

Italian aster *(A. amellus)* blooms in lavender-blue shades. Prefers full sun and alkaline soil. 1–2 feet tall. Zones 3–8.
New England aster *(A. novae-angliae)* is abundant along roadsides in early fall. To 5 feet tall. Cultivars include 'Barr's Blue', 'Harrington's Pink', 'Red Star', and 'September Ruby'. Zones 3–8.
New York aster *(A. novi-belgii)* comes in a similarly wide range of colors. To 4 feet tall. Cultivars include 'Coombe Violet', 'Crimson Brocade', and white 'Mt. Everest'. Zones 4–8.

Astilbe (a-STIL-bee)
Astilbes

Plant type: Perennial	
Bloom time: Summer	
Best location: Full sun or light shade; slightly moist soil	
Diseases: Mildew, wilt	
Garden pests: Aphids, Japanese beetles, mites	
Good garden companions: Hostas, purple coneflower (*Echinacea purpurea*), wintercreeper (*Euonymus fortunei*)	
Propagation: Divide in early spring.	
Zones: 3–8	

Topped by feathery-plumed flowers that stand over attractive fernlike foliage, astilbes range in height from a few inches to several feet. They come in many shades of pink, red, and purple, as well as white and cream. The flowers look better and last longer in partial shade. Most behave nicely in a sunny, moist border, although a few of the older types spread quickly and outgrow their spot. Dig and divide them every 2–4 years. By choosing cultivars that bloom at different times, you can have blossoms for most of the summer.

Astilbe 'White Wings'

Astibles are excellent choices for flower borders and partly shaded paths; dwarf kinds are ideal for rock gardens.

GROWER'S CHOICE

Dwarf Chinese astilbe *(A. chinensis* var. *pumila)* is a low-growing, spreading variety with rose-pink flowers and reddish green foliage. Grows well on dry soil and makes a good groundcover. 1 foot tall.

Hybrids. Most other popular astilbes are hybrids, including early-flowering pink 'Amethyst' (30 inches tall); early-blooming 'Fanal', with bright carmine-red flowers (30 inches tall); midsummer-flowering peachy pink 'Peach Blossom' (26 inches); and midsummer-flowering white 'Deutschland' (24 inches).

Astilbe 'Peach Blossom'

Aurinia saxatilis

Aurinia saxatilis
(aw-RIN-ee-a saks-a-TIL-is)

Basket-of-gold, goldentuft

Plant type: Perennial
Bloom time: Spring to early summer
Best location: Full sun; well-drained, good garden soil
Diseases: Clubroot, leaf rot, wilt
Garden pests: Flea beetles
Good garden companions: Perennial candytuft *(Iberis sempervirens),* red tulips
Propagation: Division in late summer or fall (easy), or cuttings in early summer (also easy). Except for double forms, basket-of-gold also starts readily from seed. For best results, sow seed in August and let it winter over in a protected place.
Zones: 4–8

This low-growing evergreen perennial is ideal in the rock garden or border or as an edging for flower beds, shrub borders, and paths. Smothered in masses of small, golden yellow flowers, the species usually grows about 1 foot tall. Cut back after blooming for longer life.

GROWER'S CHOICE

Basket-of-gold *(A. saxatilis),* including 'Citrina' (also sold as 'Sulphurea'), with lemon yellow blooms (8 inches); 'Compacta', with bright yellow blooms over dense growth on cascading plant (to 10 inches); 'Flore Pleno', with bright yellow, double flowers (to 8 inches); 'Sunny Border Apricot', with peach-yellow flowers (to 10 inches).

Baptisia (bap-TIZ-ee-a)
False indigos

Plant type: Perennial
Bloom time: Late spring to early summer
Best location: Full sun; dry soil
Diseases: Leaf spot, mildew, rust
Garden pests: Not common
Good garden companions: Meadow sage *(Salvia pratensis)*
Propagation: Divide in early spring; sow seed in spring or fall
Zones: Varies (see below)

Unusual pealike flowers in spikelike clusters, followed by interesting seedpods. Blue false indigo is especially attractive in a blue-and-white garden.

GROWER'S CHOICE

Blue false indigo *(B. australis)* is a particularly hardy species, with vivid blue flowers and prominent dark seedpods. It makes a nice hedge or back-of-the-border plant but dies back immediately after even a mild frost. 3–5 feet tall. Zones 3–9.
White false indigo *(B. alba)* has white flowers. 2–3 feet tall. Zones 4–9.
Yellow false indigo *(B. tinctoria),* with yellow flowers, is a good plant for a wildflower bed. 3–4 feet tall. Zones 5–9.

Baptisia australis

Begonia (beh-GON-ee-a)
Begonias

Plant type: Bulb (tuber) or tender perennial

Bloom time: Summer

Best location: Light shade; fertile, well-drained soil. Plant tubers so the tops are 3 inches below the soil surface.

Diseases: Powdery mildew, rot

Garden pests: Mealybugs, mites, thrips, whiteflies

Good garden companions: Dwarf marigolds, dwarf zinnias

Propagation: Divide tuberous-rooted kinds in early spring by cutting the tubers apart, leaving at least one bud on each piece. Plant seeds of wax begonias in early spring, or take cuttings in summer.

Zones: Varies (see below)

Begonia grandis

Hardy begonia (*B. grandis*) bears fragrant pink or white flowers in summer. 2 feet tall. Zones 6–9.

Tuberous begonias (*B. × tuberhybrida*) have spectacular, brilliant, usually double blooms in various forms, including rose and camellia. Some are fragrant; many have attractive, fancy leaves. Use upright types in borders and pendulous ones in hanging baskets, planters, and window boxes. Most are not frost-hardy; to overwinter, dig, dry, and store tubers in a frost-free area.

Wax begonias (*B. Semperflorens hybrids*) are tender perennials with fibrous roots, single or double flowers, and green, reddish, or bronze leaves. 8–12 inches tall. Cocktail Series red, pink, or white flowers are sun-resistant.

Bellis perennis
(BEL-iss pe-REN-iss)
English daisy

Plant type: Perennial usually grown as a biennial

Bloom time: Spring and summer

Best location: Full sun, but tolerates light shade; good garden soil

Diseases: Blight, leaf spot, rot

Garden pests: Nematodes

Good garden companions: Violas (*Viola*), catmint (*Nepeta × faassenii*)

Propagation: Divide in early spring or after flowering (easy); seed is generally sown during summer for flowers the following year.

Zones: 4–8

At 2–8 inches tall, English daisy is ideal for rock gardens or for edging paths and borders. It prefers cool weather but may need some winter protection in Zones 3–5. The single or double red, pink, or white flowers begin to bloom in early spring. Although the botanical name suggests that English daisies are peren-

Bellis perennis

nials, most gardeners grow them as biennials and sow seed each year. You can also start seed in late winter and grow them as annuals. In some places they self-sow enough to become weedy.

Many cultivars, including Super Enorma Series with double, 3-inch flowers, and Tasso Series with double red, pink, or white blooms and quilled petals.

Bergenia (ber-JEEN-ee-a)
Bergenias, elephant's ears

Plant type: Perennial

Bloom time: Early spring

Best location: Full sun with afternoon shade; sandy, slightly alkaline soil

Diseases: Leaf spot

Garden pests: Slugs

Good garden companions: Smoke tree (*Cotinus coggygria*)

Propagation: Seed; division in early spring or fall

Zones: 3–8

These handsome Asian natives are good at the front of a border. Their glossy leaves, up to 1 foot across, often turn bronze in fall; they are evergreen in Zone 6 and warmer areas. The showy pink, white, or purple-pink flowers bloom in clusters on short, red stems 12–18 inches tall. Need winter protection in Zones 3–6.

B. stracheyi has fragrant pink flowers. 1 foot tall.

Leather-leaved bergenia (*B. crassifolia*), popular on West Coast, has many cultivars in pink and red shades. 18 inches tall.

Purple heart-leaved bergenia (*B. cordifolia* 'Purpurea') has purple-red flowers and reddish green leaves. 2 feet tall.

Bergenia cordifolia

Boltonia asteroides
(bowl-TOE-nee-a as-ter-OY-deez)
Boltonia

Plant type: Perennial

Bloom time: Late summer and fall

Best location: Light shade or full sun; good garden soil

Diseases: Anthracnose, leaf spot, mildew, rust

Garden pests: Relatively pest-free

Good garden companions: 'Burgundy' blanket flower (*Gaillardia* × *grandiflora* 'Burgundy')

Propagation: Division in spring (easy); seed

Zones: 4–9

Boltonia asteroides

Tall-growing boltonia produces an abundance of daisy-shaped, 1-inch-wide pink, white, or lavender flowers in late summer, when many other perennials have gone by. It is a valuable background plant in a border. Thinning out some of the stems in early summer will help encourage sturdier plants, but even so, you will probably need to stake them. You will also need to divide them regularly to keep the clumps from getting too large.

GROWER'S CHOICE

B. asteroides 'Snowbank', a popular white-flowered cultivar, is shorter than the species. 4 feet tall.

B. asteroides var. *latisquama* 'Pink Beauty' has light pink blooms. 5 feet tall.

Brachyscome iberidifolia
(bra-kee-KOH-mee i-be-ri-di-FOH-lee-a)
Swan River daisy

Brachyscome iberidifolia

Plant type: Annual

Bloom time: Midsummer to fall

Best location: A sheltered location in full sun; well-drained, fertile soil

Diseases: Seldom troubled

Garden pests: Snails and slugs

Good garden companions: Pair blue cultivars with white astilbes

Propagation: Sow seed in spring

Compact masses of finely cut leaves are covered with 1½-inch, fragrant, daisy-type flowers that have yellow centers and purple, blue, or white petals. To 1 foot. Native to Australia, New Zealand, and New Guinea, it blossoms best in cooler summer weather. It is a good choice for both containers and borders.

GROWER'S CHOICE

'Blue Star'
'White Splendor'

Bracteantha bracteata
(brak-tee-AN-tha brac-tee-AH-ta) syn. *Helichrysum bracteatum*
Strawflower

Plant type: Short-lived perennial

Bloom time: Summer to fall

Best location: Full sun; moist, well-drained soil

Diseases: Downy mildew

Garden pests: Seldom troubled

Good garden companions: 'Crater Lake Blue' Hungarian speedwell (*Veronica austriaca* subsp. *teucrium* 'Crater Lake Blue')

Propagation: Sow seed in spring

Zones: 10–11

Commonly grown as annuals, these old-fashioned favorites bear red, yellow, pink, or white daisylike flowers with papery, petal-like bracts and are 1–5 feet tall. Strawflowers are good in the border or in cutting gardens and for dried flowers.

GROWER'S CHOICE

Bright Bikinis Series, with double blooms in many colors. 1 foot tall.

Monstrosum Series, also with double blooms in many colors. 3 feet tall.

Bracteantha bracteata **Monstrosum Series**

Brassica oleracea
(BRA-si-ka oh-le-RAY-see-a)
Ornamental cabbage and kale

Plant type: Biennial grown as an annual
Bloom time: Late summer to fall
Best location: Full sun; fertile, alkaline soil
Diseases: Black leaf spot, mildew, damping-off, rust
Garden pests: Cutworms, cabbage butterfly, root maggots, aphids, leaf miners
Good garden companions: Fall-blooming asters and chrysanthemums
Propagation: Sow seed in early spring

Brassica oleracea **'Red Feather'**

Showy rosettes of rounded to deeply toothed leaves in shades of red, white, and pink; colors intensify as weather cools in fall. Usually 12–18 inches tall.

GROWER'S CHOICE

Color Up cabbage hybrids have pink, red, or white centers. 10–12 inches tall.
Peacock Series kale hybrids, 1-foot-wide heads, with red or white centers.
'Red Feather' kale has a large, lacy head with deeply notched leaves.

Browallia
(bro-WAL-ee-a)
Sapphire flowers, bush violets

Plant type: Tender perennials and annuals
Bloom time: Summer
Best location: Full sun or partial shade; fertile, well-drained soil
Diseases: Leaf spot, tomato wilt virus
Garden pests: Whiteflies, aphids
Good garden companions: Pair blue cultivars with white phlox or bellflowers (*Campanula*)
Propagation: Sow seed in early spring for summer blooms

Sapphire flowers have bushy stems with slightly sticky leaves and many blue, violet, or white flowers. They grow to 2 feet tall. These shrubby tropical plants are grown as annuals in borders and containers.

GROWER'S CHOICE

B. americana bears blue-violet or white flowers. 24 inches tall.
B. speciosa includes 'Dawn Blue' (light blue; 18 inches); 'Silver Bells' (white; 12 inches); 'White Troll' (white; 10 inches).

Browallia americana

Brunnera macrophylla
(BRUN-er-a mak-roh-FIL-la)
Siberian bugloss

Plant type: Perennial
Bloom time: Spring to early summer
Best location: Light shade; moist, well-drained, fairly fertile soil
Diseases: None
Garden pests: Quite pest-free
Good garden companions: Hostas, 'Pink Ridge' creeping phlox (*Phlox stolonifera* 'Pink Ridge')
Propagation: Seed; division in early spring; root cuttings
Zones: 3–8

This native of Siberia has interesting leaf variegations and clusters of small, intense blue flowers that resemble forget-me-nots (*Myosotis*). Siberian bugloss works well as a groundcover or combined with woodland plants in a lightly shaded border. It grows 18 inches tall.

GROWER'S CHOICE

'Hadspen Cream' has narrow, creamy white leaf edges.
'Variegata' has wide white borders on green leaves.

Brunnera macrophylla **'Hadspen Cream'**

Buddleia davidii

Buddleia (BUD-lee-a)
Butterfly bushes

Plant type: Deciduous shrub

Bloom time: Summer

Best location: Full sun; well-drained, fertile soil

Diseases: Leaf spot, dieback

Garden pests: Caterpillars, spider mites, weevils

Good garden companions: Purple coneflower (*Echinacea purpurea*), white border phlox (*Phlox paniculata*)

Propagation: Midsummer semi-hardwood cuttings; seed

Zones: 6–9

These spreading shrubs are ideal for attracting butterflies to your yard. Grow them as a hedge around a garden specifically for butterflies, or mix them into your beds and borders.

GROWER'S CHOICE

B. alternifolia bears rounded clusters of very fragrant pink flowers. To 12 feet. *B. davidii* bears fragrant lilac-like clusters of white, pink, purple, or lilac flowers; to 10 feet tall. Catalogs list many cultivars of this species, varying in flower color and size. In the northern parts of its range, it may die back to the ground during a cold winter, but it usually comes back from the roots. *B. × weyeriana* has fragrant yellow blossoms. To 12 feet.

Calendula officinalis
(ka-LEN-dew-la oh-fi-si-NAL-is)

Calendula, pot marigold

Plant type: Annual

Bloom time: All summer

Best location: Full sun or light shade; fertile, well-drained soil

Diseases: Leaf spot, rust, cucumber mosaic virus, mildew

Garden pests: Slugs, aphids

Good garden companions: 'Blue Boy' bachelor button (*Centaurea cyanus* 'Blue Boy'), zinnias

Propagation: Sow seed in early spring

Calendula officinalis 'Prince Mix'

Showy, easy-to-grow plant with orange, yellow, gold, or reddish single or double daisylike blooms for most of the growing season. 1 to 2 feet tall. Sometimes self-sows, although the colors of the seedlings may not be as good as the hybrids. Grow them in the cutting garden, in pots, or in the flower border.

Callirhoe involucrata
(ka-lee-ROH-ee in-vo loo-KRAH-ta)

Poppy mallow

Plant type: Perennial

Bloom time: All summer

Best location: Sun; well-drained soil

Diseases: Powdery mildew, rust

Garden pests: Spider mites, aphids

Good garden companions: Lamb's ears (*Stachys byzantina*), Texas bluebonnet (*Lupinus texensis*)

Propagation: Seed; 4-inch stem cuttings in early summer

Zones: 4–6

These low-growing (6–12 inches tall) plants have abundant, 2-inch-wide, poppy-shaped blossoms in bright reddish pink with white throats. They are good choices for large borders, wildflower plantings, and rock gardens and for planting at the top of a slope. Their stems are trailing, and their deep, carrotlike roots, which can withstand drought

Callirhoe involucrata

conditions, make them especially useful for seashore plantings. They grow rapidly but are sometimes short-lived and in some locations are biennial. Mature plants are difficult to transplant.

Callistephus chinensis

(ka-LEE-ste-fus chin-EN-sis)

China aster

Plant type: Annual

Bloom time: Summer to fall

Best location: Full sun; moist, well-drained, slightly alkaline soil

Diseases: Powdery mildew, aster yellows, wilt, rust

Garden pests: Blister beetles, aphids, spider mites, galls

Good garden companions: Dwarf kinds in containers with edging lobelia (*Lobelia erinus*); in the garden, with purple bellflowers (*Campanula*)

Propagation: Sow seeds indoors in early spring for early summer blooms

These annuals produce colorful single, semi-double, or double chrysanthemum-like blooms in shades of pink, purple, white, and blue-white. They are 10 to 30 inches tall. Deadhead to keep them blooming longer; in mild seasons, they will bloom well into the winter. Good with perennials and annuals in a sunny border or in a cutting garden.

Callistephus chinensis 'Matsumoto Blue'

Calluna vulgaris

(ka-LOO-na vul-GAH-riss)

Heather

Calluna vulgaris 'Kinlochruel'

Caltha palustris

(KAL-tha pa-LUS-tris)

Marsh marigold, cowslip

Plant type: Perennial

Bloom time: Spring

Best location: Full sun or light shade; wet soil

Diseases: Rust, powdery mildew

Garden pests: Not common

Good garden companions: Water forget-me-not (*Myosotis scorpioides*)

Propagation: Divide in early spring or late summer

Zones: 3–6

The bright yellow wildflowers of marsh marigold are well known to those who explore bogs and other wet places. Their attractive, bright green, heart-shaped leaves are sometimes eaten as "boiled greens." They are ideal for a wet natural garden, but they may also be worth a try in normal soil if it isn't too dry. They need little care and grow to 1 foot in height.

Plant type: Evergreen shrub

Bloom time: Summer

Best location: Full sun; well-drained, humus-rich, acidic soil. Protect with a mulch of evergreen branches where snow cover is not reliable (Zones 3 and 4).

Diseases: Rare

Garden pests: Occasional spider mites

Good garden companions: Low-growing, blue-foliaged junipers, such as *Juniperus squamata* 'Blue Carpet'

Propagation: Layer in spring; take semi-hardwood cuttings in summer

Zones: 5–7

Heather is a low (18-inch-tall), spreading plant prized for its colored foliage as well as for its spikelike clusters of tiny flowers, which are enclosed by colorful sepals. The species has green foliage and pink, white, or red flowers. Among the many cultivars, foliage and bloom colors vary. Prune in early spring to keep neat. Good for covering slopes or rocky hillside gardens.

GROWER'S CHOICE

C. palustris var. *alba* has white flowers. 10 inches tall.

'Flore Pleno' has double yellow blooms. 10 inches tall.

Caltha palustris

Calycanthus floridus

Calycanthus floridus

(ka-lee-KAN-thus FLO-ri-dus)

Carolina allspice, sweetshrub

Plant type: Deciduous shrub

Bloom time: Summer

Best location: Full sun in the North and partial shade in the South; fertile, moist soil, rich in organic matter

Diseases: Leaf spot, powdery mildew, dieback

Garden pests: Few problems

Good garden companions: Blue and white cultivars of French hydrangea (*Hydrangea macrophylla*)

Propagation: Plant seed as soon as it is ripe in the fall; layer; or take softwood cuttings in early summer.

Zones: 5–9

This attractive, 6- to 10-foot-tall shrub has deep reddish blooms resembling small water lilies; they are usually fragrant, as are the leaves, which have a clove scent when crushed. Combine with other shrubs in a border.

GROWER'S CHOICE

'Athens' has very fragrant yellow flowers.

Camassia (ka-MA-see-a)
Quamashes, wild hyacinths

Plant type: Bulb

Bloom time: Late spring to summer

Best location: Sun or light shade; moist, well-drained, humus-rich soil

Diseases: Leaf spot, leaf smut

Garden pests: Few insect troubles

Good garden companions: Japanese primrose (*Primula japonica*)

Propagation: Break off offshoots and plant in late summer, or sow seeds in a cold frame as soon as they are ripe.

Zones: 4–9, unless indicated otherwise below

These moisture-loving bulbs produce spikes of tiny, star-shaped, blue or white blooms. They are good in wildflower gardens, borders, and cutting gardens. Plant 4–5 inches deep.

GROWER'S CHOICE

Camass (*C. cusickii*) has steel blue, plumy flowers. 2 feet tall. Zones 3–9. *C. leichtlinii* 'Alba' has white blooms; 'Coerulea' has dark blue blooms. 2–4 feet tall.

Quamash (*C. quamash*) has bright blue flowers. 10–30 inches tall. 'Orion' has darker blue, larger flowers. 30 inches tall.

Camassia cusickii

Camellia (ka-MEE-lee-a)
Camellias

Camellia japonica 'Mathotiana Rubra'

Plant type: Broad-leaved evergreen shrub

Bloom time: Winter to late spring

Best location: Filtered light; moist, well-drained, acidic, humus-rich soil. Likes a deep mulch of rotted leaves. Where not hardy, grow in a cool greenhouse and move potted plants outside in summer to a sheltered spot.

Diseases: Anthracnose, canker, leaf spot, root rot

Garden pests: Scale, spider mites, leafhoppers, aphids

Good garden companions: Siberian bugloss (*Brunnera macrophylla*)

Propagation: Take semi-hardwood cuttings in late summer; graft in very early spring; layer in early summer

Zones: 7–9

These glossy-leaved shrubs produce beautiful pink, red, or white flowers in many different forms and sizes, from just over 2 inches to more than 5 inches across.

GROWER'S CHOICE

Common camellia (*C. japonica*) grows 10–20 feet tall. Many cultivars are available.

Campanula
(cam-PAN-yew-la)

Bellflowers

Plant type: Perennial and biennial

Bloom time: Varied; some throughout the summer

Best location: Full sun preferred, but in hot climates, it also will grow in light shade; likes good, well-drained garden soil.

Diseases: Crown rot, leaf spot, root rot, rust

Garden pests: Aphids, slugs, thrips

Good garden companions: Tall bellflowers with Miss Wilmott's ghost (*Eryngium giganteum*); low-growers with dwarf Chinese astilbe (*Astilbe chinensis* var. *pumila*)

Propagation: Division of perennials in early spring; seed. To assure a continuous supply of the biennials, plant seed every year.

Zones: Varies (see below)

Campanula medium 'Champion Pink'

The bell-shaped, tubular, or star-shaped flowers of this large group of plants come in a wide variety of colors, and the plants grow from a few inches to several feet tall. Some form clumps, while others are spreading, trailing, or upright. Most are extremely attractive in a border or rockery, but some, such as peach-leaved bellflower, can become invasive and are better for wild gardens or country roadside plantings. If given plenty of room to grow, bellflowers will show their appreciation by blooming heartily. A winter mulch of evergreen boughs will help keep the crowns from being crushed by snow, which can make them susceptible to early spring rot. Tall campanulas may need staking.

GROWER'S CHOICE

Adriatic bellflower (*C. garganica*) has bright blue, star-shaped, summer blooms and prefers light shade. 2–6 inches tall. Zones 4–7.

Bluebell or harebell (*C. rotundifolia*) has blue or purple flowers in summer. This species was brought to North America by English and Scottish settlers and is now naturalized in some places. 5–12 inches tall. Zones 4–8.

Canterbury bells (*C. medium*) is the most spectacular and well-known species of this group. The biennial plants bear distinctly bell-shaped white, pink, blue, or purple flowers in early summer. 2–3 feet tall. Its cultivar 'Calycanthema' has a saucerlike rim at the base of each flower. Champion Series includes blue and pink cultivars. To 26 inches tall. Zones 5–8.

Carpathian harebell (*C. carpatica*) comes in many cultivars with blue or white flowers borne all summer. 2–10 inches tall. Zones 3–7.

Clustered bellflower (*C. glomerata*) has large leaves and white, purple, or blue early summer flowers. 18 inches tall. Zones 3–8.

Fairies' thimbles (*C. cochleariifolia*) is a dwarf species with long-blooming blue or lavender flowers. 3 inches tall. Zones 5–7.

Milky bellflower (*C. lactiflora*) bears lavender, blue, or white flowers through summer and thrives in either sun or partial shade. 3–5 feet tall. Zones 5–7.

Campanula carpatica

Peach-leaved bellflower (*C. persicifolia*) has blue, pink, white, or lavender flowers in early to midsummer. It spreads quickly and can become weedy. 2–3 feet tall. Zones 3–8.

Serbian bellflower (*C. poscharskyana*) is a compact species with pale lavender flowers all summer. It is often planted in hanging baskets. 6–10 inches tall. Zones 4–7.

Canna (CA-na)
Cannas

Plant type: Bulb (rhizome)

Bloom time: Late summer to fall

Best location: Full sun; good garden soil

Diseases: Blight, leaf spot, rust

Garden pests: Caterpillars, slugs, snails, spider mites

Good garden companions: 'Tall Boy' hosta, fall-blooming asters

Propagation: Divide rhizomes in early spring, and plant inside in pots for early blooms. Seed is possible but takes several years to reach blooming size.

Zones: 8–11

Some cannas have long, colorful leaves, and the flowers, formed by petals and sepals joined in a basal tube, are in vivid shades of red, yellow and pink. Plant 2 inches deep from the base of the rhizome. They grow from 3 to 10 feet tall, and those too large for most home gardens are suitable for parks and large estates. In areas colder than Zone 8, dig up the rhizomes before hard frosts, and store in barely moist peat moss in a frost-free place for spring planting. Various species have been mixed by interbreeding, so most cannas are identified only by cultivar names.

Canna 'Cleopatra'

TALL GROWERS

'**King Humbert**', scarlet flowers with bronze leaves; 8 feet tall.

'**King Midas**', yellow; 5 feet tall.

'**President**', red; 4 feet tall.

'**Wyoming**', frilled orange flowers with bronze leaves; 6 feet tall.

DWARF CULTIVARS (2–3 FEET)

'**Cleopatra**', a medium-height canna; grows well in water.

Futurity Series, with burgundy foliage and a range of flower colors.

'**Pfitzer's Chinese Coral**', coral pink.

'**Picasso**', yellow with deep red spots.

Caryopteris × clandonensis 'Dark Knight'

Caryopteris × clandonensis
(kah-ree-OP-te-ris clan-do-NEN-sis)

Blue spirea, bluebeard

Plant type: Deciduous shrub

Bloom time: Late summer and early fall

Best location: Sun or light shade; light, well-drained, moderately fertile soil

Diseases: Few problems

Garden pests: Tarnished plant bugs

Good garden companions: Curry plant (*Helichrysum italicum* subsp. *serotinum*)

Propagation: Layer; take softwood cuttings in late spring

Zones: 6–9

Prized for its aromatic foliage and blue flowers, this compact (3-foot-tall) shrub is a good choice for beds and borders.

GROWER'S CHOICE

'**Blue Mist**', with light blue flowers.

'**Dark Knight**', with dark blue blooms and silvery foliage.

'**Worcester Gold**', with purple-blue flowers and yellow foliage.

Cassia marilandica

(KAH-see-a ma-ri-LAN-di-ka)

Wild senna

Cassia marilandica

Plant type: Perennial
Bloom time: Late summer
Best location: Full sun; moist soil
Diseases: Dieback, rot, powdery mildew
Garden pests: Lacebugs, nematodes, scale, mites
Good garden companions: Monkshoods (*Aconitum*)
Propagation: Divide large clumps in spring with a saw or hatchet; sow seed as soon as it is ripe
Zones: 4–8

Wild senna has attractive, yellow-green, fernlike leaves and clusters of yellow, bowl-shaped flowers followed by fruits in 4-inch-long pods. The semi-woody branches die to the ground in winter. Fast-growing enough to be used as an herbaceous hedge; also good for a border or wildflower planting. Wild senna grows best when left undisturbed for years. 3–4 feet tall.

Catananche

(ka-ta-NAN-chee)

Cupid's darts

Plant type: Short-lived perennial, often used as an annual
Bloom time: Varies (see below)
Best location: Sun; sandy garden soil
Diseases: Powdery mildew
Garden pests: Quite free of pests
Good garden companions: Pair blue cupid's dart with baby's breaths (*Gypsophila*)
Propagation: Seed indoors in late winter for blooms the same year; division; root cuttings.
Zones: 3–8

These daisylike flowers are a good addition to the garden and useful for cutting and drying.

Catananche caerulea

GROWER'S CHOICE

C. caerulea, with rich blue flowers on 3-foot-tall stems in mid- to late summer, is the most common species; 'Alba' is a white cultivar. Plant in masses for the best display.

C. caespitosa is a dwarf alpine with yellow flowers in spring. 2–4 inches tall.

Catharanthus roseus

(ka-tha-RAN-thus)

Madagascar periwinkle

Catharanthus roseus

Plant type: Tender evergreen perennial
Bloom time: Summer
Best location: Full sun or partial shade; fertile, well-drained soil
Diseases: Yellows, blight, tomato wilt virus, stem rot
Garden pests: Indoors, whiteflies and spider mites; outdoors, few problems
Good garden companions: Good in containers with edging lobelia (*Lobelia erinus*) or in the ground with compatible shades of lavatera (*Lavatera trimestris*).
Propagation: Grow from seed planted in spring; take summer cuttings; layer where hardy
Zone: 10; grown as an annual where not hardy

This low-growing, spreading plant bears pink, red, or white flat-faced flowers (similar to vinca) and shiny leaves. Many series and cultivars are available, varying in height and color. Fine for the front of a border, in containers, or as houseplant. 1–2 feet tall.

Celosia spicata

Celosia (se-LOH-see-a)
Celosias, cockscombs

Plant type: Tender perennial usually grown as annual

Bloom time: Summer

Best location: Full sun; well-drained garden soil

Diseases: Root rot, leaf spot

Garden pests: Few problems

Good garden companions: Blue balloon flower (*Platycodon grandiflorus*)

Propagation: Plant seeds inside in early spring for earliest blooms

Celosias are pretty in the garden and excellent as cut or dried flowers.

GROWER'S CHOICE

C. argentea has clusters of tiny bright red, orange, yellow, or pink flowers, either in plumes (Plumosa group) or broad, crinkled heads (Cristata group). The foliage may be green, bronze, or deep red. 6 inches to 4 feet tall.

Spike celosia *(C. spicata)* has dense, 5-inch-long, pink or purplish flower spikes. 2–3 feet tall.

Centaurea
(sen-TO-ree-a)
Centaureas

Plant type: Perennial or annual

Bloom time: Early to midsummer

Best location: Full sun; average garden soil

Diseases: Stem rot, rust, wilt, yellows

Garden pests: Aphids, leafhoppers

Good garden companions: Cranesbills (*Geranium*); bearded iris; white phlox

Propagation: Division in early spring; seed

Zones: Varies (see below)

Of the hundreds of centaureas, only a few species are regularly planted. Most came from Europe or Asia, but some have become naturalized (and occasionally weedy) in North America. The flowers of the popular species are long-lasting and good for cutting and attract butterflies and bees. All are very hardy and easy to grow; in fact, many need to be kept under control by preventing them from going to seed and by dividing them frequently.

GROWER'S CHOICE

Annual bachelor's buttons *(C. cyanus)*, also called cornflower, has deep blue, pink, red, or white flowers in summer. 8 inches to 3 feet tall.

Dusty miller *(C. cineraria)* is prized for its velvety, silver foliage. It is often planted in borders, rock gardens, and containers. 8–30 inches tall. Zones 7–9; usually grown as an annual.

Giant knapweed *(C. macrocephala)* is another perennial, with large, thistlelike yellow flowers that attract butterflies in midsummer. 4–5 feet tall.

Mountain bluet or **perennial cornflower** *(C. montana)* has bright blue spidery flowers for over a month in early summer. It may rebloom if cut down after flowering. Tends to spread rapidly. 'Alba' has white flowers; 'Rosea' is pink. 18–24 inches tall.

Persian centaurea *(C. dealbata)* is a perennial with pink, white, or red flowers in midsummer. 1–2 feet tall. Zones 4–8.

Centaurea montana

Centranthus ruber

(sen-TRAN-thus ROO-ber)

Red valerian, Jupiter's beard

Centranthus ruber 'Albus'

Plant type: Perennial

Bloom time: Late spring to early fall

Best location: Full sun; well-drained, alkaline garden soil

Diseases: None

Garden pests: Rarely bothered by pests

Good garden companion: Large-flowered tickseed (*Coreopsis grandiflora*)

Propagation: Division in early spring; cuttings in early summer; seed

Zones: 5–8

This long-blooming perennial bears clusters of tiny, fragrant, red, pink, or white flowers and grows to 3 feet. Although hardy and easy to grow, red valerian needs excellent drainage in order to survive the winter. Pretty in either a border or wild garden, it is also a good cut flower, producing more blooms when it is cut frequently. Red and pink cultivars often self-sow and must be weeded out where not wanted. White cultivars include 'Albus' and 'Snowcloud'; both are 2 feet tall.

Ceratostigma plumbaginoides

Ceratostigma

(se-ra-toh-STIG-ma)

Leadworts, plumbagos

Plant type: Perennial or deciduous shrub

Bloom time: Late summer into fall

Best location: Full sun, though tolerates light shade; good, well-drained soil

Diseases: Powdery mildew

Garden pests: Not common

Good garden companions: 'Autumn Joy' sedum (*Sedum* 'Autumn Joy')

Propagation: Divide clumps in spring; take softwood cuttings in early summer

Zones: 6–9; Zone 5 with winter protection

GROWER'S CHOICE

Chinese plumbago (*C. willmottianum*) is a deciduous shrub with clusters of pale blue, 1-inch-wide blooms. 3 feet tall.

Leadwort (*C. plumbaginoides*) has long-lasting cobalt blue flowers that arrive late in the season, when flowers of that color are scarce. The mounded green foliage turns reddish bronze as the flowers fade. Useful as a rock garden plant or border edge, it is also a good groundcover, since it spreads quickly in regions with a long growing season. 12–18 inches tall.

Cerastium (se-RA-stee-um)

Cerastiums

Plant type: Perennial

Bloom time: Late spring and summer

Best location: Full sun; well-drained garden soil

Diseases: Rare

Garden pests: Spider mites

Good garden companions: 'Dropmore' catmint (*Nepeta* × *faassenii* 'Dropmore')

Propagation: Seed; division in early spring; cuttings taken right after flowering

Zones: 3–7

These low-growing perennials are useful for a rock garden or terrace, next to garden steps, on steep banks, or at the front of the border. Cut back after flowering to keep them compact.

GROWER'S CHOICE

Snow-in-summer (*C. tomentosum*) is a vigorous spreader that gets its common name from the great mass of snowy, small white flowers that completely cover the woolly, silvery gray foliage. 3–6 inches tall. Does well in poor, dry soil.

Taurus cerastium (*C. biebersteinii*) is similar but has larger blooms.

Cerastium tomentosum

Chaenomeles
(chay-NO-mee-lees)
Flowering quinces

Plant type: Deciduous shrub

Bloom time: Spring

Best location: Sun or light shade; moderately fertile, well-drained soil

Diseases: Canker, apple mosaic, fireblight, rust

Garden pests: Scale

Good garden companions: White-flowering plums (*Prunus*)

Propagation: Seeds in fall; layering in autumn; softwood cuttings in summer

Zones: Varies (see below)

These early-blooming, usually thorny-stemmed shrubs flower in shades of red, orange, pink, or white, followed by fruits that are edible when cooked. Use them as groundcovers, in a shrub border, or on a slope.

GROWER'S CHOICE

C. speciosa comes in many cultivars, varying in height and flower color. From 3–8 feet tall and spreads up to 15 feet wide. Zones 5–8.

Japanese flowering quince (*C. japonica*) is a thorny-stemmed species that grows 3 feet tall and spreads to 6 feet. Cultivars include 'Jet Trail', with white flowers; 'Minerva', with large cherry-red blooms; and 'Orange Delight', with orange-red flowers. Zones 4–9.

Chaenomeles speciosa

Chelone obliqua

Chelone (chay-LOH-nee)
Turtleheads

Plant type: Perennial

Bloom time: Late summer into early fall

Best location: Full sun, though best if shaded from afternoon sun; moist or swampy soil

Diseases: Leaf spot, powdery mildew, rust

Garden pests: Slugs

Good garden companions: Asters, Russian sage (*Perovskia atriplicifolia*)

Propagation: Seed; cuttings; division in spring

Zones: Varies (see below)

The turtleheads are unusual plants for the wild garden, perennial border, or streamside. Their oddly shaped pink, purple, or white flowers resemble a turtle's head with its mouth open. The bitter-tasting leaves were once used to make a medicinal tea.

GROWER'S CHOICE

Pink turtlehead (*C. lyonii*) has rose-pink blooms. 2–3 feet tall. Zones 3–8.

Rose turtlehead (*C. obliqua*) bears pink or purplish blooms. 1–3 feet tall. Zones 5–9.

White turtlehead (*C. glabra*) has white to pale pink blooms. 2–3 feet tall. Zones 4–8.

Chionodoxa
(ky-oh-noh-DOCK-sa)
Glory-of-the-snows

Plant type: Bulb

Bloom time: Early spring

Best location: Full spring sun; good, well-drained garden soil

Diseases: Rarely affected

Garden pests: None serious

Good garden companions: Other low-growing spring bloomers, including crocuses, grape hyacinths (*Muscari*), and squills (*Scilla*)

Propagation: Division of offsets in summer; seed

Zones: 3–8

Low-growing (4–8 inches in height) plants with clusters of small blue, white, or pink star-shaped flowers. They naturalize easily under deciduous trees.

GROWER'S CHOICE

C. forbesii has bright blue flowers with white centers. 'Alba' has white blooms; 'Pink Giant', pink.

C. luciliae is similar to *C. forbesii*, with fewer but slightly larger flowers that are blue with white centers.

Chionodoxa forbesii

Chrysanthemum
(kri-SAN-the-mum)

Chrysanthemums

Plant type:	Perennial
Bloom time:	Varies
Best location:	Sun; rich soil
Diseases:	Leaf spot, mildew, wilt, yellows
Garden pests:	Aphids, borers, leaf miners, mites, nematodes
Good garden companions:	Dwarf cannas, perennial asters
Propagation:	Division; tip cuttings in spring and early summer planted in moist, sandy soil
Zones:	Varies

The popular garden mums (*C. × morifolium*) are a mainstay of the fall border because they bloom for a long time in many different colors and forms. Some are upright; others form cushions or mounds. The tips of young plants need pinching back several times in late spring and early summer to make them bushy and well branched. In Zones 3 and 4, cease all pinching by July 1, or fall frost may hit the plants before they have a chance to bloom. In warmer zones, continue pinching until mid-July or until the plant is well branched and bushy. Feed generously for the best blossoms.

Other than pinching, garden mums need no special care until they begin to bloom. Then you should keep the faded flowers picked for best appearance and longer flowering. To get the best blossoms on the large-flowering kinds, pick off all buds except for those at the end of each stem. All the plant's energy will then go into developing a few big, stunning, long-stemmed flowers.

Until recently, the common large-flowered garden mums could be grown only in Zone 5 and warmer locations, because they couldn't withstand subzero temperatures, and only a few of the cushion and pompom types bloomed before early northern frosts. Fortunately, both hardier and earlier-blooming cultivars have been developed in recent years, and now Zone 3 gardeners can successfully grow many cushion and pompom mums,

and even some of the larger-flowering kinds. Most of the spoon, daisy, and quill mums still bloom too late and are too tender for planting in Zone 4 and colder regions. The same applies to the exhibition mums, including the giant "football" types. These florist mums are raised primarily in greenhouses or by southern gardeners. Gardeners everywhere still have thousands of cultivars from which to make selections, and the full-color pictures in plant catalogs can make planning the fall garden a real delight.

Northern gardeners find that even hardy mums benefit from a winter mulch of evergreen boughs or similar material. Some people dig up and pot their plants and store them in a cold frame or root cellar over the winter. Because mums are so susceptible to winter injury and disease, many gardeners do not try to save their old plants but instead order new rooted cuttings each spring. Still others wait until late summer and buy potted blooming plants to use around the foundation of their homes or to set near spots in their borders where earlier-flowering perennials have died back.

To help prevent disease, split clumps apart early each spring and replant the small divisions. Better yet, if you have a greenhouse, pot up some divisions in fall, then take cuttings from them in spring and plant outside later. Whether you save your plants or buy them new, you can better control disease if you set mums in a new place each year, so any pathogens that might have wintered over in the soil around old plants will not easily find your new ones.

Several species of chrysanthemums are now found under other genus names: **Feverfew** (formerly *C. parthenium*): See *Tanacetum parthenium*.
Painted daisy (formerly *C. coccineum* or *Pyrethrum coccineum*): See *Tanacetum coccineum*.
Shasta daisy (formerly *C. maximum × C. superbum*): See *Leucanthemum × superbum*.

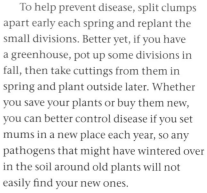
Chrysanthemum 'Prato'

Chrysanthemum 'Luciane'

Cimicifuga
(si-mih-si-FEW-ga)

Bugbanes, snakeroots

Plant type: Perennial

Bloom time: Varies (see below)

Best location: Partial shade; moist soil

Diseases: Leaf spot, rust

Garden pests: Nematodes, tarnished plant bugs

Good garden companions: Hostas, ferns

Propagation: Seed; division in spring

Zones: Varies (see below)

Cimicifuga simplex

These elegant, tall, upright plants have white, bottlebrush-like flowers that provide a wonderful autumn display at the back of a moist border or in a woodland garden. Although the unpleasant odor of bugbanes repels insects, a person has to get very close to find it offensive. They are not difficult to grow but are hard to propagate, which means you may have difficulty finding them at a nursery. Although they prefer shade, they will tolerate full sun if given moist soil rich in organic matter. It takes several years for them to reach their best, so don't disturb them once planted.

GROWER'S CHOICE

American bugbane (*C. americana*) is a well-known, odiferous, native wildflower that blooms in mid- to late summer. 2–8 feet tall. Zones 3–8.

Autumn snakeroot (*C. simplex*) blooms in early to midfall, with white flowers on arching stems. 3–5 feet tall. Cultivars include 'Brunette', with purplish leaves, and 'White Pearl', with fernlike, deep green foliage. Zones 4–8.

Black cohosh (*C. racemosa*), also called black snakeroot, is another native, with creamy white blooms in midsummer. 6–7 feet tall. Zones 3–8.

***C. japonica*,** also sold as *C. acerina*, is similar to American bugbane but shorter and later-blooming, from late summer to midfall. 2–3 feet tall. Zones 4–8.

Clarkia (KLAR-kee-a)

Satin flowers

Plant type: Annual

Bloom time: Summer

Best location: Sun or light shade; moist, well-drained, moderately fertile, slightly acid soil. Prefers areas with cool nights.

Diseases: Root rot, botrytis, rust, powdery mildew

Garden pests: Few

Good garden companions: Dusty miller (*Senecio cineraria*)

Propagation: Plant seed in early spring.

GROWER'S CHOICE

C. amoena (formerly *Godetia amoena*) grows in many heights, up to about 30 inches. Its cultivars, in many series, have cup-shaped flowers with thin, satiny petals in pink, red, or lavender-pink, often with white margins. Good cut flowers.

***C. breweri* 'Pink Ribbons'** has fragrant, purplish pink flowers. 1 foot tall.

Royal Bouquet Series, which are cultivars of *C. unguiculata* (formerly known as *C. elegans*), have ruffled, double blooms in pink, mauve, or red. To 3 feet tall.

Clarkia unguiculata

Claytonia virginica

Claytonia (klay-TOH-nee-a)
Spring beauties, mayflowers

Plant type: Bulb (corm)

Bloom time: Spring

Best location: Deciduous woods or other location that gets spring sun and summer shade; well-drained, woodsy, moist, humus-rich soil

Diseases: Rust, downy mildew

Garden pests: Aphids

Good garden companions: Canadian wild ginger (*Asarum canadense*), yellow adder's tongue (*Erythronium americanum*)

Propagation: Plant seed in the fall; divide the corms in spring after they bloom.

Zones: Varies (see below)

GROWER'S CHOICE

Carolina spring beauty (*C. caroliniana*) is similar to spring beauty but hardy only in Zones 5–9. 1 foot tall.

Spring beauty (*C. virginica*) bears small, pink-white, darker-veined, fragrant blooms that close on cloudy days and at night. 6–12 inches tall. Zones 3–8.

Clematis
(KLEH-ma-tiss or kleh-MA-tiss)
Clematis

Plant type: Perennial or vine

Bloom time: Varies (see below)

Best location: Sun to light shade; loamy garden soil, with a pH of 6.5 or higher. A mulch is desirable to keep the roots cool.

Diseases: Blight, crown gall, canker, mildew, rust

Garden pests: Caterpillars, mites, nematodes

Good garden companions: Perennial types with astilbes and foam flower (*Tiarella cordifolia*); vining types with climbing roses

Propagation: Division or stem cuttings for both types; seed for perennials only

Zones: 4–8 for most

HERBACEOUS PERENNIAL CLEMATIS

Quite different from the vining species, the herbaceous garden types are woody to semi-woody, with lacy flowers. 2–5 feet tall. Most bloom over a long period; the flowers are attractive for cutting.

GROWER'S CHOICE

C. heracleifolia* var. *davidiana has tubular blue flowers and is attractive in a blue-and-white garden. Needs support. 3 feet tall. Zones 3–8.

Ground clematis (*C. recta*) bears fragrant white flowers from midsummer to fall. Will climb if given support. 4–6 feet tall. Zones 3–7.

Solitary blue clematis (*C. integrifolia*) is probably the best herbaceous species, with blue, bell-shaped flowers on slender stems in summer. 18–24 inches tall. Zones 3–7.

VINING CLEMATIS

One of the best flowering vines, clematis has an array of bloom colors and many sizes, from ½ to 8 inches in diameter. The flowers may be saucer-shaped, star-shaped, bell-shaped, or tubular and are followed by attractive seedheads. The stems cling to trellises, arbors, and wire fences by wrapping their leaf stems around the support. Clematis need

Clematis 'Henryi'

afternoon shade on their roots to do well, hence they enjoy the east side of a building.

Three general types exist. The first group blooms in late winter and early spring, where the climate permits, on shoots formed the previous year. *C. macropetala* and *C. montana* are two examples. The second group flowers in late spring and early summer on shoots grown the previous year and may flower again in late summer on the current year's growth. Some popular hybrids are white 'Henryi', pink-mauve 'Nelly Moser', and blue-purple 'Richard Pennell'. The third group blooms in summer and early fall on the current season's growth. Clematis in this group are the best choice for growers in Zones 3 and 4, where clematis vines usually die to the ground each fall but still regrow so rapidly the following spring that they

Cleome hassleriana
(klee-O-mee has-la-ree-AH-na)

Spider flower, cleome

Plant type: Annual
Bloom time: Summer
Best location: Full sun; light, fertile, well-drained soil
Diseases: Rust, leaf spot, mildew
Garden pests: Aphids, spider mites, whiteflies
Good garden companions: Blue or purple monkshoods (*Aconitum*)
Propagation: Plant seeds in spring. Self-sows enough to be weedy in warm areas.

Tall plant with pungently aromatic flowerheads of spidery petals in pink, rose, white, and violet-pink, topped by prominent, long stamens. 3–5 feet tall.

GROWER'S CHOICE

'Rose Queen'
'White Queen'

Cleome hassleriana

Clethra alnifolia
(KLETH ra al ni FOH-lcc-a)

Sweet pepperbush, summersweet

Plant type: Deciduous shrub
Bloom time: Late summer to early fall
Best location: Light shade; moist, well-drained, fertile, acidic soil rich in organic matter
Diseases: Root rot
Garden pests: Rare
Good garden companions: Wild bergamot (*Monarda fistulosa*)
Propagation: Seeds in early spring; softwood cuttings in summer
Zones: 3–9

This upright shrub produces small, fragrant white flowers in spikelike clusters and is 6–8 feet tall. Good for a lightly shaded border. Prune in late spring to shape.

GROWER'S CHOICE

'Hummingbird' is more compact. 2–3 feet tall.
'Pink Spires' has light pink blossoms.

Clethra alnifolia

Clematis 'Elsa Späth'

are able to fill a trellis with blooms by midsummer. Some of these are pink 'Comtesse de Bouchard', magenta 'Ernest Markham', deep purple 'Jack-manii', and red 'Mme. Edouard Andre'.

In early spring, cut back groups 1 and 2 to shape, cut out any damaged or winter-killed shoots, and thin excess new shoots. Do all other pruning to shape and control after they have stopped blooming. In group 3, cut back to about 1 foot from the ground when the vines die down after the fall frosts.

Cobaea scandens
(KOH-bee-a SKAN-denz)

Cup-and-saucer vine

Cobaea scandens

Plant type: Tender perennial vine

Bloom time: Summer to fall

Best location: Full sun; moist, well-drained, fertile soil in sheltered spot

Diseases: Seldom affected

Garden pests: Few problems

Good garden companions: Climbing roses, autumn snakeroot (*Cimicifuga simplex*)

Propagation: Plant seed indoors in spring for earliest results; take softwood cuttings in summer.

Zones: 9–10

This vigorous vine clings to trees and trellises with tendrils; climbs to 30 feet or more. Produces fragrant, bell-shaped lavender to purple flowers over a long season. *C. scandens* f. *alba* has white flowers. Evergreen where hardy; grow as annual in cooler zones.

Colchicum (KOL-chi-kum)

Autumn crocuses

Plant type: Bulb (corm)

Bloom time: Early to midfall

Best location: Sun; fertile, well-drained garden soil

Diseases: Botrytis

Garden pests: Slugs

Good garden companions: Wormwoods (*Artemisia*), thymes

Propagation: Divide corms when dormant; plant seed when ripe.

Zones: 3–9

Despite their name, these plants are not true crocuses. The foliage of many species appears in spring and dies back in early summer, then the plant blossoms in the fall. Most are low-growing, with pink or rosy purple goblet-shaped flowers. They are excellent in a rock garden, at the front of a border, or at the base of trees. Most need a protective mulch in order to survive winter in the North, but otherwise they are easy to grow. Plant the corms 4 inches deep in late summer, and fertilize them in spring so they will make lush growth before the leaves die. The corms are extremely poisonous.

GROWER'S CHOICE

C. speciosum **'Album'** is a vigorous white-flowered cultivar. 7–10 inches tall. **Meadow saffron (*C. autumnale*)** is the most common species, with lavender-pink blooms. 6 inches tall. **'Waterlily'** is a popular hybrid, with double, purplish pink blooms. 4–6 inches tall.

Colchicum 'The Giant'

Consolida ajacis

Consolida ajacis
(kon-SO-li-da a-JA-kis)

Larkspur

Plant type: Annual

Bloom time: Summer

Best location: Full sun; light, fertile, well-drained soil

Diseases: Crown rot, powdery mildew

Garden pests: Slugs, snails

Good garden companions: Purple larkspur with pink lavatera (*Lavatera trimestris*), feverfew (*Tanacetum parthenium*)

Propagation: Sow seed inside, or as early as possible outside, for blooms throughout a long season.

Larkspurs bear delphinium-like clusters of violet, blue, rose, white, or pink single or double flowers. They are 1–4 feet tall. Plants in the Dwarf Hyacinth Series grow only 18 inches tall; Giant Imperial Series cultivars reach 2–3 feet in height. Cultivars vary in color shades, heights, and bloom size. Excellent for a cottage garden or mixed border.

Convallaria majalis

(kon-va-LAH-ree-a mah-JAH-lis)

Lily-of-the-valley

Plant type: Bulb (rhizome)

Bloom time: Late spring to early summer

Best location: Light to moderate shade; rich, somewhat acid soil

Diseases: Leaf spot, stem rot

Garden pests: Weevils

Good garden companions: Japanese spurge *(Pachysandra terminalis),* lesser periwinkle *(Vinca minor)*

Propagation: Division in summer or fall (easy)

Zones: 2–7

Nearly every garden has a place for delightfully fragrant, old-fashioned lily-of-the-valleys. Although they will grow under large trees, results will be better where there is less competition for moisture and nourishment. Plant with their bases 1 inch deep. Under good conditions, they quickly naturalize and cover a large area with a rich green carpet. They need little care, but dig clumps and separate whenever blooms become sparse. All parts are poisonous, so keep both growing plants and cut flowers away from small children who might want to taste them.

Lily-of-the valley plants commonly have broad green leaves and fragrant, white, bell-like flowers. 8 inches tall.

GROWER'S CHOICE

C. majalis **var.** *rosea* has pinkish blooms. **'Giant Bells'** and **'Fortin's Giant'** are tall with large flowers. To 1 foot tall.

Convolvulus tricolor

Convolvulus tricolor

(con-VOL-vew-lus TRY-ko-lor)

Dwarf morning glory

Plant type: Annual, except in the tropics

Bloom time: Summer

Best location: Full sun; poor to good soil

Diseases: Leaf spot, rust

Garden pests: Aphids

Good garden companions: Moss rose *(Portulaca grandiflora),* New Guinea impatiens

Propagation: Plant seed in early spring.

Zones: 9–10

Not to be confused with the annual morning glory vine *(Ipomoea),* this bushy annual bears white-and-yellow throated, funnel-shaped flowers, 1½ inches in diameter; it is 12–16 inches tall. Each bloom lasts only a day, but if they are deadheaded, the plants bloom over a long period. Plant with rock garden and alpine plants or in containers on a deck or terrace.

GROWER'S CHOICE

'Red Ensign', with dark red blooms
'Rose Ensign', with deep rose blooms
'Royal Ensign', with large dark blue blooms

Convallaria majalis

Coreopsis (ko-ree-OP-sis)
Tickseeds

Plant type:	Perennial or annual
Bloom time:	All summer
Best location:	Sun or light shade; well-drained garden soil
Diseases:	Root rot, virus
Garden pests:	Leaf miners, mites
Good garden companions:	Blue sage (Salvia × sylvestris), monkshoods (Aconitum)
Propagation:	Division (easy); seeds planted early will often bloom the first year, making it possible to grow the perennial types as annuals.
Zones:	4–9

Tickseeds are so named because their seed resembles a tick, which belies the beauty of these bright, daisylike, yellow-toned flowers. They are a delight in any garden, blooming early and for most of the summer in cool areas; they may stop blooming for a period during hot weather. Tickseeds may self-sow and become weedy, although perennial cultivars are less troublesome than annuals.

They make excellent cut flowers. Keep the fading blooms picked to maintain blossoms over a long time. Because they are somewhat susceptible to frost, a mulch is recommended to protect the roots of perennials in northern zones.

GROWER'S CHOICE

Calliopsis (C. tinctoria) is an annual with showy yellow flowers marked with deep red or dark brown. 2–4 feet tall.
C. auriculata 'Nana' is a dwarf perennial with orange-yellow blooms. 8 inches tall.
Lance-leaved coreopsis (C. lanceolata) is similar to C. grandiflora but shorter. 'Brown Eyes' has yellow flowers with a dark maroon center. 12–30 inches tall.
Large-flowered coreopsis (C. grandiflora), a perennial, has many fine cultivars; single, semi-double, or double yellow flowers. Often short-lived; use as an annual or let self-sow. 3 feet tall.
'Limerock Ruby', a hybrid, has dark red flowers.
Pink coreopsis (C. rosea), a perennial, has single pink blooms throughout the summer. 'Sweet Dreams' has pink-and-white flowers. 2 feet tall.

Coreopsis 'Limerock Ruby'

Thread-leaved coreopsis (C. verticillata) bears yellow flowers throughout the summer over very lacy foliage. 1–3 feet tall. It spreads by underground stems and is very drought-resistant. 'Moonbeam', a perennial, has pale yellow flowers. 18 inches tall.

Cornus stolonifera

Cornus (KOR-nus)
Dogwoods

Plant type:	Deciduous shrub
Bloom time:	Late spring to early summer
Best location:	Full sun; well-drained, moist, fertile soil
Diseases:	Powdery mildew, blight, rot, canker
Garden pests:	Scale, sawflies, weevils, thrips, borers
Good garden companions:	Hydrangeas, spireas
Propagation:	Divide bunchberry in spring or fall; take hardwood cuttings of woody-stemmed types.
Zones:	Varies (see below)

This genus includes many species ranging widely in size and form. Several shrubby species are grown for their winter stem color or interesting leaves.

GROWER'S CHOICE

Bunchberry (C. canadensis) is a ground-cover with white flowers in late spring. To 6 inches tall. Zones 2–7.
Flowering dogwood (C. florida) is a beautiful tree with white or pink flowers in late spring. To 20 feet tall. Zones 5–8.
Red osier dogwood (C. stolonifera), a vigorous shrub that can be invasive, produces small, dull white blooms in late spring and early summer, followed by white berries in summer and fall and red fall leaves and stems. 5–7 feet tall. 'Flaviramea' has yellow twigs. Zones 2–8.
Red-twig dogwood (C. alba) has white blooms in early summer, followed by white fruits, with orange, red, or purple fall foliage and red twigs in winter. Several cultivars have variegated foliage, including 'Spaethii', with yellow-edged leaves. To 10 feet tall. Zones 2–8.

Corydalis (ko-RI-da-lis)
Corydalis

Plant type: Perennial or biennial

Bloom time: Varies (see below)

Best location: Sun or light shade (except where noted below); rich, moist soil

Diseases: Rust, downy mildew

Garden pests: Aphids, slugs, snails

Good garden companions: Ferns, hostas

Propagation: Division in fall; seed sown as soon as it ripens in summer

Zones: Varies (see below)

Relatives of bleeding hearts *(Dicentra)*, which they resemble in both leaf and flower, corydalis are smaller plants with smaller flowers that are usually blue, yellow, or white. They are good rock-garden or wildflower-garden plants.

GROWER'S CHOICE

Blue corydalis *(C. flexuosa)* has true-blue flowers in late spring and early summer, then goes dormant during the hot months. Needs light shade. 1 foot tall. Zone 5–8.

C. ochroleuca has creamy white blooms from late spring to early summer; self-sows freely. 1 foot tall. Zones 6–8.

Ferny corydalis *(C. cheilanthifolia)* has fernlike foliage and bears yellow flowers from spring into summer; self-sows freely. To 1 foot tall. Zones 5–7.

Yellow corydalis *(C. lutea)* has blue-green foliage and golden yellow blooms from late spring through summer; self-sows freely. 15 inches tall. Zones 5–7.

Corydalis cheilanthifolia

Cosmos (KOS-mos)
Cosmos

Plant type: Annual

Bloom time: Summer

Best location: Full sun; moist, well-drained fertile soil

Diseases: Powdery mildew, stem canker, botrytis

Garden pests: Aphids

Good garden companions: Bachelor's buttons *(Centaurea cyanus)*

Propagation: Plant seeds inside in early spring or outdoors after frosts are over.

Many series and cultivars of cosmos are available as seed.

GROWER'S CHOICE

C. bipinnatus has tall (up to 5-foot) stems with lacy leaves and pink, white, or rose-magenta blossoms. The flowers of 'Sea Shells' have fluted petals. Sonata Series cultivars are much shorter, at about 1 foot in height.

Cosmos bipinnatus 'Sonata White'

C. sulfureus has a bushier habit, with ferny leaves and flowers in shades of yellow-orange and red. 24–30 inches tall. 'Bright Lights' has semi-double flowers. Klondike Series includes dwarf cultivars (to 15 inches) with yellow or orange flowers.

Cotinus coggygria
(ko-TY-nus ko-GIG-ree-a)
Smokebush

Plant type: Deciduous shrub

Bloom time: Early summer

Best location: Full sun or light shade (full sun for purple-leaved kinds); moist, well-drained, fertile soil

Diseases: Powdery mildew, verticillium wilt

Garden pests: Few problems

Good garden companions: Dwarf false cypress *(Chamaecyparis obtusa* 'Compacta'), autumn olive *(Elaeagnus umbellata)*

Propagation: Layer in spring; take softwood cuttings in early summer; plant seed in containers in fall.

Zones: 4–8

This is a showy shrub or small tree with plumy clusters of pinkish gray flowers that resemble smoke puffs, as well as colorful fall foliage later in the season. Usually grows to 15 feet.

Cotinus coggygria 'Royal Purple'

GROWER'S CHOICE

'Daydream' has brownish pink blooms on well-branched plants.

'Flame' has green foliage that turns bright orange-red in fall. To 20 feet tall.

'Royal Purple' has purple leaves that turn deep red in the fall.

Cotoneaster 'Coral Beauty'

Cotoneaster

(ko-toh-nee-AS-ter)

Cotoneasters

Plant type: Deciduous or evergreen shrub

Bloom time: Spring to summer

Best location: Full sun; fertile, well-drained soil

Diseases: Powdery mildew, rust, canker, fire blight

Garden pests: Slugs, spider mites, snails, scale

Good garden companions: Rockspray cotoneaster with variegated winter-creeper (*Euonymus fortunei* 'Variegatus'); *C. multiflorus* with flowering shrubs, such as viburnums

Propagation: Layer in spring; take root cuttings in early summer; plant seed when ripe in fall.

Zones: Varies (see below)

These deciduous shrubs bear cup- or saucer-shaped pink or white flowers, followed by red, yellow, or black fruits.

GROWER'S CHOICE

'Coral Beauty', a hybrid evergreen, with bright orange fruit in fall. To 6 feet tall; Zones 7–8.

C. multiflorus, deciduous and very upright. To 15 feet tall. Zones 5–7.

Rockspray cotoneaster *(C. horizontalis),* a deciduous groundcover, with a low, spreading growth habit and good red fall color. 3 feet tall. Zones 4–8.

Crinum (KRY-num)

Crinums

Plant type: Bulb

Bloom time: Late summer to fall

Best location: Full sun; humus-rich, well-drained, moist soil

Diseases: Anthracnose, red leaf spot, mosaic virus

Garden pests: No serious problems

Good garden companions: Dahlias, chrysanthemums, asters

Propagation: Split off offsets in spring; sow seeds as soon as ripe.

Zones: 7–10

In spring, plant with bulb neck just above soil. North of Zone 7, dig, dry, and store crinum bulbs indoors over winter.

GROWER'S CHOICE

C. asiaticum bears fragrant white flowers in spring and summer. 2 feet tall. Zones 8–11.

Crinum asiaticum

C. × *powellii* is a beautiful hybrid with 4-inch-wide umbels of showy, fragrant, pink flowers on leafless stems. To 5 feet tall. 'Album' is pure white.

'Ellen Bosanquet', a hybrid, has very fragrant reddish purple flowers. 2 feet tall.

Crocosmia (kro-KOZ-mee-a)

Crocosmias, montbretias

Plant type: Bulb (corm)

Bloom time: Mid- to late summer

Best location: Sun or light shade; good garden soil

Diseases and garden pests: Few problems

Good garden companions: Wormwoods (*Artemisia*), purple-leaved dahlias

Propagation: Divide corms in early spring; sow seed as soon as it is ripe.

Zones: 6–9; can survive colder spots in a sheltered place

Originally from South Africa, this delightful plant was little noticed for years because most books described it as hardy only in the warmest parts of North America. It has become naturalized in Great Britain, however, and a plant given to us several years ago still thrives in our Zone 3 garden. The corms don't like the soil around them to freeze for long periods, so mulch heavily unless you have a deep snow cover. Plant 3–4 inches deep.

Crocosmia 'Lucifer'

Crocosmias have green, irislike leaves and clusters of scarlet, orange, orange-yellow, or orange-red flowers on arching stems over a long period. They are 2–3 feet tall.

GROWER'S CHOICE

'Emily McKenzie', bright orange blooms

'Jackanapes', also known as 'Fire King', orange-red and yellow bicolored blooms

'Lady Hamilton', yellow blooms

'Lucifer', bright red blooms

Crocus (KRO-kus)
Crocuses

Plant type: Bulb (corm)

Bloom time: *Spring bloomers:* early spring. *Fall bloomers:* early autumn.

Best location: Full sun; average soil

Diseases: Rot, rust, scab

Garden pests: Aphids, mites; chipmunks, mice, and squirrels may eat corms.

Good garden companions: Miniature daffodils and species tulips with spring crocuses; 'Autumn Joy' sedum for fall-bloomers

Propagation: Divide spring-flowering crocuses after blooming in autumn, and fall bloomers after their foliage dies down

Zones: Varies (see below)

Plant 4 inches deep, in late fall for spring bloomers and in early spring for fall bloomers. Mulch over winter unless constant snow cover is certain in Zones 3–4.

SPRING-BLOOMING CROCUSES

There are many spring-blooming species in a wide range of colors and of varying hardiness. Although spring crocuses are often planted in lawns, it is not the best spot for them, because their foliage should not be mowed until it dies naturally.

GROWER'S CHOICE

Dutch crocus *(C. vernus)* blooms later and is larger, in white and shades of purple. 4–6 inches tall. Zones 3–8.

Snow crocus (Chrysanthus hybrids) are the familiar yellow, purple, or white 2-inch-tall flowers that are often hailed as the harbingers of spring. Zones 3–8.

FALL-BLOOMING CROCUSES

Though often confused with *Colchicum*, also called autumn crocuses, the late-flowering true crocuses are smaller (3–6 inches tall), with blue, lavender, rose, and white blooms. The foliage may appear with the flowers or may emerge in spring and die back in summer.

GROWER'S CHOICE

C. pulchellus has lilac-colored flowers with a honeylike fragrance. 4 inches tall. Zones 5–8.

C. speciosus is one of the earliest fall crocuses to bloom, and one of the best, with violet-blue or white flowers. 4–6 inches tall. Zones 3–8.

Saffron crocus *(C. sativus)* has rich purple flowers and bright red parts called styles, which are the source of the prized culinary saffron. It takes thousands of the flowers to yield one ounce of the spice. 2 inches tall. Zones 6–8.

Crocus vernus

Cyclamen hederifolium

Cyclamen
(SY-kla-men or SIK-la-men)
Cyclamens

Plant type: Bulb (tuber)

Bloom time: Varies (see below)

Best location: Light to medium shade; humus-rich, fertile soil

Diseases: Botrytis

Garden pests: Mites, weevils

Good garden companions: *C. coum* with snowdrops *(Galanthus nivalis)*; fall-flowering species with 'Ruby Glow' sedum

Propagation: Plant seeds as soon as they are ripe, and place in total darkness until they sprout.

Zones: Varies (see below for hardy species)

Most of these beautiful plants from southern Europe and Asia grow only a few inches tall, with colorful, nodding, butterfly-shaped flowers and round or kidney-shaped leaves. Tender types are often grown in pots as houseplants; hardy types are good in rock gardens. Plant 1 inch deep.

GROWER'S CHOICE

Baby cyclamen *(C. hederifolium)* bears fragrant pink or white blooms and silver-mottled foliage; blooms late summer and fall. 4–6 inches tall.

***C. cilicium*,** with pink or white flowers and gray-mottled leaves, blooms late summer and fall. 2 inches tall.

C. coum blooms in early spring, with pink, red, or white flowers over plain or silver-splashed leaves. 2–3 inches tall. All three of these are hardy in Zones 5 (with winter protection) through 9.

Cytisus (sy-TI-sus)
Brooms

Plant type: Shrub
Bloom time: Midspring to early summer
Best location: Full sun; poor, dry, acidic soil
Diseases: Botrytis, root rot
Garden pests: Spider mites
Good garden companions: Smoke bush
(Cotinus coggygria 'Royal Purple'), blue
Siberian iris (Iris sibirica)
Propagation: Plant seeds in the spring;
take cuttings in summer
Zones: 6–8

These short, shrubby plants, most 4–5 feet tall, produce quantities of pealike red, yellow, pink, or white blooms. They resent being moved, so start new plants in pots and move to where they will grow.

Cytisus scoparius 'Moonlight'

C. × praecox has many pale yellow blooms in mid- to late spring. 'Allgold' has deep yellow flowers, while 'Warminster' (also known as Warminster broom) is light yellow.
Hybrids include 'Killiney Red', with deep red flowers; 'Golden Sunlight', with pale yellow blooms; and 'Hollandia', with red-and-cream flowers.
Normandy broom *(C. scoparius f. andreanus)* has yellow flowers with red tips.
Scotch broom *(C. scoparius),* a well-known species, has bright yellow flowers. 'Moonlight' has large, pale yellow flowers. 30 inches tall.

Dahlia (DAH-lee-a)
Dahlias

Plant type: Bulb (tuber)
Bloom time: Midsummer to fall
Best location: Full sun; deep, well-drained,
fertile soil rich in organic matter
Diseases: Dahlia mosaic, powdery mildew,
smut, leaf spot, rot, gall, mold
Garden pests: Thrips, mites, aphids, beetles,
slugs
Good garden companions: Brazilian
vervain (Verbena bonariensis)
Propagation: Cut the tubers apart in spring
before planting, making sure there is at
least one bud on each section.
Zones: 9–10 (grown as an annual elsewhere)

The various dahlia species grow from a few inches to 6 feet in height. Plant tubers of tall-growing dahlias 6 inches deep; short species, 2–3 inches deep. Tall kinds may need staking, and all need watering during dry periods. The brightly colored flowers are single, semi-double, or double, ranging in diameter from the 2-inch Mignon types to the 10-inch Giant types. Dahlias are further classified according to

Dahlia 'Happy Face'

the shape and petal form of the flower-head, including Single, Anemone, Ball, Cactus, Collarette, Decorative, Fimbriated, Novelty, Orchid, Peony, and Waterlily. There are thousands of cultivars, and all are excellent for cutting. 'Happy Face' is a cactus type; 6–8 inches tall. The so-called seed or bedding-plant dahlias are grown as annuals. Feature dahlias in a bed of their own or use in mixed borders, as foundation plantings, or as a flowering hedge alongside a garage or shed. The tubers must be dug and stored for the winter in a frost-free location in all but Zone 9 and warmer regions.

Daphne × burkwoodii
(DAF-nee berk-WOO-dee-eye)
Burkwood daphne

Plant type: Semi-evergreen shrub
Bloom time: Spring or early summer;
possibly again in fall
Best location: Full sun or light shade;
neutral or slightly alkaline garden soil
Diseases: Wilt, blight, rot, viruses
Garden pests: Scale, aphids
Good garden companions: Virginia bluebells
(Mertensia virginica)
Propagation: Softwood cuttings in summer;
ripe seed in summer
Zones: 5–8, but will grow in sheltered spots
in colder zones

This low-growing (3- to 5-foot-tall), bushy plant, bears small fragrant, pinkish white, lilaclike clusters of flowers, followed by red fruits. Keep roots cool with mulch.

'Albert Burkwood', with pink-white blooms on a rounded bush.
'Carol Mackie', with leaves that have yellow margins that later turn white.

Daphne × burkwoodii 'Carol Mackie'

Delphinium
(del-FIN-ee-um)

Delphiniums

Plant type: Perennial

Bloom time: Early to midsummer

Best location: Sun (but tolerate light afternoon shade); rich, slightly alkaline garden soil

Diseases: Mildew, botrytis, blight, leaf spot, rust, rot

Garden pests: Aphids, cutworms, cyclamen mites, slugs

Good garden companions: 'Miss Lingard' meadow phlox (Phlox maculata 'Miss Lingard'), false sunflower (Heliopsis helianthoides). Dark blue delphiniums look especially good with rose-pink lavateras and red-flowering clematis vines, like 'Ernest Markham'.

Propagation: Seed (see below); stem cuttings in early summer

Zones: 3–7, except where noted

With their tall spires of blue, purple, lilac, pink, and white flowers, each with a "bee" formed by the sepals, delphiniums have long been important accent plants in the border. The advice to a beginning gardener once was: "Plant the delphiniums first; then designing the rest of the border will be easy." New hybrids have made delphiniums even more desirable, and though they may need more care than many other plants, they are worth the trouble.

Unfortunately, the best cultivars seem to have the most trouble with diseases. Give these plants plenty of space to allow the good air circulation necessary to prevent mildew. Protect those that grow tall from wind by placing them near a hedge, fence, wall, or building; each stalk may need to be staked separately (see page 116). After blooming, cut down the stalks; in areas where the growing season is long enough, they will bloom again in late summer or early fall.

If you buy hybrid plants, get those propagated from seed rather than by division, because they are more vigorous. Plant them in spring. Potted plants or those dug with a ball of soil at the nursery are preferable, because bare-root plants often have a poor survival rate. Overgrown clumps of the long-lived species should be split up every four or five years to keep them thriving.

The best way to get vigorous, healthy plants is to start them yourself from seed. Plant only fresh seeds, because those over a year old are not likely to grow. Sow fresh seeds during the summer in a shady spot, and mulch the seedlings over winter. Alternatively, store seed in sealed plastic bags in the refrigerator, then plant it in midwinter, either in a greenhouse or under grow lights, or wait and plant outdoors in a seedbed in the spring.

Delphiniums have been hybridized to such a degree that the species origin of many cultivars is blurred, so most are sold under cultivar names.

GROWER'S CHOICE

Belladonna Group cultivars have spikes with loose, branched flowers. 3–4 feet tall. They include 'Bellamosum', with dark blue flowers, and 'Moerheimii', with white flowers.

Chinese or Siberian delphinium (*D. grandiflorum*) is a low, spreading plant with bright blue, white, or lavender flowers. It is perennial but usually grown as an annual or biennial. 10–24 inches tall. Zones 4–7.

Delphinium '**Blushing Brides**'

Delphinium '**Royal Aspirations**'

Connecticut Yankee Series plants are shorter, with blue, white, lavender, or purple flowers. To 2 feet tall.

Elatum Group cultivars (from *D. elatum*) are among the best and include pale blue 'Blue Dawn', white 'Butterball', pink 'Blushing Brides', purple 'Royal Aspirations', and 'Magic Fountains'.

Pacific Hybrids' gigantic size and spectacular color compensate for the fact that they are fragile and difficult to stake. The plants tend to be short-lived in warm climates, but in Zones 3 and 4, they often live for many years. We have seen 10-year-old Pacific Hybrids reach a height of 10 feet in northern gardens. Most come fairly true from seed and have large, semi-double blooms in a wide spectrum of colors. Good cultivars are 'Astolat' (pale pink to raspberry rose) and 'Blue Bird', as well as the Round Table Series, which includes very dark purple 'Black Knight', white 'Galahad', lavender 'Guinevere', and violet 'King Arthur'.

Scarlet larkspur (*D. cardinale*) is a California native with bright scarlet flowers. It is longer-lived than the hybrids but quite susceptible to diseases such as mildew and rust. To 6 feet tall. Zones 7–8.

Deutzia crenata var. nakaiana

Deutzia (DOOT-zee-a)
Deutzias

Plant type: Deciduous shrub

Bloom time: Spring to midsummer

Best location: Full sun; slightly moist, fertile soil

Diseases: Leaf spots may occur

Garden pests: Few problems

Good garden companions: Purple lilacs (Syringa)

Propagation: Softwood cuttings in summer; seed in a cold frame in fall

Zones: 5–8; may be killed back to the ground in very cold winters

Deutzias bear a profusion of small, white or pink, star- or cup-shaped flowers that are often fragrant. An excellent choice for a shrub border, deutzias need pruning right after blooming to maintain a good shape. They grow to 7 feet in height.

GROWER'S CHOICE

D. crenata var. nakaiana 'Nikko', with reddish purple fall foliage. 2 feet tall. **'Magicien'**, a hybrid, with white-edged pink flowers. 5 feet tall. **Slender deutzia (D. gracilis)** is a bushy upright shrub with white flowers. 3 feet tall.

Dianthus (dye-AN-thus)
Pinks

Plant type: Perennial, biennial, or annual

Bloom time: Various (see below)

Best location: Full sun; well-drained, slightly alkaline soil. Choose a site with good air circulation.

Diseases: Leaf spot, stem rot, root rot, rust

Garden pests: Aphids, slugs

Good garden companions: 'Crater Lake Blue' Hungarian speedwell (Veronica austriaca subsp. teucrium 'Crater Lake Blue'), cranesbills (Geranium)

Propagation: Perennials: Division in spring; stem cuttings in midsummer; seed. Biennials: Seed. The seed is very easy to gather, and plants often self-sow. If you grow more than one color, however, the colors of the seedlings will likely vary because of cross-pollination.

Zones: 3–8, unless noted otherwise

In Greek, *dianthus* means "divine flower," and so it is. The carnation *(D. caryophyllus)* is but one member of this large family of hundreds of species, many of which have a spicy fragrance similar to that of cloves, as well as grass-like foliage. The greenhouse carnation is not hardy enough to grow in northern gardens, but other pinks are excellent garden plants and cut flowers. Nearly all are low-growing, rarely exceeding 2 feet in height.

Divide perennial pinks each year to keep them healthy. Biennials need replanting every year, and even though they may live more than two years, the second blooming is not usually as good. Avoid mulching, because their stems need air circulation, and organic mulches may encourage disease. Most species are relatively short lived.

GROWER'S CHOICE

China pink (D. chinensis), a tender perennial treated as an annual, has spicy-scented, fringed flowers in pink, red, or white, sometimes with a purple center. 2 feet tall.

Grass pink (D. plumarius), a perennial and excellent choice for edging, has fragrant white, pink, or red flowers over gray-green foliage. 12–15 inches tall.

Lilac pink (D. superbus), a short-lived perennial best grown as a biennial, has very fragrant, lilac-pink flowers; prefers light shade. 8 inches tall.

'Loveliness', a hybrid, is very fragrant, with unusual pinwheel blooms in pale pink, violet, or white, often with contrasting eyes. A short-lived perennial often grown as an annual. 18 inches tall. Zones 5–7.

Maiden pink (D. deltoides) forms a tight, low mat of green foliage covered with pink, white, or red flowers in early summer. A strong grower and bloomer, this perennial is good for rock gardens. 6–8 inches tall.

Sand pink (D. arenarius) has pink or white flowers, often with purple bases. This perennial grows well in partial shade. 6–12 inches tall.

Sweet William (D. barbatus), a well-known biennial or short-lived perennial, blooms in many colors over a long period in early summer. Plant same-color masses for best effect. Among our favorites are dwarfs 'Wee Willie' and 'Indian Carpet' and standards 'Newport Pink' and bronze-leaved 'Dunnet's Dark Crimson'. Dwarfs, 4–6 inches; standards, 1–2 feet.

Dianthus barbatus

Dicentra

(dye-SEN-tra)

Bleeding hearts

Plant type: Perennial

Bloom time: Spring, except as noted

Best location: Light shade; moist, fertile, humus-rich, alkaline soil

Diseases: Leaf spot, mildew, wilt

Garden pests: Aphids, slugs

Good garden companions: Fragrant Solomon's seal (Polygonatum odoratum), hostas

Propagation: Division directly after blooming or in very early spring (fastest method); seed; stem and root cuttings

Zones: 3–8

Bleeding hearts have been garden favorites for centuries, and few plants attract more attention when they are in full bloom. For the longest period of bloom, plant them in a spot with morning sunshine and light afternoon shade. The east side of a building is ideal.

Dicentra spectabilis 'Alba'

GROWER'S CHOICE

Dutchman's breeches (D. cucullaria) has white flowers with yellow tips. It flourishes in partial shade and alkaline soil. 10 inches tall.

Fringed bleeding heart (D. eximia) is an excellent edging plant, with lacy leaves and pink flowers all summer. 18 inches tall. 'Snowdrift' and 'Alba' have white blooms; 'Bacchanal' is deep crimson.

Old-fashioned bleeding heart (D. spectabilis) has heart-shaped flowers that hang gracefully from long, arching stems in colors that range from pink to bright red. 2–4 feet tall. Leave plenty of room for the plant to grow, since it can reach 3–4 feet across. In many areas, it dies down after blooming. 'Alba', with white flowers, is somewhat less vigorous.

Squirrel corn (D. canadensis) is a wildflower that grows from a small rhizome, with greenish white, red-tipped flowers in early spring. It is good for a rock garden or shade garden with fertile, humus-rich soil. 1 foot tall.

Western bleeding heart (D. formosa) is similar to fringed bleeding heart, with deep pink blooms. It is well suited to the West Coast and may need to be controlled in spots that it likes. 20 inches tall.

Dictamnus albus

(dik TAM nus AL-bus)

Gas plant

Plant type: Perennial

Bloom time: Early summer

Best location: Sun or light shade; rich soil

Diseases: None serious

Garden pests: None serious

Good garden companions: Monkshoods (Aconitum), foxgloves (Digitalis), low-growing delphiniums

Propagation: Seed (best, but it takes 3–4 years before bloom); division of the woody, carrotlike roots (difficult, and new plants establish slowly); root cuttings in early summer

Zones: 3–8

The flowers and foliage of the gas plant smell somewhat like an old-fashioned stomach tonic mixed with lemon, and the flowers are followed by clusters of attractive but equally strong-smelling seedpods. There is no middle ground:

You either like or strongly dislike gas plants and their unusual odor, but either way, you must admit they are interesting.

The 2- to 3-foot-tall plants typically have spikes of white flowers with dark veins, but D. albus var. purpureus has purplish pink blooms with dark veins and long stamens. They grow in shrubby mounds of leathery-textured, glossy green foliage. Once planted, gas plants are long lived but should not be disturbed, because they bloom best only after they are well established. They are attractive either as single specimens or in groups of three or more. Leave at least 3 feet of space between new plants.

Perhaps you can better appreciate the pungent odor that gives the plant its name if, on a hot summer evening when the air is still, you hold a lighted match next to the ripe seedpods and watch the volatile oils ignite in a flash of light. People with delicate skin sometimes get a rash from this oily substance when they touch the plant.

Dictamnus albus var. purpureus

Digitalis (di-ji-TAH-lis)
Foxgloves

Plant type: Perennial or biennial

Bloom time: Early to midsummer

Best location: Sun or light shade; average garden soil that is neither wet over winter or very dry

Diseases: Anthracnose, leaf spot, mildew, root and stem rot

Garden pests: Aphids, Japanese beetles, mealybugs

Good garden companions: Foxgloves of other colors; catmint (*Nepeta × faassenii*)

Propagation: Sow seeds (easy); divide perennial kinds in spring or fall.

Zones: 3–8, unless noted otherwise

These tall (1½–6 feet), handsome plants have spiky racemes of bell-shaped flowers in pink, purple, yellow, or white shades, often speckled inside the bells.

No one could have admired foxglove more than we until the day a clump dropped its seeds over a fence, and the plants spread so rapidly that in a few years our entire orchard was a sea of brightly colored blooms. Beautiful, yes, but we strongly advise picking the flowers

Digitalis purpurea 'Primrose Carousel'

before they scatter their seed, except for a very few of the best ones, which you may want to save and sow as replacements. Foxgloves are biennials or short-lived perennials and able to produce a lot of

seed. If plants self-sow, thin the seedlings to 1–2 feet apart.

The plants are most effective when planted in masses of the same color and equally attractive in a formal border or a semi-wild garden. They respond well if given extra fertilizer and benefit from a light winter mulch where there is little snow cover.

GROWER'S CHOICE

Common foxglove (*D. purpurea*) is usually a biennial; 3–6 feet tall. The many cultivars have spectacular colors and blooming habits. The florets on Excelsior hybrids emerge from the stalk at right angles, rather than downward. 'Sutton's Apricot' is apricot-peach. 'Primrose Carousel' has pale yellow flowers all the way around the stalk; comes true from seed. 30 inches tall. Zones 4–8.

Grecian foxglove (*D. lanata*) has small cream or tan flowers with yellow markings; perennial. 2 feet tall.

Strawberry foxglove (*D. × mertonensis*) has pink blossoms; perennial. 3–5 feet tall.

Yellow foxglove (*D. grandiflora*) is perennial. 30 inches tall.

Doronicum
(do-RON-ih-kum)
Leopard's banes

Plant type: Perennial

Bloom time: Spring to early summer

Best location: Sun in cool climates or light shade in warm ones; moist, rich garden soil

Diseases: Mildew

Garden pests: Aphids, Japanese beetles, mealybugs

Good garden companions: Virginia bluebells (*Mertensia pulmonarioides*), lungworts (*Pulmonaria*), spurge (*Euphorbia palustris*)

Propagation: Division every two or three years just after flowering (best method); seed.

Zones: Varies (see below)

Leopard's banes, among the first daisy-types to flower, add a bright spot to the early spring border or woodland garden. Their yellow flowers grow on branched stems above the heart-shaped leaves, making them good cut flowers; of 5 inches to 4 feet in height. For extra-early blooms, dig plants in late fall, pot and store in a cool root cellar, then bring them into a warm, sunny room in late winter. Leopard's banes die to the ground in summer.

GROWER'S CHOICE

D. austriacum has yellow, 2-inch flowers and hairy leaves. 4 feet tall. Zones 5–8.

D. columnae 'Miss Mason' has 3-inch flowers. To 2 feet tall. Zones 3–8.

D. × excelsum 'Harpur Crewe' has 4-inch flowers. 2 feet tall. Zones 4–8.

D. orientale 'Goldcut' is very early; tolerates shade and cool temperatures; 2 feet

Doronicum orientale 'Goldcut'

tall. 'Magnificum' has showy 2-inch flowers. To 2 feet tall. Zones 5–8.

D. plantagineum, with 2- to 5-inch-wide flowers, is useful in large gardens because of its size. 3 feet tall. Zones 4–8.

Echinacea (e-ki-NAY-see-a)
Coneflowers

Plant type: Perennial	
Bloom time: Midsummer to fall	
Best location: Sun (but tolerates light shade); average garden soil. Stands dry conditions.	
Diseases: Leaf spot, viruses	
Garden pests: Japanese beetles	
Good garden companions: False sunflower (*Heliopsis helianthoides*), Russian sages (*Perovskia*)	
Propagation: Division. Plants grown from seed usually do not come true.	
Zones: 3–9	

A worthy addition to mid-to-late summer gardens, coneflowers bear large, daisy-like, pink, red, purple, or white flowers, with central cone-shaped disks, often with reflexed petals. Plants are long lived but need dividing when the clumps get too large (usually every 3–4 years). Separate more vibrant shades by inter-planting paler shades.

Echinacea purpurea

GROWER'S CHOICE

Narrow-leaved purple coneflower (*E. angustifolia*) has pink or white blooms. 3–4 feet tall.
Pale coneflower (*E. pallida*) has pink or white blooms. 3–4 feet tall.
Purple coneflower (*E. purpurea*), is the most common rose-purple-blooming species. 3–4 feet tall. 'Magnus' has dark rose-purple blossoms up to 7 inches across. Compact 'Kim's Knee High' has huge pink flowers and reblooms in the fall. 20 24 inches tall.

Echinops sphaerocephalus

Echinops (E-ki-nops)
Globe thistles

Plant type: Perennial	
Bloom time: Mid- to late summer	
Best location: Full sun or light shade; nearly any soil	
Diseases: Crown rot	
Garden pests: Japanese beetles	
Good garden companions: Wild bee balm (*Monarda fistulosa*), 'David' phlox	
Propagation: Division of clumps; root cuttings; seed (easy, but plants may differ in growth habit from parent)	
Zones: 3–9	

With their unusual globelike, blue or gray-blue flowers and spiny, woolly leaves, these hardy perennials are as attractive to people as to the bees that cluster around them. If picked before they reach full bloom, they make excel-lent dried flowers. As children, we tried to fool the other kids into thinking the unopened buds were porcupine eggs.

Globe thistles are easy to grow in nearly any soil and withstand dry conditions better than most other perennials. Divide them frequently to keep them under con-trol and healthy. Our neighbor had a plant of giant globe thistle that grew to the size of an old-fashioned lilac (*Syringa vulgaris*) bush every year after it had died to the ground over the winter. It made a spec-tacular sight when in bloom, and fortu-nately, it didn't crowd out anything else because it was at the corner of her house.

GROWER'S CHOICE

***E. bannaticus* 'Taplow Blue'** is an outstanding cultivar with bright blue flowers. 3–4 feet tall.
E. sphaerocephalus grows 6 feet tall, with large, grayish blooms.
Small globe thistle (*E. ritro*) is a more reasonably sized plant for most gardens at 1–3 feet in height. 'Veitch's Blue' has very dark blue globes.

Enkianthus perulatus

Enkianthus
(en-kee-AN-thus)

Enkianthus

Plant type: Deciduous shrub
Bloom time: Midspring to early summer
Best location: Full sun or light shade; moist, well-drained, acidic soil
Diseases: Not common
Garden pests: Not common
Good garden companions: Underplant with purple heart-leaved bergenia (*Bergenia cordifolia* 'Purpurea').
Propagation: Layer in fall or spring; take semi-hardwood cuttings in summer.
Zones: Varies (see below)

These unusual shrubs bear umbels of tiny, bell-shaped, creamy yellow, red, or white flowers. Some have attractive red to orange fall foliage. Ideal for open areas and woodland gardens.

GROWER'S CHOICE

E. perulatus, with white urn-shaped flowers, has bright red foliage in fall. To 6 feet tall. Zones 6–8.
**Redvein enkianthus (*E. campanulatus)* has red-veined yellow flowers. 'Red Bells' has creamy yellow blossoms with red tips and veins. To 15 feet tall. The form *albiflorus* has white flowers. Zones 5–8.

Epimedium
(e-pi-MEE-dee-um)

Bishop's hats, barrenworts

Plant type: Perennial
Bloom time: Spring into summer
Best location: Light shade (tolerates full sun); good, moist, well-drained soil in sheltered spot
Diseases: Occasionally subject to viruses
Garden pests: Weevils
Good garden companions: White daffodils and other white-flowered spring bloomers
Propagation: Division of clumps in either fall or spring
Zones: 5–9

These low-growing plants have heart-shaped leaves and delicate red, pink, yellow, or white flowers, some of which resemble bishops' hats. They are among the finest dwarf perennials for the border or rock garden or as a groundcover in a Zone 5 or warmer climate. Never allow them to dry out. Mulch around the plants rather than cultivate, because the roots are shallow and can be easily damaged.

GROWER'S CHOICE

**Alpine barrenwort (*E. alpinum)* has reddish yellow flowers in mid- to late spring and colorful fall foliage. 6–12 inches tall. *E. × versicolor* has tiny pink and yellow flowers in mid- to late spring. 1 foot tall. The cultivar 'Sulfureum' has dark yellow flowers and makes a fast-growing groundcover. 8–12 inches tall.
**Long-spur barrenwort (*E. grandiflorum),* from Japan and Korea, bears pink, yellow, or white flowers in early summer. 9–12 inches.
**Persian barrenwort (*E. pinnatum)* has vivid yellow blooms from late spring through early summer. 8–12 inches.
**Red barrenwort (*E. × rubrum)* bears bright crimson flowers in spring, with reddish foliage that turns red-brown in fall. 1 foot tall. Zones 4–8.

Epimedium grandiflorum

Eranthis (e-RAN-this)
Winter aconites

Plant type: Bulb (tuber)

Bloom time: Late winter and spring

Best location: Light shade or full sun; humus-rich, fertile, moist soil

Diseases: Smut

Garden pests: Slugs and snails

Good garden companions: Snowdrops (*Galanthus*)

Propagation: Divide clumps after blooming; plant seeds in cold frame in spring.

Zones: 4–8

These woodland plants, though initially slow-growing, eventually form carpets of 1-inch, buttercup-shaped yellow flowers. For spring color in a woodland garden, plant the tubers in fall, with the base of tubers 2–3 inches below the soil surface.

Eranthis hyemalis

GROWER'S CHOICE

E. cilicica has flowers up to 1½ inches wide. 2–3 inches tall.

E. hyemalis naturalizes quickly, especially in alkaline soil. 2–3 inches tall.

Erica (EH-ree-ka)
Heaths

Plant type: Evergreen shrub

Bloom time: Varies (see below)

Best location: Full sun; well-drained, acidic soil

Diseases: Powdery mildew, wilt, rot

Garden pests: Few problems

Good garden companions: Low-growing conifers such as spreading junipers and yews (*Taxus*); heather (*Calluna vulgaris*)

Propagation: Layer in spring; take cuttings in midsummer.

Zones: Varies (see below)

Erica carnea 'Springwood Pink'

Many species of heaths exist, and some of the tropical kinds grow as trees. The evergreen shrubs grown in the temperate zones have urn- or bell-shaped flowers in white or shades of pink, red, or gold, held in spiky or domed clusters. Use as a groundcover on sunny slopes or in a shrub border.

GROWER'S CHOICE

Scotch heath or bell heather (*E. cinerea*) blooms throughout the summer. 2 feet tall. Zones 6–8.

Spring heath (*E. carnea*), the most widely planted species, blooms in late winter and early spring. The many cultivars vary in hardiness, bloom form, and foliage color. Most bloom over a long period in shades of pink, magenta, or white. Tolerate slightly alkaline soil. Heights from 6–12 inches. Zones 5–7. The blossom color of 'Springwood Pink' deepens with age. 16 inches tall.

Eremurus (eh-reh-MEW-rus)
Desert candles, foxtail lilies

Plant type: Perennial

Bloom time: Summer

Best location: Sun; well-drained, sandy soil

Diseases: Few problems

Garden pests: Slugs

Good garden companions: Beach wormwood (*Artemisia stelleriana*), sea lavender (*Limonium latifolium*)

Propagation: Divide in late fall; plant seed as soon as it is ripe. Protect young plants over the winter in a cold frame or greenhouse.

Zones: Varies (see below)

These tall-growing perennials from Asia have a growth habit similar to that of yuccas, with spikes of star-shaped pink, yellow, or white flowers that reach 4–8 feet above short, succulent foliage. Once established, they should not be disturbed. Protect them from high winds, and give them a mulch over winter. These unusual plants may be hard to find, but they are well worth growing and are interesting plants for the back of the border.

GROWER'S CHOICE

E. × isabellinus cultivars come in many beautiful colors. To 8 feet. Zones 6–9.

Himalayan foxtail lily (*E. himalaicus*) bears white flowers on tall spikes in June. To 6 feet tall. Zones 5–8; worth a try in Zone 4.

Orange desert candle (*E. stenophyllus*) blooms in July, with deep yellow flowers that age to orange. 3–5 feet tall. Zones 6–9.

Eremurus × isabellinus

Erigeron pulchellus

Erigeron (ee-RIH-je-ron)
Fleabanes

Plant type: Perennial, biennial, or annual
Bloom time: All summer
Best location: Full sun with afternoon shade; nearly any soil, but alpine species need excellent drainage
Diseases: Leaf spot, mildew, rust, yellows
Garden pests: Aphids
Good garden companions: Sea hollies *(Eryngium),* wormwoods *(Artemisia)*
Propagation: Cuttings; seed; division of plants in spring
Zones: 5–8

These easy-to-grow plants produce 2-inch, asterlike, single or semi-double flowers in shades of pink, purple, white, yellow, orange, or lavender, with yellow centers. Some species are good for a mixed border; others, for a rock garden. Divide perennials every 3–4 years.

GROWER'S CHOICE

'Azure Fairy', a hybrid perennial, has semi-double lavender flowers. About 18 inches tall.
Beach aster *(E. glaucus)*, a perennial, bears reddish purple blooms; salt-tolerant (native to West Coast seaside). 1 foot tall. 'Albus', white; 'Elstead Pink', lavender-pink.
'Foersters Liebling', a hybrid perennial, has bright reddish pink, semi-double blossoms. 2 feet tall.
Oregon fleabane *(E. speciosus)*, the most common, has lavender-blue flowers; perennial; 2 feet tall.
'Pink Jewel', a hybrid, has flowers in various shades of pink; perennial; 2 feet tall.
Robin's plantain *(E. pulchellus)* has pink, blue, or white flowers; biennial or short-lived perennial; 2–2 ½ feet tall.

Erodium (ee-ROH-dee-um)
Heron's bills

Plant type: Perennial
Bloom time: Summer
Best location: Full sun; dry, somewhat alkaline, gravelly soil
Diseases: Stem rot, leaf gall
Garden pests: Few
Good garden companions: *Geranium cinereum,* other rock-garden plants
Propagation: Sow seed; divide plants in early spring; separate small offshoots with a bit of root attached in midsummer.
Zones: Varies (see below)

Heron's bills are low-growing (3- to 18-inch-tall) plants bearing single, 5-petaled flowers that are pink to purple, and sometimes white or yellow, followed by seedpods that resemble a heron's bill. Related to cranesbills *(Geranium),* they are good rock-garden or edging plants and also go with trailing plants in tubs or planters. All benefit from winter protection in the North.

GROWER'S CHOICE

E. chrysanthum has pale yellow flowers and silvery, fernlike foliage. 6 inches tall. Zones 6–8.
E. corsicum has pink blooms on mat-forming plants. 3 inches tall. Zones 4–8.

E. manescaui has purple flowers; blooms all season. 8–12 inches tall. Zones 6–8.
E. × variabile has large wavy leaves and dark red flowers with purple-red veins all summer long. 5 inches tall. 'Roseum' has deep pink flowers. To 3 inches. Zones 5–8.

Erodium corsicum

Eryngium giganteum

Eryngium (ee RIN-jee-um)
Sea hollies

Plant type:	Perennial
Bloom time:	All summer
Best location:	Full sun. Those with taproots need sandy, loamy, well-drained soil; those with fibrous roots need moist, fertile soil.
Diseases:	Powdery mildew, root rot
Garden pests:	Snails and slugs
Good garden companions:	White phlox, snapdragons (Antirrhinum majus), wormwoods (Artemisia)
Propagation:	Sow seed as soon as it ripens; divide clumps; take cuttings
Zones:	Varies (see below)

Sea hollies are striking, thistlelike plants 2–4 feet tall with blue or white flowers and spiny blue-gray foliage. They grow wild on sand dunes, as the name implies, and the hybrids are interesting in the perennial or wildflower border. The leaves and flowers make good fillers in bouquets and may be easily dried. Once planted, they should not be disturbed. Sea hollies can self-sow and spread over an area with alarming speed, so keep the fading flowerheads picked.

GROWER'S CHOICE

Amethyst sea holly (E. amethystinum), which is tap-rooted, is one of the best available species, with steel gray leaves and blue-purple flowers from June to late August. About 2 feet tall. Zones 3–8.
Flat-leaved sea holly (E. planum) is another tap-rooted species but is less attractive and better suited to a wildflower border, with small, light blue flowers in mid- to late summer. To 3 feet. Zones 5–9.
Miss Willmott's ghost (E. giganteum) is a fibrous-rooted biennial or short-lived perennial with green flowers that become silvery blue. To 3 feet tall. Zones 5–8.
Rattlesnake master (E. yuccifolium) is a tap-rooted species with greenish white flowers. 4 feet tall. Zones 4–8.

Erysimum (ee-RI-si-mum)
syn. *Cheiranthus*
Wallflowers

Plant type:	Most are short-lived perennials grown as biennials.
Bloom time:	Spring to early summer
Best location:	Full sun; poor to moderately rich, well-drained, alkaline soil
Diseases:	Rust, downy mildew, clubroot
Garden pests:	Slugs, caterpillars
Good garden companions:	Lady's mantle (Alchemilla mollis)
Propagation:	Seed; cuttings in early summer
Zones:	Varies (see below)

Vivid-colored wallflowers with their spicy-scented blooms brighten spring walls, rock gardens, and borders. Most are yellow, orange, or red, but cultivars come in pink, mauve, and white. They failed in our heavy-soil border but thrive in a well-drained, raised bed.

GROWER'S CHOICE

'Bowles Mauve', a hybrid, has mauve flowers and gray-green leaves. To 30 inches. Zones 6–10.
English wallflower (E. cheiri) has yellow-orange blooms. 12–30 inches tall. Cultivars include 'Ivory White' and orange-red 'Fire King'. Zones 3–7.
E. linifolium is an evergreen perennial. 6–24 inches. Zones 7–9.
Siberian wallflower (E. × allionii) is a hardy biennial. Keep the blooms picked for bright orange flowers nearly all summer. To 20 inches tall. Zones 3–7.
Western wallflower (E. asperum) has bronze-yellow blooms. Good for West Coast gardens. 1 foot tall. Zones 5–8.

Erysimum linifolium 'Variegatum'

Erythronium

(eh-rith-RO-nee-um)

Trout lilies, dogtooth violets, adder's tongues

Plant type: Bulb

Bloom time: Early spring

Best location: Light shade; moist, well-drained soil, or in thin grass under deciduous trees

Diseases: Few problems

Garden pests: Slugs

Good garden companions: Spring beauty (*Claytonia virginica*), crocuses, grape hyacinths (*Muscari*)

Propagation: Divide the clumps after flowering.

Zones: 3–9

Clumps of these short, dainty, lily-shaped blooms in shades of yellow, pink, white, and violet spell spring in many areas of North America and brighten up wildflower and rock gardens. Many have marbled foliage, which accounts for the name "trout lily." Plant 4 inches deep.

GROWER'S CHOICE

European dogtooth violet (*E. dens-canis*) has pink, lavender, or white blooms. 6 inches tall.

Fawn lily (*E. californicum*) is a California native with creamy white flowers, one to three on a stem. To 1 foot tall.

'Pagoda', a hybrid, is golden yellow, with 4 or 5 blossoms per stem. To 15 inches tall.

Yellow adder's tongue (*E. americanum*), native to the eastern U.S., has yellow flowers and brown-marbled green leaves. 3–6 inches tall.

Eschscholzia californica

Erythronium americanum

Eschscholzia californica

(esh-SHOLT-zee-a kal-i-FOR-ni-ka)

California poppy

Plant type: Tender perennial usually grown as an annual

Bloom time: Spring and summer

Best location: Full sun; drained, poor soil

Diseases: Root and stem fungal diseases

Garden pests: Rare

Good garden companions: Purple or blue lupines (*Lupinus*)

Propagation: When frosts are over in the spring, plant seed where plants are to grow. May self-sow.

Zones: 8–10

Fernlike foliage and cuplike, fragrant flowers in gold, yellow, orange, or red distinguish these plants. Good for rock gardens or annual beds. The cultivars listed below are all less than 1 foot tall.

GROWER'S CHOICE

'Ballerina', semi-double or double flowers.

'Carmine King', reddish pink.

'Milky White', cream-colored.

Thai Silk Series, brightly colored single or semi-double flowers.

Euonymus (ew-AH-ni-mus)
Euonymus

Plant type: Evergreen or deciduous shrub or vine

Bloom time: Flowers are inconspicuous.

Best location: Full sun or light shade; moist, well-drained soil. Evergreens like a sheltered location.

Diseases: Dieback, leaf spot, powdery mildew

Garden pests: Mites, aphids, leaf miners, mealybugs. Euonymus scale can be devastating.

Good garden companions: Variegated vines good with deciduous trees; shrubs with cotoneasters.

Propagation: Seeds are difficult to start, but softwood cuttings root easily in summer, and layering is easy in spring.

Zones: Varies (see below)

Euonymus alatus 'Compactus'

Grown mostly for the shiny leaves, winged fruits, or (on some) the blazing red fall color.

GROWER'S CHOICE

Burning bush (*E. alatus*) has excellent fall color and small purplish fruits. The stems have odd, corky "wings" that are obvious after leaves drop. 10–18 feet tall. Dwarf burning bush (*E. alatus* 'Compactus') is a more compact form. 4–8 feet tall. Zones 4–9.

Japanese spindle tree (*E. japonicus*) is a popular small tree and ornamental shrub in the South. Grows to 12 feet. Zones 6–9.

Wintercreeper (*E. fortunei*) is a clinging vine or mound-forming sub-shrub, and the hardiest of the evergreen vines. As a climber, it can reach 15 feet in height. Left to sprawl, it makes a good groundcover. Many cultivars vary in foliage color: Some are variegated, while others are gold, red, or purple in fall. Zones 5–9.

Eupatorium
(ew-pa-TO-ree-um)
Eupatoriums

Plant type: Perennial

Bloom time: Late summer into fall

Best location: Full sun (tolerates light shade); average to rich, well-drained to evenly moist soil

Diseases: Crown rot, mildew, leaf spot

Garden pests: Aphids, leaf miners, scales

Good garden companions: New England aster (*Aster novae-angliae*), goldenrods (*Solidago*)

Propagation: Seed; division of clumps in spring

Zones: Varies (see below)

Eupatoriums produce fuzzy pink, purple, or white flowerheads that attract butterflies. Many native hardy eupatoriums were once valued as medicinal herbs, and they still deserve a place in the wildflower garden. Some of them are even suited to the perennial border, although they may spread a little too vigorously there.

GROWER'S CHOICE

Boneset (*E. perfoliatum*) has large white blooms tinged with lavender and prefers wet sites. 5 feet tall. Zones 3–8.

Joe-Pye weed (*E. maculatum*) bears large clusters of purplish flowers. 6 or more feet. It prefers damp sites. 'Atropurpureum' has deep purple flowers, 'Bartered Bride' is pure white, and 'Gateway' is purplish red. Zones 3–8.

Mistflower (*E. coelestinum*), also known as hardy ageratum, has coarsely toothed leaves and tiny blue or violet-blue flowers in flat, 2- to 4-inch-wide clusters. Thrives in light, sandy soil. Grows up to 3 feet. Zones 3–8.

Eupatorium maculatum 'Gateway'

Euphorbia (ew-FOR-bee-a)
Spurges

Plant type: Perennial or annual	
Bloom time: Varies (see below)	
Best location: Full sun; dry, sandy soil	
Diseases: Fungal and viral diseases occasionally	
Garden pests: Mealybugs, mites, nematodes, aphids	
Good garden companions: Cosmos, purple coneflower (*Echinacea purpurea*)	
Propagation: Division in early spring; seed; cuttings	
Zones: Varies (see below)	

This large genus includes annual and perennial plants, succulents, shrubs, and trees, many of them weeds. It also includes the Christmas poinsettia (*E. pulcherrima*). Spurge stems contain a milky sap that can irritate sensitive skin. Just as on poinsettias, what seem to be the flowers on other spurges are actually colored upper leaves called bracts, which surround small, inconspicuous blooms. Spurges look good in borders, rock gardens, and woodland beds, but watch them carefully, because some can spread quickly.

GROWER'S CHOICE

Cushion spurge (*E. polychroma*, also known as *E. epithymoides*) forms spreading mounds to about 2 feet, covered with golden yellow bracts in spring to midsummer. Its foliage turns rose-purple shades in fall. 1–2 feet tall. 'Purpurea' has pale yellow bracts and purple stems. Zones 4–8.

Cypress spurge (*E. cyparissias*) has very narrow leaves that resemble conifer needles, along with bright yellow bracts. It is so much at home in North America that it has often spread through cemeteries and abandoned farms. 8–18 inches tall. Zones 4–9.

Flowering spurge (*E. corollata*) is a perennial European wildflower with showy white bracts and small white flowers in mid- to late summer. 3 feet tall. Zones 4–7.

Myrtle spurge (*E. myrsinites*) is a trailing evergreen perennial with bright yellow bracts in spring. It is a good rock plant that prefers difficult, dry places. 4 inches tall. Zones 5–8.

Snow on the mountain (*E. marginata*) is an annual. It has greenish white flowers from late summer to fall, nestled atop attractive leaves with white margins. 2–4 feet tall.

Eustoma grandiflorum 'Flamenco Blue'

Eustoma grandiflorum
(ew-STOH-ma gran-di-FLOR-um)
Prairie gentian, lisianthus

Plant type: Tender perennial, grown as an annual where not hardy	
Bloom time: Summer	
Best location: Full sun; well-drained, slightly alkaline soil	
Diseases: Wilt, mold, canker	
Garden pests: Few problems	
Good garden companions: Wormwoods (*Artemisia*)	
Propagation: Plant seed in fall.	
Zones: 8–10	

This lovely plant produces gray-green leaves topped with attractive, bell-shaped, pale purple flowers; it is 2–3 feet tall. The species may need staking, but cultivars tend to stay more compact.

GROWER'S CHOICE

Echo Series plants have double flowers. **Flamenco Series** have longer stems. **Heidi, Lisa,** and **Yodel Series** make good cut flowers, with blooms in white or rose as well as purple-blue.

Euphorbia polychroma

Filipendula (fi-li-PEN-dew-la)
Meadowsweets

Plant type: Perennial

Bloom time: Early to midsummer

Best location: Full sun to light shade; rich, moist, well-drained garden soil

Diseases: Leaf spot, mildew, rust

Garden pests: Few problems

Good garden companions: Daylilies (*Hemerocallis*), Siberian iris (*Iris sibirica*)

Propagation: Seed; division in early spring

Zones: 3–9 for most

Fragrant white or light pink clusters of small, feathery flowers grace the tops of meadowsweets' sturdy stems. Although there are many species, only a few are found in nurseries or grown in gardens. Most appreciate moisture and need extra water during their blooming season, though dropwort prefers dry, alkaline soil.

GROWER'S CHOICE

Dropwort (*F. vulgaris*) has loose clusters of tiny white flowers. 18–24 inches tall. 'Multiplex' has double, creamy white flowers; 'Rosea' has pink blooms.

Queen-of-the-prairie (*F. rubra*) includes the cultivar 'Venusta', which features large plumes of rose-pink flowers. 6–8 feet tall.

Siberian meadowsweet (*F. palmata*) has two good cultivars: 'Elegantissima' (also sold as 'Elegans'), with pale pink flowers. 'Rubra', with reddish blooms. 3–4 feet tall.

Filipendula rubra 'Venusta'

Forsythia × intermedia

Forsythia (for-SI-thee-a)
Forsythias

Plant type: Deciduous shrub

Bloom time: Early spring (yellow flowers appear before leaves)

Best location: Light shade to full sun; ordinary garden soil

Diseases: Leaf spot, gall, mosaic virus

Garden pests: Nematodes

Good garden companions: Flowering almond (*Prunus dulcis*)

Propagation: Split up clumps in early spring or fall; take softwood cuttings in early summer.

Zones: Varies (see below)

Golden yellow forsythia blooms are harbingers of spring in many areas. The flower buds are often killed by sub-zero temperatures, which makes some kinds difficult to grow in cold zones, although they may bloom below snow line. Prune them after blooming.

GROWER'S CHOICE

Common forsythia (*F. × intermedia*) includes 'Arnold Giant', with clear yellow flowers. 5 feet tall. Zones 6–9.

'New Hampshire Gold', a hybrid, with bright yellow blooms. 6–8 feet tall. Zones 4–8.

'Northern Gold', a hybrid, clear yellow blossoms. 6–8 feet tall. Zones 6–9.

'Vermont Sun', a hybrid, with bright yellow flowers. 8 feet tall. Zones 4–8.

Weeping forsythia (*F. suspensa*) has clusters of yellow blooms on arching branches. To 10 feet tall. Zones 6–8.

Fothergilla major

Fritillaria (fri-ti-LAH-ree-a)
Fritillaries

Plant type:	Bulb
Bloom time:	Spring to early summer
Best location:	Full sun in well-drained garden soil
Diseases:	Leaf spot, rust
Garden pests:	Few problems
Good garden companions:	For short species, pansies (*Viola × wittrockiana*); for tall species, tulips in compatible colors
Propagation:	Break off offsets in early fall and plant.
Zones:	Varies (see below)

Bell-, saucer-, or tube-shaped flowers, usually pendant, are often checkered. Plant bulbs at 4 times their depth. Few of the many species are used in gardens.

GROWER'S CHOICE

Checkered lily or guinea-hen flower (*F. meleagris*) has checkered purple-and-white blooms. Checkered lilies are good for cool woodland areas and naturalizing. 1 foot tall. Zones 3–8.

Crown imperial (*F. imperialis*) is the showiest, with up to eight orange, red, or yellow bells topped by upright, leaflike bracts on each stem. Even deer and rodents spurn their unpleasant odor. 2–3 feet tall. 'Aurora' has burnt orange/red flowers. Zones 4–8.
F. verticillata has long-lasting, green-white flowers. 12–30 inches. Zones 4–8.
Persian fritillary (*F. persica*) has spike-like clusters of deep purple, bell-shaped blooms. 3–4 feet tall. Zones 6–8.
Yellow fritillary (*F. pudica*) has fragrant yellow blossoms. 6 inches tall. Zones 3–8.

Fritillaria verticillata

Fritillaria imperialis 'Aurora'

Fothergilla (fo-thar-GIL-la)
Fothergillas

Plant type:	Deciduous shrub
Bloom time:	Late spring
Best location:	Full sun, light shade; rich, well-drained, acidic soil
Diseases:	Rare
Garden pests:	Rare
Good garden companions:	Lavender cotton (*Santolina chamaecyparissus*), dwarf blue spruce (*Picea pungens* f. *glauca* 'Montgomery')
Propagation:	Plant seed in cold frame in fall; take softwood cuttings in summer.
Zones:	5–8

This deciduous shrub bears fragrant, bottlebrush-like, white or pink blooms before or as the leaves appear. Brilliant fall color.

GROWER'S CHOICE

F. gardenii, dwarf, to 3 feet. Cultivar 'Blue Mist' has bluish foliage.
F. major grows slowly, up to 8 feet.

Fuchsia (FEW-sha)
Fuchsias

Plant type: Tender shrub, grown as an annual where not hardy

Bloom time: Summer

Best location: Full morning sun, afternoon light shade; fertile, moist, well-drained soil

Diseases: Blight, gall, mold, rust, Verticillium wilt

Garden pests: Whiteflies, aphids, mites, scale, nematodes

Good garden companions: Spotted deadnettle (Lamium maculatum)

Propagation: Softwood cuttings in early summer; seed in spring

Zones: 9–10 for most

Fuchsia 'Stanley Cash'

Fuchsias are either upright or trailing. The unusual tubular flowers with long stamens are ordinarily pendant in clusters at the ends of the stems. Often the petals and sepals are of different colors, mostly in shades of red, pink, purple and white. Hummingbirds love them. Plant with the base of stem 2 inches below soil surface. In addition to the trailing fuchsias that do well in hanging baskets and the upright kinds that thrive in tubs and the flower border, there are many species of deciduous and evergreen shrubs and trees with thousands of cultivars.

GROWER'S CHOICE

F. magellanica has red flowers throughout the summer (year-round in frost-free climates). Grows to 10 feet. Hardy in Zones 7–10.

Gaillardia (gay-LAR-dee-a)
Blanket flowers

Plant type: Perennial, hardy annual, or biennial

Bloom time: All summer

Best location: Full sun; rich, warm, sandy, well-drained soil

Diseases: Leaf spot, yellows

Garden pests: Beetles, leafhoppers

Good garden companions: White boltonia or Japanese silver grass (Miscanthus sinensis)

Propagation: *Annuals, biennials, and common perennials:* Seed in spring. *Cultivars:* Root division in early spring or cuttings in late summer from new shoots that appear at the base. *For a large number of plants:* Dig up the entire clump in the fall, cut the roots into small pieces, and plant them in flats in a cool greenhouse for overwintering.

Zones: 4–8

These showy, long-stemmed flowers with their large, daisylike blooms are a worthwhile addition to any garden, not only because of their beauty, but because they stay in bloom all summer. Blooms come in singles or doubles in various combinations of red, yellow, orange, and gold. They are fairly hardy but appreciate a heavy mulch for winter protection in the North. Dwarf cultivars start at 6–8 inches, but most grow from 15–36 inches tall.

GROWER'S CHOICE

Blanket flower (G. × grandiflora), a hybrid, is a short-lived perennial. The many selections include compact Goblin and Monarch strains and dwarf 'Baby Cole' (8 inches). 'Kobold' is 12 inches tall. **Common blanket flower (G. aristata)** is a perennial with yellow flowers that sometimes have a red base. 30 inches tall. *G. pulchella* is an annual. Cultivars in the Plume Series have double red or yellow flowers. 1 foot tall.

Gaillardia × grandiflora 'Kobold'

Galanthus (ga-LAN-thus)
Snowdrops

Plant type: Bulb	
Bloom time: Late winter to early spring	
Best location: Light shade; average garden soil	
Diseases: Blight	
Garden pests: Bulb flies, nematodes	
Good garden companions: Crocuses; glory-of-the-snows (*Chionodoxa*)	
Propagation: Offsets separated after blooming but before foliage disappears in spring; seed	
Zones: 3–8	

Unfazed even by snow surrounding them when they are in full bloom, the drooping, 1-inch, white blossoms of snowdrops are one of the first flowers of spring. The foliage disappears by summer. Most naturalize easily. Plant 3 inches deep, 3 inches apart. 6–10 inches tall. Many are considered endangered in the wild, so buy only from nurseries that propagate them commercially.

GROWER'S CHOICE

Common snowdrop *(G. nivalis)* has small, sweet-scented flowers. There are many cultivars, including the double 'Flore Pleno'. 4 inches tall.

Giant snowdrop *(G. elwesii)* has large flowers. 5–10 inches tall.

Galanthus nivalis

Galium odoratum

Galium odoratum
(GA-lee-um oh-do-RAH-tum)
Sweet woodruff

Plant type: Perennial	
Bloom time: Spring	
Best location: Sun or light shade; moist soil	
Diseases: Rust, mildew, leaf spot, scorch	
Garden pests: Rare	
Good garden companions: Interplant sweet woodruff with spring bulbs.	
Propagation: Divide in spring; plant seed as soon as it is ripe.	
Zones: 4–8	

This low-growing (6- to 8-inch-tall) herb has tiny, fragrant, star-shaped white flowers and graceful, dark green, whorled foliage. Sweet woodruff makes a good groundcover and woodland plant. It is a native of Europe and Africa and may need winter protection in the North. The fresh leaves are traditionally used to flavor May wine and are sometimes laid among stored clothes for their pleasant hay scent and to repel insects.

Gazania (ga-ZAY-nee-a)
Gazanias

Plant type: Tender perennial, grown as annual	
Bloom time: Summer	
Best location: Full sun; light, sandy soil	
Diseases: Rot, leaf spot, mildew	
Garden pests: Mealybugs	
Good garden companions: Blue floss flower (*Ageratum houstonianum*), speedwells (*Veronica*)	
Propagation: Plant seed indoors in late winter. Set out after frosts end.	
Zones: 8–10	

Daisylike flowers bloom over a long season in many bright colors, including white and shades of red, yellow, orange, and pink, and grow 8–10 inches tall. They close in cloudy weather. Most seed is sold in mixed colors, but you can also find single colors, such as 'Daybreak Red

Gazania rigens 'Sunshine Mix'

Stripe', with a red stripe in the center of each golden yellow petal. Pinching off the spent flowers will extend the bloom period.

Geranium macrorrhizum

Geranium sanguineum

Geranium (ge-RAY-nee-um)
Cranesbills, hardy geraniums

Plant type: Perennial

Bloom time: Summer, except in hottest periods

Best location: Full sun or light shade for large species, full sun for small species; average, but not dry, garden soil

Diseases: Leaf spot, mildew, rust, viruses

Garden pests: Slugs, leaf miners

Good garden companions: Lamb's ears (Stachys byzantina)

Propagation: Seed (easy); division of cultivars in early spring

Zones: Varies (see below)

Don't confuse this hardy garden plant with the other plants commonly called geraniums and often used in window boxes, as bedding plants, or as houseplants. They are members of the genus *Pelargonium*.

The name cranesbill refers to the bill-like extensions on the seed capsules of many species in this genus. Clump-forming types have deep green foliage and grow in mounds up to 2 feet in diameter, with small, 1- to 2-inch, cup-shaped pink, lavender, blue, white, or purple blossoms that appear over the surface. Their size and shape make them good plants for the front of a flower or shrub border or along garden paths. Many short species are ideal for rock or wildflower gardens. Split off parts of the clumps every 3–4 years to keep them healthy and under control. Deadhead frequently to keep them blooming.

GROWER'S CHOICE

Bigroot geranium *(G. macrorrhizum)* has fragrant foliage and red fall color, along with clusters of pink to white blooms in early summer. 18 inches tall. Good for dry, shady spots. There are many cultivars, including 1-foot-tall 'Variegatum', with cream-streaked foliage. Zones 4–8.

Bloody cranesbill *(G. sanguineum)* has magenta flowers for most of the summer. 8 inches tall. It self-sows so easily that it may become weedy. There are many culti-

vars varying in height and flower colors, including 1-foot-tall white 'Album'; 9-inch-tall reddish pink 'Max Frei'; and 6-inch-tall pale pink *G. sanguineum* var. *striatum*. Zones 4–8.

Dalmatian cranesbill *(G. dalmaticum)* has clusters of pink flowers in summer. 6 inches tall. Zones 5–7.

Gray-leaved cranesbill *(G. cinereum)* has evergreen gray-green foliage and white or light pink flowers in late spring and early summer. 6 inches tall. 'Ballerina' has deep purple-red-veined flowers. Zones 5–8.

Lilac geranium *(G. himalayense)* has lavender-blue flowers in early summer. Excellent groundcover. 12–20 inches tall. Zones 4–8.

'Wargrave Pink' cranesbill *(G. × oxonianum* 'Wargrave Pink'*)* has pink flowers from late spring into fall. To 2 feet tall. Zones 4–8.

Gerbera jamesonii
(GER-ba-ra jaym-SOH-nee-eye)

Transvaal daisy,
Barberton daisy

Plant type: Tender perennial, grown as an
annual

Bloom time: Summer

Best location: Full sun; well-drained, fertile
soil

Diseases: Blight, rot, anthracnose,
mildew

Garden pests: Thrips, mites, leaf miners,
aphids

Good garden companions: Wormwoods
(*Artemisia*)

Propagation: Plant seed indoors early for
planting outside after frosts are over.

Zones: 8–10

These large (1–2 feet tall), long-lasting,
daisylike, single or double flowers reach
3–6 inches in diameter. The many cultivars come in shades of pink, purple, red,
yellow, and orange, with yellow centers.
Transvaal daisies are good for either the
border or the cutting garden.

Gerbera jamesonii

Geum chiloense '**Fire Opal**'

Geum (JEE-um)
Avens

Plant type: Perennial

Bloom time: Late spring to midsummer

Best location: Full sun; average garden soil
that holds moisture well but doesn't stay
wet over winter

Diseases: Leaf spot, mildew

Garden pests: Spider mites, caterpillars

Good garden companions: 'Blue Fountain'
speedwells (*Veronica* 'Blue Fountain'),
bloody cranesbill (*Geranium sanguineum*)

Propagation: Division in spring; cuttings in
early summer; seed

Zones: Varies (see below)

Avens add bright spots of orange, red,
pink, cream, or yellow to borders and
rock gardens. Many have flowers up to 1½
inches across above rosettes of fuzzy leaves.
Avens thrive where summers are cool and
winters fairly mild, although even in the
best habitat they are often short lived.
Short types are ideal for a rock garden,
taller ones for the front of the border.

GROWER'S CHOICE

G. chiloense has orange-red flowers with
bright yellow stamens. 12–20 inches tall.
'Fire Opal' has semi-double flowers on
purple stems. Zones 5–8.

'**Lady Stratheden**', a hybrid, has
semi-double, golden yellow blooms.
18–24 inches tall. Zones 5–8.

'**Mrs. J. Bradshaw**', a hybrid, has semi-
double, scarlet flowers. 18–24 inches tall.
Zones 5–8.

Purple avens (*G. rivale*) has pendant,
bell-shaped, small pink to dark red-
orange blooms. Many hybrids.
8–24 inches tall. Zones 3–8.

Gladiolus hybrid

Gladiolus (gla-dee-OH-lus)
Gladioli

Plant type: Bulb (corm)

Bloom time: Varies (see below)

Best location: Full sun, well-drained garden soil

Diseases: Yellows, scab, blight, rot

Garden pests: Thrips, aphids, mites, Japanese beetles

Good garden companions: 'David' phlox

Propagation: Divide corms; pull off small cormels in spring.

Zones: 9–10

Thousands of spectacular gladioli cultivars exist, in every color except true blue. The flowers are held in spikes and open gradually, from bottom to top. Plant 3–6 inches deep, 3–6 inches apart in spring. Where the corms are not hardy, dig them up before hard frosts and dry for winter storage in a cool, dry spot. Gladioli go well clumped with perennials in the border but are also superb in a group by themselves or in the cutting garden.

GROWER'S CHOICE

Grandiflorus types flower from late spring to fall, depending on planting time. They range from 3–5½ feet tall, with miniature blooms (bottom flowers on spike smaller than 2½ inches) to giant blooms (over 5½ inches across).

Nanus group plants bloom in early summer. To 14 inches tall.

Primulinus types flower all summer. 1–2 feet tall. Plant at two-week intervals for constant blooms.

Gomphrena
(gom-FREE-na)
Globe amaranths

Plant type: Annual

Bloom time: Summer to early fall

Best location: Full sun; well-drained, fertile soil

Diseases: Leaf spot, mold

Garden pests: Few problems

Good garden companions: Bachelor's buttons (*Centaurea cyanus* 'Blue Boy')

Propagation: Plant seeds in early spring.

All are good in the border and for cut flowers and drying.

GROWER'S CHOICE

G. globosa produces cloverlike blooms with brilliant purple, pink, or white papery bracts over a long season. To 2 feet tall. 'Buddy', a dwarf cultivar, has purple flowers. 6 inches tall.

G. haageana '**Lavender Lady**' sports lavender bracts. 2 feet tall.

'**Strawberry Fields**', a hybrid, has large bright red flowers. To 3 feet tall.

Gomphrena globosa 'Woodcreek White'

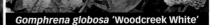

Gomphrena globosa 'Bicolor Rose'

Gypsophila (jip-SO-fi-la)
Baby's breaths

Plant type: Perennial or annual

Bloom time: Summer

Best location: Full sun; well-drained, alkaline garden soil

Diseases: Botrytis, crown gall, yellows

Garden pests: Leafhoppers

Good garden companions: Monkshoods (*Aconitum*), purple coneflowers (*Echinacea purpurea*)

Propagation: Seed; root cuttings of species in spring. Divide creeping baby's breath in spring or fall. Cleft-graft cultivars onto potted seedlings of *G. paniculata*. Shelter the new plants in a tight, shaded cold frame over the following winter until the graft has healed. Harden them off by gradually opening the frame a bit more each day, before planting them outdoors. Protect young plants over winter.

Zones: 4–9 for most; winter protection needed in Zone 3

Clouds of these tiny, lacy, star-shaped, white or pink flowers are lovely in the garden or as a filler in bouquets; they also make excellent dried flowers. The taller kinds (3–4 feet) fit into the border nicely, and the dwarf types are useful as edging or in the rock garden. Their botanic name derives from the Greek, meaning "fond of lime," so you may need to correct your soil if the pH is less than 6. They need space to grow to their full size and beauty without being moved, because their long taproots do not like to be disturbed. The outstanding cultivars are tissue-cultured or grafted. Plant grafted kinds so that the graft union is set 1–2 inches below the soil surface to encourage root formation above the graft. Pick the flowers as soon as they fade to encourage rebloom. They may need staking.

GROWER'S CHOICE

Annual baby's breath (*G. elegans*) has white or pink ½-inch flowers. To 2 feet tall. 'Lady Lace' is white; 'Rosea' is pale pink.

Common baby's breath (*G. paniculata*) usually has single white flowers; to 4 feet tall and wide. 'Perfecta' has large double white flowers for several weeks in midsummer. 3 feet tall. 'Pink Star' bears a

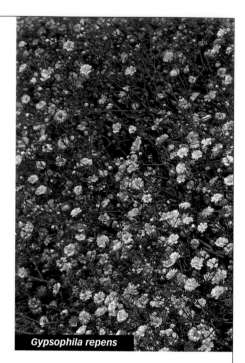

Gypsophila repens

profusion of large double pink flowers that last almost until frost; 18 inches tall. 'Snowflake' has tiny white double blooms.

Creeping baby's breath (*G. repens*) spreads a little too rapidly for the border, so it is best for a rockery or to trail over a wall. 4–6 inches tall. 'Alba' is white; 'Dorothy Teacher' is pale pink.

Hamamelis mollis

Hamamelis (ha-ma-MAY-liss)
Witch hazels

Plant type: Deciduous shrub

Bloom time: Late fall or mid- to late winter

Best location: Light shade to full sun; well-drained, humus-rich soil

Diseases: Leaf spot, powdery mildew

Garden pests: Scale, gall, aphids, leaf rollers

Good garden companions: False cypresses (*Chamaecyparis*), pyramidal American arborvitae (*Thuja occidentalis* 'Pyramidalis')

Propagation: Plant seed in pots or cold frames when ripe; bud graft cultivars on witch hazel seedlings in summer or graft in early spring.

Zones: Varies (see below)

These shrubs produce scented, spidery, yellow, orange, or reddish flowers and are 12–15 feet tall. Most have red or yellow fall foliage color. Good as a specimen and fine in a tall hedge, shrub border, or woodland planting.

GROWER'S CHOICE

Chinese witch hazel (*H. mollis*) has fragrant yellow blooms in mid- to late winter. Zones 5–9.

Common witch hazel (*H. virginiana*) has small yellow flowers in October, before the leaves fall. Zones 4–8.

H. × intermedia 'Arnold Promise' has large yellow flowers; 'Diane' is dark red. Both bloom in late winter. Zones 5–9.

Japanese witch hazel (*H. japonica*) has yellow blooms in late winter and interesting pods that explode and shoot their seeds several feet when touched. Zones 5–9.

Helenium (he-LEE-nee-um)
Sneezeweeds

Plant type: Perennial

Bloom time: Varies (see below)

Best location: Full sun; most soils, even moist ones if they are well-drained

Diseases: Leaf spot, mildew, rust

Garden pests: Few problems

Good garden companions: Asters, chrysanthemums

Propagation: Cuttings in spring; division is possible, but because plants tend to be short-lived, seed is better. Sow as soon as it ripens in summer.

Zones: 4–8 for most

This plant gets its botanical name from Helen of Troy; the common name arose because the dried flowers were formerly ground into a dust that stimulated sneezing. Sneezeweeds are closely related to sunflowers *(Helianthus)*, and their large, flat, and sometimes reflexed yellow, crimson, bronze, or variegated blooms are similar to those of its relative, but smaller and more abundant. They are long-lasting cut flowers and excellent for a large border. In bloom, their colors complement fall chrysanthemums and autumn leaves. Divide every spring to keep plants healthy.

GROWER'S CHOICE

Common sneezeweed *(H. autumnale)* blooms from late summer to midfall. To 5 feet tall.

'Moerheim Beauty', a hybrid, has deep red summer blooms that fade to gold. 3 feet tall.

Orange sneezeweed *(H. hoopesii)* has clear yellow or orange blooms in early summer. 2–3 feet tall. Zones 3–8.

'Pumilum Magnificum', a hybrid, has yellow flowers in late summer to midfall. 3 feet tall.

'Riverton Beauty', old favorite hybrid, has red-centered, lemon yellow flowers from late summer into fall. 4 feet tall.

Helenium autumnale 'Moerheim Beauty'

Helianthemum
(he-lee-AN-the-mum)

Sun roses, rock roses

Plant type: Evergreen or semi-evergreen shrub

Bloom time: Usually early to midsummer; may bloom again later if cut back after the first bloom

Best location: Full sun; light, dry, somewhat alkaline soil

Diseases: None serious

Garden pests: None serious

Good garden companions: Sea thrift *(Armeria maritima)*, rock soapwort *(Saponaria ocymoides)*

Propagation: Division; cuttings taken in early summer (easy)

Zones: 6–8

These shrubby, evergreen plants have 1-inch flowers that resemble those of a single rose. They do best if severely cut back after blooming and benefit from winter protection in northern areas.

Their compact size (4–20 inches tall) makes them good at front of the border, along paths, or in a rock garden. The plants listed below are among the many hybrids.

GROWER'S CHOICE

'Buttercup' has golden yellow flowers. To 1 foot tall.

'Fire Dragon' is coppery red. 8–12 inches tall.

'Orange Surprise' is pale orange. 4 inches tall.

'Raspberry Ripple' has white blooms with purple centers. 8 inches tall.

'Roseum' has clear pink flowers. 16 inches tall.

'Stoplight' is rose red. 8–12 inches tall.

'Wisley White' bears creamy white flowers with prominent yellow centers in mid- to late summer. To 1 foot tall.

Helianthemum hybrid

Helianthus (he-lee-AN-thus)
Sunflowers

Plant type: Perennial or annual

Bloom time: Midsummer to fall

Best location: Full sun; rich, deep, moist, well-drained garden soil

Diseases: Crown gall, leaf spot, mildew, stem rot

Garden pests: Aphids, beetles

Good garden companions: Adam's needle (*Yucca filamentosa*), other sunflowers

Propagation: *Annuals:* Sow seeds in spring. *Perennials:* Divide roots in early spring or late fall; take softwood cuttings in early summer.

Zones: 5–9 for perennials

This large genus includes the familiar annual sunflower, as well as a wide variety of perennials with yellow or gold blossoms. Many attract bees, and birds love the seeds. Easy to grow, some are valuable for flower gardens, while others are ugly weeds. Some can grow as tall as 15 feet, but even the shorter ones are so coarse and conspicuous that they are usually suitable only for planting in the back of a border. For best results, add generous amounts of manure or other fertilizer. Divide the perennial clumps every year. Some need winter protection in the North.

GROWER'S CHOICE

H. × *multiflorus* has 5-inch-wide flowerheads from late summer into fall; grows 5–6 feet tall. Perennial. The cultivars 'Flore Pleno', 'Loddon Gold', and 'Soleil d'Or' all have double yellow flowerheads.

Maximilian sunflower (*H. maximilliani*), native to the Midwest, has 3-inch-wide yellow blossoms and blooms later than other sunflowers, often into October; grows to 10 feet tall. It tolerates dry soil. Perennial.

Sunflower (*H. annuus*) is an annual with yellow or red daisylike blooms that have center disks of yellow, purple, or brown. Many have flowerheads a foot or more in diameter. Numerous cultivars. 3–15 feet.

Thin-leaved sunflower (*H. decapetalus*) is a perennial species that is appropriate for most plantings, with 3-inch-wide yellow blooms late summer to fall. Grows 4–5 feet tall.

Helianthus annuus

Helianthus annuus

Heliotropium arborescens

(he-lee-o-TROH-pee-um ar-bo-RESS-enz)

Heliotrope, cherry pie

Plant type: Tender shrubby perennial, usually treated as an annual

Bloom time: Summer

Best location: Full sun; moist, well-drained, fertile soil

Diseases: Leaf spot, rust

Garden pests: Whiteflies

Good garden companions: 'Coronation Gold' yarrow (*Achillea* 'Coronation Gold')

Propagation: Plant seed in spring; take cuttings in summer.

Zones: 10–11

Clusters of small, vanilla-scented, deep lavender-blue flowers are the reason for this plant's popularity with both people and butterflies. It grows to 4 feet tall where it is hardy but only 18 inches tall as an annual or in a container.

GROWER'S CHOICE

'**Alba**' has white flowers.
'**Marine**' has deep violet flowers.

Heliotropium arborescens

Helleborus × hybridus

Helleborus (he-le-BO-rus)

Hellebores

Plant type: Perennial

Bloom time: Winter to early spring

Best location: Winter sun/summer shade; rich, well-drained soil

Diseases: Leaf spot, mildew, black rot

Garden pests: Slugs

Good garden companions: Snowdrops (*Galanthus*), grape hyacinths (*Muscari*), netted iris (*Iris reticulata*), dwarf evergreens

Propagation: Division; seed in a cold frame or greenhouse as soon as ripe (seedlings may take 2 or more years to bloom)

Zones: Varies (see below)

The cup-shaped or saucer-shaped hellebore flowers listed here are single and usually pendant, in shades of pink, purple, green, and white. They are best grown in groupings in a woodland garden or rock garden or at the front of a perennial or shrub border.

GROWER'S CHOICE

Bear's foot hellebore (*H. foetidus*) has bell-shaped, 1- to 2-inch, green blooms sometimes rimmed with maroon and long, handsome, leathery, evergreen leaves with an unpleasant odor when crushed. 18–24 inches tall. Zones 5–8.

Christmas rose (*H. niger*) has white or pinkish, 2- to 3-inch, saucer-shaped flowers with green centers that last a month or more. Although it doesn't often live up to its name by blooming on December 25, Christmas rose may flower at various times during the winter in mild climates and in early spring in the North. Give it winter protection in the North. When planting, set crowns 1 inch beneath the soil. After it has been moved, it may take years to become established enough to bloom well again. 1 foot tall. Zones 4–8.

Lenten roses (*H. × hybridus*, often sold as *H. orientalis*) bloom from mid- or late winter into spring, with saucer-shaped flowers in a range of colors. 12–18 inches tall. Zones 6–8.

Hemerocallis

(he-me-ro-KA-lis)

Daylilies

Plant type: Perennial

Bloom time: Varies from early summer to fall

Best location: Full sun (tolerates afternoon shade); fertile, well-drained soil with a near-neutral pH

Diseases: Leaf streak, spring sickness, rust

Garden pests: Japanese beetles, mites, thrips, tarnished plant bug, deer

Good garden companions: Common monkshood *(Aconitum napellus)*, 'David' phlox

Propagation: Divide in early spring or late summer after bloom period. Root the small proliferations (called *slips*) that develop on the flower stalks in moist sand or sandy soil in summer. Plants grown from the seed of hybrids vary greatly but are often worthwhile. For hybridizing technique, see page 84.

Zones: Dormants: 2–9. Evergreens: 6–10. Semi-evergreens: 4–9 for most.

Hemerocallis hybrid

A mid-twentieth century entry for the rather ordinary daylily would have merited only a short description, but since that time, the rust-colored tawny daylily *(H. fulva),* yellow lemon lily *(H. flava),* and common early orange daylilies such as *H. dumortieri* have been hybridized into more than 40,000 cultivars, many of which deserve a prominent place in every garden. Most of the qualities of the old-time daylilies — vigor, hardiness, dependability, pest and disease resistance, and ease of culture — have not been lost in the new hybrids. The daylily has often been described as the perfect flower.

Unlike true lilies *(Lilium),* each daylily flower lasts only a day. Some open in the morning and fade at dusk; others stay open until midnight. A few bloom in the evening and last through the next day. Each plant produces so many buds, however, that most plants stay in bloom for several weeks. If you plant a number of different cultivars, it is possible to enjoy daylily blossoms for the entire summer and early fall.

Hemerocallis **'My Sweet Love'**

Daylilies are classified as dormant, evergreen, or semi-evergreen. The dormants are hardy and do well throughout North America. Evergreens and semi-evergreens vary widely in frost resistance. The flower size varies from miniature, or smaller than 3 inches in diameter, to large, or more than 4½ inches. A plant's height refers to the length of the flower stem (scape), which is either low (1–2 feet), medium (2–3 feet), or tall (over 3 feet.) A dwarf is any plant with a scape less than 1 foot in height. Daylilies are also classified as diploid or tetraploid. The "tets," as they are called, have double the number of chromosomes of diploids, usually resulting in larger and heavier flowers. To get the best daylily blooms, you may need to water frequently during the growing season and divide them every 6–10 years.

GROWER'S CHOICE

Although there are a few classic daylilies that many nurseries sell, most have their own special assortment, and it is wise to visit them at different seasons to see what is blooming that would fit into your own garden design. The following tried-and-true standbys are well worth considering.

For mass plantings. Consider some of the inexpensive, older, vigorous kinds that have withstood the test of time, such as the yellow 'Hyperion'; red 'Autumn Red' and 'Gusto'; orange 'Talisman' and 'Manila Moon'; orchid or purple 'Grape Harvest' and 'Sugar Candy'; pink 'Neyron Rose' and 'Pink Swan'; peach 'Diamond Anniversary' and 'Formal Affair'; or yellow-green 'Green Ice' and 'Green Flutter'.

For edgings and rock gardens. Dwarf cultivars are a good choice, including red 'Little Zinger' and 'Siloam Red Toy'; pink 'Little Delight'; or yellow 'Little Butterfly', 'Renee', and 'Stella D'Oro', as well as the related Stellas that bloom off and on all summer.

As background plants. Look for tall (5- to 6-foot) *H. altissima* cultivars, such as 'Autumn Minaret', 'Challenger', and 'Statuesque'.

For Borders or Foundations. The following cultivars are suitable in both the North and the South. We list only the predominant color; many flowers are actually combinations of two or more shades. Check catalog descriptions for further information about size, flower shapes, and height of plant. Bloom times are categorized as "early in the growing season," "midseason," and "late."

★ *Early.* Bright red 'Firecup'; lavender-rose 'Grandways'; yellow with pink 'Silver Circus'.

★ *Midseason.* Near white 'Astolat'; white 'Gentle Shepherd'; creamy white 'Ice Carnival'; buff with coral 'Abstract Art'; pale pink 'Pink Snow Flakes'; rose-peach 'Lovely Dancer'; rose-pink 'Peppermint Lounge'; pink with purple eye 'Prairie Charmer'; red 'Grandfather Time'; dark red 'American Revolution'; orange-yellow with red halo 'Radiant Greetings'; bright orange-yellow 'Rocket City'; rich yellow 'Double Gold'; yellow 'Hudson Valley' and 'Susan Elizabeth'; light yellow 'Prairie Moonlight'; pink-orchid-yellow 'Disneyland'; purple-lavender with wine eye 'Royal Flair'; pale orchid 'Helen Connelley'; purple 'Chicago Royal'; lavender-blue 'Prairie Blue Eyes'.

★ *Late.* Pink-white 'World of Peace'; red 'August Flame'; yellow 'Chicago Brave'; purple with white stripes 'Bold Baron'.

Hemerocallis **'Cherry Candy'**

Heuchera (HEW-ka-ra)
Coral bells, alumroots

Plant type: Perennial

Bloom time: Summer

Best location: Full or nearly full sun for coral bells, and partial shade for alumroots; rich, moist soil

Diseases: Stem rot

Garden pests: Mealybugs, weevils

Good garden companions: Lamb's ears (*Stachys byzantina*), hostas

Propagation: Sow seed inside during late winter (will bloom in 2 years); divide any time (if done in late summer or fall, overwinter plants in a cold frame until they develop a good root system).

Zones: 3–8

We have seen large flower borders completely edged with coral bells (*Heuchera sanguinea*), and they were an impressive sight. The leafy evergreen clumps of this dainty plant, only a few inches tall, are attractive and compact. The spikes of tiny, bell-shaped flowers reach above the leaves on 1- to 2-foot stems and attract hummingbirds. The plants need mulch and may require winter protection in cold areas where snow cover is uncertain. Coral bells make good rock garden plants; a clump tucked here or there along a border is also effective because of its interesting foliage and long season of bloom.

GROWER'S CHOICE

Alumroot (*H. americana*) has greenish flowers and is grown primarily for its mounds of attractive evergreen foliage. '**Black Beauty**', a hybrid, has white flowers and purple leaves. 24 inches tall. **Coral bells (*H. sanguinea*)** cultivars are numerous. Most bloom in early summer in shades of red, pink, or white. ***H. brizoides*** includes 'Green Ivory', with green-and-white flowers, and 'Raspberry Regal', with bright red blooms all summer. 30–42 inches tall in bloom. ***H. micrantha*** var. ***diversifolia*** '**Palace Purple**' stands out for its exceptional purple-red foliage, rather than its small white blooms. To 2 feet tall in bloom. '**Persian Carpet**', a hybrid, has reddish leaves edged in dark purple. '**Pewter Veil**', a hybrid, has silver-mottled purple leaves. '**Velvet Night**', a hybrid, has purple-black foliage.

Hibiscus moscheutos 'Anne Arundel'

Hibiscus (hi-BIS-kus)
Hibiscus, rose mallows

Plant type: Perennial or shrub

Bloom time: Midsummer to fall

Best location: Sun; rich, moist soil

Diseases: Leaf spot, gall, rust

Garden pests: Aphids, Japanese beetles, scale

Good garden companions: Blue oat grass (*Helictotrichon sempervirens*), yellow coneflowers (*Rudbeckia*)

Propagation: Seed (if started inside in midwinter, it will produce blooms the first year, so plants may be grown as annuals); division of cultivars in spring

Zones: Varies (see below)

Plants in the *Hibiscus* genus vary from small wildflowers to the tropical trees that are grown indoors as large houseplants in the North.

GROWER'S CHOICE

Common rose mallow (*H. moscheutos*) hybrids are real show-stoppers. Woody perennials, the flowers make excellent mammoth bouquets. The flat, 6- to 8-inch-wide flowers come in range of

Heuchera 'Black Beauty'

colors, including white, pink, and red. Their size and the plant's height (3–6 feet tall) make them impressive but usually suitable only for large gardens. Set them 3–4 inches deep, so they will be slow to sprout in the spring and thus not get nipped by late frosts. Unfortunately for northern gardeners, rose mallows bloom late and are not easy to cover, so they often get caught by an early fall frost. The roots are tender, which makes it necessary to provide a protective mulch over the winter. 'Frisbee' is an early-blooming cultivar. 'Anne Arundel' grows to 4 feet tall. Zones 5–10.

Shrub and tree hibiscus species range from the rose-of-Sharon *(H. syriacus),* a shrub that grows up to 10 feet tall in Zones 5–9, to Hawaiian white hibiscus *(H. arnottianus),* a shrub or tree that reaches 25 feet but requires a Zone 10 climate. Tall species make good background or accent plants in the border, cottage garden, or cutting garden. Tender kinds make showy houseplants that may be moved to a porch or terrace for the summer. *H. syriacus* 'Diana' has large (to 5-inch) white flowers.

Hosta 'Carol'

Hibiscus syriacus 'Diana'

Hosta (HA-sta)
Hostas, plantain lilies

Plant type: Perennial

Bloom time: Summer

Best location: Light shade; deep, rich, moist soil

Diseases: Crown rot, leaf spot, viruses

Garden pests: Caterpillars, slugs, nematodes

Good garden companions: Ferns, astilbes, 'White Swan' purple coneflower (*Echinacea purpurea* 'White Swan')

Propagation: Division in early spring; seed (seedlings will be variable)

Zones: 3–8

These hardy perennials produce blue, lavender, or white blooms, some of which are fragrant, on tall stalks, but most gardeners choose them because they have beautiful foliage and prosper in shady locations. Hundreds of cultivars are available, ranging in size from dwarfs to giant-sized specimens, with mounds of leaves in many shapes in interesting green, yellow, blue, and variegated shades.

Low-maintenance plants, hostas often thrive where other desirable plants refuse to grow. They look nice on a shady bank, along a woodland path, and as an edging for a shrub or wildflower garden. They are also useful beneath trees and as foundation plants on the shady side of buildings, hedges, or high fences. Although they prefer light shade, they will grow in full sun if the soil is moist, deep, and well supplied with organic matter and nutrients.

GROWER'S CHOICE

The many cultivars have not been well classified, and you may find the same plant with several different names. If you can't find a specific kind at your garden center, it may have one that is very similar but bears a different name. The numerous hosta species are better defined. *Note:* The height refers to the foliage.

August lily *(H. plantaginea)* has light green leaves accented with fragrant white flowers in late summer and fall. 2 feet tall. It makes a good groundcover but needs winter protection in northern areas if heavy snow cover is uncertain. Its cultivar 'Aphrodite' has double flowers.

'Carol' has dark green leaves edged with white. 20 inches tall.

'Decorata' has dark green leaves with white margins and dark purple-blue flowers in midsummer. It spreads quickly, and its dwarf habit makes it a good edging plant. 1 foot tall.

'Fortunei' has lavender to white flowers over dark green leaves in midsummer. 2 feet tall.

'Fortunei Albomarginata' has green leaves with irregular white margins and pale lavender flowers in mid- to late summer. 3 feet tall.

'Fortunei Hyacinthina' has blue-green leaves with small white margins and lavender flowers in summer. 2 feet tall.

'Fragrant Bouquet' is a popular selection with cream-edged, green leaves and fragrant white blooms in late summer. 18 inches tall.

'Frances Williams', with large bluish leaves that have irregular gold margins, and bluish white summer flowers, is a favorite of many gardeners. 2 feet tall.

H. montana 'Aureomarginata' has narrow, shiny, dark green leaves edged in yellow. 28 inches tall.

H. sieboldiana bears blue-green, heart-shaped leaves, with pale lavender blooms in early summer. 3 feet tall.

H. ventricosa has shiny green leaves, with large purple blooms in late summer. 20 inches tall.

'Lancifolia' has narrow, lance-shaped, green leaves and purple flowers in late summer. 18 inches tall.

'Patriot' is a showy selection with attractive dark green foliage with large wavy white margins and purple-blue summer flowers. 18 inches tall.

'Royal Standard' has pale green, heart-shaped leaves and fragrant white blooms in late summer and fall. 2 feet tall.

'Undulata' has wavy green leaves variegated with yellow and white, and lavender to blue flowers in July. 2–3 feet tall.

'Undulata Univittata' bears green leaves with creamy white centers and pale purple flowers in late summer. 2 feet tall.

Popular Hosta Cultivars by Foliage Color

BLUE. 'Elegans', 'Halcyon', 'Hadspen Blue', 'Love Pat'

GOLD OR VARIEGATED WITH YELLOW. 'Golden Tiara', 'Gold Standard', 'Kabitan' (good as an edging or in moist rock gardens; less than 1 foot tall); 'Piedmont Gold', 'Sum and Substance'

WHITE VARIEGATION. 'Francee', 'Frosted Jade', 'Great Expectations', 'Patriot'

Hosta 'Frances Williams'

Hosta montana 'Aureomarginata'

Hyacinthoides hispanica

Hyacinthoides

(hy-a-sin-THOY-deez)

syn. *Endymion*

Bluebells

Plant type: Bulb

Bloom time: Early spring

Best location: Sun to partial shade; well-drained, moderately rich soil. Set bulbs 3–4 inches deep.

Diseases: Blight, mosaic, rot

Insects: Aphids

Good garden companions: Daffodils, tulips

Propagation: Separate bulbs after blooming; plant seed in spring.

Zones: 4–9

These low-growing, spring-flowering, bulbous plants are close relatives of the genus *Scilla,* and several of them were formerly classified in that genus. Spreading rapidly by offsets and seed, they naturalize well. Their clusters of bell-shaped blue, white, or pink blooms beautify a wildflower garden or shrub border.

GROWER'S CHOICE

English bluebell (*H. non-scripta*, formerly *Endymion non-scriptus, Scilla non-scripta,* and *S. nutans)* has narrow, scented, blue or white flowers. 8–15 inches tall.

Spanish bluebell (*H. hispanica*, formerly *Endymion hispanicus, Scilla hispanica,* and *S. campanulata)* produces blue flowers above clumps of glossy green leaves. 12–16 inches tall. 'Rosabella' has lavender-pink flowers. 'Excelsior' has violet-blue flowers with pale blue stripes and is somewhat larger, reaching 20–24 inches in height.

Hyacinthus orientalis

(hy-a-SIN-thus o-ree-en-TAH-lis)

Hyacinth

Plant type: Bulb

Bloom time: Spring

Best location: Sun or light shade; fertile, well-drained soil.

Diseases: Bulb rot, botrytis

Garden pests: Bulb flies, mites, nematodes

Good garden companions: Tulips, grape hyacinths *(Muscari),* daffodils

Propagation: Home gardeners usually have the best results buying commercially grown bulbs, but it is possible to separate old clumps after blooming and pull off small bulblets to replant.

Zones: 5–9; may survive with winter mulch in Zones 3 and 4

These short, 8-to 10-inch plants produce very fragrant spring flowers in bright shades of pink, blue, red, yellow, and white. Set 8 inches deep, 4–8 inches apart in fall. Mulch heavily in winter in cold climates. Avoid planting hyacinths where they may be exposed to prolonged wetness over winter, because they tend to rot easily. You can force them indoors for late winter blooms. Many cultivars available; choose by the colors that appeal to you.

Hyacinthus orientalis

Hydrangea (hy-DRAN-jee-a)
Hydrangeas

Plant type: Shrub or vine

Bloom time: Mid- to late summer

Best location: Sun or light shade; well-drained, fertile, moist soil. White-flowering hydrangeas need a pH of 6–7 or the flowers will have a greenish tinge. For pH requirements of other species, see below.

Diseases: Leaf diseases, powdery mildew, rust, mold

Garden pests: Slugs, rose chafers

Good garden companions: For white-flowering hydrangeas, 'Royal Purple' smoke bush (*Cotinus coggygria* 'Royal Purple'); Shubert chokecherry (*P. virginiana* 'Shubert')

Propagation: Layering in spring; softwood cuttings in summer; hardwood cuttings in winter; split-off offshoots fall or spring

Zones: Varies (see below)

Hydrangeas produce large, showy bloom clusters, usually consisting of big sterile flowers and tiny fertile ones. They are useful additions to the landscape or shrub border and make good foundation plants and hedges. All species of the hydrangeas listed below have many cultivars.

GROWER'S CHOICE

Climbing hydrangea (*H. petiolaris*) is a woody-stemmed vine that clings to stone and brick walls and buildings, climbing to 50 feet. It has large domed clusters of small white florets in early summer. Zones 5–9.

French, big-leaved, or florist's hydrangea (*H. macrophylla*) blooms in shades of pink, purple, or blue in mid- to late summer. The species is divided into two groups: *Hortensias* (or mopheads) have rounded flowerheads of sterile flowers; *Lacecaps* have flat flowerheads with small, fertile flowers in the center and large, sterile ones

Hydrangea macrophylla 'Mariesii Variegata'

surrounding them. For pink blooms, soil needs a pH of 6 or higher; for blue, soil needs a pH of 5.5 or less. Many colorful cultivars are available. Up to 6 feet tall. Zones 6–9. 'Mariesii Variegata', a Lacecap with variegated foliage, has up to 8-inch-wide flowers from midsummer to early fall and is 3 feet tall.

Hills-of-snow (*H. arborescens*) is a popular, hardy, early-summer bloomer producing 6-inch, flat or domed clusters of white florets. 3–5 feet tall. 'Annabelle' is a compact cultivar; 'Grandiflora' has smaller florets but larger flowerheads. Zones 3–9.

Oak-leaved hydrangea (*H. quercifolia*) has interesting orange peeling bark, white flowers in midsummer, some of which change to pink, and bronze-purple foliage in fall. 6 feet tall. Zones 5–9.

PeeGee hydrangea (*H. paniculata* 'Grandiflora') has large, showy, conical flower clusters that start off white in late summer, then change to pink, and then to bronze, lasting well into the fall. The flowers are often dried for winter bouquets. PeeGee hydrangea is easily pruned to grow as a small tree, 10–20 feet tall. It prefers a pH of 6 or higher. 'Brussels Lace' grows only to 5 feet. Zones 3–8.

'Preziosa', a hybrid, blooms in mid- to late summer, with round, 4- to 5-inch-wide clusters of white flowers that become deep blue, red, or lavender when the soil is acidic. 5 feet tall. Zones 6–8.

Tea-of-heaven (*H. serrata*) blooms from summer into fall, with Lacecap-type flowerheads that have pink or blue sterile and fertile flowers. 4–5 feet tall. Zones 6–9.

Hydrangea quercifolia

Hypericum (hy-PEH-ree-kum)
St. John's worts, Aaron's beards

Plant type: Perennial or shrub
Bloom time: Early summer to fall
Best location: *Tall species:* Sun, with light shade in the afternoon; fertile, moist, well-drained soil. *Dwarf species:* Full sun; sandy soil.
Diseases: Mildew, root rot, anthracnose
Garden pests: Scale, thrips
Good garden companions: 'Butterfly Blue' scabious (*Scabiosa* 'Butterfly Blue'), purple-flowered clematis vines
Propagation: Division of roots; cuttings in early summer; seed
Zones: Varies (see below)

These shrubby plants, with bright golden flowers usually 2 to 3 inches in diameter, bloom profusely in a warm spot, but the flowers last longer if they are lightly shaded from the afternoon sun. They are evergreen or semi-evergreen in mild climates.

Hypericum cerastioides

GROWER'S CHOICE

Aaron's beard (*H. calycinum*), a dwarf shrub, has bright yellow, 3- to 4-inch-wide flowers midsummer to fall. It is a good groundcover in light shade. 2 feet tall. Zones 5–9.

'Hidcote', a hybrid, is a popular evergreen or semi-evergreen shrub with large golden flowers from midsummer to fall. To 4 feet tall. Zones 6–9.

H. cerastioides is a perennial with small yellow flowers in late spring and early summer; good for rock gardens. 5–6 inches tall. Zones 6–9.

H. frondosum is a shrub with bright yellow blooms, each with a thick center of golden stamens in mid- to late summer. To 4 feet tall. 'Sunburst' is a cultivar with reddish flaking bark. Zones 6–8.

Perforate St. John's wort (*H. perforatum*) is a weedy perennial with many small yellow blooms for much of the summer. It is good for meadow or wild gardens and is used as a medicinal herb. 2–3 feet tall. Zones 3–9.

Iberis sempervirens

Iberis (i-BE-ris)
Candytufts

Plant type: Perennial or annual
Bloom time: Spring and early summer
Best location: Full sun; rich, well-drained soil
Diseases: Clubroot
Garden pests: Caterpillars, slugs, scale
Good garden companions: 'Blue Clips' Carpathian harebell (*Campanula carpatica* 'Blue Clips')
Propagation: *Perennials:* Division, cuttings in early summer. *Annuals:* Seed (but plants grow slowly).
Zones: Varies (see below)

These low-growing plants, many with woody stems, are some of the best early-blooming plants. They form a dense mat covered with clusters of small, ½-inch-wide, white or sometimes pink, lavender, or red flowers. Candytufts like frequent watering but do not like to be disturbed once they are established. They are usually planted as an edging in a flower border or in a rock garden.

GROWER'S CHOICE

Globe candytuft (*I. umbellata*) is an annual, forming a mound covered with fragrant white, pink purple, red, or bicolored blooms. 6–12 inches tall.

Perennial candytuft (*I. sempervirens*) is an evergreen woody plant with 2-inch-wide clusters of small white or lavender-tinted flowers. 6–12 inches tall. 'Autumn Snow' flowers again in fall. 'Little Gem' grows only 6 inches tall. Zones 3–9.

Rock candytuft (*I. saxatilis*) is a popular perennial for rock gardens with small white flowers. 6 inches tall. Zones 7–9.

Rocket candytuft (*I. amara*) is an annual with fragrant, ½-inch-wide, white or lavender flowers, in 4- to 6-inch domed racemes. To 16 inches tall.

Impatiens walleriana 'Super Elfin Blue Pearl'

Impatiens (im-PAY-shenz)
Impatiens, patience plants

Plant type: Tender perennial, used as annual where not hardy

Bloom time: Summer

Best location: Light shade; moist, well-drained, humus-rich soil

Diseases: Mold, wilt, leaf spot

Garden pests: Caterpillars, mites, aphids

Good garden companions: 'Halcyon' hosta, sweet woodruff (Galium odoratum)

Propagation: Plant seed in spring.

Zones: 9–10

These brightly colored, five-petaled flowers may be single, semi-double, or double and are borne either singly or in clusters. They are excellent as bedding plants for edging gardens or paths or in containers, particularly in lightly shaded locations.

GROWER'S CHOICE

Common impatiens (I. walleriana), also known as busy Lizzies, bloom in a wide range of colors and grow up to 2 feet tall. There are many series in various sizes, including the compact Accent Series, 8 inches; Deco Series, 9 inches; and Super Elfin Series, 10 inches.
New Guinea impatiens have white, pink, red, or salmon flowers and green leaves. Often shaded with red or marked with yellow. Tolerates more sun than its relatives. 14 inches tall.
Rose balsam (I. balsamina) has white, pink, red, or purple flowers held close to the stem. 30 inches tall. Cultivars in the Tom Thumb series are more compact, growing to 1 foot.

Ipheion uniflorum
(I-fee-on ew-ni-FLO-rum)
Spring starflower

Plant type: Bulb

Bloom time: Spring

Best location: Full sun or light shade; humus-rich, well-drained fertile soil.

Diseases: Few problems

Garden pests: Snails and slugs

Good garden companions: 'Rolf Fiedler' as an underplanting for daffodils

Propagation: Plant seed in spring; divide bulbs in summer

Zones: 6–9

This 5- to 8-inch-tall plant has bluish white, star-shaped, 1-inch-wide, fragrant blooms and grasslike foliage that smells like garlic when crushed. Plant bulbs in fall, with their bases 3 inches deep; mulch heavily where winter tempera-

Ipheion uniflorum

tures are low. Naturalizes easily in lawns or woods where hardy.

GROWER'S CHOICE

'Album', pure white
'Froyle Mill', violet
'Rolf Fiedler', clear blue. 4–5 inches tall
'Wisley Blue', lilac

Ipomoea (i-po-MEE-a)
Morning glories, ornamental sweet potatoes

Plant type: Annual, or tender perennial vine used as an annual

Bloom time: Summer

Best location: Full sun; well-drained soil, in sheltered spot

Diseases: Wilt, leaf spot, rot, rust

Garden pests: Japanese beetles

Good garden companions: Wormwoods (Artemisia)

Propagation: Plant seed in spring.

Zones: 9–11

Annual morning glories are fast-growing vines that twine around a trellis, fence, lamppost, or other support and produce large trumpet-shaped flowers.

GROWER'S CHOICE

Common morning glory (I. purpurea) has 2- to 3-inch-wide blue, purple-red, pink, or white blooms. 7–10 feet.
I. tricolor has 3-inch-wide blooms, in bright blue or purple with white centers.

Cultivars include 'Crimson Rambler', cerise; 'Flying Saucers', white with blue streaks; 'Heavenly Blue', sky blue; and 'Pearly Gates', white.
Ornamental sweet potato (I. batatas), a tender perennial, is grown not for flowers or food but for its attractive foliage. Used as a groundcover or in containers. Needs to be kept moist. Leaves have their best color in light shade. 'Blackie' has dark purple-black leaves; 'Margarita' is yellow-green. Only 6–10 inches tall, but it may spread 3–5 feet in a season.

Ipomoea tricolor 'Heavenly Blue'

Iris (EYE-ris)
Irises

Plant type: Rhizome or bulb

Bloom time: Late spring to midsummer (various species)

Best location: Full sun; soil and moisture requirements vary according to species

Diseases: Rot, leaf spot, rust, scorch

Garden pests: Thrips, aphids, nematodes, borers, weevils

Good garden companions: Peonies, daylilies (Hemerocallis), cranesbills (Geranium)

Propagation: Divide the bulbs or rhizomes after flowering.

Zones: Varies (see below)

Iris sibirica 'Caesar's Brother'

One kind of iris or another should be in every garden. Not only do irises fill a void between spring bulbs and summer flowers, but also, their beauty is too startling to miss. Irises take their name from the Greek goddess of the rainbow, and they come in a wide variety of lovely colors. All have flat, sword-shaped foliage and a flower form consisting of three outer petals (falls) and three inner petals (standards), which are often upright.

GROWER'S CHOICE
RHIZOMATOUS IRISES

Rhizomatous irises have rhizomes on or close to the soil surface. They are divided into three horticultural groups, depending on the appearance of the falls.

✳ Bearded irises have a "beard" — a row of hairs — at the base of the falls.

✳ Beardless irises, including Japanese iris (*I. ensata*) and Siberian iris (*I. sibirica*), have smooth falls.

✳ Crested irises, including *I. cristata* and *I. japonica,* have a central serrated ridge at the base of the falls.

The rhizomatous irises need full sun. Plant the bearded types with the soil barely covering the rhizomes. Plant the beardless types with the rhizomes slightly below the soil surface. All need dividing often so the roots do not become crowded.

Bearded hybrids, once called German iris (*Iris × germanica*), come in many colors and color combinations. They range in size from 8-inch-tall miniature dwarfs to tall beardeds up to 4 feet in height. Each bloom lasts only 2–3 days in warm weather, but since the buds open over a long period, one clump may be in flower for weeks in early summer. Zones 3–9.

Dwarf bearded iris (*I. pumila*) is dark blue and blooms in early summer. Cultivars come in white, red, lavender, and yellow. 6 inches tall. Zones 3–9.

Dwarf crested iris (*I. cristata*) grows only to 4 inches tall, with pale lilac, purple, pink, or white flowers in late spring. It is good in the rock garden or the front of the border. Zones 3–8.

Flags. Irises were once called "flags," but the term now usually refers to either blue flag (*I. versicolor*), a blue-flowering iris, or yellow flag (*I. pseudacorus*), with yellow flowers. Although both of these beardless, rhizomatous irises thrive in shallow water, they also grow in moist soil. Blue flag grows to 3 feet tall; yellow flag, from 3–5 feet. Both bloom in midsummer. Unlike other irises, they can tolerate soil that is wet in winter. Zones 3–9.

Japanese iris (*I. ensata,* formerly *I. kaempferi*) grows 2–3½ feet tall, with beardless, orchidlike, flat-topped blooms in various colors. It blooms later than other irises, in June and July, and prefers acid soil. Zones 3–9.

Siberian iris (*I. sibirica*) has beardless blooms that all tend to come at one time in early summer. There are many cultivars, with purple, blue, pink, or white flowers. This vigorous grower likes acidic soil. 2–3 feet tall. Zones 3–9.

BULBOUS IRISES

The following irises bloom from early spring to midsummer, then are dormant.

Juno irises bloom in early to midspring. 6–24 inches tall. Zones 5–9.

Netted iris (*I. reticulata*) has violet-and-white blooms in early spring. It is a good choice for naturalizing. 6–10 inches tall. Zones 3–8.

Xiphium group includes Spanish, English, and Dutch irises, with blue, yellow, or white flowers from spring into summer. Plant them 3–4 inches deep in a sunny spot. 1–3 feet tall. Zones 5–9.

Itea virginica
(eye-TEE-a ver-JI-ni-ka)

Virginia sweetspire

Itea virginica 'Henry's Garnet'

Plant type: Deciduous shrub

Bloom time: Summer

Best location: Full sun, light shade; well-drained, moist, rich, somewhat acidic soil

Diseases: Rare

Garden pests: Rare

Good garden companions: European cranberry bush (*Viburnum opulus*)

Propagation: Softwood cuttings in late spring; seed when it is ripe

Zones: 5–9

This good-looking 5- to 10-foot tall native shrub has an upright-then-arching form, with creamy white fragrant flowers in narrow clusters up to 6 inches long. The green leaves turn purple to red fall foliage. Virginia sweetspire is interesting in a shrub border or woodland planting.

GROWER'S CHOICE

'Henry's Garnet' has bigger flowers and spectacular fall color; only 4 feet tall.

Kalmia latifolia
(KAL-mee-a)

Mountain laurel

Plant type: Broad-leaved evergreen shrub

Bloom time: Late spring to early summer

Best location: Full sun if soil is moist, or light shade; moist, humus-rich, well-drained, acidic soil

Diseases: Blight, leaf spot, gall, powdery mildew

Garden pests: Scale, weevils, lace bugs

Good garden companions: 'Silver Queen' wintercreeper (*Euonymus fortunei* 'Silver Queen')

Propagation: Layering in summer; softwood cuttings in spring

Zones: 5–9

This bushy shrub bears clusters of cup- or bowl-shaped white, pink, or red flowers, often with markings, above glossy evergreen foliage. It is an excellent choice for shrub borders and, at 6–10 feet tall, makes a good backdrop for flower gardens.

GROWER'S CHOICE

'Bullseye', white with red-purple ring.
'Carousel', white flowers, with pink or red inside.
'Elf', pink buds, white blooms. 3 feet tall.
'Olympic Fire', red buds open to pink.
'Silver Dollar', large white flowers.

Kalmia latifolia 'Carousel'

Kerria japonica

Kerria japonica
(KE-ree-a ja-PA-ni-ka)

Japanese kerria

Plant type: Deciduous shrub

Bloom time: Mid- to late spring

Best location: Sun or light shade; well-drained, moist, fertile soil

Diseases: Fireblight, twig blight, canker

Garden pests: Few problems

Good garden companions: 'Miss Kim' lilac (*Syringa pubescens* subsp. *patula* 'Miss Kim')

Propagation: Division in fall; softwood cuttings in summer

Zones: 4–9

This pretty shrub produces an abundance of golden yellow, saucer- or cup-shaped, 1- to 2-inch-wide flowers. It grows 6–10 feet in height and is a good choice for early color in a woodland planting or shrub border.

GROWER'S CHOICE

'Golden Guinea' has large, 2½-inch-wide flowers.
'Picta' has variegated foliage. 5 feet tall.
'Pleniflora' has attractive double flowers.

Kniphofia (ni-FOH-fee-a)

Torch lilies, red-hot pokers, tritomas

Plant type: Perennial

Bloom time: Varies (see below)

Best location: Full sun to light shade; ordinary, well-drained garden soil

Diseases: Leaf spot, crown rot

Garden pests: Nematodes, thrips

Good garden companions: White-flowered cultivars of border phlox (*Phlox paniculata*)

Propagation: Divide or plant seed in spring; seedlings may take years to bloom.

Zones: Varies (see below)

Torch lilies are not commonly grown, but they give a bright glow to the border. Their blooms have a straight-as-a-poker form, with little tubular flowers tightly clustered around the stem and held well above the grasslike foliage. The flowers come in combinations of brilliant red, orange, white, and yellow, as well as solid colors. Hummingbirds and bees love them. In Zones 3 and 4, mulch them heavily or move them into a cold frame for the winter.

GROWER'S CHOICE

'Alcazar' has orange flowers in early summer. 42 inches tall. Zones 5–9.

Common torch lily (*K. uvaria*) gets its name from its flame-colored, orange-red flowers. 4 feet tall. It blooms from mid-summer to fall. 'Flamenco' is easy to grow from seed and blooms in several different colors. 30 inches. It is good for cutting. Zones 6–9.

'Earliest of All' has orange-red blooms in late spring and early summer. 2 feet tall. Zones 5–9

'Ice Queen' has yellowish white flowers in fall. To 5 feet tall. Zones 6–9.

Kolkwitzia amabilis 'Pink Cloud'

Kniphofia uvaria

Kolkwitzia amabilis

(kol-KWIT-zee-a a-MAH-bi-lis)

Beautybush

Plant type: Deciduous shrub

Bloom time: Late spring to early summer

Best location: Full sun; well-drained, fertile soil

Diseases: Rare

Garden pests: Rare

Good garden companions: 'Royal Purple' smoke bush (*Cotinus coggygria* 'Royal Purple')

Propagation: Chip off rooted suckers in spring; take softwood cuttings in early summer.

Zones: 3–8

Beautybush is a tall, vase-shaped shrub that bears a profusion of small, pink, bell-shaped blooms with yellow throats. It grows to 10 feet in height.

GROWER'S CHOICE

'Pink Cloud' bears clear, light pink flowers.

Lamium (LAY-mee-um)
Dead nettles

Plant type: Perennial	
Bloom time: Late spring into summer	
Best location: Light to deep shade; well-drained soil. Will grow in dry shade.	
Diseases: Leaf spot, mildew	
Garden pests: Relatively pest-free	
Good garden companions: Bugleweed (*Ajuga reptans*)	
Propagation: Divide plants in spring; plant seed of species.	
Zones: 3–8	

Though this genus includes some terrible weeds, some species make nice groundcovers and woodland plants. And they don't bite when touched, like stinging nettles *(Urtica dioica)*; hence the name "dead nettles." Their snapdragon-like pink or white flowers blossom over a long period, but they are grown primarily for their attractive foliage. These plants are most effective if planted as a groundcover beneath trees and tall shrubs.

GROWER'S CHOICE

Spotted dead nettle *(L. maculatum),* with silver-marked green leaves, is the most commonly recommended species for garden use. 8–12 inches tall. 'Beacon Silver' has pink flowers and very silvery leaves; 'Chequers' has purplish pink flowers over silver-centered green leaves; 'White Nancy' has white flowers and silvery leaves.

Yellow archangel *(L. galeobdolon)* is extremely invasive, with bright yellow flowers in late spring and silver-and-green leaves on long, trailing stems that take root wherever they touch the ground. 'Hermann's Pride', with yellow blooms and silver-streaked foliage on more upright stems, is less invasive than the species. To about 1 foot tall.

Lamium maculatum 'White Nancy'

Lantana camara 'Radiation'

Lantana (lan-TAN-a)
Lantanas, shrub verbenas

Plant type: Evergreen shrub, used as an annual where not hardy	
Bloom time: All summer	
Best location: Full sun; well-drained, moist, fertile soil	
Diseases: Root knot, rust, virus, leaf spot	
Garden pests: Indoors: Mites, whiteflies	
Good garden companions: Phlox, French hydrangea (*Hydrangea macrophylla*)	
Propagation: Plant seed in spring; take semi-hardwood cuttings in summer.	
Zones: 8–10	

Where lantanas are not hardy, grow them as annuals or bring them inside for the winter. They are good in the border, the seaside garden, or shrub plantings.

GROWER'S CHOICE

L. camara produces flat, domed, or round clusters of small, often bicolored flowers in various color combinations. 3–6 feet tall. Cultivars include 'Feston Rose', with bicolored pink-and-yellow bloom clusters; 'Goldmine', with golden yellow flowers; and 'Radiation', with orange-and-red clusters. 'Cream Carpet' is a compact (1-foot-tall) selection with creamy white flowers.

Weeping lantana *(L. montevidensis)* is a spreading, mat-forming shrub with blooms in shades of pink or lavender. 10–36 inches tall.

Lathyrus
(LA-thi-rus)
Sweet peas

Plant type: Perennial or annual vine or shrub

Bloom time: Summer to late fall

Best location: Sun, light shade; rich soil

Diseases: Anthracnose, mildew, root rot, leaf spot

Garden pests: Aphids, spider mites

Good garden companions: A tight hedge of American arborvitae (*Thuja occidentalis*) as a background

Propagation: Soak seed overnight before planting. Since seedlings transplant poorly, it is best to start them in peat pots or where they will grow.

Zones: Varies (see below)

Although we think of sweet peas as vines, some species form bushy clumps. These include many cultivars of *L. odoratus*, such as the Explorer group (2 feet tall).

GROWER'S CHOICE

Annual sweet pea (*L. odoratus*) is a garden favorite, with often-fragrant pink, lavender, red, or white flowers. With support, the climbing stems can reach anywhere from 30 inches to 6 feet, depending on the cultivar. Cut off the spent flowers frequently to prevent seed formation and promote a longer blooming season.

Everlasting pea (*L. grandiflorus*), with rose-purple or red flowers, is not nearly as well-known as its annual relative. It also needs support but, once planted, is long-lived and does not like to be disturbed. This perennial vine grows 6 feet tall with support. Zones 6–9.

Perennial pea vine (*L. latifolius*) has rose-pink flowers and grows 6–9 feet tall with support. Cultivars include white-flowered 'White Pearl' and bright pink 'Rose Queen'. Zones 3–9.

Lathyrus latifolius

Lavandula angustifolia

Lavandula angustifolia
(la-VAN-dew-la an-gus-ti-FOH-lee-a)
English lavender

Plant type: Perennial

Bloom time: Midsummer

Best location: Full sun; light, fertile, well-drained, alkaline soil

Diseases: Leaf spot, root rot

Garden pests: Caterpillars, nematodes, tarnished plant bugs

Good garden companions: 'Wargrave Pink' cranesbill (*Geranium endressii* 'Wargrave Pink')

Propagation: *Cultivars:* Take cuttings in early summer; divide plants in early spring. *Species:* Start seeds indoors in late winter and set seedlings outside after frosts are over.

Zones: 4–8

Lavender was once grown in nearly every garden, and its special fragrance is still prized in the border, as well as in soaps and lotions. The flowers make lovely bouquets or may be dried and used in potpourri or placed among stored linens. Lavender can also be used as a foundation plant, in a rock garden, or as a compact, untrimmed hedge. Lavender doesn't entirely die back during the winter and does best in a sheltered location. It needs winter protection when grown in the North.

English lavender produces shrublike but low-growing plants with silvery, needle-shaped, aromatic foliage and blue-violet flowers. They can reach up to 3 feet in height in ideal conditions but are usually shorter in the cool North.

GROWER'S CHOICE

'Hidcote' is a compact form with deep purple flowers. To 20 inches tall.

'Lady' flowers the first year from seed, with purple-blue blooms. To 10 inches tall.

'Rosea' has pink flower spikes. 15 inches tall.

Lavatera trimestris

Lavatera trimestris

(lah-va-TER-a try-MESS-tris)

Lavatera

Plant type:	Annual
Bloom time:	Summer
Best location:	Full sun; well-drained, light, fertile soil
Diseases:	Leaf spot, rot
Garden pests:	Scale
Good garden companions:	'Crater Lake Blue' Hungarian speedwell (*Veronica austriaca* subsp. *teucrium* 'Crater Lake Blue'), blue China aster (*Callistephus chinensis*)
Propagation:	Plant seed in spring.

These members of the mallow family produce a profusion of showy, funnel-shaped, open blooms, 3–4 inches across, in shades of pink, lavender, rose, or white. At 3–4 feet tall, they are excellent in the cutting garden or border and as annual foundation plants.

'**Loveliness**', rose-pink, to 3 feet tall.
'**Mont Blanc**', white, to 20 inches.
'**Pink Beauty**', pale pink with purple centers, 2 feet.
'**Ruby Regis**', deep reddish pink, 26 inches.
'**Silver Cup**', pink with dark veins, 30 inches.

Leucanthemum × superbum

(loo-KAN-the-mum soo-PER-bum)
syn. *Chrysanthemum × superbum*

Shasta daisy

Plant type:	Perennial
Bloom time:	Summer
Best location:	Sun or light shade; moist but well-drained, fertile soil
Diseases:	Leaf spot
Garden pests:	Earwigs, nematodes, aphids, slugs
Good garden companions:	Common monkshood (*Aconitum napellus*)
Propagation:	Divide clumps in spring; plant seed for species.
Zones:	3–8

As desirable in the garden as it is in arrangements, shasta daisy is vigorous, prolific, and easy to grow. The white-petaled, yellow-centered flowers of shasta daisy may be single or double. Shastas need good drainage; cultivars benefit from winter protection. Divide often, perhaps every other year if they are growing well, otherwise they'll be very short-lived.

Leucanthemum × superbum

'**Alaska**', an old favorite, bears huge single flowers. 2–4 feet tall.
'**Becky**' has large, 3- to 4-inch flowers over a long season and attractive foliage.
'**Little Silver Princess**' (often sold as 'Little Princess') is a shorter version of 'Alaska'. 1 foot tall.
'**Phyllis Smith**' is semi-double with twisted petals. 2–3 feet tall.

Leucojum vernum

(loo-KOH-jum VER-num)

Spring snowflake

Plant type:	Bulb
Bloom time:	Spring
Best location:	Sun; moist, fertile, well-drained soil
Diseases:	Few problems
Garden pests:	Slugs
Good garden companions:	Daffodils, tulips
Propagation:	Divide bulbs after the leaves die down in spring, or plant seed.
Zones:	3–8

These tiny white flowers on 8- to 12-inch stems are one of the first bloomers of spring. They make a nice edging plant and compete well with grass without getting weedy. It doesn't hurt to mow the foliage after blooming.

Leucojum vernum

Leucothoe fontanesiana

(loo-KOH-tho-ee fon-ta-nee-zee-AH-na)

Drooping leucothoe

Plant type: Evergreen shrub in the South; semi-evergreen in the North
Bloom time: Spring
Best location: Light to deep shade; well-drained, acidic, humus-rich soil
Diseases: Powdery mildew, anthracnose, tar spot
Garden pests: Scale, lace bugs
Good garden companions: Sargent juniper (*Juniperus sargentii*)
Propagation: Chip off rooted suckers in spring; take softwood cuttings in summer; sow seeds in spring.
Zones: 5–8

Drooping leucothoe is an upright-growing shrub with arching branches and clusters of ¼-inch-wide, cylinder-shaped, waxy white flowers. The shiny green leaves turn a beautiful purple bronze in fall. It grows up to 6 feet tall but looks best when kept shorter. Drooping leucothoe is good for a woodland planting or shady shrub border.

GROWER'S CHOICE

'Nana' grows only 1–2 feet tall.
'Rainbow' (also known as 'Girard's Rainbow') has green leaves with cream and pink markings that are especially noticeable in spring.
'Scarletta' has red-purple in spring that turn green in summer.

Leucothoe fontanesiana

Lewisia rediviva

(loo-IS-ee-a re-di-VEE-va)

Bitterroot

Plant type: Perennial wildflower
Bloom time: Early to late spring
Best location: Full sun; humus-rich, well-drained soil. Needs moisture when in leaf and blooming, dryness when dormant in summer.
Diseases: Rot, rust
Garden pests: Mealybugs, slugs, snails
Good garden companions: Pasque flower (*Pulsatilla vulgaris*)
Propagation: Sow seed in fall; divide roots in spring.
Zones: 4–10

Meriwether Lewis, best known for his role in the Lewis and Clark expedition, collected specimens of this and many other plants when he explored the

Lewisia rediviva

Louisiana Purchase. Its fleshy, edible tap-root gives it the common name. In the spring, spectacular white, pink, or rose, 2-inch-wide flowers bloom on 4- to 6-inch stems that arise in center of a rosette of fleshy leaves. The plant dies back to the ground in midsummer, then the leaves reappear in fall. Bitterroot is a fine rock-garden plant.

Liatris (lee-A-tris)

Gayfeathers

Plant type: Perennial
Bloom time: Varies (see below)
Best location: Sun or light shade; light, moist, well-drained soil
Diseases: Leaf spot, rust, rot
Garden pests: Slugs and snails
Good garden companions: Common monkshood (*Aconitum napellus*)
Propagation: Seed in fall; division in early spring
Zones: 3–8

Gayfeathers have many tiny lavender-pink flowers held in fuzzy-looking spikes. Unlike most spiky flowers, which open from the bottom, gayfeathers' blooms start at the top. They are excellent butterfly attractors and good for drying. In the garden, gayfeathers are attractive when planted in groups in a border. They need no fertilizer.

GROWER'S CHOICE

Blazing star (*L. spicata*) blooms from late summer into early fall, with purplish pink flowers. To 5 feet tall. 'Blue Bird' has long-lasting, bluish purple flowers. 'Floristan White' has white blooms. 'Kobold' has rich purple-pink spikes on compact stems. 18–24 inches tall. **Kansas gayfeather** (*L. pycnostachya*) has pink-purple flowers in midsummer. 4–5 feet tall. 'Alba' is a white cultivar. *L. ligulistylis* bears pink spikes over a long summer season. 3–5 feet tall. **Tall gayfeather** (*L. scariosa*) has red-purple flowers in early fall. 2–4 feet tall. 'White Spires' is a white cultivar.

Liatris spicata

Lilium (LI-lee-um)
Lilies

Plant type:	Bulb
Bloom time:	Varies (see below)
Best location:	Full sun, light afternoon shade in hot climates; well-drained soil that never becomes waterlogged
Diseases:	Blight, botrytis, crown rot, mold, rust
Garden pests:	Aphids, borers, nematodes, thrips
Good garden companions:	Colored lilies with white 'David' border phlox (*Phlox paniculata* 'David'); white lilies with blue and purple delphiniums
Propagation:	See box on facing page
Zones:	3–8 for most

Lilies are among the most beloved of all garden perennials. You could create an entire border featuring these beautiful plants, which range in size from miniatures to showy 7-foot-tall specimens that sometimes hold 20–30 flowers. Lily blooms have many forms: They may be recurved (like the turk's cap lily), trumpet-shaped, upward-facing, outward-facing, or hanging like bells. Some are tiny, while others are 8 inches in diameter. Some, like the Orientals, are very fragrant, and they come in every imaginable color except pure blue. Flower colors are often best if the plants receive light shade during the heat of the afternoon. The many different species make it possible to have blooms from late spring until midfall.

Lily bulbs are more fragile than those of tulips or daffodils and should never be allowed to dry out. If you can't plant the bulbs immediately, store them in moist peat moss in plastic bags and plant as soon as possible. Put a little fertilizer in the bottom of the hole and set each bulb so its top is about 5 inches below the surface of the soil. (An exception is Madonna lilies, which should be only 1 inch below the surface.)

Apply a small amount of garden fertilizer around the shoots each spring, but do not give them excessive amounts of manure or nitrogen fertilizer.

Lilium 'Avalanche'

Most lilies prefer neutral to acidic soil, though a few, such as *L. candidum,* need alkaline soil.

Most lilies that grow over 3 feet tall need staking, but their stems are surprisingly sturdy, given the weight of the blooms. Begin to stake the plants as soon as buds form. To allow nutrients to return to the bulbs before winter, let the stems die down naturally, rather than cutting them immediately after blooming.

Most plants are hardy throughout the continental United States and southern Canada, although the Madonna types should be mulched in the North.

GROWER'S CHOICE

It would be difficult to list all the lily species, to say nothing of the myriad cultivars that have been developed. Even dedicated collectors find they can not begin to amass all the named cultivars now in existence, to say nothing of keeping up with new introductions. Most nursery catalogs carry only a few of the most popular species; to find others, contact a nursery that specializes in lilies. If you have plenty of room, you may want to plant early, midseason, and late kinds in a variety of heights, colors, and bloom forms. There are species that are especially suited for wild gardens, such as the attractive wood lily *(L. philadelphicum),* with purple-spotted, red-and-orange flowers. Others are ideal for scented or cutting gardens.

Vigor varies widely among the hundreds of lily hybrids, and the conditions where they are growing can affect their longevity, too. Unfortunately, some of the newer hybrids are short lived no matter where you grow them. It is still worth growing them, though, because their spectacular beauty outweighs the trouble and expense of frequent replacement. Many gardeners, however, prefer to grow species and cultivars that will prosper for years, so they choose old favorites like 'Bright Star', 'Corsage', 'Elegans', 'Enchantment', Henry lily *(L. henryi),* 'Paisley', regal lily *(L. regale),* 'Sutter's Gold', 'Thunderbolt', and tiger lily.

Lilies are classified into nine divisions, as follows:

American hybrids. These hybrids are derived from native species. They may have recurved petals or trumpet-shaped blooms.

Asiatic hybrids. These easy-to-grow beauties, derived from Asiatic species, are among our favorites. They are usually unscented. The Mid-Century hybrids are extremely vigorous, especially 'Enchantment', which, with its orange-red blooms, is considered by many to be one of the best. 'Avalanche' is pure white.

Candidum hybrids. Derived from the Madonna lily *(L. candidum)* and other European species, these bear single or clustered flowers that usually have recurved petals.

Longiflorum hybrids. Characterized by clusters of large, trumpet-shaped, fragrant blooms, this group is derived from the well-known Easter lily *(L. longiflorum). Note:* Easter lily *(L. longiflorum)* is too tender to survive winter in most of the North. If you get one at Easter, plant it outside for the summer, then dig it up in the fall and plant the bulb in a pot. Store it in a cool basement until midwinter, then place in a sunny window. With luck, it may blossom the day before Easter!

Martagon hybrids. Derived from *L. martagon,* these hybrids bear clusters of flowers with reflexed petals.

Oriental hybrids. Derived from East Asian species such as *L. japonicum* and *L. speciosum,* these hybrids bear clusters of large, usually fragrant, trumpet-shaped flowers. This group includes Imperials, with attractive red and gold markings on white flowers, and Olympics, with fragrant white blooms. These are ideal for containers or raised beds where they can have the excellent drainage they require.

Other hybrids. These are hybrids achieved by crossing plants classified in different divisions.

True species. Among the many species is the well-known tiger lily *(L. lancifolium,* formerly *L. tigrinum),* often used for mass plantings. It has become so well adjusted that it has naturalized in many places. This group also includes the regal lily, with fragrant flowers that are rose-purple on the outside and white inside. This garden

Lilium henryi

favorite is useful for mass plantings.

Trumpet and Aurelian hybrids. Developed from Asiatic species, these hybrids produce clusters of scented flowers in a range of forms.

Propagating Lilies

Propagate your lilies in several different ways:

PLANT SEEDS to propagate species, since they come true from seed, or to see what you get from hybrid crosses. Some lily seeds, such as those of Regal and Mid-Century hybrids, sprout easily and grow rapidly, but others may take many months to start.

DIVIDE THE BULBS. Large bulbs often split in the middle. Pull them apart and replant. Although such bulbs usually bloom the first year after planting, they need an additional year to reach full size again.

HARVEST THE BULBLETS. Small bulblets form around the main bulb (the underground stem) and along creeping roots that roam through the surrounding soil. Break them off and plant them in spring or fall to start new plants. A few types of lilies spread rapidly in this way, including the Mid-Century hybrids. Such clumps need dividing regularly or they will deteriorate into numerous tiny plants that bloom sparingly, if at all.

PEEL SCALES. Peel off the outside scales of a bulb and plant them in light soil. In a short time, each one will form a new bulb and grow into a plant. Set these new bulbs at the proper depth the following fall or spring.

PLANT BULBILS. Small bulbils form along the stalks of certain lilies, such as tiger lily *(L. lancifolium).* If you want a lot of new plants, pull off the flower buds before they open so the plant will direct more energy into the production of bulbils. Plant them as soon as they are fat and begin to fall from the plant.

Limonium
(lee-MO-nee-um)
Sea lavenders, statice

Plant type: Perennial

Bloom time: Mid- to late summer

Best location: Full sun; light, well-drained soil

Diseases: Leaf spot, rust

Garden pests: Aphids, mites, nematodes

Good garden companions: Annual baby's breath *(Gypsophila elegans)*

Propagation: Seed (easy); root cuttings. Divide perennials in spring but with care, because the plant does not like to be disturbed. Sometimes self-sows.

Zones: Varies (see below)

Papery, colorful, long-lasting blooms above low rosettes of foliage make these plants desirable for borders and rock gardens. The flowers also make nice fillers in floral arrangements and dried bouquets. These plants are ideal for seashore plantings because they are not damaged by ocean spray.

Limonium latifolium

Limonium sinuatum

GROWER'S CHOICE

Sea lavender *(L. latifolium)* has purple-blue flowers in late summer. 2 feet tall. 'Nanum' is 9 inches tall. Zones 4–9.
Statice *(L. sinuatum)* has clusters of tiny blue, pink, or white flowers from summer into fall. Cultivars bloom in many other rich colors, including yellow, orange, and rose, as well as various pastels. Those in the Petite Bouquet Series are only 12 inches tall; other cultivars range from 18-30 inches tall. Statice is hardy in Zones 8 and 9 but is usually grown as an annual.

Linaria purpurea

Linaria (li-NAH-ree-a)
Toadflaxes

Plant type: Perennial or annual

Bloom time: Spring to midsummer

Best location: Full sun; will grow in poor, rocky soil

Diseases: Crown rot, leaf rot, root rot, mildew

Garden pests: Aphids, mites, nematodes

Good garden companions: 'Sarah Bernhardt' pink peony with 'Canon J. Went' toadflax

Propagation: Seed in fall; division of spreading tuberous roots in early spring

Zones: Varies (see below)

Although butter-and-eggs *(L. vulgaris)* is a common wildflower and perennial roadside weed, the garden species of this genus are much more respectable and desirable. Their snapdragon-like flowers are attractive, and the plants are easy to grow.

GROWER'S CHOICE

Alpine toadflax *(L. alpina)* is a fine perennial rock-garden plant with clusters of tiny purple-and-yellow flowers. 3 inches tall. Zones 4–9.
L. maroccana is an annual with masses of purple, ½-inch-long flowers. 'Northern Lights' produces a mix of bright colors, including white and shades of purple, pink, yellow, and orange. 1–2 feet tall.
L. purpurea, a perennial, has rich purple flowers in spikelike clusters. To 3 feet tall. 'Canon J. Went' is a pink cultivar. Zones 5–8.
L. reticulata, an annual, has deep purple flowers. 2–4 feet tall. 'Aureo-purpurea' is deep purple. 'Crown Jewels' has orange, red, or yellow blooms and is more compact at 9 inches tall.

Linum (LY-num)
Flaxes

Plant type: Perennial or annual
Bloom time: All summer
Best location: Full sun; light, fairly fertile, well-drained soil
Diseases: Anthracnose, wilt, rot
Garden pests: Aphids, slugs, snails
Good garden companions: 'Blue Sapphire' perennial flax with basket-of-gold (*Aurinia saxatilis*)
Propagation: Seed; cuttings; division in early spring
Zones: 5–8 for most

Several perennial flaxes are worth a spot in the flower border or rock garden. Each small golden, blue, or white flower lasts only a day, but if they are picked before they go to seed, the plants will keep producing new flowers all summer. The plants do not like their roots disturbed by cultivation, so a permanent mulch around them is advisable. All are evergreen, a bit woody, and somewhat tender in the North, so they need winter protection.

Linum lewisii

GROWER'S CHOICE

Flowering flax *(L. grandiflorum),* an annual, has rose, white, or red flowers, depending on the cultivar. 15–30 inches tall.
Golden flax *(L. flavum),* a perennial, has 1-inch-wide, funnel shaped, yellow flowers. 1 foot tall. 'Compactum' is 6 inches tall.

Perennial flax *(L. perenne)* has lovely blue flowers early to midsummer over feathery, blue-green leaves. 6–24 inches tall. 'Blue Sapphire' has azure-blue blooms. 1 foot tall.
Wild blue flax *(L. lewisii),* a hardy perennial wildflower, has clusters of light blue, 1½-inch-wide flowers atop 1- to 3-foot-tall stems.

Liriope muscari 'Variegata'

Liriope (li-REYE-oh-pee)
Lilyturfs

Plant type: Bulb (tuber or rhizome)
Bloom time: Late summer to fall
Best location: Sun or shade; moist, slightly acidic, well-drained, moderately fertile soil
Diseases: Rot, anthracnose, leaf spot
Garden pests: Slugs
Good garden companions: 'Variegata' blue lilyturf with yellow or red daylilies (*Hemerocallis*)
Propagation: Divide in early spring.
Zones: 5–10

Native to the Orient, these small evergreen plants can withstand exposure to saltwater spray. Their blooms resemble those of grape hyacinths *(Muscari)* and rise above grasslike leaves growing from tubers or rhizomes.

GROWER'S CHOICE

Blue lilyturf *(L. muscari),* a tuberous plant, grows in tight clumps, with lavender or white flowers. It is often used as an edging for paths, as a groundcover, or in a shaded rock garden. 12–20 inches tall. 'Variegata' has purple flowers and green leaves with yellow margins. Zones 5–10.
Creeping lilyturf *(L. spicata),* a rhizomatous perennial, has light lavender blooms. To 1 foot tall. Zones 4–10. Though not particularly competitive with grass, it can become invasive in its favorite spots, so it is best used as a groundcover.

Lobelia cardinalis

Lobelia (lo-BEE-lee-a)
Lobelias

Plant type: Perennial, biennial, or annual
Bloom time: Midsummer to fall
Best location: Sun or light shade; moist, fertile soil
Diseases: Blight, leaf spot, rot, rust
Garden pests: Aphids, leafhoppers, nematodes, wireworms
Good garden companions: White New England asters (*Aster novae-angliae*), such as 'Wedding Lace'
Propagation: Plant seed in early fall in a cold frame; divide plant roots in spring.
Zones: Varies (see below)

The tubular, two-lipped flowers of lobelias are attractive to hummingbirds. Many species are ideal for naturalizing in the wildflower garden and as perennial border plants, if the soil is damp. In cold areas, plant in a protected location, and mulch heavily around the plants for the winter unless you are certain of a deep snow cover. Plants tend to self-sow and are short lived.

GROWER'S CHOICE

Blue lobelia (*L. siphilitica*) has long, spikelike clusters of blue flowers. 2–4 feet tall. *L. siphilitica* f. *albiflora* has white blooms.

Cardinal flower (*L. cardinalis*), a semi-aquatic perennial wildflower, has long, erect, spikelike clusters of scarlet-red flowers through summer. 3–4 feet tall. 'Ruby Slippers' has deep red flowers. Zones 3–9.

Edging lobelia (*L. erinus*) is a low-growing perennial grown as an annual. Its short clusters of intense blue, white, purple, red, or pink flowers brighten up window boxes or other containers. Some cultivars have a bushy habit, while others are trailing; most are 4–6 inches tall.

***L.* × *gerardii* 'Vedrariensis'** has purple flowers that last for many days when cut. 3–4 feet tall. Zones 8–9.

L.* × *speciosa hybrids have larger flowers than the other perennial species, in shades of red, pink, or purple-blue. Some have reddish green foliage. They can be perennial but are often grown as annuals or biennials. To 4 feet tall. Zones 3–9.

Lobularia maritima
(lob-ew-LAH-ree-a ma-ri-TY-ma)
Sweet alyssum

Plant type: Annual
Bloom time: Summer
Best location: Full sun; well-drained, moderately fertile soil
Diseases: White blister, downy mildew, clubroot
Garden pests: Flea beetles, slugs
Good garden companions: Pansies (*Viola* × *wittrockiana*)
Propagation: Plant seed in spring.

This low-growing (2- to 12-inch-tall), mound-forming, free-flowering plant bears clusters of tiny, fragrant, white blooms. Cut back after the first flush of flowers to encourage reblooming. Excellent edging plant, especially for seaside areas.

GROWER'S CHOICE

'**Carpet of Snow**', white, 4 inches tall.
'**Royal Carpet**', violet-purple, 6 inches tall.

'**Snow Crystals**', white, 8 inches tall.
'**Wonderland Rose**', rose-pink, 3–6 inches tall.

Lobularia maritima 'Snow Crystals'

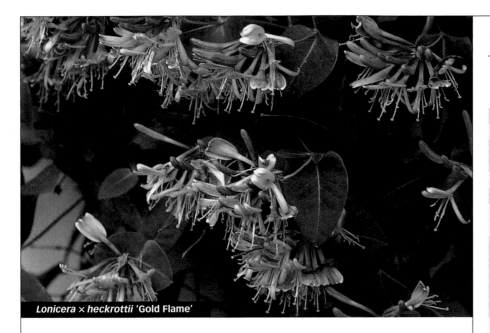

Lonicera × heckrottii 'Gold Flame'

Lonicera (la-ni-SER-a)
Honeysuckles

Plant type: Deciduous shrub or vine

Bloom time: Varies (see below)

Best location: Full sun or light shade; shrubs need well-drained ordinary soil; vines like moist, fertile, well-drained soil. Japanese honeysuckle (L. japonica) is a vigorous evergreen or semi-evergreen vine that can grow to 30 feet with support. It spreads quickly and can become invasive, so is not a good choice for most gardens.

Diseases: Dieback, mildew, blight, leaf spot

Garden pests: Scale, leaf rollers, aphids

Good garden companions: Golden elderberry (Sambucus nigra 'Aurea') with bush-type honeysuckles, 'Jackmanii' clematis with vining honeysuckles

Propagation: *Shrubs:* Take softwood cuttings early summer; chip off rooted suckers in spring or fall. *Vines:* Layer in spring; take softwood cuttings in early summer.

Zones: Varies (see below)

Honeysuckles are shrubs or vines that produce tubular or funnel-shaped, often fragrant blooms in spring or summer, followed by berries.

GROWER'S CHOICE
SHRUBS

Box-leaved honeysuckle (L. nitida) is evergreen, with white blooms in spring followed by purple berries. 11 feet tall. 'Baggesen's Gold' has bright golden foliage and is only 5 feet tall. Zones 6–9.

'Freedom' has white flowers with a touch of pink in early summer, followed by red berries. 10–12 feet tall. Zones 4–7.

'Honeyrose' has red flowers in early summer, followed by dull-red berries. 10 feet tall. Zones 4–7.

L. fragrantissima is a deciduous or semi-evergreen shrub with fragrant white flowers in late winter and early spring, followed by red berries. To 6 feet tall. Zones 5–8.

Tatarian honeysuckle (L. tatarica), a deciduous type, has pink, red, or white blooms in late spring to early summer, followed by red berries. To 12 feet. 'Arnold Red' has an abundance of bright red flowers and red fruits. Zones 3–8.

VINES

Common honeysuckle (L. periclymenum) has fragrant white to yellow flowers in mid- to late summe. 22 feet tall with support.

'Dropmore Scarlet' trumpet honeysuckle (L. × brownii 'Dropmore Scarlet') has tubular scarlet flowers all summer. To 12 feet with support. Zones 3–8.

L. × heckrottii 'Gold Flame' is a vigorous, 15–foot-long, deciduous or evergreen vine, with fragrant pink exterior blooms; orange-yellow inside.

Lunaria annua
(loo-NAH-ree-a AN-new-a)
Honesty, money plant

Plant type: Biennial

Bloom time: Late spring and early summer

Best location: Full sun or light shade; average soil with a pH of 6.5 or higher

Diseases: Canker, clubroot, leaf spot

Garden pests: Few problems

Good garden companions: 'Alba Variegata' honesty with Russell Hybrid lupines

Propagation: Plant seed in early spring where you want them to grow permanently, because they are not easy to transplant. They should bloom and "make money" the next year.

Zones: 3–9

The white or purple-magenta flowers of honesty are pretty and sweetly scented, but the 3-foot-tall plants are grown mostly for the 1- to 2-inch-wide coin-like seed pods, which are used in dried arrangements. To get the "coins," gently rub off the outer covering when it is dry and brown to find the silvery treasure within. A good spot for honesty plants is the wild garden, where they sometimes self-sow.

GROWER'S CHOICE

'Alba Variegata' has white blooms and white-margined foliage.
'Munstead Purple' has red-purple blooms.

Lunaria annua

Lupinus (loo-PY-nuss)
Lupines

Plant type: Perennial or annual

Bloom time: Early to midsummer

Best location: Full sun; moist but well-drained soil. Prefer cool nights.

Diseases: Blight, mildew, virus

Garden pests: Aphids, tarnished plant bugs

Good garden companions: Lamb's ears (*Stachys byzantina*), 'Miss Lingard' meadow phlox (*Phlox maculata* 'Miss Lingard')

Propagation: Division; stem cuttings in spring. Our favorite method is to raise hybrids from seed, planted in peat pots for easier transplanting.

Zones: 4–8 for most

Even though they have gone wild in some places and become rather common, lupines are some of the best garden perennials. They have small, pealike flowers in brilliant red, pink, purple, yellow, white, or blue, often with bicolor shades, on 18-inch flower spikes that top their 3- to 4-foot stems. Although the colorful hybrids are less vigorous, they are best for the flower border.

Set lupines at least 2 feet apart, because the clumps get large, and once established, it is best not to move or divide them. Where they are happy, they are easy to grow. They especially enjoy the cool, dewy nights of the Northeast and Pacific Northwest but are never happy in a wet spot. If you don't let them produce seed after they bloom in early summer, you may get a second bloom later in the season.

GROWER'S CHOICE

L. luteus 'Yellow Javelin' is an annual with yellow spikes. 2 feet tall.

Popsicle hybrids have 10- to 12-inch flower spikes. To 2 feet tall.

Russell hybrids come in many colors and bicolors. To 3 feet tall

Texas bluebonnet (L. texensis) is an annual with deep blue-purple flowers. 1 foot tall.

Wild lupine (L. perennis), a perennial, is fine for natural gardens, to cover slopes, and for planting on banks near streams.

Lychnis (LIK-nis)
Campions, catchflies

Plant type: Perennial or biennial

Bloom time: Early spring to late summer

Best location: Full sun or light shade; sandy, rich, somewhat dry soil

Diseases: Leaf spot, rot, rust

Garden pests: Whiteflies

Good garden companions: 'Royal Blue' Hungarian speedwell (*Veronica austriaca* subsp. *teucrium* 'Royal Blue') with rose campion

Propagation: Plant seed in spring; divide plants in early spring.

Zones: 4–8

There are many species and cultivars in this genus, each quite different and worth planting in the border.

GROWER'S CHOICE

German catchfly (L. viscaria) bears brilliant magenta blooms from early to midsummer. It has a sticky substance on its stems just below the flower. 18 inches tall. 'Splendens Plena' is a dazzling rosy crimson.

Maltese cross (L. chalcedonica) has bright orange-red blooms on 3- to 4-foot-tall stems in midsummer. Each floret in the round head resembles a small cross. It is long lived, is easy to grow, and seeds freely. 'Alba' is a white cultivar.

Rose campion (L. coronaria) is a biennial or short-lived perennial with silvery gray leaves and crimson-pink flowers in late summer. 24–30 inches tall.

'Vesuvius' Arkwright's campion (L. × arkwrightii 'Vesuvius') has star-shaped, bright scarlet flowers from early to midsummer. 18 inches tall.

Lycoris squamigera

(li-KO-ris skwah-MI-je-ra)

Magic lily,
resurrection lily

Plant type: Bulb	
Bloom time: Late summer and early fall	
Best location: Full sun; well-drained, ordinary garden soil. Plant in summer or very late fall when dormant, with the top of the bulb neck just below the soil surface.	
Diseases: Leaf scorch	
Garden pests: Nematodes	
Good garden companions: Purple-pink chrysanthemums, such as 'Barbara'	
Propagation: Divide bulbs after the flowers die down in fall.	
Zones: 3–8	

Lycoris squamigera

These members of the amaryllis family have daffodil-like leaves that come up early in the spring. By summer these turn yellow and disappear, until the sudden appearance in early fall of 2- to 3-foot-tall stalks, each topped with several rose-colored, funnel-shaped blooms. We prefer to use one of their other names: "naked ladies." Although they are not considered hardy in the North, they have grown for nearly four decades in our garden in northern Vermont, withstanding occasional temperatures of –40°F, sometimes with little snow cover.

Lysimachia clethroides

Lysimachia (li-si-MAH-kee-a)

Loosestrifes

Plant type: Hardy perennial	
Bloom time: Varies (see below)	
Best location: Sun, but will tolerate light shade, especially in hot climates; moist, well-drained soil	
Diseases: Leafspot, rust	
Good garden companions: Bee balm (Monarda didyma)	
Propagation: Divide roots in late fall or in early spring; plant seed.	
Zones: 3–8	

Many of these plants in the primrose family are wild and rather weedy. The species that follow are all useful in wild gardens, and especially in spots where it is difficult to grow other perennials, such as a bog garden. But be sure they are kept under control or they may decide to inherit your earth. If you have dry soil, they may be less invasive.

GROWER'S CHOICE

Golden creeping Jenny (*L. nummularia* 'Aurea') is vinelike in growth, with golden blooms and yellow leaves throughout the summer. It is a useful groundcover in wet places, such as alongside streams. 2 inches tall.

Gooseneck loosestrife (*L. clethroides*) has various other common names, including shepherd's crook and Japanese loosestrife. It grows from 2–3 feet tall, with hairy leaves and white flowers in midsummer that are good for cutting.

Yellow loosestrife (*L. vulgaris*) is a European native but has made itself so much at home in the Colonies that many wonder why it was ever invited. Its yellow, cuplike blooms on leafy, upright, 3-foot-tall stems are attractive in early summer, however, and it grows well where better-behaved perennials will not.

Malva sylvestris 'Zebrina'

Malva (MAL-va)
Mallows

Plant type: Perennial

Bloom time: Early summer to frost

Best location: Full sun; well-drained soil

Diseases: Leaf spot, mildew, rot, rust

Garden pests: Caterpillars

Good garden companions: Double-
flowered feverfew *(Tanacetum
parthenium* 'Plenum')

Propagation: Plant seeds in spring; divide
named cultivars in spring or fall.

Zones: 4–8 for most

Many mallows are common weeds, but a
few of the hardy perennials are good for
the border, where they produce attractive
cup-shaped pink, lavender, or white
flowers that are up to 3 inches wide.

Their petals have irregular edges, and
the blooms vaguely resemble those of a
single rose. In fact, some common names
for *Malva* are skunk rose, musk rose, and
musk mallow.

GROWER'S CHOICE

**Hollyhock mallow *(M. alcea)* and musk
mallow *(M. moschata)*** are similar in
appearance, each with white to lavender-
pink blooms and 3–4 feet tall. Both bloom
from early to midsummer until fall.
M. alcea* var. *fastigiata has deep pink
flowers and grows to 3 feet in height.
M. sylvestris has purple-pink, 2½-inch-
wide blooms and grows to 4 feet tall.
'Primley Blue' has pale blue flowers with
deep blue veins and grows to 1 foot tall.
Zones 5–8. 'Zebrina' has purple-striped
pink or white flowers. 36–48 inches tall.

Mandevilla
(man-da-VIL-la)
Mandevillas

Plant type: Tender vine

Bloom time: Summer

Best location: Sun, with shade at midday;
well-drained, fertile, moist soil

Diseases: Mold, rot, leaf spot

Garden pests: Mealybugs, whiteflies,
spider mites

Good garden companions: Morning glories
(Ipomoea)

Propagation: Plant seeds early and transplant after frosts are over. Where hardy,
take softwood cuttings in early summer.

Zones: 10–11

Twining, woody-stemmed, tropical
vines bear clusters of fragrant, funnel-
shaped flowers and climb to 10–20 feet,
with support. In temperate zones, they
may be grown as annuals to decorate
arbors, lampposts, or mailboxes.

GROWER'S CHOICE

Chilean jasmine *(M. laxa)*, with white
2- to 3-inch flowers, is one of the hardiest species in the genus and can stand
light frosts for a short period.
***M. × amoena* 'Alice du Pont'** has bright
pink, 3- to 4-inch-wide flowers.
M. splendens has deep pink flowers, up
to 4 inches wide, with yellow and white
centers.

Mandevilla × amoena 'Alice du Pont'

Matthiola
(ma-thee-OH-la)

Stocks

Plant type: Tender perennial or biennial

Bloom time: Summer

Best location: Full sun; moist, well-drained, slightly alkaline soil

Diseases: Damping off, blight, rot

Garden pests: Aphids, cabbage worms

Good garden companions: China aster (*Callistephus chinensis*)

Propagation: For longest season of bloom, plant seeds inside in late winter and set plants outside after frosts are over.

Stocks are old-fashioned flowers that remain popular in the garden. Native to southern Europe, they are usually grown as annuals in areas with frosts.

The spiky clusters of pink, white, or purple blooms are pleasantly clove-scented and make good cut flowers.

GROWER'S CHOICE

Common stock *(M. incana)* comes in a variety of bright and pale colors. 30 inches tall. Seed is available in many series that produce double or single blooms. A popular one is the Ten Week Mixed, an early-blooming series with usually double flowers in shades of lavender, pink, red, and white. From 8–36 inches tall. Harmony Series stocks make good container plants, as they are only 9–12 inches tall. **Evening-scented stock** *(M. longipetala* **subsp.** *bicornis)* has purplish pink flowers that are scented at night. This species is popular in lighted gardens for its after-dark flowers and fragrance. To 1 foot tall.

Matthiola incana 'Harmony'

Mertensia pulmonarioides
(mer TEN-zee-a pul-mon-ay-ree-OY-deez)

syn. *M. virginica*

Virginia bluebells

Plant type: Perennial

Bloom time: Early spring

Best location: Spring sunshine and light summer shade; moist, well-drained, humus-rich soil

Diseases: Leaf spot, mildew, rot

Garden pests: Slugs

Good garden companions: Late-blooming daffodils, such as 'Actaea'

Propagation: Divide in early spring or fall; plant seed in fall.

Zones: 3–7

Virginia bluebells is a delightful wildflower and a lovely, early-blooming border perennial. The clusters of small, ball-like buds are bright reddish purple and become deep blue in full bloom, so the plants seem to have two different kinds of flowers at once. They grow

1–2 feet in height. They naturalize well under deciduous shrubs or trees, if the shade is not too deep, and are good choices for the wildflower garden or the front of a shady border. After blooming, they die back for the summer, so mark the spot with a stake if you intend to dig in the area or move or divide the plants later.

Mertensia pulmonarioides

Mirabilis jalapa
(mee-RAH-bi-lis ja-LAH-pa)
Four o'clock

Plant type: Tender perennial; treat as
an annual

Bloom time: Summer

Best location: Full sun; well-drained,
fertile soil

Diseases: Leaf spot, rust

Garden pests: Few problems

Good garden companions: 'Silverdust'
dusty miller (Senecio cineraria 'Silverdust')

Propagation: Plant seed or divide tubers
in spring, where hardy.

Zones: 8–11

Mirabilis jalapa

These bushy, 2- to 3-foot plants produce
trumpet-shaped, 1- to 2-inch-wide, pink,
red, yellow, or white fragrant flowers that
are sometimes streaked or striped with
contrasting colors. They open in late
afternoon and fade by morning. Keep
watered for best blooms. Where not
hardy, grow as an annual, or dig in fall,
store the tuberous roots indoors for the
winter, and replant in spring.

Muscari (mus-KAH-ree)
Grape hyacinths

Plant type: Bulb

Bloom time: Early spring

Best location: Full sun, light shade; well-
drained, fertile soil

Diseases: Rot, viruses

Garden pests: Nematodes

Good garden companions: Tulips

Propagation: Dig and separate the bulb
clumps frequently to keep them healthy.
Grow species from seed.

Zones: 3–8

A harbinger of spring, grape hyacinths
feature blue or purple flowers clustered
like tiny grapes atop each stalk. At 4–8
inches tall, they are excellent in rock
gardens or as edging or naturalized in
the lawn. Plant bulbs 2 inches deep in
early fall, spaced 3 inches apart. They
need little care and spread readily, both
by offsets and seed, even becoming
weedy in some places. Don't mow until
leaves have died down.

Muscari armeniacum

Monarda (mo-NAR-da)
Bee balms, bergamots

Plant type: Perennial

Bloom time: Mid- to late summer

Best location: Full sun or light shade; fertile,
moist, well-drained soil

Diseases: Leaf spot, mildew, rust

Garden pests: Stem borers

Good garden companions: Cranesbills
(Geranium)

Propagation: Usually by seed; propagate
named cultivars by division.

Zones: 3–8

Monarda 'Jacob Cline'

Although one sometimes sees a neglected garden where bee balms have gone
on a rampage, in a well-kept border, they
provide a bright spot of summer color.
The leaves have a minty scent, and bees
and hummingbirds are enticed by the
tubular flowers that bloom for most of
the summer. Colors range from white
and lavender-pink to clear pink and bright
red. Cut back the plants after blooming,
and divide clumps each spring to keep
them within bounds if they are planted
in the garden border; otherwise, they
send out runners and can spread rapidly.

GROWER'S CHOICE

Bee balm or **Oswego tea** *(M. didyma)*
is the best garden species. 3–4 feet tall.
Seed-grown Panorama Hybrids come in
several colors, including pink, salmon,
and bright red. If powdery mildew is a
problem in your area, look for resistant
cultivars, such as pink 'Marshall's
Delight' and red 'Jacob Cline'.

Wild bergamot *(M. fistulosa)* is a native
plant with smaller lavender or light pink
flowers. It tolerates dry soil but can rapidly become weedy. 4 feet tall.

GROWER'S CHOICE

Armenian grape hyacinth *(M. armeniacum)* includes 'Blue Spike' (double,
blue flowers); 'Early Giant' (fragrant,
light blue flowers); and 'Heavenly Blue'
(light blue blooms). 'Cantab' flowers
slightly later than the others, with light
blue blooms. Zones 4–8.

Common grape hyacinth *(M. botry-
oides)* is similar but slightly hardier. Its
flowers are bright blue, but cultivars are
white or pink. Zones 3–8.

Myosotis scorpioides

Myosotis (my-oh-SOH-tis)
Forget-me-nots

Plant type: Perennial or biennial
Bloom time: Spring to early summer
Best location: Full sun, light shade; moist, well-drained, poor to slightly fertile soil
Diseases: Gray mold, blight, mildew, rot, rust
Garden pests: Aphids, caterpillars, flea beetle
Good garden companions: Honesty (*Lunaria annua*), yellow tulips
Propagation: Plant seeds where they will grow permanently; divide perennial kinds In early spring.
Zones: 3–8

The forget-me-not has been described as an adventuresome adolescent because it continually wants to break away from home and join the wild bunch. It particularly enjoys dampness, such as that beside a stream, but it also frequents compost piles and mulch heaps. It seeds so freely that in late spring, many perennial borders are covered with these familiar dainty blue flowers with a tiny gold circle in the center.

GROWER'S CHOICE

Alpine forget-me-not *(M. alpestris)* is a short-lived perennial slightly shorter than other forget-me-nots. 4–8 inches tall.
Water forget-me-not *(M. scorpioides)* is a marginal aquatic perennial frequently seen growing in large masses near ponds and streams. To 15 inches tall.
Woodland forget-me-not *(M. sylvatica),* a biennial or short-lived perennial, is the most common. It usually has tiny blue blooms, but you can find many cultivars with white or pink flowers, too. 6–12 inches tall.

Nandina domestica

Nandina domestica
(nan-DEE-na do-MES-ti-ka)

Heavenly bamboo

Plant type: Evergreen or semi-evergreen shrub
Bloom time: Midsummer
Best location: Sheltered area in full sun; moist, well-drained soil
Diseases: Wilt, leaf spot, rot, viruses
Garden pests: Few problems
Good garden companions: Golden privet (*Ligustrum ovalifolium* 'Aureum')
Propagation: Plant seed in spring; root semi-hardwood cuttings in midsummer.
Zones: 6–10

Handsome, glossy, compound leaves are pink-bronze when unfurling, green in summer, and red-tinged in winter on this 6- to 8-foot-tall shrub. Clusters of small white flowers are followed by bright red fruits that last well into the winter. Good in a shrub border.

GROWER'S CHOICE

'Alba' has white fruit.
'Plum Passion' is purple-red in winter; evergreen. 4–5 feet tall.
'Wood's Dwarf' has excellent winter color. 18 inches tall.

Myrica pensylvanica
(mi-REE-ka pen-sil-VA-ni-ka)

Northern bayberry

Plant type: Deciduous or semi-evergreen shrub
Bloom time: Spring
Best location: Full sun or light shade; well-drained, moist, humus-rich soil; also does well in poor, sandy soil
Diseases: Rot, leaf spot, rust, dieback
Garden pests: Few problems
Good garden companions: Rugosa rose (*Rosa rugosa*)
Propagation: Softwood cuttings in early summer; seed when ripe
Zones: 4–8

Myrica pensylvanica

These 9-foot-tall shrubs are grown for their glossy, green, aromatic leaves and gray berries. The male plants produce yellowish green catkins in spring, and female plants produce the waxy berries, which are used for making candles. You must have both male and female plants to get berries. The leaves remain on the plants until late fall. Northern bayberry is a fine foliage plant for the shrub border or seashore garden.

Narcissus (nar-SI-sus)
Narcissi, daffodils

Plant type: Bulb

Bloom time: Early spring

Best location: Full sun, light shade; well-drained, fertile, deep soil

Diseases: Blight, leaf scorch, leaf spot, rot, virus, botrytis

Garden pests: Bulb flies, mites, caterpillars, mealybugs, nematodes, thrips. It is likely that none may ever bother your plants, and if they do, an all-purpose organic garden dust will probably correct the problem.

Good garden companions: Grape hyacinths (*Muscari*)

Propagation: Dig and separate the bulbs after they have died down completely. Replant at once, or dry in the sun a few hours, store in a cool dry place, and plant in early fall. For the fastest increase, plant bulbs less deep than is usually recommended. Their energy then goes into creating new bulbs, although they won't bloom as well. Start new varieties by planting seeds.

Zones: 3–8 for most

Narcissi have long been celebrated as harbingers of spring. They are easy to grow, and it's nearly impossible to have too many. They are classified in 12 divisions according to flower form: Trumpet, Large-Cupped, Small-Cupped, Double, Triandrus, Cyclamineus, Jonquilla, Tazetta, Poeticus, Wild Species, Split-Corona, and Miscellaneous. In size, they range from miniature plants under 10 inches tall to large-flowering kinds that may grow over 18 inches tall. Many are very fragrant. Colors are yellow or white, with a corona (trumpet or cup) of yellow, white, orange, pink, or red.

The terms *narcissus, daffodil,* and *jonquil* are often used interchangeably, but technically, a daffodil is a trumpet-type narcissus, so although all daffodils are narcissi, the reverse is not true. Jonquil correctly refers only to the cultivars of *N. jonquilla* and similar plants.

Most are hardy and easy to grow, and if provided with sun and good garden soil, they bloom faithfully for years in borders or rock gardens or naturalized in masses. For the best color effect, arrange in groups of a dozen or more of the same cultivar.

Plant bulbs in early fall so they have time before winter to form the mass of fibrous roots necessary for good growth. Set most 5–7 inches deep, but 2–3 inches for Jonquilla, Tazetta, Cyclamineus,

Narcissus 'Thalia'

Triandrus, and wild species (or according to package directions). Space them 3–5 inches apart, and place dried manure or other slow-acting fertilizer in the bottom of the planting hole.

To keep them flowering well, divide daffodil cultivars every 5–6 years. Many of the older kinds, such as the pink-cupped whites or double yellows, will bloom for generations without attention and, thus, are the best choices for naturalizing. Add more fertilizer each year to retain their blooming size and vigor.

Let the leaves die down naturally after blooming. Their yellowing leaves are not attractive, so it is tempting to mow or cut them off too early, but it's essential that all the nourishment in the leaves returns to the bulb before it goes dormant for the summer.

GROWER'S CHOICE

'**Altruist**', yellow with an orange cup.
'**Avalanche**', from the Tazetta group, with 10 or more fragrant flowers per bulb in midspring; 14 inches tall.
'**Cheerfulness**', late blooming; small, white, with several blooms on a stem.
'**Irene Copeland**', double white.
'**King Alfred**', a yellow trumpet.
'**Mount Hood**', a white trumpet.
'**Tahiti**', a double yellow, with a red center.
'**Thalia**', from the Triandrus group, with two 2-inch white flowers in midspring; 14 inches tall.

Narcissus 'Avalanche'

Nepeta × *faassenii* 'Dropmore'

Nepeta
(NEH-pe-ta)

Catmints

Plant type: Perennial	
Bloom time: Early summer for most; some will rebloom if cut back severely after first flowers fade	
Best location: Full sun or light shade; ordinary garden soil	
Diseases: Leaf spot, stem rot, virus	
Garden pests: Caterpillars, leafhoppers	
Good garden companions: Pink- or white-flowered scarlet sage (*Salvia splendens*)	
Propagation: Divide clumps. If you need many plants, layer or take root cuttings in late spring; grow species from seed.	
Zones: 3–9, unless otherwise noted	

Many gardeners don't realize how attractive flowering catmint is, and how well it fits into the perennial border, rock garden, or path border. Spikes of dainty blue flowers cover compact mounds of mint-green foliage, and it needs little care.

GROWER'S CHOICE

N. × *faassenii* (also known as *N. mussinii*) is a very different plant from catnip (*N. cataria),* the herb that our feline friends go wild about. Many different strains and cultivars exist, so you may want to visit a nursery when the plants are in bloom to get the most attractive ones. 'Blue Wonder', one of the most popular cultivars, grows about a foot tall; so does 'White Wonder', which has white blooms. 'Dropmore' has gray leaves and is 18 inches tall.

N. nervosa has violet-blue flowers from midsummer to fall. 2 feet tall. Zones 5–9.

'Six Hills Giant', a hybrid, is similar to *N.* × *faassenii,* with spikes of lavender-blue flowers, but it grows to 3 feet high and wide.

Nicotiana
(ni-koh-shee-AH-na)

Flowering tobaccos

Plant type: Tender perennials, treated as annuals	
Bloom time: Summer	
Best location: Full sun or light shade; well-drained, fertile soil	
Diseases: Rot, mildew	
Garden pests: Leaf miners, aphids, spider mites	
Good garden companions: 'Nicki Red' with blue delphiniums	
Propagation: Plant seed in spring.	
Zones: 9–10	

GROWER'S CHOICE

Jasmine tobacco *(N. alata)* has 2- to 4-inch-long, tubular, greenish white or greenish yellow flowers. 3–5 feet tall. Blooms usually open in early evening and are most fragrant at night. Includes day-blooming (if shaded) Nicki Series cultivars in white, rose, cream, purple, red, and greenish white. 18 inches tall. *N. sylvestris* bears long, trumpet-shaped white flowers that close in full sun. To 5 feet tall.

Nicotiana sylvestris

Nigella damascena

Nigella damascena

(ni-JEL-la da-ma-SEE-na)

Love-in-a-mist

Plant type: Annual
Bloom time: Summer
Best location: Full sun or light shade; well-drained, fertile soil
Diseases: Not common
Garden pests: Not common
Good garden companions: 'Lambrook Silver' wormwood (*Artemisia absinthium* 'Lambrook Silver')
Propagation: Plant seeds in spring.

The light blue, 2-inch-wide flowers of this pretty annual are encircled by hair-like foliage (the "mist"). The blooms are followed by decorative seed pods. All are attractive in borders and for cutting and grow to 18–24 inches tall.

GROWER'S CHOICE

'Blue Midget', only 10 inches tall.
'Cambridge Blue', with double flowers.
Miss Jekyll and Persian Jewels series cultivars bloom in shades of pink, white, or blue.

Nymphaea (nim-FAY-a)
Waterlilies

Plant type: Perennial
Bloom time: Summer
Best location: Full sun in shallow pools
Diseases: Leaf spot, rot
Garden pests: Aphids, beetles
Good garden companions: Lotus (*Nelumbo lutea*)
Propagation: Divide the roots in early spring.
Zones: 3–11 for hardy types; for tropicals, see below

Among floating plants, the waterlily is certainly the queen. These plants grow beautifully in shallow ponds, pools, tubs, or slow-moving streams.

For frost-free southern gardens and indoor pools, many tropical species are available, including both day- and night-blooming types in a wide range of vivid colors as well as white; many are fragrant. To grow tropicals in Zones 3–8, either treat them as annuals or take them indoors in winter (See The Magic Spell of Water Gardening on page 164.)

GROWER'S CHOICE

Magnolia waterlily (*N. tuberosa*), also a native, has white flowers that are 6–9 inches across, but it is only slightly fragrant. It blooms mostly in the morning and closes tight during the late afternoon and evening.

Marliac hybrids are among the best hardy waterlilies, in various shades of red, pink, yellow, and apricot.
N. **'Director Moore'**, a tropical, has deep violet-blue flowers with gold centers.
N. **'Mrs. George T. Hitchcock'**, a night-blooming tropical, has rose-pink flowers.
N. odorata, the hardy, fragrant, native waterlily, bears waxy white, 4- to 6-inch-wide blooms. It is one of the easiest waterlilies to grow. You can dig it from shallow ponds and transplant it nearly any time. Among the many cultivars available commercially are 'Pink Sensation', 'Radiant Red', and the yellow 'Sulphurea'.

Nymphaea 'Mrs. George T. Hitchcock'

Nymphaea 'Director Moore'

Oenothera

(ee-no-THEE-ra)

Sundrops, evening primroses

Plant type: Perennial or biennial

Bloom time: Summer

Best location: Full sun; well-drained, moderately fertile soil

Diseases: Leaf spot, rust, mildew

Garden pests: Aphids

Good garden companions: Catmint (*Nepeta* × *faassenii*)

Propagation: Separate clumps or plant seeds in early spring.

Zones: 3–8, unless noted otherwise

Oenothera macrocarpa 'Silver Blade'

Bright yellow is always a cheery color in the garden, and it's hard to find a brighter shade than that provided by the cup-shaped blooms of sundrops. The genus includes both day- and evening-flowering species. If yours opens in the morning, "sundrop" is probably the proper term, even though it is often called "evening primrose." These hardy, drought-tolerant plants are easy to grow, asking only for full sun and good garden soil, although they tolerate poor soil. Use sundrops in a rock garden, as an edging along steps or paths, or as a bright spot at the front of the border. They need occasional division to keep them healthy and prevent them from spreading too much.

Common sundrops (*O. fruticosa*) have rich yellow blooms for most of the summer; many cultivars. 1–3 feet tall.

Evening primrose (*O. biennis*), a native, is a 3- to 4-foot tall biennial that blooms in late afternoon and evening. Sometimes gardeners move a few of these roadside plants into their perennial borders but promptly regret it because they quickly become fast-spreading weeds. The seeds are used to make evening primrose oil. *O. pallida* has fragrant white blooms in the evening throughout the summer. 8–20 inches tall.

Ozark sundrops (*O. macrocarpa*) are a bit shorter, with large, golden blooms and attractive seedpods that can be dried. They have silvery green foliage and a sprawling habit of growth. 6–12 inches tall. Zones 5–8. 'Silver Blade' has silver-blue foliage and blooms from May through frost. 6–10 inches tall.

Opuntia compressa

(oh-PUN-tee-a com-PRE-sa)

Prickly pear

Plant type: Perennial

Bloom time: Late spring into summer

Best location: Full sun; fertile, well-drained soil

Diseases: Crown gall, rot

Garden pests: Aphids, mealybugs, mites, nematodes, scales

Good garden companions: Stonecrops (*Sedum*), yuccas

Propagation: Plant seeds; take cuttings from the older parts of the stem.

Zones: 4–10

Opuntia compressa

Most members of this large genus of cacti are suitable only for southwestern deserts or sunny northern windows, but *O. compressa* (also known as *O. humifusa*) is hardy as far north as Zone 4. Its bowl-shaped yellow flowers are followed by round or oval fruits, usually with spines: the "prickly pears." The 6- to 12-inch-tall, clump-forming plants like desert conditions: full sun and sandy soil. If you grow them in a border, add a bit of soil to raise their planting area a few inches to ensure good drainage, because they cannot tolerate wetness over the winter.

Ornithogalum
(or-ni-THA-ga-lum)
Star-of-Bethlehems

Plant type: Bulb

Bloom time: Spring to early summer

Best location: Full sun or light shade; well-drained, fertile soil

Diseases: Occasional rust, leaf spot

Garden pests: Not common

Good garden companions: Grape hyacinths (Muscari)

Propagation: Cut off offsets and plant.

Zones: Varies (see below)

Both hardy and tender species exist. Plant tender species in spring, setting the base of the bulbs 2–4 inches below the soil surface; in the fall, dig them up for winter storage. Some of the hardier kinds are good for rock gardens and for naturalizing. Star-shaped, sometimes fragrant, white or yellow flowers grow in spikes or umbels on leafless stems. Both *O. nutans* and *O. umbellatum* can be invasive, spreading rapidly by offsets. Keep them confined, if in a border, or plant them in a "wild" area where they can become safely naturalized.

GROWER'S CHOICE

Arabian star-of-Bethlehem (O. arabicum) is good as a greenhouse or house plant. 30 inches tall. Zones 8–10.

Nodding star-of-Bethlehem (O. umbellatum) bears star-shaped white flowers. 5–10 inches tall. Zones 7–10.

O. nutans has silvery white-and-green, bell-shaped blooms and leaves with a silver stripe. 1–2 feet tall. Zones 5–8.

Ornithogalum arabicum

Oxalis tetraphylla

Oxalis (ok-SAL-is)
Shamrocks, sorrels

Plant type: Bulb, tuber, or rhizome

Bloom time: *Indoors in pots:* Late winter, early spring. *Outdoors:* In late spring and summer.

Best location: Full sun or light shade; well-drained, fertile soil outdoors

Diseases: Mildew, leaf spot, rust

Garden pests: Leaf miners

Good garden companions: Wild columbine (Aquilegia canadensis)

Propagation: Divide in spring; plant seed in late winter or early spring.

Zones: Varies (see below)

Numerous species of these annual and perennial plants have small, cuplike, pink, red, yellow, or white flowers and attractive cloverlike leaves, which are sometimes sold as shamrocks. Plant 2 inches deep. Many close at night and on cloudy days.

GROWER'S CHOICE

Common woodsorrel (O. montana) has white flowers with pink veins. It is good for woodland gardens. 6 inches tall. Zones 3–8.

Good luck plant (O. tetraphylla, formerly *O. deppei),* also known as four-leaved pink sorrel, forms mounds of cloverlike, ¾- to 3-inch-long green leaves tinged with purple at the base and funnel-shaped, pink flowers. Use as a bedding or border plant, as well as in containers; it grows well in sun or shade. To 12 inches tall. Zones 7–10.

O. adenophylla has pink blooms and silvery-green leaves. It is good for rock gardens. 6 inches tall. Zones 5–8.

O. enneaphylla has fragrant, white to red, 1-inch-wide flowers over attractive clumps of foliage. 3 inches tall. 'Rosea' is light pink. Zones 6–9.

Pachysandra
(pa-kee-SAN-dra)

Pachysandras, spurges

Plant type: Evergreen perennial

Bloom time: Varies (see below)

Best location: Light to moderate shade; moist, well-drained, slightly acidic soil

Diseases: Blight, leaf spot, dieback, stem rot

Garden pests: Mites, nematodes, scales

Good garden companions: Lily-of-the-valley (*Convallaria majalis*)

Propagation: Divide plants in spring; take cuttings in early summer.

Zones: Varies (see below)

GROWER'S CHOICE

Allegheny pachysandra *(P. procumbens),* a clump-forming species, is evergreen in the South but dies back in northern winters. White blooms are held in brushy spikes rising directly from the ground in spring when new foliage appears. To 1 foot tall. Zones 6–9.

Evergreen Japanese spurge *(P. terminalis),* the most common, has masses of white flowers atop glossy, dark green foliage in early summer. Prized as a groundcover on shady banks, along woodland paths, and under trees where other plants won't grow, it needs shade to thrive; it spreads rapidly by underground stolons. 8–10 inches tall. Set plants 8–24 inches apart, depending on how quickly you need coverage. 'Green Carpet' is a compact 6 inches tall. 'Variegata' has green-and-white leaves. To 10 inches tall. Zones 4–8.

Pachysandra terminalis

Paeonia 'Best Man'

Paeonia (pay-OH-nee-a)

Peonies

Plant type: Perennial or deciduous shrub

Bloom time: Late spring to early summer

Best location: Full sun; moist, fertile, well-drained soil

Diseases: Botrytis, red spot, rot, wilt, virus

Garden pests: Scales, thrips, aphids

Good garden companions: Herbaceous peonies with 'Miss Lingard' meadow phlox (*Phlox maculata* 'Miss Lingard')

Propagation: Divide root clumps in midsummer, just after the blooms fade, and they may have a small bloom or two the next year. Make sure there are three or more "eyes" (red sprouts) on each division.

Zones: 3–8 for most; 5–8 for tree peonies

Even people who can't get excited about spring violets and forget-me-nots admire the giant flowers of peonies. The only landscaping many homes once had was a lilac bush and a dark red Memorial Day "piney" near the front door. Gardeners today can choose from hundreds of new peony cultivars that have since mostly replaced the old common peony (*P. officinalis*), which invariably fell apart soon after blooming and had a strong, unpleasant odor. Some of the modern red, pink, white, and even yellow blooms can be 10 inches across or more, and their shrublike foliage, up to 3 feet in height and width, looks attractive throughout the summer and fall.

In addition to their beauty, peonies are fragrant and long lived, seldom need dividing, and are superior cut flowers. They make nice focal points in a border, serve as attractive low hedges, and are good foundation plants in northern areas where woody shrubs may suffer badly under the weight of heavy snow.

Peonies deserve extra care to produce the most spectacular blooms. Buy good-sized plants growing in pots, if possible. If plants are bare-root, make sure there are three to five eyes or sprouts on each bare-root clump. They like full sun but also grow well on the southeast side of a building where they will get light afternoon shade and plenty of skylight. Good air circulation helps keep them healthy. Allow 3 feet of space between each clump.

Dig a hole the size of a bushel basket, and thoroughly mix several large shovelsful of well-aged manure or compost into the soil, along with a ½ cup of commercial organic fertilizer. Put most of the soil back in the hole, and set the root clump so the spot where the red sprouts emerge from the root is only an inch below the surface (2 inches in light soil). If set deeper, the plant will struggle, and it may be many years before it blooms properly. Planting too deep is the most common cause of peony failure. Tree peonies are grafted, so set the graft union about 6 inches below the surface of the soil.

Manure heaped over the plant each fall will keep it growing and blooming well. If manure is not available, a cup of commercial organic fertilizer dug in around the plant in early spring will suffice. As soon as the buds begin to develop, stake the large-flowering cultivars. One method is to place a wire or plastic hoops specially made for this purpose around a plant to hold the heavy blooms off the ground. (See page 116.) Each branch will produce several buds, so to obtain the largest flowers, pinch off all buds except for the one on the tip.

Once peonies are planted, don't disturb them. They will get bigger and more productive each year. Once every 8–10 years they may need dividing, but not more often, unless you need to start new plants or the old ones begin to deteriorate in the center. For information on how to divide and replant the tuberous roots, see page 123.

Although ants often roam over the plants, they do no damage and are merely attracted by the sweet substance in the buds. The old wives' tale that ants must be present or the flowers won't open is not true, however, and the ants may carry aphids, which can damage the plants and need to be controlled. Botrytis is the most common reason that buds do not open, and this disease can also cause new growth to turn brown and rot. If botrytis is a problem, apply a fungicide throughout the summer.

Three important peony species include Chinese peony *(P. lactiflora),* from which a great many of our double-flowering beauties originated; common red peony *(P. officinalis),* also called Memorial Day peony, from which come many single and double cultivars; and fern-leaved peony *(P. tenuifolia),* with

Paeonia 'Kansas'

Paeonia suffruticosa 'Coral Terrace'

Paeonia suffruticosa 'Largo'

lacy leaves and single, deep red blooms in mid- to late spring on 2-foot-tall plants.

Herbaceous peonies are ordinarily classified according to the shape of their blooms, although many new hybrids don't fit these classifications exactly.

* *Single-flowering*. A single row of petals.
* *Semi-double*. Similar to single flowering, but with several whorls of petals.
* *Double*. Large, spherical forms with ruffled center petals. Includes bomb type with a ball-like center of petals.
* *Japanese* or *anemone*. Single or semi-double with the stamens in the center replaced by petal-like segments.

GROWER'S CHOICE

RED SHADES

'Best Man', deep red, late-season
'Big Ben', dark red, bomb
'Cherry Hill', maroon-red, semi-double
'Felix Crousse', bright red, double
'Kansas', bright red, double
'Karl Rosenfield', dark red, double
'Nippon Beauty', dark red, yellow edge, Japanese
P. officinalis, red, double
'Red Charm', deep red, bomb

WHITE BLOOMS

'Bowl of Beauty', white, double
'Festiva Maxima', white with red flecks, double
'Le Cygne', one of the most famous white doubles
'White Wings', white, single

PINK SHADES

'Doreen', bright pink, Japanese
'Doris Cooper', light pink, double
'Dresden Pink', medium pink, double
'Monsieur Jules Elie', bright pink, double

'Mrs. Franklin D. Roosevelt', rose-pink, double
'Sarah Bernhardt', deep pink, double
'Solange', buff-pink, double

YELLOW SHADES

'Laura Dessert', creamy yellow center, white outer petals with pink tone
P. mlokosewitschii (Molly the Witch), single, bowl-shaped, yellow

OTHER

Tree peony *(P. suffruticosa)* is an exquisite small woody shrub, rather than an herbaceous perennial, growing 4–7 feet tall. Cultivars have 2- to 12-inch-wide single, double, or semi-double fragrant flowers in mid- to late spring in pink, red, lavender, white, or yellow. In Zones 5 and 6, grow in sun; in Zones 7 and 8, in shade. Includes the cultivars 'Largo', which bears rose-pink blossoms with a striking rose and gold center, on very study stems; and 'Coral Terrace', with large (to 8-inch), ruffled, coral-pink blossoms; 4–5 feet tall.

Papaver rhoeas 'American Legion'

Papaver (pa-PAH-ver)
Poppies

Plant type: Perennial or annual

Bloom time: Varies (see below)

Best location: Full sun; moderately fertile, well-drained soil

Diseases: Botrytis, blight, leaf spot, mildew, virus

Garden pests: Aphids, leafhoppers, nematodes, tarnished plant bugs

Good garden companions: Oriental poppy with purple or lavender bearded irises

Propagation: Divide perennial poppies when they are dormant, just after blooms have faded; plant seeds of annuals and biennials where they are to grow.

Zones: Varies (see below)

The term "poppy" is used for several plants not in the *Papaver* genus: California poppy *(Eschscholzia californica)*, plume poppy *(Macleaya cordata)*, Welsh poppy *(Meconopsis cambrica)*, and blue or Himalayan poppy *(M. grandis)*. Here, we list three popular *Papaver* species.

GROWER'S CHOICE

Arctic or Iceland poppies *(P. croceum,* also known as *P. nudicaule)* are less showy than the Orientals, grow to a height of 1 foot, and come in shades of yellow, white, and orange in both single and double blooms. Most are fragrant, and they make nice edgings. If kept picked,

they will bloom all summer if it's not too hot. Plant Iceland poppy seeds in a permanent location, as they do not transplant well. Although perennial, many gardeners treat them as biennials. Plants often self-sow, however, so once established, you need only thin out the seedlings in spring. Zones 2–8.

Field or Flanders poppy *(P. rhoeas)* is one of the leading species of annual poppies. It is red, and cultivars come in many bright colors in singles, doubles, and semi-doubles at 3–4 feet tall. 'American Legion' is a classic single, with a white or black cross at the center. The popular Shirley Series is also part of this species.

Oriental poppy *(P. orientale)* is a spectacular flower in the early summer garden. These long-lived plants grow from 2–4 feet tall, on stems that tend to sprawl. Although usually bright orange, the huge blooms also come in red, bright and pale pink, and white, sometimes with a dark blotch. If non-orange cultivars set seed, the vigorous seedlings usually produce mostly orange flowers and crowd out the cultivars. Plant Oriental poppies in rich soil and, if possible, in a spot where other plants hide them after they bloom, die down, and become dormant. New growth appears soon after the old leaves have died, however, and this is the only good time to divide them. The flowers, as well as their distinctive seed pods, are good in arrangements. Zones 3–8.

Pelargonium
(pe-lar-GO-nee-um)
Geraniums

Plant type: Tender perennial

Bloom time: All year, as long as the temperature is above 45–50°F

Best location: Full sun; well-drained, fertile soil

Diseases: Black leg, mold, mildew, viruses, blight

Garden pests: Caterpillars, mites, thrips, mealybugs

Good garden companions: 'Snow Crystals' sweet alyssum *(Lobularia maritima 'Snow Crystals')*

Propagation: Softwood cuttings in spring or fall. Seeds of most kinds do not usually come true.

Zones: 8–10

Pelargonium echinatum

These geraniums are the houseplants our grandmothers grew on their windowsills — not to be confused with hardy geraniums, which are commonly called cranesbills (Geranium). They are colorful flowering plants that are excellent in the border, in containers, and for mass planting. They are divided into four main groups, distinguished by different foliage:

* *Ivy-leaved geraniums.* Leaves resemble those of English ivy (*Hedera helix*) on trailing stems.

* *Regal or Martha Washington geraniums.* Rounded leaves that may be toothed or lobed.

* *Scented geraniums.* Foliage that releases scent when brushed.

* *Zonal geraniums (P. × hortorum).* Rounded leaves are often bicolored or multicolored with zones of dark green or red. May be either seed-raised or propagated by cuttings.

There are many beautiful geranium selections, varying in height, flower color, leaf shape and markings, and (in the case of scented geraniums) fragrance. Rather than give specific recommendations, we suggest checking out those available at from local sources and buying those that appeal to you.

Pelargonium 'Vancouver Centennial'

Penstemon (PEN-steh-mon)
Beardtongues

Plant type:	Perennial, sub-shrub
Blooming time:	All summer
Best location:	Sun or light shade; well-drained, rich soil
Diseases:	Rust, root rot
Garden pests:	Aphids, caterpillars, nematodes
Good garden companions:	Lavenders
Propagation:	Plant seed in early spring; divide in fall. Take cuttings in late summer.
Zones:	Varies (see below)

More than 250 brightly colored species of this native genus grow throughout North America. Most need protection in northern regions where there is no certainty of snow cover. Their common name comes from the tubular flower, which appears to have whiskers protruding from its open mouth. Throughout most of the summer, showy small flowers on thin, 1- to 2-foot-tall stalks burst forth in shades of pink, purple, red, white, or yellow. Like many perennials, they require adequate moisture but don't like their roots to be wet for long periods. The blossoms make good cut flowers.

GROWER'S CHOICE

Beardlip penstemon (P. barbatus) has bright red flowers throughout the summer. 3–6 feet tall. 'Rose Elf,' 18 inches tall, and 'Prairie Fire', with bright orange-red flowers on 2-foot-tall stems, are popular cultivars. Zones 4–9.

Foxglove penstemon (P. digitalis) has white blooms. 'Husker Red' has red leaves when young. 2–4 feet tall. Zones 2–8.

P. hirsutus has lavender blooms. 20–36 inches tall. Zones 3–9.

Platte River penstemon (P. cyananthus) is a good species for wildflower gardens. 1–2 feet tall, with blue flowers. Zones 3–7.

Rocky Mountain penstemon (P. strictus), also good for wildflower gardens, has deep purple-blue flowers from late spring to early summer. 24–30 inches tall. Zones 3–10.

Penstemon strictus

Perovskia (pe-ROF-skee-a)
Russian sages

Plant type: Perennial

Bloom time: Late summer to early fall

Best location: Full sun; well-drained, moderately fertile soil

Diseases: Few problems

Garden pests: Few problems

Good garden companions: Oak-leaved hydrangea (*Hydrangea quercifolia*)

Propagation: Softwood cuttings in late spring

Zones: 6–9

Grown for their interesting silvery gray foliage and panicles of small, tubular, blue flowers borne on 4-foot stems.

GROWER'S CHOICE

P. **'Blue Spire'** is a heavy bloomer with 12-inch panicles of violet-blue flowers.
P. **'Hybrida'** bears 16-inch panicles of dark lavender-blue flowers; 3 feet tall.

Perovskia **'Blue Spire'**

Persicaria
(per-sih-CAY-ree-a)

syn. *Polygonum*

Fleeceflowers, knotweeds

Plant type: Perennial

Bloom time: Midsummer to fall

Best location: Full sun to light shade; moist, well-drained, moderately fertile soil

Diseases: Few problems

Garden pests: Slugs, snails, aphids

Good garden companions: White lavatera (*Lavatera trimestris*)

Propagation: Plant seeds of species; divide cultivars in spring.

Zones: 3–8

Clusters of long-lasting, tiny, pink, red, or white bell or cup-shaped flowers stand above the leaves of these distinctive, easy-to-grow plants. Although some species make good border plants, others may be too spreading or invasive and are better suited for naturalizing.

GROWER'S CHOICE

Himalayan knotweed (*P. affinis*) bears spikes of red flowers that fade to pink and evergreen foliage that turns red in fall. Grows up to 10 inches tall, spreads 2 feet wide. Both 'Darjeeling Red' and 'Superba' have pink buds that bloom red.
Snakeweed (*P. bistorta*) has 2- to 3-inch-long pale pink spikes of bell-shaped blossoms; semi-evergreen. 30 inches tall. 'Superba' has long-lasting, showy, 3-inch-long, lilac-pink spikes. 3 feet tall.

Persicaria bistorta **'Superba'**

Petunia (pe-TOO-nee-a)
Petunias

Plant type: Tender perennial grown as an annual

Bloom time: Summer

Best location: Full sun or light shade; well-drained, fertile soil

Diseases: Mosaic virus

Garden pests: Flea beetles, whiteflies

Good garden companions: 'Colchester White' dusty miller (*Centaurea cineraria* 'Colchester White')

Propagation: Plant seeds or take cuttings.

Common hybrid petunias (*P. × hybrida*) are free-flowering plants with single, double, fringed, ruffled, dwarf, and other types of blooms in many colors available from seed. They are usually divided into the following groups:

* *Grandiflora.* Large blooms up to 4 inches across, best grown in containers where rain will not hit them directly.
* *Multiflora.* Smaller but more numerous 2-inch-wide blooms that stand up to weather, making them ideal for a border.
* *Floribunda.* 3- to 4-inch-wide blooms on compact plants.
* *Milliflora.* 1½-inch-wide flowers covering 8-inch-tall mounds.

GROWER'S CHOICE

Because so many new cultivars are introduced regularly, replacing existing ones, a few of the most popular petunia series are listed here instead.

Petunia **'Ramblin' Nu Blue'** is one of a new petunia series that offers a fascinating crawling growth habit, in this case 2–3 feet. This is the first wave-type petunia with a deep blue flower, which comes early and covers the entire plant. Excellent for containers, window boxes, or hanging baskets. 8–10 inches tall.

GRANDIFLORA GROUP

Cloud Series, with flowers up to 5 inches across; 1 foot tall.

Petunia 'Ramblin' Nu Blue'

Petunia 'Pink Wave'

Philadelphus
(fi-la-DEL-fus)
Mock oranges

Plant type: Deciduous shrub
Bloom time: Early summer
Best location: Full sun preferred, but will grow in light shade; well-drained, fertile soil
Diseases: Mildew, rust, botrytis
Garden pests: Scale
Good garden companions: Smoke bush (*Cotinus coggygria*)
Propagation: Take softwood cuttings in early summer; chip off suckers in spring or fall.
Zones: Varies (see below)

Mock oranges are grown for their pretty white flowers with yellow stamens and their orange-blossom fragrance.

GROWER'S CHOICE

'Buckley's Quill', a hybrid, bears very fragrant double flowers with ragged-edged petals. 6 feet tall. Zones 5 8.
P. × virginalis 'Minnesota Snowflake' has double, fragrant blooms. 8 feet tall. Zones 3–7.
Sweet mock orange (*P. coronarius*) has very fragrant single blooms. To 9 feet tall. 'Aureus' has bright yellow leaves; 'Variegatus' has green leaves heavily edged in creamy white. Zones 3–7.

Philadelphus hybrid

Flash Series, wide range of colors with creamy centers; to 16 inches tall.
Hula Hoop Series, early bloomers of many colors with ruffled white margins; 1 foot tall.
Picotee Series, pink, deep purple, red, or blue with ruffled white margins; 9–18 inches tall.
Razzle Dazzle Series, bicolors of white with red, blue, or rose; 1 foot tall.
Ultra Series, early flowering in many colors, some with central stars; 1 foot tall.
Wave Series, plants grow to only 6 inches tall but spread 3–5 feet.

MULTIFLORA GROUP

Carpet Series, many excellent colors including reds and oranges; 10 inches.

Celebrity Series, compact, in many colors; to 1 foot.
Duo, wide mixture, some bicolors; to 1 foot.
Horizon, range of colors, many with halos or white, pink, or red throats; 12–14 inches.
Merlin, compact 8- to 10-inch plants.
Plum Series, 2½-inch flowers in many colors including yellow; 12 inches.
Polo Series, vivid colors, some bicolors with veining; 10 inches.

FLORIBUNDA GROUP

Celebrity Series, large 3-inch blooms on 8- to 10-inch plants over long season. Comes in various shades of pink, red, blue as well as "Ice" shades with veins.
'Chiffon Morn', pink with white throat.

MILLIFLORA GROUP

Fantasy Series, small 1- to 1½-inch flowers cover compact 6- to 8-inch mounds. Many colors, including blue and ivory.

Phlox (FLOKS)
Phlox

Plant type: Perennial or annual
Bloom time: Varies (see below)
Best location: Full sun; light, well-drained garden soil for most (see exceptions below)
Diseases: Mildew, leaf spot, rot
Garden pests: Beetles, mites, tarnished plant bugs
Good garden companions: Border phlox with 'Superba' Chinese astilbe (*Astilbe chinensis* 'Superba'); moss pink with rock cress (*Arabis caucasica*)
Propagation: Grow annual phlox from seed. For perennial phlox, divide the clumps in fall or early spring, or take stem cuttings in early summer. Moss pink layers easily. Border phlox grows well from root cuttings (see below).
Zones: Varies (see below)

Phlox paniculata 'Bright Eyes'

When phlox is mentioned, most people think of the tall-growing, brightly colored border phlox, but other important members of this family are also worthwhile additions to the garden.

Phlox thrive in rich, deep garden soil and need adequate moisture, especially at blooming time. Most prefer full sun but will tolerate light afternoon shade; wild blue phlox and creeping phlox prefer partial shade. Always cut off the fading flowerheads before any seeds form, especially on border phlox; its seedlings almost always produce flowers of a muddy magenta color.

The biggest weakness of phlox is the susceptibility of some species and cultivars to powdery mildew, which is encouraged by high humidity. Because the disease is difficult to treat, prevention is the best cure. First, choose mildew-resistant cultivars, if available. Good air circulation is essential, so space the tall plants at least 2 feet apart, and avoid planting them right next to walls, fences, and hedges. Thin out the stems of upright species while they are still short, leaving only four or five stems per clump. This will permit the plants to dry out more quickly after a rain or dewy night but still provide a good display of flowers.

Thinning also encourages stronger stems and larger flowers.

If you need lots of new border phlox plants, try this trick: In early summer, cut straight down a foot or so into the soil with a spade, about 2 inches from the outermost stems of a mature clump. Don't dig up the clump, though; you only want to cut some of the roots. Many of the severed roots will grow into new little plants, which you can dig and transplant the following spring.

GROWER'S CHOICE

Annual phlox *(P. drummondii)* blooms in late spring in shades of pink, red, purple, and white, with single or double flowers. 4–18 inches tall.

Border phlox *(P. paniculata),* the classic, blooms from midsummer into fall, with large, domed clusters of flat-faced flowers in white or shades of red, orange, pink, or purple. To 4 feet tall. 'David' is a mildew-resistant, white-flowered selection. 'Bright Eyes' is pale pink, with deep rose centers. Zones 3–8.

Carolina phlox *(P. carolina)* has pink or purple blossoms in summer. 3–4 feet tall. Zones 4–8.

Creeping phlox *(P. stolonifera)* has ground-covering, dark green leaves and purple-blue flowers; prefers partial shade. 4–6 inches tall. Zones 4–8.

Meadow phlox *(P. maculata)* has fragrant lavender or white blooms from early to midsummer. 3 feet tall. The mildew-resistant selection 'Miss Lingard' has pure white flowers that make a nice contrast to blue delphiniums. Zones 3–8.

Moss pink or moss phlox *(P. subulata)* covers slopes and rock gardens in late spring with carpets of tiny pink, lavender, red, white, or blue flowers. 2–5 inches tall. Zones 3–8.

Wild blue phlox *(P. divaricata),* also called woodland phlox, blooms in late spring, covering the plant with flowers in white or shades of blue. 12–14 inches tall. This species is especially good for planting in shady wildflower gardens and in rockeries. 'Fuller's White' is a white-flowered cultivar. 10 inches tall. Zones 3–8.

Phlox divaricata

Physalis alkekengi
(FI-sa-lis al-ke-KEN-jee)

Chinese lantern

Plant type: Perennial

Bloom time: Summer; showy seed pods in fall

Best location: Sun or light shade; ordinary, well-drained soil

Diseases: Wilt, leaf spot, rust

Garden pests: Striped beetles, flea beetles

Good garden companions: New England aster *(Aster novae-angliae)*

Propagation: Plant seed or divide in spring.

Zones: 3–8

Chinese lantern grows to about 2 feet tall, with tiny white blooms in summer followed by bright red berries enclosed in 2-inch-long, bright orange, lantern-shaped, papery seedpods that are good for drying. Unfortunately, because it spreads both by long rhizomes and seeds, Chinese lantern can become a wretched weed, so plant it where it can be contained. This perennial needs little care except for keeping it under control. For winter bouquets, pick the stems just after the pods turn orange, dry them hanging upside down, in a shaded dry spot with good air circulation.

Physalis alkekengi

Physostegia virginiana
(fy-so-STEF-gee-a ver-ji-nee-AH-na)

False dragonhead, obedient plant

Plant type: Perennial

Bloom time: Midsummer to fall

Best location: Sun or light shade; moist, humus-rich soil

Diseases: Mildew, rust

Garden pests: Aphids

Good garden companions: 'Autumn Joy' sedum *(Sedum 'Autumn Joy')*

Propagation: Divide clumps; plant seeds in spring.

Zones: 3–8

The flowers of false dragonhead are striking: 6- to 10-inch flower spikes covered with small snapdragon-like rosy pink, lilac, or white blooms arranged in rows on four sides of the stiff, square, 4-foot stems. It is also called obedient plant because the hinged florets stay in whatever position they are placed when moved laterally. They are attractive in shady borders, along streams, and in wildflower gardens. Although these hardy plants prefer moist soil, they also do well in dry soil, although they don't get as tall. Under the right conditions, they spread rapidly.

GROWER'S CHOICE

'**Crown of Snow**', white blooms. 2 feet.
'**Miss Manners**', pure white flowers; spreads less than some. 30 inches tall.
'**Rosea**', pink flowers. 2 feet tall.
'**Variegata**', bright pink flowers over creamy margined leaves.

Physostegia virginiana '**Miss Manners**'

Pieris (pee-AY-ris)
Pieris, andromedas

Plant type: Evergreen shrub

Bloom time: Early spring

Best location: Full sun or light shade; well-drained, fertile, acidic soil

Diseases: Dieback, canker, rot

Garden pests: Lace bugs, nematodes

Good garden companions: Variegated Japanese pieris with purple-leaved barberry (*Berberis thunbergii* f. *atropurpurea*)

Propagation: Softwood cuttings in early summer; layering in spring; seed as soon as it is ripe

Zones: Varies (see below)

GROWER'S CHOICE

'Forest Flame', a hybrid, is large, growing to 12 feet tall and spreading 6–8 feet. Zones 6–9.

Japanese pieris (*P. japonica*), sometimes called lily-of-the-valley bush, has drooping clusters of small, waxy, white flowers. 9–12 feet tall. Among its many cultivars are 'Christmas Cheer', with pink flowers, and 'Daisen', with red flowers. 'Variegata' has green leaves edged with white. 'Little Heath' grows only 2 feet tall, with white-edged leaves that are pink when new. Zones 5–8.

Mountain pieris (*P. floribunda*), like other members of this genus, is closely related to rhododendrons. Its new leaves are often pinkish or reddish in early spring, later turning dark green, and it has upright-growing clusters of small, pink or white flowers. To 6 feet tall. Zones 5–8.

P. formosa has bronze-red leaves when young and nodding white flower clusters. To 15 feet tall. Zones 7–9.

Pieris japonica

Platycodon grandiflorus

Platycodon grandiflorus
(pla-tee-KOH-don gran-di-FLOH-rus)
Balloon flower

Plant type: Perennial

Bloom time: Midsummer

Best location: Full sun; light, well-drained garden soil

Diseases: Root rot

Garden pests: Slugs and snails

Good garden companions: Sweet William (*Dianthus barbatus*)

Propagation: Grow from seed, because the plant is difficult to divide.

Zones: 3–8

Balloon flower gets its name from its flower buds, which look like small balloons just before they open. In full bloom, it resembles a bellflower (*Campanula*), with deep purple-blue, 2-inch-wide flowers. This excellent border plant is 1 to 2 feet-tall, long lived, easy to care for, and not invasive.

Because balloon flower sprouts late in the spring, mark the spot where you place it so you won't accidentally plant something else in the apparently empty space. Try to choose a permanent planting spot, because the long taproot makes it difficult to transplant successfully. A winter mulch is beneficial. The blooms make good cut flowers but will last longer if their stems are singed with a match before being placed in water.

GROWER'S CHOICE

Japanese bellflower (*P. grandiflorus* subsp. *mariesii*) has blue flowers; 18 inches tall.

'Mother of Pearl' is light pink.

P. grandiflorus* f. *apoyama is dark violet-blue; 8 inches tall. Fuji hybrids have 2½-inch blue, white, or pink blooms on 2- to 2½-foot-tall stalks. Excellent for cutting.

Polemonium

(po-li-MOH-nee-um)

Jacob's ladders, Greek valerians

Plant type: Perennial

Bloom time: Late spring to midsummer

Best location: Full sun or light shade; fertile, moist, well-drained soil

Diseases: Leaf spot, mildew, rust, wilt

Garden pests: Few problems

Good garden companions: 'White Wonder' catmint (*Nepeta* × *faassenii* 'White Wonder')

Propagation: Divide plants in early spring; take stem cuttings in early summer; plant seeds in spring or fall

Zones: 3–9

Jacob's ladder makes an excellent blue spot in the border or in a blue-and-white garden. Clusters of small, flat or bell-shaped flowers grace the top of stems bearing fernlike leaflet pairs that have been compared to the rungs on a ladder.

GROWER'S CHOICE

Creeping Jacob's ladder (*P. reptans*) is similar to *P. caeruleum* but has a more mounded form, with bright blue flowers. It grows to about 1 foot tall.

Jacob's ladder (*P. caeruleum*), also called Greek valerian, bears attractive purple-blue flowers atop upright stems. 1–3 feet tall. 'Album' has white flowers. 'Brise d'Anjou' has lavender-blue blooms and a cream-colored edge around each leaflet. **'Lambrook Mauve',** a hybrid, forms a tidy clump 18 inches tall and wide, with light blue flowers in spring. *P. boreale*, a dwarf alpine plant with purple-blue flowers, is suitable for rock gardens and shady banks. To 1 foot tall.

Portulaca grandiflora **'Sundial Pink'**

Polemonium reptans

Portulaca grandiflora

(por-tew-LAH-ka gran-di-FLOH-ra)

Moss rose

Plant type: Annual

Bloom time: Summer

Best location: Full sun; light, dry, sandy soil

Diseases: Rust, black stem rot

Garden pests: Scale

Good garden companions: 'Hidcote' lavender (*Lavandula angustifolia* 'Hidcote')

Propagation: Plant seed in spring. Seed is very fine, so cover lightly.

This low-growing (4–8 inches tall), spreading plant produces bright pink, purple, apricot, red, or white flowers, either single or double, above rosettes of succulent fleshy foliage. The flowers open in sunlight and close at night. Moss rose is good as an edging plant, in a rock garden, or for adding a spot of color to almost any dry landscape.

GROWER'S CHOICE

Calypso Mixed, Sundance Hybrids, and Sundial are popular series; most of their members have double flowers in a wide range of colors.

Potentilla (poh-ten-TIL-la)
Cinquefoils

Plant type: Deciduous shrub or perennial

Bloom time: All summer

Best location: Full sun, light shade; light, well-drained, moderately fertile soil

Diseases: Leaf spot, mildew, rust

Garden pests: Aphids, weevils

Good garden companions: Perennial cinquefoils with Carpathian bellflower (*Campanula carpatica*); shrubby cinquefoil with peegee hydrangea (*Hydrangea paniculata* 'Grandiflora')

Propagation: Divide the spreading perennial cinquefoils in spring. Grow species from seed; some cultivars, such as 'Miss Willmott,' will also come true. Divide shrubby cinquefoil in spring or fall, or take softwood cuttings in early summer.

Zones: Varies (see below)

Fortunately the herbaceous perennial-garden species of this genus bear little resemblance to the native creeping cinque-foil (*P. canadensis*), which is a common weed all over the East. They do resemble strawberries in their trailing growth habit and leaf shape, but cinquefoils are much more colorful, with red, yellow, or white five-petaled blossoms. They do not like extreme heat and are less hardy than either the wild or shrubby forms, needing winter protection when grown in Zones 3 and 4. A good addition to the perennial border or rockery, and fine edging plants, they need to be divided often to stay healthy.

GROWER'S CHOICE

Himalayan cinquefoil (*P. atrosanguinea*) has cultivars that produce single or double flowers in bright orange, red, and yellow. 18–30 inches. Zones 5–8.

Nepalese cinquefoil (*P. nepalensis*) has dark red, 1-inch blooms. 1–3 feet tall. 'Miss Willmott' grows to 1 foot tall, with rose-pink flowers with dark throats. Zones 4–8.

P. alba, a long-blooming, white-flowering species, is a neat 3-inch-tall plant for rock gardens. Zones 5–8.

Shrubby cinquefoil (*P. fruticosa*) blooms for most of the summer and is a fine addition to the shrub or mixed border. 'Abbotswood' grows 3 feet tall and spreads to 4 feet, with white flowers. 'Coronation Triumph', with bright yellow flowers, blooms early and continues for an extra long season. 3–4 feet tall. 'Gold Drop' has fernlike foliage and golden flowers. 2–3 feet tall. 'Goldfinger' has 2-inch-wide, showy flowers on a compact bush. 3–4 feet tall. 'Mango Tango' has yellow flowers with an orange-red blush. 2 feet tall. 'McKay's White' is clear white. To 30 inches tall. 'Pink Beauty' has clear pink flowers. 2 feet tall. 'Princess' (also sold as 'Pink Princess') is pale pink. 2 feet tall. 'Royal Flush' is also pink; 18 inches tall. Zones 2–7.

Three-toothed cinquefoil (*P. tridentata*) is a low-growing species often planted in rockeries, with tiny white blossoms that appear throughout the summer. 6–12 inches tall. Zones 3–8.

Potentilla fruticosa **'Pink Beauty'**

Potentilla fruticosa **'Abbotswood'**

Primula × polyantha

Primula (PRI-mew-la)
Primroses

Plant type: Perennial

Bloom time: Spring

Best location: Preferred light conditions vary with species, but all prefer afternoon shade; moist, well-drained humus-rich, slightly acidic soil

Diseases: Anthracnose, leaf spot, rot, rust, yellows

Garden pests: Aphids, beetles, mealybugs, mites, red spiders, slugs

Good garden companions: Japanese primrose with ostrich fern (*Matteuccia struthiopteris*)

Propagation: Divide cultivars in late summer or spring; grow species from seed.

Zones: Varies (see below)

These cheery, low-growing plants have been hybridized into hundreds of forms, colors, and color combinations. A border of primroses in bloom is a joyous sight, and these plants will reward you handsomely if you provide the environment that each kind prefers. The conditions that best suit them are those found in Great Britain and the Pacific Northwest, because they enjoy cool weather and moist soil. The species listed below thrive in partial shade, especially during the hottest part of the day, and are averse to deep cultivation or other kinds of root disturbance.

Primroses are divided into several groups. Here are the five most important:

★ *Acaulis.* Large flowers usually held singly among or just above rosettes of evergreen or semi-evergreen foliage.

★ *Auricula.* Umbels of large blooms rise above leathery, evergreen leaves that may be covered with a yellow or white mealy substance. Garden auriculas are colorful and often fragrant; show auriculas have a circle of white paste at the center of each bloom; alpine auriculas have a golden or light center.

★ *Candelabra.* Tiers of flowers surround a tall stem.

★ *Polyanthus.* Umbels of many flowers above rosettes of foliage.

★ *Juliana.* Small, hardy plants with colorful flowers that bloom in early spring.

GROWER'S CHOICE

Auricula primrose (*P. auricula*) grows to 8 inches tall and has evergreen leaves. Early in the spring, it produces clusters of fragrant, single blooms in many colors, often with contrasting centers. Zones 3–8.

English or common primrose (*P. vulgaris*) has yellow blooms, often scented, with evergreen foliage. 6–8 inches tall. Zones 4–8.

Himalayan or drumstick primrose (*P. denticulata*) has foliage with whitish meal on the undersides and globelike violet flowerheads. 12–18 inches tall. *P. denticulata* var. *alba* is white; 'Rubra' is deep purple-red. Zones 2–8.

Japanese primrose (*P. japonica*) is a candelabra type, with one to six pink, red, purple, or white flowers. 8–24 inches tall. It is a favorite with gardeners because it is so easy to grow and propagate, and it blooms over a long season. 'Miller's Crimson' and 'Postford White' are two popular cultivars. Zones 3–8.

Julia primrose (*P. juliae*) has tiny, 3-inch-tall flowers that are excellent in masses. Zones 3–8.

Polyanthus Group contains some of the largest flowering primroses, with huge umbels of single or double, often ruffled, 2-inch-wide blossoms in bright and pastel shades. To 6 inches tall. Zones 4–8.

Siebold primrose (*P. sieboldii*) will grow in more sunlight than most primroses. They go dormant and the foliage disappears in summer. 8–12 inches tall. Zones 3–8.

Primula japonica

Pulmonaria longifolia 'E. B. Anderson'

Pulmonaria

(pul-mo-NAH-ree-a)

Lungworts

Plant type: Perennial

Bloom time: Early spring

Best location: Sun or light shade; moist soil rich in humus

Diseases: Mildew

Garden pests: Slugs

Good garden companions: Old-fashioned bleeding heart *(Dicentra spectabilis)*

Propagation: Divide after the plants have bloomed.

Zones: Varies (see below)

Lungworts are among the first perennials in the border to bloom in spring. Their tiny, bell-shaped flowers decorate low-growing clumps of hairy green leaves that may be spotted like a trout or, as early physicians pointed out, diseased lungs. All are very hardy and easy to grow, and they form a clump rapidly yet do not become weedy.

GROWER'S CHOICE

Bethlehem sage *(P. saccharata)* has pointed leaves dappled with white; cultivars have blooms in red, white, blue, or pink. 6–15 inches tall. 'Mrs. Moon', an old favorite, has large pink flowers that fade to deep blue. Zones 4–8.

Blue or cowslip lungwort *(P. angustifolia)* has unspotted green leaves and pink buds that open into trumpet-shaped blue flowers. 6–10 inches tall. 'Munstead Blue' is deep blue. Zones 4–8.

Common lungwort *(P. officinalis)* has light green leaves with white spots and small rose-red flowers that gradually turn blue-purple. 1 foot tall. 'Cambridge Blue' has pink buds and pale blue blooms; 'Sissinghurst White' has pink buds and pure white blooms. Zones 6–8.

'Excalibur', a hybrid, has clumps of silvery white leaves and large blue flowers. 12–14 inches tall. Zones 4–8.

Longleaf lungwort *(P. longifolia)* has narrow, dark green, silver-spotted leaves. Zones 5–8. 'E. B. Anderson' is bright blue.

Pulsatilla vulgaris

(pul-sa-TIL-la vul-GAH-ris)

Pasque flower

Plant type: Perennial

Bloom time: Spring to early summer

Best location: Sun; extremely well-drained, fertile soil

Diseases: Few problems

Garden pests: Snails and slugs

Good garden companions: Edelweiss *(Leontopodium alpinum)*

Propagation: Plant seed when it is ripe.

Zones: 3–8

Nodding, bell- or cup-shaped flowers above fine, fernlike foliage are the features of these unusual plants. Ornamental seed heads follow the blooms, then the foliage dies back to the ground in midsummer. Pasque flower is ideal for rock gardens.

GROWER'S CHOICE

Pasque flower *(Pulsatilla vulgaris)*, 8–12 inches tall, with lavender flowers. *P. vulgaris* f. *alba,* with white flowers. 'Rode Klokke', with maroon-red blooms.

Pulsatilla vulgaris

Puschkinia scilloides var. *libanotica*

Puschkinia scilloides

(push-KIN-ee-a skil-LOY-deez)

Striped squill

Plant type: Bulb
Bloom time: Early spring
Best location: Full sun or light shade
Diseases: Viruses
Garden pests: Few problems
Good garden companions: Grape hyacinth (*Muscari armeniacum*)
Propagation: Divide bulbs after blooming.
Zones: 3–8

Striped squill bears clusters of bell-shaped white or pale blue flowers with dark blue stripes on 4- to 8-inch stems. Related to *Scilla,* which is also called squill, it is excellent for naturalizing, rock gardens, or border edgings. Plant 4 inches deep in well-drained, fertile soil. *P. scilloides* var. *libanotica* is usually not striped; prefers partial shade. 6–8 inches tall. Zones 5–9.

Ranunculus

(rah-NUN-kew-lus)

Buttercups

Plant type: Bulb (tuber or rhizome)
Bloom time: Varies (see below)
Best location: Varies (see below)
Diseases: Mildew, rust, viruses, leaf spot
Garden pests: Leaf miners, mites, snails, slugs
Good garden companions: Persian buttercup with 'Lambrook Silver' wormwood (*Artemisia absinthium* 'Lambrook Silver')
Propagation: Divide the roots or tubers in early spring. Seeds are also possible.
Zones: Varies (see below)

Ranunculus contains more than 400 species, including annuals, biennials, and perennials that grow in a variety of habitats and from rhizomes, tubers, or fibrous roots. The cup- or saucer-shaped yellow wild buttercup (*R. acris*) is familiar to us all, but there are also pink, red, orange, and white species.

GROWER'S CHOICE

Aconite buttercup (*R. aconitifolius*) grows 2–3 feet tall. Its leaves resemble those of monkshoods (*Aconitum*), and the tall flower stalks have white, saucer-shaped blossoms in late spring and early summer. It likes sun or light shade and moist, rich, well-drained soil. 'Flore Pleno' is an attractive double white selection, and 'Luteus Plenus' is a double yellow. Zones 5–9.

Mountain buttercup (*R. montanus*) has single, yellow, 1-inch-wide flowers in late spring and does not spread rapidly. 3–6 inches tall. It is good in well-drained soil in a sunny rock garden. 'Molten Gold' has cup-shaped, yellow-gold flowers and is 4 inches tall. Zones 4–8.

Persian buttercup (*R. asiaticus*) has large pink, red, yellow, or white flowers with purple centers in late spring and early summer. To 18 inches tall. It needs full sun, well-drained soil, and a dry, dormant period in summer. Grow it as an annual in Zones 3–6, or dig, dry, and store the tubers inside over the winter like gladiolus corms. Bloomingdale Series cultivars have 4-inch-wide double blooms and grow to 10 inches tall. Zones 7–10.

Ranunculus asiaticus Bloomingdale Series

Rhododendron
(roh-doh-DEN-dron)
Rhododendrons, azaleas

Plant type: Evergreen, semi-evergreen, or deciduous shrub

Bloom time: Varies

Best location: Full sun or light shade; well-drained, humus rich, acidic soil (pH 4.5–5.5)

Diseases: Powdery mildew, rust, blight, bud blast

Garden pests: Whiteflies, aphids, weevils, leafhoppers, scale, caterpillars, lace bugs

Good garden companions: Chinese astilbe (*Astilbe chinensis* var. *davidii*), mountain laurel (*Kalmia latifolia*)

Propagation: Plant seed; layer or divide plants in spring; root semi-hardwood cuttings in late summer.

Zones: Varies (see below)

The thousands of rhododendron and azalea species and cultivars vary not only in size, from low-growing creepers to huge trees, but also in leaf texture, bloom size, shape, color, hardiness, and time of blooming. They require acidic soil and prefer the moist Zone 8 conditions of Great Britain and the Pacific Northwest, but a few are hardy in the Northeast as far north as Zones 3 and 4. For in-depth information on these remarkable plants, consult a book on rhododendrons or visit a nursery that specializes in them. Some are ideal for each garden situation, shrub border, rock garden, woodland garden, and even containers. 'Day Spring' is an evergreen azalea that blooms very early. *R. obtusum* 'Amoenum' has wine-red leaves in winter. 15–18 inches tall. Zones 7–9.

Ricinus communis

Ricinus communis
(ri-SIH-nus KOM-mew-nis)
Castor bean

Plant type: Tender perennial, grown as annual in the North

Bloom time: Summer

Best location: Full sun; well-drained, fertile soil

Diseases: Botryris, blight, rot, wilt, leaf spot

Garden pests: Mites

Good garden companions: 'Mother of Pearl' border phlox (*Phlox paniculata* 'Mother of Pearl')

Propagation: Soak seed for 24 hours before planting in pots in early spring indoors. Set out after frosts are over.

Zones: 9–10

This fast-growing tropical plant has small greenish yellow flowers, followed by reddish round seed pods with spines; it is grown mostly for its huge, glossy, reddish bronze or reddish purple leaves, up to 16 inches in diameter. It is rumored that it attracts mosquitoes to itself and away from humans, although all parts, including the seeds, are very poisonous. Growing up to about 6 feet tall as an annual and 30 feet tall where hardy, it may need staking. An interesting plant for the back of the border.

GROWER'S CHOICE

'Carmencita' has bright red flowers and seed pods.

Rhododendron obtusum 'Amoenum'

Rhododendron 'Day Spring'

Rosa (ROH-sa)
Roses

Plant type:	Shrub
Bloom time:	Varies
Best location:	Full sun, in deep, well-drained, fertile soil
Diseases:	Black spot, mildew, canker, rust
Garden pests:	Aphids, Japanese beetles, leafhoppers, thrips, rose chafers, spider mites, sawflies
Good garden companions:	Clematis, catmint (*Nepeta* × *faassenii*)
Propagation:	Layer in spring; take cuttings in early summer; plant seeds in fall, but don't expect them to come true. Most roses are budded commercially.
Zones:	Varies

Rosa 'Graham Thomas'

Roses have been called the queen of flowers, and many beautiful books have been devoted entirely to them. You will find information about using roses in your garden, as well as a garden designed just for roses, in Part 2 (pages 208–211). Here, we give some advice about how to plant and care for them.

THE SITE. Prepare your new rose bed carefully, in a spot with full sun or where the plants will get at least six hours of sunlight each day. Roses need rich soil with plenty of organic matter, so if your soil is not already enriched, add compost or well-rotted manure. The bed needs good drainage, too, and a pH of 5.8–6.3. Space the plants so air can circulate freely among them. Keep the garden clean, too, so bugs and disease can't thrive in nearby plant debris, old prunings, or weeds.

PLANTING. Roses are sold either potted or bare-root, wrapped in moss with a plastic covering. Follow the planting directions that come with them, and never let them dry out. Plant potted roses just as you would a container-grown shrub (see page 63). If the plant is bare-root, cut back the canes by at least half if they haven't already been pruned. Most roses are grafted on the rootstock of a wild rose and it is important to plant them with the graft union area 2–3 inches below the soil level in northern climates

and slightly above the soil level in the South. Water them well.

Mound the soil around the canes as a mulch to retain moisture until new roots have developed and their new shoots appear through the mound. Then gently wash away the mound of soil and hollow out a shallow saucer in the soil around the base of the plant to catch future waterings. Spread mulch 2–3 inches deep, leaving a mulch-free space 4 inches in diameter around the stems to help prevent disease.

PRUNING. When you prune, use sharp pruners and make cuts on an angle, ¼ inch above an outward-facing bud. Remove any shoots that emerge from below the graft, since they come from the rootstock rather than the good rose. Each spring, cut off any dead canes a few weeks before the plants leaf out, and snip back any that are growing out of balance. During the blooming season, pick off the side buds of hybrid tea roses if you want the largest blooms, leaving only the tip buds. Remove all flowers as soon as they start to fade. Each group of roses has specific pruning

requirements, both for maintenance and renewal of the bush. As you become more involved with the huge world of roses, you'll want a book specifically on the subject to guide you at pruning time.

FERTILIZING. Roses are heavy feeders, and for the best blooms they will need plenty of nourishment, first in early spring before the buds swell, and then at least every three weeks throughout the spring and early summer months. Use a balanced fertilizer or a complete rose food.

PESTS AND DISEASE. Inspect your plants frequently for signs of disease and harmful insects. Viruses, powdery and downy mildew, rust, black spot, canker, and other diseases are possible invaders, as are a long list of insects, from spider mites and aphids to rose chafers and Japanese beetles. Experts recommend an intensive spray program beginning in early spring, treating the entire plant periodically with a combination of fungicides, insecticides, and miticides. Use organic sprays whenever possible.

Rudbeckia (rud-BEH-kee-a)
Orange coneflowers, black-eyed Susans

Plant type: Perennial or biennial

Bloom time: Midsummer to frost

Best location: Full sun; fertile, well-drained soil

Diseases: Crown rot, leaf spot, mildew, rust

Garden pests: Aphids, beetles, sawflies, tarnished plant bugs

Good garden companions: Gloriosa daisy with white-flowered border phlox *(Phlox paniculata)*

Propagation: Start biennial kinds from seed; divide perennial cultivars in spring or fall

Zones: Varies (see below)

This large genus of the daisy family includes annuals, biennials, and perennials, many of which are valuable, easy-to-grow border plants. Black-eyed Susans grow wild and gardeners often dig up these bright blooms from roadsides and move them to their flower border, without realizing that most are annual or biennial and will die shortly after blooming. They are ideal plants for a wildflower garden, however, if allowed to reseed.

GROWER'S CHOICE

Black-eyed Susan (R. fulgida) includes many selections offered by perennial nurseries, such as *R. fulgida* var. *sullivantii* 'Goldsturm', with 5-inch-wide, golden yellow blossoms. 2 feet tall. Zones 3–9. At 6–8 feet, it grows too tall for most small borders. New, shorter *B. laciniata* hybrids are better for backyard plantings. Zones 3–9.

Gloriosa daisy (R. hirta), with bright blooms in orange, yellow, red, or bicolored tones, gives the garden a full-of-bloom appearance in mid- to late summer, when other flowers are scarce. The 3-foot-tall plants have double, semi-double, or single blooms. Since they are short lived, they must be replaced every few years, but they grow easily from seed and, if started early, bloom the same year. 'Indian Summer' has 6- to 9-inch-wide yellow blooms. 3 feet tall. 'Sonora' is mahogany-red and yellow. 16 inches tall. 'Toto' is a compact selection with golden yellow 2- to 3-inch blooms. To 1 foot tall. Zones 3–8.

Golden glow (R. laciniata var. hortensia) is so durable that after decades of neglect, its double yellow flowers still bloom beside the cellar holes of old farms and abandoned country schoolhouses. In rich soil, it often needs staking.

R. maxima has somewhat drooping flowerheads with quite large, cone-shaped, brown centers. 5–6 feet tall. Zones 4–9.

Rudbeckia maxima

Rudbeckia hirta

Salvia pratensis

Salvia (SAL-vee-a)
Sages

Plant type: Perennial, annual, or shrub
Bloom time: Varies (see below
Best location: Sun to light shade; moderately fertile, well-drained soil
Diseases: Leaf spot, mildew, wilt
Garden pests: Aphids, beetles, plant bugs, whiteflies
Good garden companions: 'Moonshine' yarrow (*Achillea* 'Moonshine')
Propagation: Biennial and perennial species grow readily from seeds. Propagate cultivars by cuttings, or divide in early spring.
Zones: Varies (see below)

This large genus includes not only the common culinary sage (*S. officinalis*) and the familiar red and blue annual sages, but also excellent perennial species for the border. These vigorous growers reach 2–5 feet in height, with masses of small blue, pink, or lavender two-lipped flowers on long spikes. Most have square stems and bloom for long periods, and many have aromatic foliage.

GROWER'S CHOICE

Clary sage (*S. sclarea*), usually grown as a biennial, blooms from late spring to summer in shades of pale lavender, blue, or pink. 3 feet tall. Zones 4–9.

Meadow clary (*S. pratensis*) bears spikes of lavender-blue blooms in early summer. To 3 feet tall. Zones 3–9.

Mealycup sage (*S. farinacea*) is a perennial usually grown as an annual, with spikes of deep purple-blue flowers from midsummer into fall. 2–4 feet tall. The tiny white hairs that cover the stems produce a mealy look. Compact 'Blue Bedder' is only 1 foot tall. 'Victoria', a vivid purple-blue, and 'Strata', with bicolored blue and white blooms, are attractive cultivars. Zones 8–10.

Perennial hybrid sage (*S. × sylvestris*) blooms with violet spikes over a long period from early to late summer. 2–3 feet tall. Exceptional cultivars are 'Blue Queen', deep blue; 'May Night', deep violet blue; and 'Rose Queen', rosy pink with gray-green leaves. Zones 5–9.

Scarlet sage (*S. splendens*), a perennial usually grown as an annual, grows 1–2 feet tall. Its many series include the compact, 10-inch-tall Firecracker and Sizzler Series in shades of pink, purple, orange, white, and red.

Violet sage (*S. × superba*) is a perennial with spikelike clusters of purple flowers that bloom from midsummer to fall. Zones 5–9.

Sanvitalia procumbens
(san-vi-TAH-lee-a pro-KUM-benz)
Creeping zinnia

Plant type: Annual
Bloom time: Summer
Best location: Full sun; deep, rich soil
Diseases: Not common
Garden pests: Not common
Good garden companions: Purple petunias
Propagation: Plant seeds in spring.

Creeping zinnia bears ¾-inch-wide, yellow, daisylike flowers with dark centers on 6- to 8-inch-tall trailing plants. Excellent as a groundcover and for edging paths and flower beds, as well as for container growing. Cultivars include 'Aztec Gold', bright yellow with a green eye; 'Gold Braid', yellow blooms, 2–4 inches tall; 'Mandarin Orange', semi-double orange blooms on compact, spreading plants to 4 inches tall.

Sanvitalia procumbens 'Aztec Gold'

Saponaria 'Bressingham'

Saponaria
(sa-poh-NAH-ree-a)
Soapworts

Plant type: Perennial
Bloom time: Varies (see below)
Best location: Sun; fertile, moist, slightly alkaline, well-drained or sandy soil
Diseases: Seldom troubled
Garden pests: No serious pests
Good garden companions: Rock soapwort with 'Sunny Border Blue' speedwell (*Veronica* 'Sunny Border Blue')
Propagation: Seed; division in early spring; cuttings in late summer
Zones: 3–8

The genus includes both short rock-garden plants and tall border species. It is so named because the juice of crushed leaves and stems of some species can be used to create a soaplike lather.

GROWER'S CHOICE

Bouncing bet (*S. officinalis*) has become a weed in much of the United States. Pink, red, or white blooms appear throughout summer. Best in a wildflower garden, where it can be kept under control. 30 inches tall. **'Bressingham'** is a hybrid with bright pink flowers; good in rock gardens. 3 inches tall. Zones 5–8.
Rock soapwort (*S. ocymoides*), covered with small, pink flowers in early summer, is ideal for rock gardens and for trailing over walls. 8 inches tall. **'Splendens'** has deep rose blossoms; **'Rubra Compacta'** is deep red. Cut back after flowering to keep plants compact.

Saxifraga (saks-IF-ra-ga)
Saxifrages

Plant type: Perennial
Bloom time: Varies (see below)
Best location: Most enjoy partial shade; well-drained, sandy, slightly alkaline soil
Diseases: Blight, gray mold, leaf spot, mildew, rust
Garden pests: Aphids, mealybugs, mites
Good garden companions: London pride with Siberian iris (*I. sibirica*)
Propagation: Divide plants in early spring.
Zones: Varies (see below)

An entire book could be written describing the immense *Saxifraga* genus, which consists of hundreds of named species divided into various sections, each with different characteristics. Their forms and growth habits vary from succulent to mossy types, and their flowers come in many different colors. In Latin, *saxifraga* means "rock breaking," and as the name implies, most are small plants suitable for the rock garden.

GROWER'S CHOICE

Aizoon saxifrage (*S. paniculata*), a mat-forming Arctic alpine, has flat panicles of tiny creamy white or sometimes pink flowers in early summer. 6 inches tall. Zones 2–7.
Jungfrau saxifrage (*S. cotyledon*) bears interesting white flowers with red veins in May and June. 2 feet tall. Zones 4–6.
London pride (*S. × urbium*) is an attractive, summer-blooming ground-cover much used in England. It has large rosettes of leathery leaves and small star-shaped pink flowers. 1 foot tall. Enjoys moist, shady spots. 'Aureopunctata' has variegated foliage. Zones 6–7.
Pyrenean saxifrage (*S. longifolia*) produces rosettes of silvery green leaves, with white flowers in summer. 2 feet tall. Zones 6–9.
S. × geum grows in broad rosettes of round, shiny, leathery leaves with small white flowers. 8–12 inches tall. Zones 5–8.
Strawberry geranium or mother of thousands (*S. stolonifera*) is a favorite houseplant, although it's sometimes planted outdoors where it is hardy. It grows in rosettes of somewhat rounded leaves, with airy clusters of white flowers in summer. 1 foot tall. 'Tricolor' has green leaves heavily marked with white and pink. Zones 6–9.

Saxifraga stolonifera

Scabiosa (ska-bee-OH-sa)
Pincushion flowers, scabiosas

Plant type: Perennial or annual

Bloom time: Summer

Best location: Sun in the North, partial shade in the South; well-drained, moderately rich, neutral to alkaline soil

Diseases: Blight, leaf spot, mildew, rust

Garden pests: Aphids, mealybugs, mites, slugs

Good garden companions: 'Moonbeam' coreopsis

Propagation: Divide cultivars in spring. Seed produces the strongest plants, however, and a large proportion should closely resemble the parent.

Zones: Varies (see below)

Scabiosa atropurpurea **'Blue Cockade'**

These plants were given the botanical name *Scabiosa* because they were once considered to be a cure for the disease known as scabies. And they were dubbed "pincushion flower" because their domed shape resembles that of a pincushion, and in some species, the stamens stand out like pins. But such a beautiful specimen deserves more elegant nomenclature. Delicate petals surround the "cushion" of these long-stemmed, 1½- to 3-inch-wide flowers, in shades of light blue, pink, yellow, lavender, and white. Some of the tall perennial species are excellent near the front of the border, while the smaller species are ideal rock plants. They bloom for several weeks, especially if the flowers are kept picked and the plants aren't exposed to extreme heat or cold.

GROWER'S CHOICE

Annual sweet scabious (*S. atropurpurea*) has fragrant, lavender to purple, 2-inch-wide blooms on 30-inch-tall stalks. 'Blue Cockade' is purple-blue.

Pincushion flower (*S. caucasica*) is a perennial with pale blue or lavender 3-inch-wide flowers. 2 feet tall. 'Alba' has lacy white blooms; 'Fama' is clear blue; and the 'Isaac House' hybrids come in a wide range of blue shades. 'Miss Willmott' has white blooms and is an excellent cut flower. 3 feet tall. Zones 4–9.

S. stellata, an annual, has blue blooms followed by silvery seed heads used in dried arrangements. 18 inches tall.

Small scabious (*S. columbaria*) has 1½- to 2-inch-wide pink or lilac blooms from midsummer to fall. 20–30 inches tall. 'Butterfly Blue', lavender blue, is a heavy bloomer; 'Pink Mist' has deep pink flowers. Both grow 15 inches tall. Zones 3–8.

Scilla (SIL-la)
Squills

Plant type: Bulb

Bloom time: Early spring

Best location: Sun to partial shade; well-drained, moderately rich soil

Diseases: Blight, mosaic, rot

Garden pests: Aphids

Good garden companions: Daffodils

Propagation: Plant seed in spring; separate bulbs after blooming.

Zones: 3–8

Scilla bifolia

These dwarf, spring-flowering, bulbous plants are native to southern Europe and Asia. They spread rapidly, both by offsets and from seed, so they are excellent for planting in a wildflower garden or naturalizing. Set bulbs 3–4 inches deep in fall.

GROWER'S CHOICE

Siberian squill (*S. siberica*) is a widely grown species with deep blue, pendent flowers in racemes. 6–8 inches tall. 'Alba' has white blooms; other cultivars are pale blue and pink.

Twinleaf squill (*S. bifolia*) is early flowering, with starlike blue flowers. 3–6 inches tall. 'Rosea' has pink flowers.

Sedum (SEE-dum)
Stonecrops, sedums

Plant type: Perennial

Bloom time: Varies (see below)

Best location: Sun; well-drained, somewhat fertile, neutral to alkaline soil

Diseases: Crown rot, leaf spot, rot, rust

Garden pests: Mealybugs, nematodes, scale

Good garden companions: Autumn monkshood (*Aconitum autumnale*) with showy stonecrop and other upright fall bloomers

Propagation: Easy from cuttings (nearly every piece will root and grow speedily); division; seed

Zones: Varies (see below)

This large genus of succulents contains nearly 400 species. Some are well suited to the rock garden or border, some are good groundcovers, and still others are ugly weeds. Generally hardy and easy to grow, they are sometimes called "live forever." Their flowers come in a wide range of colors, and one or another is in bloom throughout the season.

Sedum 'Autumn Joy'

GROWER'S CHOICE
UPRIGHT-GROWING SPECIES

'**Autumn Joy**', a hybrid (also known as 'Herbstfreude'), is one of the best fall flowers, with light pink blooms in late summer that darken to red and then russet-bronze in fall. 2 feet tall. Zones 3–10.
'**Frosty Morn**' has light pink flowers and variegated leaves. 2 feet tall. Zones 3–9.
'**Ruby Glow**' has red blooms and blue-green leaves. 10 inches tall. Zones 5–9.
Showy stonecrop (*S. spectabile*) bears lavender-pink flowers in late summer. 18–24 inches tall. Sometimes difficult to control, it spreads rapidly through seeds, offsets, and even pieces accidentally broken off. As children, we rubbed the slippery leaves to separate the membranes and blew them up as tiny balloons. 'Brilliant' has bright pink blooms. Zones 4–9.
'**Vera Jameson**' has rosy pink blooms and arching stems with purple-red foliage. Zones 4–9.

LOW-GROWING, WIDE-LEAVED SPECIES

The following sedums are suitable for rock gardens or groundcovers.

Sedum cauticola 'Lidakense'

Kamchatka sedum (*S. kamtschaticum*) is a favorite for planting in walls where it can trail over rocks. It has tiny, yellow-orange blossoms in late summer and green leaves that turn an attractive bronze during the fall. To 1 foot tall. 'Rosy Glow' has blue-pink leaves and pink blooms late into the fall. Zones 3–7.
S. cauticola '**Lidakense**' features mounds of round, purple-edged, blue foliage, with starry pink flowers in late summer. 3 inches tall. Zones 5–8.
Two-row stonecrop (*S. spurium*) has pink-white flowers in late summer and green foliage that turns bronze-red. 4–6 inches tall. Among the fine cultivars are 'Fuldaglut', with rosy flowers and dark red foliage; 'Golden Carpet', with bright yellow flowers; 'John Creech', with pink blooms in early summer; and 'Red Carpet', with bright red flowers and brilliant red leaves throughout the season. Zones 3–9.

NARROW-LEAVED SEDUMS

Golden moss stonecrop (*S. acre*) has a mat-forming habit and bright yellow flowers in late spring. About 4 inches tall, it is a favorite for the rockery and for planting between flagstones in paths and terraces, although it can become weedy if not controlled. 'Aureum' has bright yellow leaf tips, while the variety *elegans* has silver-tipped leaves. Zones 3–8.
Leafy stonecrop (*S. dasyphyllum*), also a dwarf, has pink-streaked-white flowers in June. 1–4 inches tall. It is good in rock gardens and for planting in the dirt crevices of stone walls. Zones 7–9.

Sempervivum

(sem-per-VEE-vum)

Hens-and-chicks, houseleeks

Plant type: Perennial

Bloom time: Summer

Best location: Full sun; dry, poor to somewhat fertile, well-drained soil or in rock walls

Diseases: Rot, rust

Garden pests: Mealybugs

Good garden companions: 'Rosabella' rock cress (*Arabis × arendsii* 'Rosabella')

Propagation: Separate offsets anytime, or plant seed.

Zones: Varies (see below)

Sempervivum tectorum

These neat-looking, succulent plants with leaves in rosettes have long been favorites in terraces, rock walls, stone paths, and rock gardens, as well as for edgings for foundation plantings and perennial borders. Some mat-forming types grow so densely they make good groundcovers. The many different species and their cultivars grow from a few inches to about a foot in height, bearing rather unattractive red, purple, yellow, or greenish flowers. The plants are valued instead for their colorful foliage, which has made them popular in the creation of intricate plant mosaics in formal gardens and parkway median plantings. They also enjoy nuzzling around rocks. A little dryness is okay, because they are able to store moisture in their succulent stems. The rosettes die after they bloom, but since their offsets multiply so fast around the base of the old plant, this usually goes unnoticed. If a lot of them seem ready to bloom at one time, however, cut the buds from most of them before they open, to preserve the planting. Although they thrive in warmth, the hardy species need a cool dormant period, so if you bring them indoors for the winter as houseplants, leave them outside for several weeks first to rest.

GROWER'S CHOICE

Hens-and-chicks (*S. tectorum*), the most widely grown species, is also one of the hardiest, if grown in a sheltered location. It has clusters of 1-inch-wide, lavender-red flowers, and many cultivars have colorful leaf rosettes with red edgings. To 6 inches tall. Zones 3–8.

Houseleek (*S. montanum*) grows in dark green rosettes with sharp-pointed leaves and purplish blue flowers. 5–6 inches tall. Zones 5–8.

Spiderweb or cobweb houseleek (*S. arachnoideum*) is a popular species with showy, bright red flowers and leaves that are connected by light threads. 3–4 inches tall. Zones 5–8.

Senecio cineraria **'Silver Queen'**

Senecio cineraria

(se-NEE-see-oh si-ne-RAY-ree-a)

Dusty miller

Plant type: Tender evergreen perennial grown as an annual where not hardy

Bloom time: Beginning in summer of second year where perennial

Best location: Full sun; well-drained, moderately fertile soil

Diseases: Rust

Garden pests: Seldom troubled

Good garden companions: 'Blue Mink' floss flower (*Ageratum houstonianum* 'Blue Mink')

Propagation: Seeds in spring

Zones: 7–10

Dusty miller is grown for its feltlike, silvery or white foliage. It is 12–30 inches tall. Yellow flowers are produced in the second year after planting seed. Use in rock gardens, in containers, or as bedding plants.

GROWER'S CHOICE

'Silver Dust' has lacy, nearly white leaves. 1 foot tall.

'Silver Queen' has silvery leaves; only 8 inches tall.

'White Diamond' has broader, gray-white foliage. 12–14 inches.

Sidalcea malviflora

Sidalcea (see-DAL-see-a)

False mallows, wild hollyhocks

Plant type: Perennial

Bloom time: Summer

Best location: Sun, light shade; moderately fertile, well-drained soil

Diseases: Leaf spot, rust

Garden pests: Aphids, mites

Good garden companions: 'Veitch's Blue' small globe thistle (*Echinops ritro* 'Veitch's Blue')

Propagation: Native species by seed; named cultivars by division

Zones: 5–8

Similar to hollyhocks (*Alcea rosea*) and good for cutting, these short-lived perennials have spikelike clusters of pink or white blooms. They will bloom long into the fall if kept cut. At 2 to 4 feet tall they are attractive in borders or natural gardens.

GROWER'S CHOICE

Checkerbloom (*S. malviflora*) has 2-inch-wide flowers in shades of pink. To 4 feet tall.

'Elsie Heugh', a hybrid, has large, pink, fringed petals; 3 feet.

'Party Girl', another hybrid, produces 1½-inch-wide pink flowers over a long season. 2–4 feet tall.

Wild hollyhock (*S. candida*) is one of the hardiest, with racemes of small, white, 1-inch-wide flowers. To 3 feet tall.

Skimmia japonica

(SKI-mee-a ja-PAH-ni-ka)

Japanese skimmia

Plant type: Evergreen shrub

Bloom time: Mid- to late spring

Best location: Full sun, but can tolerate light shade; deep, rich, moist, acidic soil in a sheltered spot

Diseases: Few problems

Garden pests: Aphids, mites

Good garden companions: 'Silver Queen' wintercreeper (*Euonymus fortunei* 'Silver Queen')

Propagation: Take cuttings mid- to late summer. Plant seed in fall in a cold frame.

Zones: 7–9

Skimmia has male and female flowers on separate plants, so both are needed to

Skimmia japonica

produce fruit. Clusters of small, fragrant, white blooms, sometimes flushed with pink or red, are followed by clusters of red fruits on female plants. Decorative pink buds form in late fall. 4-inch-long, lance-shaped leaves often form clusters at the ends of the branches. The shrub may be spreading, rounded, or upright growing up to 20 feet tall and wide.

Solenostemon scutellarioides

(so-le-NAH-ste-mon ska-tel-lay-ree-OY-deez)

Coleus

Plant type: Perennial usually grown as an annual

Bloom time: Usually grown for the colorful foliage

Best location: Sheltered spot with light shade, although it tolerates some sun; deep, rich, moist, well-drained soil

Diseases: Few problems

Garden pests: Scale, mealybugs, slugs

Good garden companions: Silvermound (*Artemisia schmidtiana*)

Propagation: Seed sown in early spring, set out after frosts are over; cuttings of cultivars

Zones: 9–11

A popular tropical bedding plant, coleus has many cultivars, with various colored and shaped leaves. It may also produce tiny, inconspicuous, blue or white flowers in spikelike clusters. Plants can grow up to 3 feet tall but are more attractive if kept pinched back. Keep them moist.

GROWER'S CHOICE

'Cinders' has green leaves with red and yellow spots.

'India Frills' has small, lobed green leaves with pinkish purple and yellow markings.

'Pineapple Queen' bears yellow-green leaves with brown-purple markings.

'Purple Emperor' has ruffled, dark purple leaves with lacy margins.

'Red Trailing Queen' has deep red purple leaves with a thin green outline.

Wizard Series cultivars are compact, 8- to 10-inch-tall plants grown from seed.

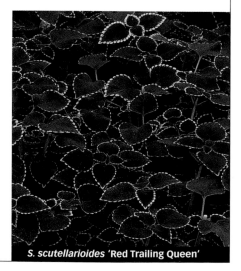

S. scutellarioides 'Red Trailing Queen'

Solidago (so-li-DAH-go)
Goldenrods

Plant type: Perennial

Bloom time: Late summer and fall

Best location: Sun, but can tolerate light shade; well-drained, moderately fertile, slightly alkaline soil

Diseases: Rust, mildew, fungus

Garden pests: Not a problem

Good garden companions: New England aster *(Aster novae-angliae)*

Propagation: Divide plants in spring.

Zones: 5–9

Nearly 100 native species of these hardy plants bloom in abundance every fall in many parts of North America, so few people consider planting them in their gardens. Certain new cultivars and hybrids, however, are less invasive, more attractive, and worthy of a spot in the border, especially since they bloom when other perennials have gone by. The plant's bad name among hay fever sufferers has been greatly exaggerated;

Solidago rugosa **'Fireworks'**

ragweed, which blooms at the same time, is usually the real culprit.

GROWER'S CHOICE

'Golden Boy' is a compact hybrid with 8-inch-long yellow plumes. 2 feet tall.

S. rugosa **'Fireworks'** has compact clumps of 3- to 4-foot-tall arching stems that resemble golden fireworks.
S. sphacelata **'Golden Fleece'** has long clusters of yellow flowers on 18-inch-tall stalks.

Spiraea japonica **'Anthony Waterer'**

Spiraea (spy-REE-a)
Spireas

Plant type: Deciduous shrub

Bloom time: Varies (see below)

Best location: Full sun; deep, rich soil

Diseases: Leaf spot, mildew, fire blight

Garden pests: Weevils, aphids, scale

Good garden companions: *S. japonica* with lamb's ears *(Stachys byzantina)*

Propagation: Divide mature shrubs in fall or spring; take softwood cuttings in early summer.

Zones: Varies (see below)

These easy-to-grow ornamental shrubs are ideal for the landscape and make good foundation plants, hedges, and specimens in the shrub border.

GROWER'S CHOICE

Bridal wreath *(S. × vanhouttei)* flowers from late spring to early summer, bearing clusters of white flowers on 6-foot-tall plants. Zones 4–8.

Japanese spirea *(S. japonica)* has many cultivars that bloom in mid- to late summer, including 'Anthony Waterer', with pink flowers, 3–4 feet tall; 'Gold-flame', with yellow foliage and pink flowers, 30 inches tall; 'Little Princess', with pink flowers and dark red fall color, 2 feet tall; and 'Neon Flash', with red flower clusters and red fall foliage, 3 feet tall. Zones 3–8.

Mellow Yellow spirea *(S. thunbergii* **'Ogon')** has small yellow leaves that turn yellow-green in summer. Zones 5–8.

S. nipponica **'Snowmound'** blooms in midspring, with pure white flowers. 4–8 feet tall. Zones 4–8.

S. thunbergii is a white, early spring bloomer. 3–6 feet tall. 'Fujino', a cultivar, has pink buds that open to white flowers. Zones 5–8.

Sprekelia formosissima

(spre-KEE-lee-a for-mo-SIS-si-ma)

Aztec lily

Plant type: Bulb

Bloom time: Spring where hardy, summer when grown as annual

Best location: Full sun; deep, rich soil

Diseases: Few problems

Garden pests: Few problems

Good garden companions: Baby's breath (*Gypsophila paniculata*)

Propagation: Divide small bulbs after blooming.

Zones: 8–10

This member of the amaryllis family grows about 1 foot tall and produces straplike leaves. The bright red flowers have three upper segments and three lower ones rolled into a cylinder for part of their length. Plant in fall with bulb neck just above soil level. Grow Aztec lily in the border where hardy or as an annual.

Sprekelia formosissima

Stachys (STA-kis)

Betonies

Plant type: Perennial

Bloom time: Early to midsummer

Best location: Full sun to light shade; well-drained, quite dry, somewhat fertile soil

Diseases: Rust, leaf spot, powdery mildew

Garden pests: Caterpillars, slugs

Good garden companions: Almost anything goes with lamb's ears, especially brightly colored flowers. Good for planting under roses.

Propagation: Divide in fall or spring, or plant seed.

Zones: 3–8

GROWER'S CHOICE

Big betony (*S. macrantha,* also known as *S. grandiflora)* has green leaves with scalloped edges and spikes of attractive lavender-pink flowers. 18–24 inches tall. 'Superba' has deep purple blooms. **Lamb's ears or woolly betony (*S. byzantina,* also sold as *S. olympica**

Stachys byzantina

or *S. lanata)* is grown mostly for its soft, furry, gray-white leaves, rather than for its spikes of small pink or lavender flowers. 18 inches tall. 'Silver Carpet', a nonflowering cultivar, spreads rapidly and makes an effective groundcover.

Stokesia laevis

(STOKS-ee-a LAY-vis)

Stokes' aster

Plant type: Perennial

Bloom time: Midsummer to fall

Best location: Full sun; light, moist, well-drained, fertile, slightly acid soil

Diseases: Leafspot

Garden Pests: Caterpillar

Good garden companions: 'Silver Brocade' beach wormwood (*Artemisia stelleriana* 'Silver Brocade')

Propagation: Seed planted in fall or early spring will bloom the first year; divide cultivars in spring.

Zones: 5–9

Native to southeastern U.S., this light blue-, pink-, or white-flowered perennial will grow in sheltered northern locations with winter protection. The 18- to 24-inch plants, with 3- to 4-inch cornflower-type blooms, are excellent for the front of the border, make long-lasting cut flowers,

Stokesia laevis 'Silver Moon'

and attract butterflies. Deadhead for a long blooming season.

GROWER'S CHOICE

'Alba' and **'Silver Moon'**, both white. **'Blue Danube'**, with large blue blooms over a long season. 12–15 inches tall. **'Honeysong Purple'**, with dark purple blooms on 1-foot stems. **'Omega Skyrocket'**, with large blue flowers on 2- to 3-foot-tall stems.

Syringa (si-RIN-ga)
Lilacs

Plant type: Deciduous shrub

Bloom time: Spring or early summer

Best location: Full sun; deep, rich, slightly alkaline soil

Diseases: Wilts, leaf spot, blight, mildew, dieback

Garden pests: Scale, borers, leaf miners

Good garden companions: Sweet mock orange *(Philadelphus coronarius)* with *S. × prestoniae* cultivars

Propagation: Divide clumps or chip off suckers in spring; take cuttings of late bloomers in early summer. Plant seeds of species in fall when ripe.

Zones: 3–8, unless noted otherwise

These upright-growing shrubs bear clusters of single or double, usually fragrant flowers in shades of red, pink, blue, white, and lavender. Use in a shrub border or as a hedge or screen.

GROWER'S CHOICE

Common, old-fashioned, or French lilac *(S. vulgaris)* blooms from late spring to early summer. 12–20 feet tall. Cultivars include 'Belle de Nancy', double pink; 'Congo', purple-red; 'Ludwig Spaeth', dark red; 'Mme. Lemoine', double white; 'President Grevy', double purple-blue; 'President Lincoln', deep purple-blue; 'Vestale', single white; 'Yankee Doodle', dark purple, only 8 feet tall. Zones 3–8.

Preston lilac (*S. × prestoniae*) flowers slightly later, in early summer, and has oval leaves. Cultivars include 'Audrey', purple-pink; 'Donald Wyman', pink; 'Isabella', pink; 'James McFarlane', clear pink; 'Minuet', pale pink; and 'Miss Canada', rose-pink. Zones 3–7.

S. × hyacinthflora blooms in mid- to late spring, with heart-shaped leaves. 15 feet tall. Among the many fine cultivars are

Syringa × hyacinthflora 'Esther Staley'

'Blanche Sweet', bluish white, pink tinged; and 'Esther Staley', lilac-pink.

***S. pubescens* subsp. *patula* 'Miss Kim'** is slow-growing, with pale purple flowers in early summer. 6–7 feet. Zones 3–7.

Syringa vulgaris 'Vestale'

Tagetes tenuifolia 'Lemon Gem'

Tagetes
(ta-JEE-teez)

Marigolds

Plant type: Annual
Bloom time: Summer
Best location: Full sun; deep, rich soil
Diseases: Stem rot, yellows, virus, fusarium wilt, botrytis
Garden pests: Aphids, leafhoppers, tarnished plant bug
Good garden companions: 'Blue Boy' bachelor's buttons (*Centaurea cyanus* 'Blue Boy')
Propagation: Plant seed early indoors and set out plants after frosts are over for longest blooming season.

These classic annuals have fernlike, fragrant foliage and flowers in various shades of yellow, orange, red, and even white. They are classified in four groups: African, French, Signet, and Triploid; each includes many series. Deadhead regularly throughout the summer to keep them neat and encourage a long blooming season. Marigolds are excellent for cutting and for edging the border.

GROWER'S CHOICE

African marigolds, derived from *T. erecta,* are the tallest, some growing to 3 feet. Their large, yellow to orange blooms reach up to 4 inches across and have a strong odor that makes them a favorite garden insect-repellent plant. African marigolds such as 'Crackerjack' are good back-of-the border plants.
French marigold hybrids, derived from *T. patula,* are usually 10–12 inches tall, but in warm climates, they may grow taller. Most flowers are double and about 2 inches across.
Signet marigolds (*T. tenuifolia*) have 1-inch-wide, single, yellow or orange flowers over very lacy foliage; include the popular Gem Series. 10–12 inches tall.
Triploid group cultivars, with many 1- to 2-inch-wide, yellow or orange flowers, often with reddish markings, are crosses of *T. erecta* and *T. patula.*

Tanacetum
(ta-na-SEE-tum)

Tanacetums

Plant type: Perennial
Bloom time: Early summer
Best location: Sun or light shade; rich, well-drained garden soil
Diseases: Few problems
Garden pests: Leaf miners, nematodes
Good garden companions: 'Moonshine' yarrow (*Achillea* 'Moonshine')
Propagation: Plant seed or divide plants in spring.
Zones: 3–9

Both species listed below have many cultivars and are hardy to Zone 3, though a light mulch over winter is good insurance. Divide the plants often to keep them healthy.

GROWER'S CHOICE

Feverfew (*Tanacetum parthenium*) has tiny white daisylike flowers that make good fillers in bouquets. Up to 30 inches tall. Often grown as an annual. 'Aureum' has green-gold foliage.
Painted daisy or **pyrethrum daisy (*Tanacetum coccineum,*** formerly *Chrysanthemum coccineum*) has pink, red, or white single or double daisylike flowers on stems up to 30 inches tall. It starts blooming in early summer and, if cut back after flowering, may rebloom.

Tanacetum parthenium 'Aureum'

Thalictrum (tha-LIK-trum)
Meadowrues

Plant type: Perennial

Bloom time: Various (see below)

Best location: Light shade; moist, rich soil

Diseases: Leaf spot, mildew, rust

Garden pests: Aphids

Good garden companions: Black cohosh (*Cimicifuga racemosa*) with tall meadowrues

Propagation: Divide in spring; seeds of most species grow readily.

Zones: 4–8, unless noted otherwise

Tall meadowrues, with their foamy clusters of pink, white, yellow, or lavender blooms, are good choices for the back of borders, in wild gardens, or along streams and other moist places. Shorter species, like *T. alpinum* and *T. kiusianum,* fit well in a shady rock garden.

GROWER'S CHOICE

Alpine meadowrue *(T. alpinum)* has white blooms in early summer. 4–6 inches tall.

Columbine meadowrue *(T. aquilegiifolium)* has feathery white, pink, or blue flowers in late spring. The name refers to its columbine-like foliage. 3–4 feet tall. 'Album' flowers have white stamens; 'Thundercloud' has dark purple stamens.

Dusty meadowrue *(T. flavum* subsp. *glaucum)* has bluish green leaves and fragrant yellow flowers in early summer; likely to need staking. 3–6 feet tall.

Kyoshu meadowrue *(T. kiusianum)* has lacy, mat-forming foliage and lavender blooms in early summer. 4–6 inches tall. Zones 5–8.

***T. minus* 'Adiantifolium'** has fernlike leaves and long-lasting yellowish flowers. To 3 feet tall. Zones 6–9.

T. rochebrunianum is a superior species with nice foliage and lavender-violet blossoms from mid- to late summer, but it usually needs staking. 3–4 feet tall. 'Lavender Mist' has purple flower stems, deep lavender flowers, and is self-supporting at 5 feet tall.

Yunnan meadowrue *(T. delavayi,* also sold as *T. dipterocarpum)* has lavender flowers in late summer. 3–5 feet tall. 'Hewitt's Double' has double, lavender-pink blooms.

Thunbergia alata

Thunbergia alata
(thun-BER-jee-a ah-LAH-ta)
Black-eyed Susan vine, clockvine

Plant type: Tender perennial vine, grown as an annual in most of the U.S.

Bloom time: All summer

Best location: Full sun; deep, rich soil

Diseases: Few problems

Garden pests: Few problems when grown outdoors

Good garden companions: Underplant with annual blue violas or perennial 'Johnson's Blue' cranesbill (*Geranium* 'Johnson's Blue')

Propagation: Seed

Growing 4–8 feet tall with support, black-eyed Susan vine produces orange-yellow or white blooms, often with purple throats.

GROWER'S CHOICE

'Alba', with dark-centered, white blooms.

Suzie hybrids, with orange or white flowers.

Thalictrum aquilegiifolium 'Album'

Tithonia rotundifolia

(ti-THO-nee-a ro-tun-di-FO-lee-a)

Mexican sunflower

Plant type: Annual

Bloom time: Late summer to fall

Best location: Full sun; deep, well-drained, rich soil

Diseases: Few problems

Garden pests: Slugs

Good garden companions: 'Fiesta del Sol' with lamb's ears (Stachys byzantina)

Propagation: Plant seed indoors, set out after frosts.

Tithonia rotundifolia

These sun- and heat-loving plants provide height for the border. Their blooms resemble those of a single dahlia: 2- to 3-inch-wide orange-yellow flowers on 3- to 6-foot-tall stalks. Tall cultivars of Mexican sunflower may need support.

GROWER'S CHOICE

'Aztec Sun' is golden yellow. 4 feet tall.
'Fiesta del Sol', orange, grows to only 30 inches.
'Torch' has red or reddish orange blooms. 4 feet tall.

Torenia fournieri

(to-REH-nee-a for-nee-AH-ree)

Blue torenia, wishbone flower

Plant type: Annual

Bloom time: Summer

Best location: Moderate shade; deep, rich soil

Diseases: Mildew, botrytis, root rot

Garden pests: Few problems

Good garden companions: Dwarf Chinese astilbe (Astilbe chinensis var. pumila)

Propagation: Plant seeds in spring indoors, set out when frost danger is past.

The bicolored blooms of this uncommon 1-foot-tall annual make it an attractive front-of-the border bedding plant. The numerous, 2½-inch-wide, tubular flowers have two lips, each with several lobes: The upper two lobes are pale violet, while the bottom three are purple, with a yellow throat. To prolong blooming time, dig and pot up a plant before frost and bring it indoors.

GROWER'S CHOICE

Clown Series cultivars are pink, white, or lavender-purple. 10 inches tall.
Duchess Series plants have a similar color range but are only 6 inches tall.

Torenia fournieri

Trillium (TRIL-lee-um)

Trilliums, wake robins

Plant type: Perennial wildflower (rhizome)

Bloom time: Spring

Best location: Light to deep shade; moist, well-drained, humus-rich soil

Diseases: Rust, fungal spots

Garden pests: Few problems

Good garden companions: Yellow adder's tongue (Erythronium americanum)

Propagation: Plant seeds when they are ripe in fall; divide rhizomes after blooming.

Zones: Varies (see below)

Trilliums have a whorl of three leaves topped with flowers that have three inner petals and three leaflike sepals. The fruit is a three-segmented berry. Excellent for wildflower or woodland gardens.

GROWER'S CHOICE

Painted trillium (T. undulatum) has beautiful white or pinkish flowers with crimson center markings. Fruit is a bright red, oval berry. 12–14 inches tall. Zones 3–7.

Purple trillium (T. erectum) is a common wildflower with purple-red, or occasionally white or yellow, strong-smelling blooms. It appears in northern deciduous woods in late spring. 10–18 inches tall. Zones 3–9.

Snow trillium or **wake robin** (T. grandiflorum) has lovely, large, pure white flowers with 3-inch-long petals that often turn a pale pink with age. Fruit is a blue-black berry. 12–14 inches tall. Zones 4–7.

Trillium grandiflorum

Triteleia
(tri-ti-LAY-a)
Triteleias

Plant type: Bulb (corm)
Bloom time: Summer
Best location: Full sun; deep, rich soil
Diseases: Rust
Garden pests: Few problems
Good garden companions: White China asters (*Callistephus chinensis*)
Propagation: Separate corms after blooming.
Zones: 7–10; grown elsewhere as an annual

These bulbs produce small, bowl-shaped, blue or white flowers. They prefer the dry conditions of the Pacific and southern states and do poorly in the humid Northeast. Plant 3–5 inches deep in spring.

Triteleia laxa 'Queen Fabiola'

GROWER'S CHOICE

Triplet lily *(T. laxa)* has trumpet-shaped flowers that are usually blue, but sometimes violet or white. 30 inches tall. 'Queen Fabiola', a deep blue, is one of the best cultivars. It grows to only 1 foot tall.
Wild hyacinth *(T. hyacinthina)* has blue, lilac, or white flowers on 30-inch-tall stems.

Tropaeolum majus
(tro-pay-OH-lum MAH-jus)
Nasturtium

Plant type: Annual
Bloom time: Summer
Best location: Full sun; good garden soil
Diseases: Viruses
Garden pests: Black aphids, serpentine leaf miner
Good garden companions: Geraniums (*Pelargonium*)
Propagation: Plant seed in spring; take cuttings of double kinds in early summer.

The funnel-shaped, spurred flowers in bright yellow, orange, or red shades are 2½ inches wide, on bushy plants or climbing or trailing vines. Many hybrid series and cultivars have single and double blooms in solid colors and bicolors. Stems of vine-types range from 4–6 feet, and are attractive either as climbers or in hanging baskets.

GROWER'S CHOICE

Alaska Series feature variegated foliage. 12 inches tall.
Jewel Series plants are bushy, growing 1 foot tall and spreading to 15 inches.
Tom Thumb Series plants are a dwarf, growing to 10 inches tall.
Whirlybird Series plants produce blooms well above the leaves. 10–12 inches tall.

Tropaeolum majus 'Alaska'

Trollius (TRO-lee-us)
Globeflowers

Plant type: Perennial
Bloom time: Varies (see below)
Best location: Sun or light shade; deep, heavy, fertile soil that stays moist
Diseases: Leaf spot, mildew
Garden pests: Few problems
Good garden companions: Alpine columbine (*Aquilegia alpina*)
Propagation: Plant seed, but seeds germinate slowly and unevenly. Divide older plants as soon as they finish flowering, but the plants spread slowly, so it cannot be done often.
Zones: 3–8

Trollius chinensis

This member of the buttercup family has been a beloved garden flower for years, and it is one of our special favorites. Its large, 2- to 3-inch-wide, bright yellow or orange, globe- or bowl-shaped blooms are held atop 2 foot-tall stalks. They brighten the spring garden and make excellent cut flowers. The clumps of toothed leaves always stay nicely compact and within bounds. Once planted, let them grow undisturbed for several years to obtain the best effect. In the North, it's best to provide some winter protection.

GROWER'S CHOICE

Chinese globeflower *(T. chinensis,* also known as *T. ledebourii)* blooms in midsummer and has semi-double, orange-yellow blooms on 3-foot-tall stems.
Common globeflower *(T. europaeus)* is yellow and blooms for a long season, from mid- or late spring to midsummer. 2 feet tall.
T. × cultorum blooms from midspring to midsummer. To 3 feet tall. Cultivars include 'Canary Bird', pale yellow; 'Earliest of All', clear yellow, 3-inch-wide blooms; 'Golden Queen', large, orange flowers that open flat; and 'Orange Globe', orange flowers that open flat.

Tulipa (TEW-li-pa)
Tulips

Plant type: Bulb	
Bloom time: Spring	
Best location: Full sun; fertile, well-drained soil	
Diseases: Anthracnose, blight, brown rot, virus	
Garden pests: Aphids, bulb flies, millipedes, mites, nematodes, wireworms	
Good garden companions: Grape hyacinth (*Muscari armeniacum*)	
Propagation: Because tulips are not easy to propagate, for most gardeners, it's better to leave this job to the professionals and buy the bulbs. Few are grown commercially outside of favored places in Holland and North American locales such as Long Island, Michigan, and the Pacific Northwest, where the climate is conducive to starting new plants.	
Zones: 3–8. Use a protective mulch in the North. In Zones 8–10, precool the bulbs in a refrigerator for 10 weeks before planting, and treat as annuals.	

Tulipa 'Shirley'

Everyone who lives in a temperate climate knows these brightly colored, popular bulb plants that are such a welcome sight after the dark, cold days of winter. Gardeners who take time to plant a few dozen, or a few hundred, of these relatively inexpensive bulbs in the fall have every right to congratulate themselves the next spring. It's hard to become bored with them because there are many species, and some species have thousands of cultivars.

The best time to plant bulbs is in late fall, once the weather cools enough so that the bulbs won't start to grow but a few weeks before the ground starts to freeze. This timing allows the bulbs to form the roots necessary to provide the nourishment they need to bloom well in the spring. For information on how to plant, see page 66.

Most tulips, unfortunately, do not continue to bloom year after year or to increase in numbers like daffodils when left in the ground. Some may survive and produce flowers again the second year,

but the blooms are usually less satisfactory, and the third year they may not bloom at all. So that we don't need to buy new bulbs each year, we dig ours each spring, dry them, and store them for fall planting. To avoid the sight of dying tops for weeks, we dig them directly after the blooms have faded, lay them flat on tilled, bare soil, then cover the bulbs with a few inches of soil but leave the tops exposed. (See page 114.) We keep the soil moist until the tops die completely, then cut them off, dry the bulbs for a few days, and store them in a cool, dry, dark place. Then we replant them in late fall, provided we remember where we stored them.

Luckily for absentminded gardeners, there are longer-lasting tulips available that produce blooms for several years when left in the ground. Some of these are the species tulips, such as the Kaufmanniana and Greigii types. Be sure to follow the accompanying cultural directions when planting them.

To outwit winter, some gardeners pot a few tulip bulbs in the fall, store them in a

cool basement, and bring them into a warm room for late-winter blooms, a process called *forcing*.

Tulips are sold under the following classifications, referred to as *groups*. Please note that the blooming seasons mentioned refer to early, mid-, or late spring, not the entire growing season.
Single Early Group. These tulips are good as bedding plants and for forcing in the late winter. 8–18 inches tall.
Double Early Group. Good for the same uses as the singles, double early tulips are not only double but also longer-lasting than the singles. 12–14 inches tall.
Triumph Group. Tall and showy, Triumphs bloom just after the early kinds. 14–24 inches tall. 'Peer Gynt' and 'Shirley' are Triumphs.
Darwin Hybrid Group. Known for their wide variety of large, squarish, single flowers with strong stems in a wide range of rich colors, Darwin hybrids bloom in mid- to late season. 20–26 inches tall.
Single Late Group. Sometimes offering several blossoms on one stem, often with

contrasting margins, this late-flowering group includes the old cottage and Darwin tulips. 18–28 inches tall.

Lily-flowered Group. Blossoms are single and goblet-shaped, sometimes with contrasting colors. They are late-flowering. 16–26 inches tall. 'China Pink' is a Lily-flowered tulip.

Fringed Group. Single flowers with fringed margins, often of contrasting color, bloom late. 1–2 feet tall.

Viridiflora Group. Tulips in this group often produce green flowers margined or blotched with other colors. They are late bloomers. 16–22 inches tall. 'Spring Green' is a Viridiflora.

Rembrandt Group. Streaks or variegations in flowers of this group are caused by a virus and are no longer propagated commercially. Late bloomers. 16–24 inches tall.

Parrot Group. Large, brightly colored, single, loosely formed flowers with ragged-edged petals tend to open wider than other tulips. Late blooming. 14–26 inches tall.

Double Late Group. Also called peony-flowering tulips, these are good choices both in the border and as cut flowers. The heavy double blooms need protection from the wind and may also need staking. Late-season bloomers. 12–24 inches tall.

Kaufmanniana Group. Opening so wide that they are often called waterlily tulips, these bloom in early to mid-season. 6–12 inches tall.

Fosteriana Group. Fosterianas are large, brilliant, early bloomers. 8–24 inches tall.

Greigii Group. These early to mid-season tulips come in shades of red or yellow with blotches or margins of another color. 6–12 inches tall.

Miscellaneous Group. This classification is for species and hybrids not listed in other groups. It includes wild species, many of them miniatures that are appropriate for a rock or wildflower garden.

Tulipa **'China Pink'**

Tulipa **'Spring Green'**

Valeriana (va-le-ree-AH-na)
Valerians, garden heliotropes

Plant type: Perennial
Bloom time: Midsummer
Best location: Sun or light shade; moist soil
Diseases: Leaf spot, mildew, rot, rust
Garden pests: Japanese beetles
Good garden companions: Joe-Pye weed (*Eupatorium maculatum*)
Propagation: Seeds; division of clumps in spring.
Zones: Varies (see below)

GROWER'S CHOICE

Common valerian (*V. officinalis*) has aromatic, fernlike foliage and 4-inch clusters of attractive, airy, white, pinkish, or lavender blooms. 4–5 feet tall. Because

Valeriana officinalis

it tends to spread, the wildflower garden is probably the best place for it. Zones 3–9. *V. phu* 'Aurea' has clumps of yellow leaves in early spring; later on, the leaves turn green. In early summer, clusters of tiny white flowers form atop 4- to 5-foot-tall stems. Zones 5–9.

Verbascum (ver-BAS-kum)
Mulleins

Plant type: Perennial or biennial
Bloom time: Varies (see below)
Best location: Sun; well-drained, slightly alkaline soil
Diseases: Mildew, leaf spot, rot
Garden pests: Nematodes
Good garden companions: Common monkshood (*Aconitum napellus*)
Propagation: Divide perennial mulleins in spring; plant seed for biennials.
Zones: Varies (see below)

Verbascum 'Gainsborough'

Although common mullein (*V. thapsus*), a tall, yellow-blooming, biennial weed with woolly leaves, is a familiar sight in dry country pastures, several more refined species and hybrids are useful in a border and for naturalizing. They have tall spikes of small, saucer-shaped flowers in shades of yellow, pink, purple, or white.

GROWER'S CHOICE

Chaix mullein (*V. chaixii*), a perennial, has 1-inch-wide yellow blooms with fuzzy purple stamens in mid- to late summer. 3 feet tall. Zones 4–9. *V. chaixii* f. *album* has white flowers; Zones 5–9. **'Gainsborough'**, a hybrid, has pale yellow flowers from early to late summer. To 4 feet tall. Zones 5–9. **'Jackie'**, a hybrid, has peach-pink blooms in summer. 18 inches tall. Zones 5–9. **Purple mullein (*V. phoeniceum*)** blooms from late spring through early summer with purple, pink, or white flowers. 4–5 feet tall. Zones 4–8. **'Summer Sorbet'**, a hybrid, has rose-pink flowers in summer. 2 feet tall. Zones 5–9. **Turkish mullein (*V. bombyciferum*)**, a biennial (though it may live longer), forms wide rosettes of woolly, silver-white leaves and spikes of bright yellow summer flowers. Zones 4–8.

Verbena (ver-BEE-na)
Verbenas

Plant type: Perennial or annual
Bloom time: Summer
Best location: Sun; moist, well-drained, fairly fertile soil
Diseases: Blight, mildew, rot, rust
Garden pests: Aphids, beetles, caterpillars, leaf miners, mites, nematodes, scale, thrips, whiteflies
Good garden companions: Purple coneflower (*Echinacea purpurea*) with Brazilian vervain
Propagation: Divide or plant seed in spring.
Zones: Varies (see below)

These sun and heat lovers produce dense clusters of small but brightly colored flowers. Most are perennials in the South and enjoyed as annuals in the North. Many are fragrant and attract butterflies and hummingbirds.

GROWER'S CHOICE

Brazilian vervain (*V. bonariensis*) has stiff, 4- to 5-foot-tall stems with 2- to 3-inch-wide clusters of purple-pink flowers, making it a good choice for the border. Zones 7–11; use as annual in North. **Hybrid verbena (*V. × hybrida*)** cultivars come in pink, red, purple, yellow, and white shades. 10–20 inches tall.

Verbena × hybrida 'Babylon White'

'Babylon White', an early bloomer, is white and a good choice for hanging baskets; 'Blue Lagoon' has light blue blooms; 'Peaches and Cream' is apricot pink-and-white; 'Quartz Burgundy' is a deep purple-red. Hybrid verbenas are hardy in Zones 9–10; further north, they're commonly grown as annuals.

Moss verbena *(V. tenuisecta)* has lacy, deeply divided leaves and lavender, purple, blue, or white blooms that are sometimes fragrant. 'Edith' is light pink. 20 inches tall. Zones 8–10, but used as an annual elsewhere.

Rose vervain *(V. canadensis)* forms carpets of foliage with a profusion of rose-colored blooms, which so completely cover the fading blooms that grooming the plant is unnecessary. 'Homestead Purple' has purple flowers. 8–18 inches tall. Although we have had success overwintering *V. canadensis* in Zone 3 with a reliable snow cover, it is usually listed as dependably perennial only to Zone 7 and is often grown as an annual in colder areas. Zones 7–9.

Verbena bonariensis

Veronica (ve-RO-ni-ka)
Speedwells

Plant type: Perennial
Bloom time: Spring through summer
Best location: Sun or light shade; moderately fertile, moist, well-drained soil
Diseases: Leaf gall, leaf spot, mildew, rust
Garden pests: Caterpillars, nematodes, scale
Good garden companions: Bloody cranesbill *(Geranium sanguineum)*
Propagation: Divide in spring; layer creeping kinds; upright types root well from cuttings; seed is possible, but the plants may not come true.
Zones: Varies (see below)

Although seldom called speedwell anymore, this plant was named for the ship that left England with the Mayflower but returned shortly because it was not seaworthy. Whatever they're called, the upside-down-icicle-shaped flowers of this large genus of annuals and perennials are favorites, especially among those who love blue. The long-blooming plants vary from low-growing creepers to 4-foot-tall spiky specimens in shades of blue, pink, red, purple, and white. If you are familiar with the weedy, creeping speedwell that takes over lawns, you may be reluctant to choose other *Veronica* species for your border or rock garden, but fortunately, many species are better behaved.

GROWER'S CHOICE

Comb speedwell *(V. pectinata)* is a low-growing rock-garden plant that has deep blue flowers with white centers in summer. 3 inches tall. 'Rosea' is pink. Zones 3–8.

Gentian speedwell *(V. gentianoides)* grows up to 18 inches tall, with pale blue flowers in early summer. It is a good rock garden plant. 'Variegata' has white variegated leaves. Zones 4–7.

Hungarian speedwell *(V. austriaca* subsp. *teucrium)* has a cultivar 'Crater Lake Blue' that is one of the deepest blues you'll ever find. 12–18 inches tall. This early-summer bloomer may sprawl somewhat, but you can stake it if necessary. Zones 4–8.

Veronica longifolia

Long-leaved speedwell *(V. longifolia)* has lavender-blue flowers from late summer to early fall. 2–4 feet tall. 'Blauriesin' (also known as 'Foerster's Blue') has deep blue spikes; 'Schneeriesin' has white spikes. Zones 4–8.

Prostrate speedwell *(V. prostrata)*, a 6-inch-tall, mat-forming perennial, has blue blooms in early summer. 'Trehane' has golden foliage. Zones 5–8.

Spike speedwell *(V. spicata)* blooms through the summer. 1–2 feet tall. 'Goodness Grows' has deep blue spikes; 'Noah Williams' has white blooms and variegated leaves; 'Red Fox' (sometimes sold as 'Rotfuchs') is rose-pink. Zones 3–8.

Viburnum (vi-BER-num)
Viburnums

Plant type: Deciduous or evergreen shrub

Bloom time: Spring

Best location: Full sun to light shade; well-drained, rich soil

Diseases: Powdery mildew, botrytis, rust

Garden pests: Scale and snowball aphids are persistent pests on the snowball and certain other viburnums

Good garden companions: 'Shubert' chokecherry (*Prunus virginiana* 'Shubert'), peegee hydrangea (*Hydrangea paniculata* 'Grandiflora')

Propagation: Plant seeds from the berries when ripe in the fall; take softwood cuttings in early summer; divide shrubs in spring.

Zones: Varies (see below)

There are many viburnum species and cultivars, ranging in height from a few inches to 30 feet. Most bloom in spring, with clusters of small, white or pinkish white, sometimes fragrant flowers, followed by red, blue, or black berries in late summer. Many have fall foliage color.

GROWER'S CHOICE

American highbush cranberry (*V. trilobum*) has white flowers in spring and showy, red, edible fruit in the fall. To 12 feet tall. It is deciduous, with yellow to red fall color. 'Alfredo' is a compact variety, to 6 feet tall. Two cultivars have been selected for better-tasting fruit: 'Andrews' ripens early, 5–6 feet tall; 'Wentworth' ripens later, 10–12 feet tall. Zones 2–7.

Arrowwood viburnum (*V. dentatum*) blooms in late spring and early summer, with white flowers that are followed by deep blue fruits. The fall color of this deciduous species ranges from yellow to red. 10 feet tall. Zones 3–8.

Burkwood viburnum (*V. × burkwoodii*) has pink buds, white flowers from mid- to late spring, and red berries that turn black in fall. It is semi-evergreen in mild climates. 6–8 feet tall. 'Anne Russell' is a dwarf cultivar, 5 feet tall. Zones 4–8.

European cranberry bush (*V. opulus*) has white flowers from late spring to early summer, followed by large, red berries. Deciduous, usually with red fall foliage. 6–12 feet tall. 'Compactum' is a dwarf. 5 feet tall. Zones 3–8.

Koreanspice viburnum (*V. carlesii*) has pink buds, white or pink flowers mid- to late spring, and red berries that ripen to black; deciduous. 8 feet tall. Zones 5–8.

Linden viburnum (*V. dilatatum*) has white, flat-topped flowers from late spring to early summer, red berries, and colorful fall foliage; deciduous. 10–12 feet tall. Zones 5–8.

Snowball bush (*V. opulus* 'Roseum') has balls of white flowers in early summer; no fruit. To 12 feet tall. Zones 3–8. *V. sieboldii* has shiny, dark green leaves, small clusters of white flowers, and red fruit that ripens to black. 12 feet tall. Zones 5–8.

Viburnum sieboldii

Vinca minor

Vinca (VING-ka)
Periwinkles

Plant type: Evergreen perennial

Bloom time: Spring

Best location: Light shade; grows in ordinary soil but thrives in sites that are moist and rich in potash

Diseases: Canker, dieback, botrytis blight and other molds, rot, yellows

Garden pests: Aphids, beetles, leafhoppers

Good garden companions: Good underplanting for deciduous trees

Propagation: Division is possible any time during the growing season if kept watered after planting.

Zones: Varies (see below)

With their shiny, oval, mostly evergreen leaves, these creeping plants are superb groundcovers and useful along shaded woodland paths. In early spring, they bear five-petaled, lavender-blue flowers.

GROWER'S CHOICE

Greater periwinkle (*V. major*) is good as an annual, trailing, container, or window-box plant in the North, and it is useful as a perennial groundcover in Zones 7–11. It grows 10–18 inches tall. The cultivar 'Variegata' has green leaves with irregular white margins.

Lesser or common periwinkle (*V. minor*) has lavender-blue flowers and glossy, green leaves. 8 inches tall, it grows well in sun in northern climates but does best in shade even there, although it may not bloom as heavily. 'Bowles White' has pinkish buds and white blooms. 'Multiplex' has double, bright purple flowers. Zones 3–9.

Viola (vee-OH-la)
Violets, pansies

Plant type:	Annual, biennial, or perennial
Bloom time:	Spring through fall, if flowers are deadheaded
Best location:	Sun or light shade; moist, fertile, well-drained soil
Diseases:	Anthracnose, mildew, rot
Garden pests:	Aphids, beetles, caterpillars, cut-worms, mites, nematodes, sawflies, slugs
Good garden companions:	White sweet alyssum (*Lobularia maritima*)
Propagation:	Violets and pansies, when started inside in late winter from seed, will bloom the same year. Or sow seeds outside in well-drained, raised beds in late summer, and protect with a heavy mulch for over the winter. Propagate horned violet and sweet violet by division.
Zones:	Varies (see below)

Many adults can remember the delight they felt as children when they first discovered a patch of purple, white, or yellow violets growing in a park or woodland. These tiny, fragile, colorful blooms have enchanted people for centuries. The wide variety of violas ensures there is one that will thrive in nearly any location. From tiny roadside violets to giant pansies, they offer an enormous range of sizes and colors. Prized for their early-blooming, brightly colored flowers and because they last over a long period, violas are versatile as well. They are charming in the rock garden, make good edging plants for the border, and also work well in front of larger perennials or shrubs in a foundation planting. Pick the fading flowers for a long season of bloom, and pinch back the stems from time to time to keep the plants from getting leggy. Native violets, such as *V. canadensis* and *V. pedata* (see below), are excellent in a wildflower bed or a rock garden. Choose kinds that grow naturally in soil and light conditions similar to those where you will plant them. Some species are biennials or short-lived perennials and depend on regular seeding to reproduce themselves.

Viola 'Sorbet Yellow Frost'

Viola 'Sorbet Yellow Delight'

GROWER'S CHOICE

Bird's-foot violet *(V. pedata)* has pale purple flowers. It requires slightly acid soil, spring sun, and summer shade. 2 inches tall. Zones 3–8.

Common pansy *(V. × wittrockiana)* includes some uncommon beauties. Large flowers (2–4 inches in diameter) come either in solid colors or with contrasting "faces"; some are fragrant. Many bloom for most of the growing season, especially in cool climates, if not allowed to go to seed. Short-lived perennials, usually treated as biennials. Cultivars in many series are available. 6–10 inches tall. Zones 3–8.

Horned violet *(V. cornuta),* also called viola or tufted pansy, looks like a large violet or a small pansy. Colors usually range from purple to blue. It ordinarily lives longer than pansies but is likely to need occasional replacement unless it self-sows. It is worth planting as an annual where it is not winter-hardy; it is about 6 inches tall. Of the many cultivars, 'Jersey Gem', a deep blue, is especially attractive. Zones 7–9.

Johnny-jump-up *(V. tricolor)* has gone wild in pastures, fields, and occasionally lawns. At 3–6 inches in height, it looks like a miniature pansy. It makes a good rock garden plant, although it is difficult to control because it produces seeds prolifically. Many cultivars are available, including 'Bowles Black', with near black blooms, and 'Prince John', with yellow flowers. Zones 3–8.

Sorbet hybrids come in a variety of colors and make good edging or container plants; they are heat and cold tolerant. 6 inches tall.

Sweet violets *(V. odorata)* are used by florists as cut flowers, and nurseries sell them as potted plants. The 8-inch-tall flowers come in a wide range of colors and are very fragrant. Zones 8–9.

White Canada violet *(V. canadensis)* has white flowers with a lavender tint and yellow center and likes light shade. 12–16 inches tall. Zones 3–8.

Vitex agnus-castus

Vitex agnus-castus
(VY-teks AG-nus-CAS-tus)
Chaste tree

Plant type: Deciduous shrub

Bloom time: Late summer

Best location: Full sun or partial shade; humus-rich, well-drained, slightly alkaline soil

Diseases: Root rot, leaf spot

Garden pests: Scale

Good garden companions: Panicle hydrangea (*Hydrangea paniculata*)

Propagation: Plant seed in spring or fall; take cuttings in midsummer.

Zones: 6–9

A native of southern Europe and western Asia, the chaste tree has exotic-looking, aromatic foliage and small, fragrant, lilac, pale violet, or sometimes white flowers in spikelike clusters. It grows 8–24 feet tall. It is good in the shrub border during the times when few other shrubs are blooming.

GROWER'S CHOICE

'Silver Spire' has white flowers. *V. agnus-castus* var. *latifolia* has broader leaves and is a more vigorous grower.

Weigela (wy-GEE-la)
Weigelas

Plant type: Deciduous shrub

Bloom time: Late spring to early summer

Best location: Full sun; deep, rich soil

Diseases: Verticillium wilt, twig dieback

Garden pests: Japanese beetles, nematodes, scale

Good garden companions: Variegated weigela with lady's mantle (*Alchemilla mollis*)

Propagation: Plant seeds of species in fall; layer cultivars in spring; root softwood cuttings in early summer.

Zones: Varies (see below)

Weigela bears tubular, 1½-inch-long, bright red, white, rose, or pink blooms. It is loved by hummingbirds and is attractive in shrub and flower borders.

GROWER'S CHOICE

'**Briant Rubidor**' (often sold as 'Rubidor'), a hybrid, with yellow leaves and ruby red blooms, is somewhat hardier. 6 feet tall. Zones 4–8.

Weigela florida 'Variegata'

'**Bristol Ruby**', an old favorite, has bell-shaped, deep red flowers. 8 feet tall. Zones 3–9.
'**Carnaval**' has pink-and-white flowers. 8 feet tall. Zones 5–9.
'**Snowflake**' has pure white flowers. 4 feet tall. Zones 5–9.
W. florida has dark pink flowers with lighter-colored insides in late spring and early summer. 8 feet tall. 'Foliis Purpureis' has bronze-green foliage and red flowers. 3–5 feet tall. 'Variegata' has white or yellow-edged leaves and dark pink blooms. 4–6 feet tall. Zones 5–8.
'**Wine & Roses**' bears dark purple leaves and bright pink flowers. 6 feet tall. Zones 5–8.

Weigela florida 'Foliis Purpureis'

Wisteria floribunda

Wisteria (wis-TEE-ree-a)
Wisterias

Plant type: Deciduous twining vine
Bloom time: Summer
Best location: Full sun or light shade; well-drained, moist, rich soil
Diseases: Viruses, dieback, crown gall
Garden pests: Leaf miners, scale, mealybugs, Japanese beetles
Good garden companions: *Allium hollandicum*
Propagation: Layer in fall; take softwood cuttings in early summer.
Zones: Varies (see below)

Wisteria is one of the most attractive flowering vines. Its scented, pealike blooms in hanging clusters up to 1 foot long are followed by beanlike pods.

It can be cut back and made into a woody shrub. As a vine, the stems grow to 30 feet or more.

GROWER'S CHOICE

American wisteria *(W. frutescens)* is a native twining vine with lilac-purple flowers in summer. Zones 6–9.

Japanese wisteria *(W. floribunda)* has many cultivars, including white 'Alba'; pink 'Honbeni' (also known as 'Rosea'); and 'Royal Purple' (also known as 'Black Dragon'). Zones 5–9.

Silky wisteria *(W. brachybotrys)* has hairy leaves and fragrant blooms in white or purple with yellow markings. Zones 6–9.

Yucca (YUH-ka)
Yuccas, soapweeds

Plant type: Evergreen perennial
Bloom time: Summer
Best location: Full sun; well drained, moderately fertile soil
Diseases: Leaf spot, rust, stem rot
Garden pests: Aphids, mealybugs, mites, scale, stalk borers
Good garden companions: Purple heliotrope *(Heliotropium arborescens)*
Propagation: Species by seeds; divide cultivars by separating the suckers or offsets that form around the main plant. Plant them where they won't be disturbed for decades; they bloom best after they've become deeply rooted.
Zones: Varies (see below)

The yucca plant growing on a bank near our home always creates a lot of interest when it's in bloom, because most visitors don't expect to see a desert plant growing in the northern Vermont mountains.

GROWER'S CHOICE

Adam's needle *(Y. filamentosa)* is one of the yuccas that has acclimated beautifully to colder regions, and if any cold-dwellers are lucky enough to get a hardy strain, as we did, it will grow well even in Zone 3 and still keep its Arizona look. The large, creamy white, bell-like flowers are spectacular on the 5- to 7-foot-tall sturdy stalks that rise above sword-shaped, evergreen leaves. The threads, or filaments, on the edges of the leaves give the species its name. It may need staking to support its heavy blooms. After it has bloomed, remove the flower stem. Although it often takes years for the first flowers, they are well worth waiting for. 'Bright Edge' has green leaves with golden margins; 'Golden Sword' foliage has yellow centers and green edges. Zones 4–10.

Our Lord's candle *(Y. whipplei)* forms dense tufts of narrow, swordlike leaves and bears clusters of thousands of small, white, bell-shaped blooms in summer. Each bloom lasts only a few days, but the flowering period may continue for up to 7 weeks. The foliage grows to 3 feet tall, and the flowering stems are 6 or more feet tall. Zones 7–10.

Spanish dagger *(Y. gloriosa)* has large leaves with sharp points. The huge flowers are white but occasionally have a reddish hue. 8-foot-tall stalks. Zones 7–10.

Yucca filamentosa

Zantedeschia aethiopica

Zantedeschia
(zan-te-DEH-shee-a)
Calla lilies

Plant type: Tender bulb (rhizome)
Bloom time: Late spring; summer where hardy
Best location: Full sun to light shade; deep, rich, moist soil. Plant 3 inches deep.
Diseases: Botrytis, rot, mold, rust, virus
Garden pests: Not common
Good garden companions: August lily (*Hosta plantaginea*)
Propagation: Divide in spring; plant seed when ripe.
Zones: 9–10 unless noted otherwise

Calla lilies have large, arrow-shaped leaves and long-lasting blooms composed of a white, yellow, or pink spathe surrounding a spikelike yellow spadix. In areas with short growing seasons, start the rhizomes indoors in late winter and set them out after frosts are over. Never let them dry out completely. Dig in fall and store in cool spot over winter.

GROWER'S CHOICE

'Black Magic', a hybrid; yellow spathe with black throat. 30 inches tall.
Golden calla (*Z. elliottiana*), yellow spathe; white-speckled foliage. 2 feet tall.
'Majestic Red', a hybrid; crimson. 2 feet tall.
Pink calla (*Z. rehmannii*), pink to purple spathe. 16 inches tall.
Z. aethiopica is the florist's calla. Among its fine cultivars are the dwarf white 'Childsiana', 1½–2 feet tall; 'Green Goddess' with large green and white flowers, 2½–3 feet tall; and 'Pink Mist', white to pink, 2½–3 feet tall. This species is hardy in Zones 8–10, or even into Zone 7 with winter protection.

Zinnia (ZI-nee-a)
Zinnias

Plant type: Annual
Bloom time: Summer
Best location: Full sun; rich, well-drained soil
Diseases: Bacterial wilt, powdery mildew, blight, wilt, rot
Garden pests: Spider mites, caterpillars, mealybugs
Good garden companions: 'Orange Star' Mexican zinnia with 'Crater Lake Blue' Hungarian speedwell (*Veronica austriaca* subsp. *teucrium* 'Crater Lake Blue')
Propagation: Plant seed in spring after frosts are over.

GROWER'S CHOICE

Common zinnia (*Z. elegans*) bears double, semi-double, or single flowers that resemble dahlias. Heights vary from 6–30 inches, and colors include red, yellow, pink, white, purple, orange, and lavender. Flower forms also vary, and bloom sizes range from the 1¼-inch-wide blossoms of the Thumbelina Series to the 3- to 5-inch-wide flowers of the California Giants Series.

Mexican zinnia (*Z. haageana*, but commonly called *Z. angustifolia*) has daisylike, orange flowers, 1½ inches in diameter. To 2 feet tall. 'Orange Star' has golden orange blooms; 'Star White' is white. Excellent for the border and cutting.

Zinnia elegans

Appendices

USDA Plant Hardiness Zone Map

The United States Department of Agriculture (USDA) created this map to give gardeners a helpful tool for selecting and cultivating plants. The map divides North America into 11 zones based on each area's average minimum winter temperature. Zone 1 is the coldest and Zone 11 the warmest. Once you determine your zone, you may use that information to select plants that are most likely to thrive in your climate.

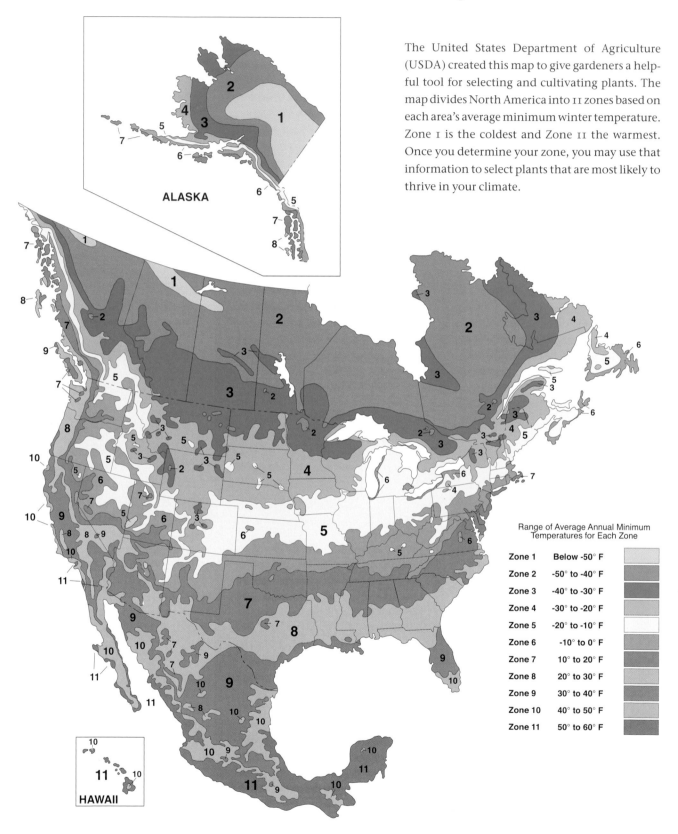

ALASKA

HAWAII

Range of Average Annual Minimum Temperatures for Each Zone

Zone 1	Below -50° F
Zone 2	-50° to -40° F
Zone 3	-40° to -30° F
Zone 4	-30° to -20° F
Zone 5	-20° to -10° F
Zone 6	-10° to 0° F
Zone 7	10° to 20° F
Zone 8	20° to 30° F
Zone 9	30° to 40° F
Zone 10	40° to 50° F
Zone 11	50° to 60° F

AHS Plant Heat-Zone Map

The American Horticultural Society (AHS) created the Heat-Zone map to provide guidance in selecting plants that tolerate the upper temperature ranges where you live. The United States is divided into 12 zones, based on the average number of days each year a region experiences *heat days,* or days when temperatures rise over 86°F (30°C), the point at which plants begin to suffer physiological damage from heat. Zone 1 has less than one heat day, while Zone 12 has more than 210 heat days. For more information, see the American Horticultural Society's website: www.AHS.org.

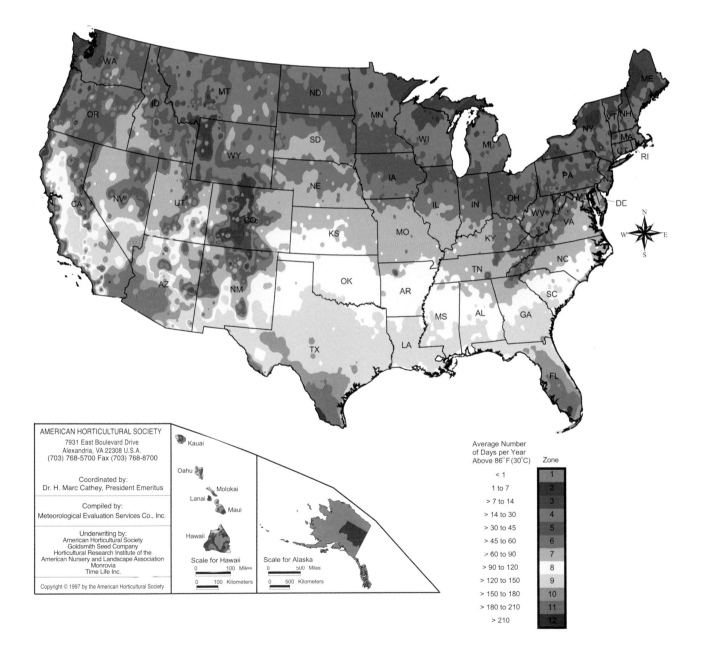

AMERICAN HORTICULTURAL SOCIETY
7931 East Boulevard Drive
Alexandria, VA 22308 U.S.A.
(703) 768-5700 Fax (703) 768-8700

Coordinated by:
Dr. H. Marc Cathey, President Emeritus

Compiled by:
Meteorological Evaluation Services Co., Inc.

Underwriting by:
American Horticultural Society
Goldsmith Seed Company
Horticultural Research Institute of the
American Nursery and Landscape Association
Monrovia
Time Life Inc.

Copyright © 1997 by the American Horticultural Society

Scale for Hawaii
0   100   Miles
0   100   Kilometers

Scale for Alaska
0   500   Miles
0   500   Kilometers

Average Number of Days per Year Above 86°F (30°C)	Zone
< 1	1
1 to 7	2
> 7 to 14	3
> 14 to 30	4
> 30 to 45	5
> 45 to 60	6
> 60 to 90	7
> 90 to 120	8
> 120 to 150	9
> 150 to 180	10
> 180 to 210	11
> 210	12

Reading List

Armitage, Allan M., *Armitage's Manual of Annuals, Biennials, and Half-Hardy Perennials* (Timber Press, 2001)

Brickell, Christopher, editor, *American Horticultural Society A–Z Encyclopedia of Garden Plants* (Dorling Kindersley, 1997)

Burrell, C. Colston, *Perennial Combinations* (Rodale Press, 1999)

Cox, Jeff, *Perennial All-Stars: The 150 Best Perennials for Great-Looking, Trouble-Free Gardens* (Rodale Press, 1998)

Cox, Jeff, and Marilyn Cox, *The Perennial Garden* (Rodale Press, 1992)

Crockett, James Underwood, *Crockett's Flower Garden* (Little, Brown, 1981)

Cullina, William, *The New England Wild Flower Society Guide to Growing and Propagating Wildflowers of the United States and Canada* (Houghton Mifflin, 2000)

Disabato-Aust, Tracy, *The Well-Tended Perennial Garden* (Timber Press, 1998)

Duthie, Pam, *Continuous Bloom* (Ball Publishing, 2000)

Ellis, Barbara W., *Shady Retreats* (Storey Publishing, 2003)

Ellis, Barbara W., *Taylor's Guide to Growing North America's Favorite Plants* (Houghton Mifflin, 2000)

Harper, Pamela, and Frederick McGourty, *Perennials* (HP Books, 1987)

Hart, Rhonda Massingham, *Deerproofing Your Yard and Garden* (Storey Publishing, 1997)

Hill, Lewis, *Secrets of Plant Propagation* (Storey Publishing, 1985)

Hillier, Malcolm, and Colin Hilton, *The Book of Dried Flowers* (Simon & Schuster, 1987)

Hobhouse, Penelope, *Color In Your Garden* (Little, Brown, 1985)

Hudak, Joseph, *Gardening with Perennials Month by Month* (Timber Press, 1993)

Jones, David, *Encyclopedia of Ferns* (Timber Press, 1987)

Lacy, Allen, *Gardening with Groundcovers and Vines* (HarperCollins, 1993)

Macunovich, Janet, *Caring for Perennials* (Storey Publishing, 1997)

Ondra, Nancy J., *Grasses* (Storey Publishing, 2002)

Pavord, Anna, *Plant Partners* (DK Publishing, 2001)

Phillips, Ellen, editor, *Rodale's Illustrated Encyclopedia of Perennials* (Rodale Press, 1999)

Roth, Sally, *Attracting Butterflies and Hummingbirds to Your Backyard* (Rodale, 2001)

Schenk, George, *The Complete Shade Gardener* (Timber Press, 2002)

Swindells, Philip, *The Master Book of the Water Garden* (Little Brown, 2001)

Tekulsky, Mathew, *The Butterfly Garden* (Harvard Common Press, 1986)

Wise Garden Encyclopedia (HarperCollins, 1990)

Wyman's Gardening Encyclopedia (Simon & Schuster, 1987)

Yang, Linda, *The City Gardener's Handbook* (Storey Publishing, 2002)

Other Sources

We do not list sources for plants or supplies, because new suppliers arrive frequently and others go out of business or change addresses. You'll find reliable mail-order sources and up-to-date information in current garden magazines and on the Internet. Some magazines we have found useful include:

Country Living Gardener
  cl-gardener.com | 800-777-0102

Fine Gardening
  www.taunton.com | 800-477-8727

Garden Design
  www.gardendesignmag.com | 877-717-8925

Gardening How-To
  visitors.gardeningclub.com | 800-324-8454

Horticulture
  www.hortmag.com | 800-258-0929

People Plants and Places
  www.ppplants.com | 800-251-1784

Plant Societies

Annual dues and addresses are subject to change.

American Daffodil Society
4126 Winfield Road
Columbus, Ohio 43220-4606
www.daffodilusa.org
Dues: $20.00

American Fern Society
Missouri Botanical Garden
P. O. Box 299
St. Louis, Missouri 63166-0299
www.amerfernsoc.org
Dues: $8.00 or $15.00

American Hemerocallis Society
Department WWW
P. O. Box 10
Dexter, Georgia 31019
www.daylilies.org
Dues: $18.00

American Hosta Society
246 Etheridge Road
Auburn, Georgia 30011
www.hosta.org
Dues: $25.00

American Penstemon Society
1569 South Holland Court
Lakewood, Colorado 80232
Dues: $10.00

American Primrose Society
P. O. Box 210913
Auke Bay, Alaska 99821
www.americanprimrosesoc.org
Dues: $25.00

American Rose Society
P. O. Box 30,000
Shreveport, Louisiana 71130-0030
www.ars.org
Dues: $37.00

Cactus and Succulent Society of America
P. O. Box 2615
Pahrump, Nevada 89041-2615
www.cssainc.org
Dues: $35.00

Delphinium Society
"Summerfield," Church Road
Biddestone, Chippenham
Wiltshire, SN14 7DP, UK
Dues: $15.00

International Waterlily and Water Gardening Society
1401 Johnson Ferry Road, Suite 328-G-12
Marietta, Georgia 30062-8115
www.iwgs.org

National Chrysanthemum Society
10107 Homar Pond Drive
Fairfax Station, Virginia 22039-1650
www.mums.org
Dues: $20.00

New England Wild Flower Society
180 Hemingway Road
Framingham, Massachusetts 01701-2699
www.newfs.org
Dues: $42.00

North American Heather Society
23930 Wax Orchard Road SW
Vashon Island, Washington 98070
www.northamericanheathersociety.org
Dues: $15.00

North American Lily Society
P. O. Box 272
Owatonna, Minnesota 55060
www.lilies.org
Dues: $20.00

North American Rock Garden Society
P. O. Box 67
Millwood, New York 10546
www.nargs.org
Dues: $25.00

Perennial Plant Association
3383 Schirtzinger Road
Hilliard, Ohio 43026
www.perennialplant.org
Dues: $80.00

Glossary

Acidic soil. Soil that tests less than pH 7. In common usage, however, it usually refers to soil with a pH of 5.5 or less.

Annual plant. One that blooms, produces seeds, and dies the same year.

Aquatic plant. Plant that lives in water.

Asexual reproduction. The propagation of a plant by cuttings, division, grafts, layers, tissue culture, or other vegetative means, rather than by seeds.

Bare rooted. A plant that is transplanted without soil attached to its roots.

Basal. The bottom or base of a plant. A basal shoot is a sprout or branch that grows near the ground. A basal cut is one made near the base or bottom of a stem or branch.

Bedding plant. A small plant, usually an annual, used in mass plantings or as an edging.

Biennial. A plant that grows from seed the first year and in the second year blooms, bears seeds, and dies.

Border. A flower bed, usually consisting of a variety of plants.

Bract. Modified leaves that surround the base of a flower so closely that they appear to be part of the bloom.

Bulb. The fleshy root of lilies, tulips, and similar plants, consisting of a bud surrounded by fleshy scales.

Bulbil. Small bulbs that form along the stems of certain plants such as tiger lilies and bladder ferns.

Bulblet. Baby bulbs that develop at the bottom of a larger bulb below the ground.

Callus. A fleshy tissue growth that forms on the cambium of a plant while a wound is healing. On cuttings it often, but not always, precedes the development of roots.

Calyx. The sepals, usually green, that form the outermost whorl of floral parts.

Clone. A new plant that is started asexually and is identical to the parent.

Cold frame. An outside seed or plant bed enclosed by a frame with a removable transparent cover. It is used to grow plants in a protected environment with no artificial heat.

Compost. Rich, porous material made of decomposed organic matter. Excellent for building up soil.

Corm. Fleshy root similar to a bulb, but solid. Gladiolus plants grow from corms.

Cormels. Small corms that form around the parent. They can be removed and planted to create new plants.

Crown. The point on a plant where the top meets the roots at, or just below, the soil line.

Cultivar. Named variety. A plant that is usually an improvement over the species and unique among other varieties. It is usually, but not always, necessary to propagate cultivars by asexual means.

Cutting. A piece of branch, leaf, or root that is separated from a plant and rooted to create a new plant with the same characteristics.

Deciduous. Describes plants that shed their leaves each year after the growing season.

Dicotyledon. A plant that produces two seed leaves at germination.

Dormancy. The period of a plant's life during which it is not growing or showing signs of life. Also refers to seeds before they sprout.

Edging plant. Usually dwarf, compact plants that are used primarily along the front of a border or along paths or steps.

Evergreen. A plant that holds its foliage throughout the year.

Eye. A bud. On perennials, it usually refers to a dormant bud growing on the root. Can also refer to the center of a flower.

Germination. The sprouting of seeds.

Grafting. The joining of the top of a plant (scion) to the roots (rootstock) of another by surgery.

Groundcover. Low-growing plants that spread rapidly by seed, underground stems that form new plants, or long horizontal top growth that layers into new plants.

Hardening off. The process by which perennials and annuals that have been started inside are gradually exposed to outdoor conditions.

Hardiness. Term used to describe a plant's ability to survive low temperatures.

Herbaceous plant. A plant with a stem above the ground that does not become woody.

Herbicide. A chemical used to kill unwanted plants or to prevent seeds in the ground from sprouting.

Humidity. The amount of moisture in the air.

Hybrid. A new plant developed by the successful cross-pollination of two plants that are genetically different.

Insecticide. A chemical used to control insects.

Island. A flower bed, surrounded by lawn or water.

Lath house. A structure made of narrow slats that provides shade for plants.

Layering. A plant propagation method whereby the stem is laid on the ground and anchored by bent wire, soil, or a stone until the section touching the soil grows roots. The rooted plant is then cut from the parent plant and nurtured as a new plant.

Lime. A calcium compound often used to raise the pH of soil.

Mature plant. A plant old enough to produce blooms and seeds.

Monocotyledon. A plant that produces only one seed leaf. Grasses, lilies, and *Hemerocallis* are examples.

Named variety. See *Cultivar*

Offshoot or offset. Small plant growing from the main stem of a perennial, just under the ground. Often these can be taken as cuttings from the parent and grown into new plants.

Panicle. Branching raceme of flowers.

Peat pellets. Small pellets of peat that swell when watered. They are often used for rooting cuttings or starting seeds.

Perennial. A plant that lives for more than two years. Commonly refers to herbaceous flowering plants, which may or may not be winter hardy.

pH. A measure of the concentration of hydrogen ions in a solution, which in gardening refers to the alkalinity or acidity of the soil. The higher numbers indicate increased alkalinity, 7 is neutral, and numbers below 7 indicate acidic soil. Most garden soils range from 5 to 6.5 in pH, and the majority of perennials grow well within this range. Some plants, however, require soil that is more acidic or alkaline than the norm.

Perlite. Soil conditioner, used to lighten heavy soil or for starting seedlings or rooting cuttings.

Petals. The colored outer parts of a flower.

Pinching. The removal of the tips of new sprouts by the fingers to create a tight, bushy, and heavier-blooming plant, as is done with chrysanthemums, or to prevent a plant from growing larger, as is often done with houseplants.

Pistil. The female reproductive organ of a flower.

Pollen. Dustlike particles produced by the male stamens on a flower. Usually brown or yellow in color, and usually spread from flower to flower by bees. The pollen of ornamental grasses is transferred by the wind.

Pollination. The fertilization of the female ova of a plant by the transfer of pollen from the male portion of the same kind of plant to a different flower, resulting in a seed. In addition to insects and wind, pollination can also be accomplished by gardeners who transfer pollen using a small paintbrush and cup.

Raceme. Stalks of flowers coming from a single, unbranched axis. The younger blooms are at the top.

Rhizome. The fleshy, horizontal roots of plants such as iris.

Rock garden. A garden of low-growing, spreading perennials grown among stone, often on a slope. Also called *a rockery*.

Root cutting. Propagating a plant by cutting a portion of its roots into small pieces and planting them. The root cuttings then grow tops and additional roots.

Rooting chemical. A chemical in powder or liquid form, into which the base of a cutting is dipped before planting in order to stimulate faster and heavier root growth.

Runner. Vinelike growths on certain plants, which produce new plants by layering or rooting where offsets or offshoots touch the soil. (See *Layering*.)

Scaling a bulb. Peeling off the outer scales of a bulb to start new plants.

Scape. The leafless stalk on which the flowers of some plants such as *Hemerocallis* are produced.

Selection. Choosing the best of a group of seedlings or wild plants for propagation or breeding.

Semi-evergreen. Partially evergreen plant that is often deciduous in the North and evergreen in the South.

Sepal. The calyx or leaflike back row of petals behind the main showy petals.

Shade. A lower degree of light, which is preferred by some plants. *Light shade* usually refers to a few hours of morning or late afternoon sun, but considerable skylight all day long. *Moderate shade* is filtered light, such as that coming through trees with light foliage, but little or no direct sun at any time. *Heavy shade* is that under trees with thick foliage.

Stamen. The male part of a flower that bears the pollen.

Succulent. A plant with fleshy leaves or roots that is capable of storing large amounts of moisture for long periods.

Subsoil. The layer of soil beneath the topsoil, usually of poor quality and lacking organic matter.

Sucker. A shoot or branch growing from the base of a plant, either above or below ground level. Plants growing from the roots of a parent plant, sometimes even a considerable distance from the parent plant, are also called suckers.

Systemic pesticide. Chemicals that a plant absorbs which then permeate it. Some kinds of insecticides, herbicides, and fungicides are produced as systemics.

Taproot. The main root of a plant, usually large and downward growing, with numerous smaller roots growing horizontally from it.

Tissue culture. The asexual propagation of plants by the rapid increase of cell growth under carefully controlled conditions of temperature, nutrition, pH, and sanitation in a laboratory.

Topsoil. The upper, usually most fertile, layer of soil.

Transpiration. The process by which a plant loses moisture through its leaves and stem.

Tuber. Fleshy root or understem, such as those of dahlia.

Turgid. A term used to describe a plant that is well supplied with water. Cuttings from turgid plants root better, and seedlings and mature plants can be more safely transplanted if they are turgid.

Umbel. Flat or rounded cluster of flowers that grows from a single point at the top of a stalk.

Viability. The ability of a bulb to grow or a seed to germinate.

Water stress. The condition whereby a plant loses water faster than it absorbs it.

Wild garden. A planting purposely planned to look natural and uncultivated. It may consist completely of native plants; natural-looking exotics may also be included.

Xeriscaping. Landscaping with drought-tolerant plants to reduce water use in dry or desert conditions.

Index

Note: Page numbers in **bold** indicate tables; page numbers in *italic* indicate photographs and illustrations.

Photography Credits

All photographs are © Joseph De Sciose, except for the following:

Global Book Publishing Pty. Limited: 219 bottom right, 228 top, 230 bottom right, 233 bottom, 241 bottom, 252 top, 258 bottom, 266 center, 271 bottom, 289 bottom left, 301 bottom, 307 bottom, 332 bottom left, 337 bottom left

MACORE Company, Inc.: 224, 225 top, 236 top right, 249 top, 250 top, 257 top, 265 top, 293 top, 299 top, 311 right, 312 bottom, 321 bottom, 340 top

Giles Prett: 60, 62 center and bottom left, 79 top left, 102, 107

© Rob Simpson/Painet, Inc.: 223 top

Storey Publishing: 96, 103, 106

© Martin Wall: 236 top left, 305 bottom

Garden Locations and Designers

Front cover: The Von Trapp Greenhouse, Waitsfield, VT

Back cover, top: Pat Nissen Garden, Dorset, VT

Bento Garden, Fairfield, CT; design by Suzanne Knutson: 36

Conservatory Garden, Central Park, New York, NY: 10

New York Botanical Garden, Bronx, NY: 25, 68 top, 112

Pat Nissen Garden, Dorset, VT: xi, 4

Philip Smith Garden, Williamstown, MA: 67

Private garden, Cold Spring, NY: 19

Private garden, Northwestern CT: 43

Suzanne Knutson Garden, Wilton, CT: ii

Von Trapp Greenhouse, Waitsfield, VT: 21, 62

Photographing for *The Flower Gardener's Bible* was an honor and a privilege. I am grateful to all the people at Storey Publishing who inspired me, and to Lewis and Nancy Hill for their vision for this important book. Over the years I've tried the patience of many gardeners when I asked about plant identification or where I might find a particular plant. But being gardeners, they were always patient and eager to share their knowledge and teach me about their plants and gardens. I am forever indebted to their generosity of time and spirit.

— *Joseph De Sciose*

Metric Conversion Chart

When the measurement given is	To convert it to	Multiply it by
inches	centimeters	2.54
feet	meters	0.305
mils	millimeters	0.254
square feet	square meters	0.093
ounces	grams	31.1
pounds	kilograms	0.373
tons	metric tons	0.907
gallons	liters	3.785
°F	°C	°F − 32 x ⅝